Second Only to Grant

Quartermaster General Montgomery C. Meigs

A Biography
By
David W. Miller

WHITE MANE BOOKS
SHIPPENSBURG, PENNSYLVANIA

Maps drawn by David W. Miller.

This White Mane Books publication
was printed by
Beidel Printing House, Inc.
63 West Burd Street
Shippensburg, PA 17257-0152 USA

E
467.1
.M44
M55
2000

The acid-free paper used in this book meets the guidelines for permanence and durability of the Committee on Production Guidelines for Book Longevity of the Council on Library Resources.

For a complete list of available publications
please write
White Mane Books
Division of White Mane Publishing Company, Inc.
P.O. Box 152
Shippensburg, PA 17257-0152 USA

Library of Congress Cataloging-in-Publication Data

Miller, David W., 1956-
   Second only to Grant : Quartermaster General Montgomery C. Meigs : a biography / by David W. Miller.
      p. cm.
   Includes bibliographical references (p.) and index.
   ISBN 1-57249-212-0 (acid-free paper)
   1. Meigs, Montgomery C. (Montgomery Cunningham), 1816-1892. 2. Quartermasters--United States--Biography. 3. United States. Army. Quartermaster Corps--Biography. 4. United States--History--Civil War, 1861-1865--Campaigns. I. Title.

E467.1.M44 M55 2000
973.7'092--dc21
[B]

                                                                        00-063298

To the grandchildren:
Wesley, Alexander, Nicholas, Spencer, and Bryan

Contents

Illustrations

Maps

A. Lincoln to Lieutenant General Scott
June 5, 1861

Doubtless you begin to understand how disagreeable it is for me to do a thing arbitrarily when it is unsatisfactory to others associated with me.

I very much wish to appoint Colonel Meigs quartermaster general, and yet General Cameron does not quite consent. I have come to know Colonel Meigs quite well for a short acquaintance, and, so far as I am capable of judging, I do not know one who combines the qualities of masculine intellect, learning, and experience of the right sort, and physical power of labor and endurance, so well as he.

I know he has great confidence in you, always sustaining, so far as I have observed, your opinions against any differing ones.

You will lay me under one more obligation if you can and will use your influence to remove General Cameron's objection. I scarcely need tell you I have nothing personal in this, having never seen or heard of Colonel Meigs until about the end of last March.

Your obedient servant,
A. Lincoln

Colonel Montgomery Meigs to his father
June 12, 1861

A Major-General commands a Corps; a Lieutenant-General commands the whole army; but the Quartermaster-General supplies the means of moving that army and his command extends from the Atlantic to the Pacific, from the Lakes to the Gulf, and, in doing so, was in "second place not in military rank but in actual real influence over the war."

Preface

In 1959 a biography of Montgomery Cunningham Meigs written by Russell F. Weigley was published by Columbia University Press. Dr. Weigley's bibliography notes that he had available to him almost weekly letters from Meigs to his father during the 1850s, and that personal material for the Civil War was scanty. Justification for a new biography arises from the availability of important new sources of information.

Since 1959 the Manuscript Division of the Library of Congress more than doubled the documents in its collection of Meigs' papers. Included are almost weekly letters from Meigs to his father during the Civil War. These open a window on Meigs' candid wartime thinking.

Meigs kept extensive shorthand journals in the 1850s, none of which had been translated when Weigley wrote his book. This has changed. William Mohr transcribed the journals for the years 1853–1859 for the United States Senate Bicentennial Commission. A copy of his translation is held in the Office of the House Curator. Although the translation, as studied and cited in this book, is "an unedited and unverified transcript of a work in progress," it gives much insight into ill feelings between Meigs and Thomas Ustick Walter, architect of the Capitol, at the time the Capitol was enlarged and a new dome constructed in the late 1850s and early 1860s. Intertwined with the Meigs-Walter arguments were conflicts between Meigs and his superior, the secretary of war, John B. Floyd. Meigs did not hold back on his true feelings in his journals.

Merely having copies of Meigs' wartime letters to his father did not help until several months of study made it possible to read what was written. As Weigley states, Meigs' handwriting was abominable. Meigs was well aware of this, having been told at various times by his wife, son, and friends that they could not read the letters he was writing to them. The story is told of General William Tecumseh Sherman receiving a paper from Meigs during the war and saying "The handwriting of this report is that of General Meigs, and I therefore approve of it, but I cannot read it."[1]

The writing problem was approached with the attitude that Meigs' father, to whom most of the wartime letters were addressed, was able to carry on a sensible correspondence on the basis of the received letters and, therefore, must have found them readable. By persevering, large parts of the letters became decipherable.

Meigs was an adaptable man. Nothing demonstrates this more than a reported conversation between Secretary of War Edwin Stanton and an unnamed senator:

> 'Mr. Secretary, I wonder how a lawyer, as you are, can keep that man Meigs where he is. Why he pays no regard to either law or justice! He is a disgrace to the army.' Stanton replied, 'Now, don't say a word against Meigs, he is the most useful man I have about me. True, he isn't a lawyer, and therefore he does many things that I wouldn't dare do.' 'Then why do you let him do them?' asked the Senator. Stanton answered, 'Somebody has to do them.'[2]

As the book is read, this assessment can be compared with a prewar determination to strictly follow the rules.

James G. Blaine, who served 20 years in Congress, agreed with Stanton as to his importance:

> Montgomery C. Meigs, one of the ablest graduates of the Military Academy, was kept from the command of troops by the inestimably important services he performed as Quartermaster-General.... Perhaps in the military history of the world there was never so large an amount of money disbursed upon the order of a single man.... The aggregate sum could not have been less during the war than fifteen hundred millions of dollars, accurately vouched and accounted for to the last cent.[3]

Acknowledgments

Thanks are given to Harry C. Ways, chief of the Washington Aqueduct from 1972 to 1991, and author of the book *The Washington Aqueduct 1852-1992*, for reading this book in its entirety in manuscript form and giving helpful corrections. His book is an invaluable source on Meigs' involvement with the aqueduct.

William C. Dickinson, president, Environmental Policy Network, a longtime student of Meigs, was willing to labor through the manuscript and pass on forthright observations that have made this a much more readable book. Martin K. Gordon, president and executive editor of White Mane Publishing Co., gave valuable guidance as to how a biography should be approached.

I also received family help. My wife, Nancy, corrected a lot of grammar, our son Eric explained some of the mysteries of computers, and son Steve and daughter-in-law Roberta gave moral support.

The published material on the Civil War is boundless and made it relatively easy to include the skeleton narrative within which Meigs' responsibilities and actions could be described. The excellent libraries of the Pentagon and Fairfax County were used for basic Civil War research.

Insofar as the personal Meigs' material is concerned, the *Official Records* of the Civil War contain the dry bones framework of the quartermaster general's contributions, but Meigs' letters to his father go beyond the factual information and give a better picture of the quartermaster general as a man. Personnel in the Manuscript Reading Room of the Library of Congress were always willing to lend a hand. The same can be said for those working in other branches of the Library of Congress: Main Reading Room, Geography and Map, and Prints and Photographs.

Curator of the House Barbara Wolanin was kind enough to let me occupy space in her office over several weeks to read the translation of the Meigs' Journals.

Chapter 1
Exile

How the mighty had fallen. For the period 1853 to 1860 Montgomery Cunningham Meigs was a revered, if controversial, army engineer constructing some of the most important public works ever placed in the nation's capital. But, on January 1, 1861, he found himself far removed from Washington City in charge of a partially completed island fortress where his mail was delivered by ship semi-monthly to Key West, Florida. The harbor of the Dry Tortugas, where Fort Jefferson was located, is more than 70 miles west of Key West in the Gulf of Mexico. The Dry Tortugas are a cluster of seven coral reefs with a name signifying an abundance of turtles and no fresh water. He had no military men under his command, nor were there any guns at the fort.[1]

This condition was the result of integrity not often found in men. He stood up to President James Buchanan and Secretary of War John Floyd, men so flexible in what they considered proper patronage that they contravened Meigs' notion of how the public treasury should be handled.

Two years before he stood on the rim of a fountain near the Capitol as a jet of water went one hundred feet into the air.[2] In his words, "No more shall the houses of the poor burn in flames for want of the means to extinguish them. And the poor and the servant will now be relieved of the unhealthy labor of carrying water from the pumps through the snowed-up streets of winter."[3] The first water passed through the Washington Aqueduct, conceived and built by Meigs, on January 1, 1859.[4] The aqueduct, designed to bring water of the Potomac River some 12 miles into the communities of Georgetown and Washington, was still a work in progress but the end was in sight. The finished project would have nine-foot diameter pipes relying on gravity feed, and the Cabin John Bridge with the greatest span for masonry construction in the world.

January 1859 also brought the culmination of another public advancement which Meigs had labored at for over five years. The United States Senate moved into its new, spacious, and ornately finished chamber in the north wing of the Capitol. The House of Representatives had moved into its new space in the south wing the preceding year.

Strange that the man most responsible for these happenings should find himself in virtual exile. But the atmosphere of September 1860, leading to his banishment, changed rapidly following Abraham Lincoln's election in November 1860. Floyd, the vain secretary of war responsible for the fall of Meigs, went south to his native Virginia in December 1860 under a barrage of criticism for what many saw as treasonable acts and the cloud of, at best, mismanagement of public funds. When Meigs wrote from Fort Jefferson that either it or Fort Taylor at Key West could be taken by men "transported in a fishing smack" and that soldiers and armaments were needed to prevent an easy takeover, Floyd told the cabinet that "he had a long rigmarole of a letter from Captain Meigs, that pestilent fellow who got trouble wherever he went, and that it was perfectly ridiculous that he wanted men and guns to defend the Tortugas and some heap of rocks, perfectly indefensible."[5]

With Floyd out of the way, General in Chief Winfield Scott, who knew the importance of holding the Tortugas, saw to it that by mid-January Fort Jefferson had a company of artillery, and by February 1 Meigs thought the fort adequately armed and manned to be able to repel any efforts to take it, and, in fact, hoped an effort would be made. Such an attack, by the 10,000 men supposedly offered by Louisiana to overwhelm Fort Jefferson, would be thrown back with a little bloodletting "that would be worth more as exhibiting the real strength" of the United States "than all the marches resolutions & acts of Congress."[6]

Not being a man constrained to a single avenue when the fate of his country was at risk, he wrote letters, seeking aid for strengthening Fort Jefferson, both within and outside the army. One to the chairman of the Military Committee of the House of Representatives stressed the importance of Jefferson if a conflict should develop with either England or France, and suggested that the Pensacola Navy Yard, seized by Florida after it seceded on January 10, 1861, not be retaken, but that $500,000 be appropriated to build a dry dock at Jefferson.[7] The scale of his thinking was carried over to the Civil War.

Meigs, a believer in a just God, never thought that he would be long in the Dry Tortugas. With the return of Congress in December 1860, he expected his supporters to bring pressure to bear to have him returned. With Floyd gone the principal force wanting him in exile was removed. Also gone though was his friend and stalwart supporter over the last seven years, Jefferson Davis. Davis announced to Congress the secession of Mississippi on January 9 and then, on January 21, 1861, withdrew from the Senate.

Meigs had no respect for those in high government positions who left the Union to join the Confederacy. As to the four members of

Buchanan's cabinet who left to align themselves with their seceding states, Meigs thought they made a "pitiable spectacle" and would be scorned by historians as trying to "wreck the country in whose high counsels they sat only to violate their sworn allegiance."[8]

Orders for Meigs' return to Washington were issued on January 28, reached him on February 12, and found him back in Washington by February 20, 1861. Over the next four years he labored, unstintingly, to bring the Union back together. The enemy was led by its president, Jefferson Davis, with whom Meigs had had few disagreements in the past. By the time Lincoln was sworn in as president on March 4, 1861, the only military forts in the South still held by Union forces were Fort Sumter at Charleston, Fort Taylor (Key West), Fort Jefferson (Dry Tortugas), and Fort Pickens near Pensacola, Florida.[9]

Chapter 2
Family, Duty, Honor, Country

Montgomery Cunningham Meigs' strait-laced approach to life was certainly influenced by the importance of honor and family drummed into him by his father, Charles Delucena Meigs, who believed there was a "rigid duty incumbent upon [his children] to do whatever might be in their power to promote [the family's] honorableness before men." Montgomery and his brothers were warned "not to disgrace the stock from which" they came.[1] In his later years Charles Meigs wrote into the family Bible.

My desire is that you should carefully preserve, each one of you, the record of our family.

If all men could be induced to preserve their family records, *discarding without mercy every member of their blood-line whose conduct might stain it*, society would derive great security, and virtue a strong support from that course. [Emphasis added.][2]

The American bloodline for Montgomery started with Vincent Meigs, a Puritan, who came from England "for conscience sake" and settled in New Haven, Connecticut, around 1640. In a time when to have 10 children was not unusual, his descendants swelled to over 1,400 by 1900. One branch of the family tree included Montgomery's great-grandfather, Return Meigs (1708–1782), and grandfather, Josiah Meigs (1757–1822).[3]

Josiah, a graduate of Yale (1778), was a part owner of a newspaper, a lecturer and professor at Yale, and a strong supporter of Thomas Jefferson in an anti-Jefferson atmosphere. Conflicts over politics led to his resigning from Yale and going to Athens, Georgia, where he was president of the nascent University of Georgia. His wife bemoaned Athens as in "the backwoods of Georgia only twelve miles from the Cherokee Indians." Josiah's contempt for Georgians, "whom he considered rude and uncivilized," and frankness of speech made enemies. He escaped Georgia, at age 55, when President James Madison appointed him surveyor general of the United States in 1812, and two years later was made commissioner of the General

Land Office of the United States at Washington and lived out his life there. Until his death he was president of Columbian Institute, the predecessor of George Washington University, and professor of experimental philosophy at the institute.[4]

Montgomery had the remains of his grandfather transferred from the Congressional Cemetery in Washington to the Arlington National Cemetery where Josiah's grave is adjacent to that of Montgomery.[5]

Montgomery's father, born in 1792, lived through the end of the Civil War, dying in 1869. He was a physician and author, spending most of his adult life in Philadelphia. He married Mary Montgomery, the daughter of a Philadelphia merchant, on March 15, 1815, and took her to Georgia where he practiced medicine. Their stay in Georgia was long enough for their eldest son (Montgomery) to be born, but was cut short when Mary was "shocked by some of the scenes incident to the slavery system," and the doctor had attacks of "bilious fever."[6]

As a six-year-old, according to his mother, Montgomery was

> very large for his age; high tempered, unyielding, tyrannical towards his brothers; very persevering in pursuit of anything he wishes; very soon tires of his play things, destroying them appears to afford him as much pleasure as their first possession; is not vexed with himself for having broken them, is very inquisitive about the use of everything, delighted to see different machines at work, appears to understand their different operations when explained to him and does not forget them; remembers the particulars of many incidents that occurred two or three years ago, and many things that I had not supposed he noticed. He seems to observe everything that passes; does not read yet, and is not very fond of learning.[7]

In 1874 Montgomery said, "I seem to see much in this portrait of the boy of 6 years which is true now of the man of 58."[8]

The Philadelphia of Montgomery's youth was described by his brother Emlen:

> [P]eople depended on wood for fuel. Gas was unknown. Food was chiefly supplied by farmers, who brought it to the city in wagons. There were no railroads, and a snow storm often meant a blockade for some days of the city's supplies, which almost caused a famine for fuel, which, with many articles of food, would double in price in a day or two.
>
> ...The well-to-do used sperm oil lamps and sperm candles, and the poorer classes used tallow dip candles. Coal oil was unknown. The country people used to produce fire by flint and steel, as there were no matches.

Philadelphia had about 120,000 inhabitants in the 1820s. Emlen described his school days as being somewhat brutal; Samuel Crawford, who ran a classical academy, had "implicit faith in the virtues of his rattan," and was a celebrated flogger. On occasion Emlen was flogged eight times a day, sometimes, Emlen thought, chiefly "for [Crawford's] own exercise."[9]

Whether Montgomery had a similar school experience is not known. He attended the School of the Franklin Institute, a preparatory school for the University of Pennsylvania, was at the university when 15, and the following year entered West Point at the age of 16.[10]

Montgomery's memories of his parents reflect a happy childhood:

> [Mother] by her good sense, [perfectly] true & honest character, was a balance wheel to [father], a man liable to be carried away by impulse, a nervous man, excitable & ardent, not difficult to be discouraged & cast down....

* * * * *

> We are indebted to her for the physical constitutions, which have kept us in good health for so many years, for the teaching and example which have instilled into us & made a part of our characters, the honesty & integrity & faith in the right which have shielded us from temptation to anything mean or untrue. For our industry & perseverance in our lines of business.
>
> In short I attribute to my Mother most of what has been good in my own character and career. Father gave me my mechanical likings, instincts I may say.[11]

When Montgomery entered the United States Military Academy at West Point, New York, in 1832, the grey line of graduates was not long— from 1802 through 1831 there were 633. With the experience of heavily relying on military officers from Europe during the Revolutionary War, George Washington expressed a need for "academies, one or more, for the instruction of the art military."[12]

Sentiment in Congress was different: "standing armies in time of peace are inconsistent with the principles of republican government, dangerous to the liberties of a free people, and generally converted into destructive engines for establishing despotism." In 1785 the United States Army had no more than 100 officers and men.[13]

Threats from abroad led Thomas Jefferson and Congress, in 1802, to establish a military academy at West Point, the largest fort in the United States. In the early years, even though 10 cadets attached to the corps of engineers and 40 to the artillery were authorized, a smaller number actually were in residence.[14]

President James Madison supported improvements at the academy— in 1810 he told Congress:

In a country, happily without the opportunities [for practice in war], seminaries where the elementary principles of the art of war can be taught without actual war, and without the expense of extensive and standing armies, have the precious advantage of uniting an essential preparation against external dangers, with a scrupulous regard to internal safety.[15]

The War of 1812 changed Congress' attitude. It passed a law reorganizing the academy. A requirement was for each cadet to "receive a regular degree from an academical staff" and on graduation to be commissioned as an officer in the army. The number of cadets was increased to 250. At the start of the War of 1812 the academy had only graduated a total of 71 cadets, an inadequate number to lead an army of 145,000 which was planned. West Point officers performed well during the war, compared to other officers, and Madison decided the academy should be an independent body with a permanent superintendent reporting to the secretary of war through the chief of engineers.[16]

With the appointment of Captain Sylvanus Thayer as superintendent in 1817, the academy, over the next 16 years with Thayer as its head, took on many features surviving to the present. Summer encampments were substituted for summer vacations, at least one year of service in the army was required upon graduation, and the corps a graduate was to serve in was based on performance at the academy. In order of prestige, the scientific corps, engineers, topographical engineers, and ordnance, received those with the highest class ranking. The line of the army (artillery, infantry, and cavalry) took the rest.[17]

Cadets were not only ranked according to their academic skills, but also on their conduct. A system of demerits was instituted with the weight of demerits for a particular infraction being heavier as a cadet went from the first to the last year. Hazing of new cadets was not a part of Thayer's academy. An effort was made to have each cadet recite in every class every day, and to group them in small sections, of about a dozen, according to their abilities. He also relied on recent academy graduates for part of the teaching.[18]

Although cadets were graded each day by their instructors, consolidated monthly reports sent to the chief of engineers, and extracts furnished to the parents, the class standing was determined by general examinations covering all their subjects twice a year—in January before the academic board, made up of professors and the superintendent, and in June by the academic board and a board of visitors (invited each year by the secretary of war). The board of visitors in essence graded the academy each year in its report to the War Department.[19]

These general examinations were rigorous. Each cadet was tested for about one hour on each subject before the board of visitors and the academic board. Four cadets would be working on problems at the same time. Each prepared answers on blackboards—while one recited to explain the answer arrived at on his blackboard, the other three would be preparing answers to their questions on their blackboards. The examinations extended over a two-week period. When not being examined, the other cadets, in the group being examined, sat on benches facing the academic board and the board of visitors.[20]

Thayer's curriculum emphasized science—the most important subject being civil engineering. Prior to 1828 West Point was the only American school teaching engineering, and in the 1820s and 1830s was the premier engineering school in the United States.[21]

The quality of the graduates, and their ability to fill a demand for engineers to supervise, plan, and build internal improvements (bridges, harbors, railroads, canals), led to friction when Andrew Jackson became president. His supporters did not like the government giving a free education to officers who left the army after a compulsory period of postgraduate service (one year when Meigs graduated in 1836 but changed to four years in 1838). From the officers' standpoint leaving made sense with West Point turning out more officers than the army needed, and, for those who stayed, there was little chance for promotion. In addition, the pay often was markedly better outside the army.[22]

A strained relationship between the president's mansion and the academy prompted Thayer to resign in 1833. Thayer was superintendent for Meigs' first year and Major Rene E. DeRussy for his remaining three years. DeRussy relaxed the discipline somewhat but made no significant changes otherwise.[23]

Meigs' entry class of 66 members slimmed to 49 at the time of graduation in June 1836. Academically he did well—numbers 6, 3, 1, and 5 in class standing for years 1 through 4. A different story on conduct—his first year 174 out of a total of 210 cadets; for the remaining years it was 143 out of 242, 172 out of 240, and 138 out of 196. Since cadets were not recommended for discharge from the academy until they had more than two hundred demerits for any one year, he was never in danger—his demerits for each of the years were 113, 74, 126, and 131.[24]

Perhaps because he got so many of them, near the end of his army career Meigs expressed a dislike for the demerit system. He thought it "pulled down the active, the enterprising, and put up at their expense the stolid, the namby pamby, the men having no distinguishing traits of character."[25]

Undoubtedly gratifying to Montgomery was the presence of his uncle, John Forsyth of Augusta, Georgia, on the board of visitors at the end of his first year. John was a distinguished man having been a member of Congress and in 1833 was a United States senator. Most of his sons and daughters, during the Civil War, were either married to, or were members of the Confederate army.[26]

The 1836 June examination for the first class was in mathematics, French, natural philosophy, drawing, engineering, chemistry & mineralogy, rhetoric & moral philosophy, tactics, artillery, and conduct. If "conduct" had not been a factor, Montgomery would have been second in his class instead of fifth. He lost over one hundred points in "conduct" to three of those who finished higher than he did—this was out of a total of 1,900 plus scored by each of the top five. In two subjects Montgomery excelled over the top four: drawing and chemistry & mineralogy.[27]

Montgomery was fortunate in having as assistant teacher of drawing Seth Eastman who made a reputation as an artist, concentrating on Indian life and landscapes, as well as a career army officer. Drawing at West Point included working on the human figure, studies in landscape, sketches from nature, topography, and the use of pen, pencil, India ink, and colors. Meigs enjoyed painting and sketching throughout his life.[28]

A Thayer objective was to keep the cadets busy. However, being busy did not include the forbidden—no drinking, cards or chess, gambling, use of tobacco, reading of novels, bathing in the river, or playing a musical instrument. He also believed in keeping them on the post—summer furloughs for the third class was the only time a cadet left the academy during his four years.[29]

Cadets did not find themselves removed from a disciplinary state very often. For meals they were assigned to tables and marched to and from. On entering the dining room they stood behind their chairs and sat when ordered to do so. They rose when the time allotted for the meals was over and marched back to their barracks. Cadets were to be in their rooms when not in class or in formation. Lounging on beds was discouraged—the mattress was folded and bedding placed on top of the mattress. Rooms could house from two to six cadets.[30]

Their drafty rooms, which were heated by a fireplace, were inspected several times a day, and cadets were required to be in their rooms when not in class. From reveille to tattoo proper uniform was required. Water was carried to the rooms from outdoor taps or wells. Large "sinks" were located near barracks and summer camp areas for human waste. Parades were scheduled for each afternoon, including Sundays. Free time came on Saturday afternoons and Sundays after chapel.[31]

At times the cadets reverted to what was natural for young men. In January 1836 six cadets removed a reveille gun, called the "old waker," to a location between the barracks and fired a one-gun salute, breaking most of the windows on one side of the barracks. The gun was then dismantled and reassembled on the fourth floor of the barracks.[32]

Excitement pulsed through the academy in December 1835, when a unit of soldiers was massacred by Seminole Indians. The cry went up for "Early Graduation"—the entire first class volunteered for immediate assignment to Florida, but the assignment was not made.[33]

Thayer worked hard to instill in the cadets a sense of duty and honor, and would have heartily embraced the academy motto of "Duty, Honor, Country" adopted in the late 1800s—a motto exemplified by Montgomery Meigs' life.[34]

Chapter 3

Seasoning

Graduation with a class standing of number five gave Montgomery leverage to get into the most sought after branch of the army, the Corps of Engineers. Although initially commissioned as a second lieutenant in the artillery a year later he was transferred to the corps.[1]

The army then was small, about seven thousand spread all over the country with approximately one hundred assigned to each post. Although there was a commanding general, Alexander Macomb, ready to be the field leader in time of war, absent a war the line of authority went from the secretary of war to those in the field. Staff components (quartermaster general, adjutant general, inspector general, commissary generals of purchases and subsistence, paymaster general, surgeon general, chief of engineers, chief of ordnance) acted reasonably independently and reported to the secretary of war.[2]

In 1836 the army was engaged in one of the sadder episodes of U.S. history. President Andrew Jackson wanted Indians in the East to trade their land for land west of the Mississippi River. Congress passed the Indian Removal Act in 1830 which allowed the government to trade land in the West for Indian land in the East. Between 1829 and 1837, Jackson's time as president, close to 20 different treaties to that end were signed, albeit, the legitimacy of some of the treaties could be questioned. The Removal Act itself does not sound too bad, but subsequent avoidance of its terms does not put the white rulers in a good light. The new Indian lands were guaranteed "forever" by the United States to the Indians, and it would be lawful for the president to protect the Indians in their new lands. In the 1850s 50 some new treaties were negotiated with Indians removed to the Mississippi Valley or west of the river whereby the United States ended up with 174 million acres of land.[3]

Although the Seminoles in Florida signed treaties respecting their removal, there was no agreement as to what the treaties required. The Second Seminole War was the culmination of many conflicts between the

Indians, whites, and government efforts to remove the Seminoles to Oklahoma. The conflicts escalated to war with the massacre of over one hundred soldiers on December 28, 1835, and soaked up most of the military academy class of 1836. Only the top six in the class went into the Corps of Engineers. The remainder were commissioned either in the artillery (31), infantry (7), or dragoons (4), virtually all of whom were sent to Florida to fight the Seminoles.[4]

The Seminole War, which continued until 1842, was a grueling affair in which few battles were fought but much guerrilla type action occurred. The cost to the regular army was heavy with "1,466 deaths, of which 328 were killed in action." As in the Civil War, most of the deaths came from disease. In the end about four thousand Seminoles had been shipped to the West, some withdrew into the Everglades, and others settled in the prescribed Indian reservation in Florida.[5]

The oppressive Indian removal policy included relocating the Cherokee Indians out of their settled areas in the Southeast in 1838 and 1839 over the so-called Trail of Tears to Oklahoma with a loss of one-fourth of their Nation. Such actions and minor wars were not the business of the Corps of Engineers.[6]

An aftermath of the War of 1812 was a congressional decision to build coastal and border fortresses. In 1818 Secretary of War John Calhoun assigned supervision of work on fortifications to the Corps of Engineers with the actual work provided by private businesses. Even though the passage of time lessened Congress' concern and the appropriations for such work, it was still going on in 1837 when Meigs joined the corps. In addition to work on fortifications, the corps also performed duties relating to civil public works such as improvements of rivers and harbors.[7]

In 1836 the Corps of Engineers only had 23 officers—one brigadier general (Gratiot), one colonel (Totten), one lieutenant colonel (Abert), two majors (Thayer & DeRussy), six captains, six first lieutenants, and six second lieutenants. In 1838 the authorized size of the corps increased to 43.[8]

Meigs got a first lieutenancy early (July 1838) but was to stay at that rank for the next 14 years. During these 14 years there were other West Point graduates toiling in the corps who became well known with the Civil War—Robert E. Lee (class of 1829), Pierre G.T. Beauregard (class of 1838), Henry Halleck (class of 1839), William Rosecrans (class of 1842), George B. McClellan (class of 1846). Through most of this period the chief of engineers was Joseph G. Totten (class of 1805) who held that job during most of the Civil War, dying in April 1864 at the age of 75. Ulysses S. Grant (class of 1843), a mediocre student graduating number 21 in a class of 39, was on active duty during these years, but in a less distinguished branch, the infantry. William T. Sherman (class of 1842) served in the artillery, and Jefferson Davis (class of 1828), another mediocre student (23 out of 33), was an infantryman-dragoon.[9]

Jefferson Davis resigned his commission in 1835 and eloped with Colonel Zachary Taylor's daughter, who tragically died of malarial fever three months later. Davis gained hero status, and Taylor's respect, as commander of a Mississippi volunteer regiment in the Mexican War.[10] Grant, Sherman, Halleck, McClellan, and Rosecrans all left the army in the 1850s—it was a time of no promotions as the army went back from 22,000 in the Mexican War to about 11,000, and the higher ranking officers stayed on.[11]

Meigs' assignments for the first few years after graduation kept him in the Washington and Philadelphia area except for a short period in 1837 when he assisted Captain Robert E. Lee who was assigned to superintend improvements of the Mississippi River and the harbor at St. Louis. This assignment gave him a touch of the frontier.[12]

Lee and Meigs traveled together by steamer in the summer of 1837 from Pittsburgh to St. Louis, arriving on August 5. St. Louis' population in 1821, when Missouri was admitted to the Union, of 5,600 people grew to 16,469 in 1840. Although not large in 1837, it was booming—during the 12 months following September 1837, Lee reported upwards to five hundred homes were built and 162 steamboats used the port.[13]

Meigs was not impressed with the hotel in which they stayed. He had a touch of homesickness and described the hotel room as having dirty walls covered with peeling white wash, a smell he hoped to kill with a cologne he had carried with him across the mountains—the atmosphere was said to be "phaugh!" But there were matters of interest. He saw a group of Indian chiefs "in full costume...with scarlet blankets & Buffalo robes and painted faces—not caricatures" like those seen in Philadelphia. There were plenty of deer and he hoped to give a good account of himself with a rifle he purchased for $25 that was capable of killing a buzzard at 85 yards. He anticipated using the rifle from horseback; it was short and suitable for that type use which was the way they hunted in the area. He was also impressed with a western catfish of two feet and a half, and later was able to get in some fishing.[14]

Their first undertaking was to survey the rapids on the Des Moines River. Lee called the country around the Des Moines River "beautiful" with a great future, and Meigs made some watercolors of the area. Later, they returned to St. Louis and worked on plans to protect the St. Louis harbor from being cut off from deep water. Meigs handled the mapping required. As winter approached they returned to Washington.[15] Meigs did not work for Lee again but years later remembered Lee as

> one with whom nobody ever wished or ventured to take a liberty, though kind and generous to all his subordinates, admired by all women, and respected by all men. He was the model of a soldier and the beau ideal of a Christian man.[16]

For the next four years Meigs was on duty in Philadelphia working on Fort Delaware and improvements of harbors in the Delaware River and Bay, and occasionally at the office of the Engineer Department in Washington. During this time he met, courted, and married Louisa Rodgers, the daughter of Commodore John Rodgers, the hero of the War of 1812, on May 2, 1841.[17] What did he see in Louisa? Plenty. Describing himself as "sober and serious by nature," he extolled her traits: she was "everything that was fascinating," with elegant manners, "appearance pleasing but not much beauty." She sang well, "amiable, intelligent, sprightly," and, as he thought before he loved her, everything necessary to make a good wife.[18]

In September 1841 he was ordered west to erect a new fort near Detroit. He stayed there for the next eight years as superintending engineer with additional responsibilities for fortifications along the Lake Frontier. While in Detroit he was at times called back to Washington during the winter to help in the office of chief engineer.[19] The time in Detroit was not all devoted to fortifications. Four children were born: John Rodgers (February 1842), Mary Montgomery (August 1843), Charles Delucena (January 1845), and Montgomery (February 1847).[20]

The Mexican War (1846–1847) came and went without his active participation. For a career military officer, to miss out on what might be the only war of his lifetime, and the chance for higher rank and to add luster to the Meigs line, was a disappointment. He did have some excitement though. In June and July 1845, Brevet Brigadier General Totten, chief of engineers, told him to push forward rapidly with the fort. Then, in a "strictly confidential" message of September 3, 1845, Meigs was told that "[t]he present state of our political relations makes it quite important that information as to the neighboring Colony should be collected on every point that could be useful in a military way in the event of hostilities."[21]

The political atmosphere was indeed electric. The issue of the northern boundary for the Oregon area had been festering since 1842. Those in the western part of the United States wanted to annex the area up to the border of Russia's Alaska (54 degrees, 40 minutes North). President John Tyler offered England a northern boundary of 40 degrees latitude, but England insisted on a northern line along the north bank of the Columbia River.

With a new, aggressive President James K. Polk elected on a Democratic platform calling for "re-occupation of Oregon, re-annexation of Texas," the argument took on new dimensions. Polk's Annual Message to Congress in December 1845 asserted that American rights up to 54–40 were "clear and unquestionable." The war with Mexico came in May 1846, and shortly after that Polk submitted a treaty making the boundary line at 49 degrees North latitude, and, after a debate in which the slogan "54–40 or fight" was heard, the Senate agreed and the matter was settled.[22]

With the completion of Fort Wayne at Detroit in 1849, Meigs moved on to supervise construction of Fort Montgomery at the outlet of Lake

Champlain. Another child, Vincent Trowbridge, was born at Rouses' Point, New York (September 1851).[23] In November 1852, the scale of his work suddenly changed. He was called to Washington which was to remain his residence for the rest of his life.

Washington was unique. It did not come into being because of any features that made it natural for people to want to congregate there. It was a creature of the Constitution of 1787 which specifies exclusive congressional legislative jurisdiction over not more than 10 square miles as the seat of government of the United States. Where the seat of government would be located was left open.[24]

Both the Northern and Southern states wanted the capital to be located within their boundaries. When the South agreed to the funding of the debts of the former colonies by the federal government, the North agreed to a location along the Potomac River. Ultimately, a 10-mile square was selected; it encompassed Georgetown, Maryland, and most of Alexandria, Virginia, which was close to President Washington's home at Mount Vernon, but otherwise consisted of mostly unsettled land on each side of the Potomac River which divides the states of Maryland and Virginia.[25]

With the location made, buildings for Congress, the president, and public offices were needed. Congress specified that these were to be located on the eastern (or Maryland) side of the Potomac. Washington selected Major Pierre Charles L'Enfant, a Frenchman who had fought against the British in the Revolution, to make "drawings of the particular grounds most likely to be approved for the site of the federal town and buildings." In petitioning Washington for the job in 1789, L'Enfant saw the task as an opportunity to acquire a reputation.[26]

L'Enfant's thinking is found in a letter to Washington dated September 11, 1789:

> No nation perhaps had ever before the opportunity offered them of deliberately deciding on the spot where their Capital city should be fixed, or of combining every necessary consideration in the choice of situation—and altho' the means now within the power of the country are not such as to pursue the design to any great extant it will be obvious that the plan should be drawn on such a scale as to leave room for that aggrandisement & embellishment which the increase of the wealth of the Nation will permit it to pursue at any period however remote....[27]

L'Enfant's plan, which has been adhered to in large measure, placed the Capitol and the president's house over a mile apart. This was a considerable distance in those days and led to criticism that it would be necessary to "employ post-horses, and establish relays" to carry messages between the president and Congress.[28]

Washington was not much of a city before the Civil War. It was situated between two pre-existing communities, Georgetown and Alexandria. By 1800 it "consisted of 109 brick houses and 263 of wood." Additionally, it had the president's house and a partially completed Capitol. The population of Washington was 3,210, of Georgetown 2,993, and of Alexandria 4,971. As provided by an act of Congress, the government moved to Washington by December 1800, from Philadelphia where it had been situated for the last 10 years.[29]

Washington grew to a population of 13,117 in 1830. Even though Washington was larger than either Georgetown or Alexandria, which had about eight thousand people each in 1830, it was spread over such a large area that it looked much less like a city than did either Georgetown or Alexandria which were confined to smaller areas.[30]

An 1834 description by an Englishwoman, Harriet Martineau, was that

> The city itself is unlike any other that ever was seen, straggling out hither and thither, with a small house or two a quarter of a mile from any other; so that, in making calls "in the city" we had to cross ditches and stiles, and walk alternately on grass and pavements, and strike across a field to reach a street.[31]

Charles Dickens traveled in the United States in 1842 and spoke well of the Capitol—"a fine building of the Corinthian order, placed upon a noble and commanding eminence." And not so well of the remainder of the city—"the City of Magnificent Intentions....Spacious avenues, that begin in nothing, and lead nowhere; streets, mile-long, that only want houses, roads and inhabitants."[32]

At the time the Meigs family moved to Washington (1852) the population was around 40,000 of whom 10,000 were African-Americans, about four-fifths being free. The population growth was greater than that, percentage wise, which had occurred in the nation as a whole. In 1830 the United States had 12.9 million people and in 1850 there were 23.2 million. Georgetown and Alexandria each still had about eight thousand population in 1850.[33]

The population tended to be close to Pennsylvania Avenue between the Capitol and the president's house or clumped around the public buildings: the president's house, which had close by the State, Treasury, War, and Navy Departments; the Capitol; City Hall; the Patent Office and General Post Office; and the Navy Yard and the Arsenal. The city, on an east-west line somewhat south of the Capitol, was divided by a "fetid and stagnant stream" that "cut off the southern portion of the city, which thus surrounded by water, went by the name of 'The Island,' much to the disgust and against the protests of its residents."[34]

The "filthy, sluggish stream" was the result of a canal built in 1815 for local traffic, and enlarged in the 1830s in an effort to participate in the expected commerce from the West, brought to the Washington area by the Chesapeake and Ohio Canal which was built between 1828 and 1851. The city of Washington wanted to have the C&O Canal, running 185 miles from Georgetown to Cumberland, Maryland, paralleling the Potomac River, terminate on the Eastern Branch (now the Anacostia River), a more navigable river than the Potomac. To this end, the improved canal went from Georgetown to the Eastern Branch. Alexandria also wanted to get into the commerce from the West. This was accomplished by the Aqueduct Bridge (now the Key Bridge) across the Potomac which was part of a canal from Georgetown to Alexandria. The Aqueduct Bridge floated canal boats. All those relying on the C&O Canal as a major commercial conduit were frustrated with the construction of the Baltimore and Ohio Railroad in the same time period which proved to be the more economical way to ship from the West.[35]

The "foul and noisome" stream had bridges over it but in traveling over them "you encountered all sights and smells that came from muddy flats, dead cats and dogs, and occasionally a human derelict who had stumbled to his death through drink."[36]

It was not easy to travel around the city. "Not a street was paved except Pennsylvania Avenue and a patch here and there." Pennsylvania Avenue was "paved with cobble stones, soon degenerating into ruts where mud and slime congregated to spoil and spatter the unwary pedestrian." There was some transportation. Stages or omnibuses "seating from twelve to sixteen persons" ran from the Capitol west to Georgetown and east to the Navy Yard, and some into North Washington and to the steamboat wharves. Most people shopped at the Center or Marsh Market: "an old frame structure...open to the four winds of heaven, dingy looking and ancient in appearance." It was located near Seventh and Pennsylvania Avenue, "separated by a narrow street from the Fish Market, which in its turn lay along the canal into whose vile depths were flung all the refuse and offal from the fish that were there cleaned."[37]

It was unhealthy to live around the Potomac Flats which were near enough to the White House that some presidents, starting with Martin Van Buren (1837–1841) and through Lincoln, did not want to live exclusively in the White House during the summer and early fall. Presidents Van Buren and Pierce (1853–1857) rented houses on the heights of Georgetown, and Buchanan (1857–1861) stayed at the Soldiers Home north of the city as did Lincoln.[38]

All in all Washington was not a pleasant city in 1852. It was a democratic city. "[D]omestic animals and people lived in perfect equality, with equal and undisturbed rights." Milch cows ran at large and geese and pigs would march through the streets. Over the next four decades Montgomery Meigs contributed significantly to its improvement.[39]

Chapter 4
The Washington Aqueduct

How do great talents arrive at a place where they can show their merit? Montgomery Meigs got his chance because of a fire and an unexpected death. In 1852 his assignment was as the superintending engineer in building Fort Montgomery for defense of the outlet of Lake Champlain, New York, and of harbor improvements in Delaware Bay and on the New Jersey coast. But events soon made him a prominent person.[1]

The Library of Congress established in 1800 played a part. After it was burned in 1814 as part of the Capitol, Thomas Jefferson, who needed the money, sold the United States his private library. Then another tragedy. On Christmas Eve 1851 fire destroyed "35,000 books; thousands of manuscripts and maps; paintings by Gilbert Stuart, John Cranch, and John Trumbull; and sculpture by Luigi Persico, Giuseppe Ceracchi, and P. J. David d'Angers."[2]

In part it is likely the fire energized Congress to appropriate $5,000 in 1852 "to enable the President of the United States to cause to be made the necessary surveys, projects and estimates for determining the best means of affording the cities of Washington and Georgetown an unfailing and abundant supply of good and wholesome water." There was a pressing need for an adequate amount of water—a population of about 58,000 was relying on cisterns, springs, and wells. For example, the president's house received water from the Franklin Park spring (near 14th and K Streets). The Capitol had a six-inch pipe connection to another spring about two and one-half miles away. In addition to the direct connection, there were brick reservoirs on either side of the Capitol.[3]

Increased demands from population growth were just part of the need for more water. Greater per capita use also contributed. Times were changing. The president's house installed fixed bathtubs after 1850. Earlier (1845) in Boston the increased use of bathtubs caused such a surge in demand for water that laws were passed against their use.[4]

After the $5,000 appropriation, President Millard Fillmore, in September 1852, assigned the job to the U.S. Army Engineer Department which tasked Captain Frederick A. Smith, deputy to the chief of engineers, to do the job. Smith died suddenly, and the job went to Lieutenant Meigs on November 3, 1852. Meigs walked on to the national scene, a scene he liked, where he was to remain the rest of his life.[5]

Congress was in a hurry. Meigs obliged with a 55-page report and bragged: "I have had but three months to survey, devise, project, and estimate three great works, either of which is well worthy the study of a year."[6] After submitting the report to the chief of engineers, General Joseph Totten, he wrote his father:

> If it is not good & does not give me a standing among engineers I shall be disappointed for it contains my brains....

> * * * * *

> I wrote it at a gallop....
> ...[T]he language seems to me as good as I am capable of inventing.[7]

Any fears were set aside when on February 14, 1853, two days after receiving the report, Totten passed it on to the secretary of war with full agreement. In March, Meigs was promoted to captain; a promotion not connected to his good work but based on 14 years of continuous service. A couple of weeks later, Jefferson Davis, the secretary of war in the new Franklin Pierce administration, put him in charge of the aqueduct and a short time later of an ongoing Capitol extension.[8]

The report laid out three source options (Rock Creek, Little Falls of the Potomac, and Great Falls of the Potomac) with the Great Falls option, which Meigs recommended, being the most expensive but also providing the largest supply of water. An advantage of the proposed course was to permit the "city [to] dispens[e], in great measure, with the labor of working fire-engines; the head being sufficient, in every part of the city, for extinguishing fires by the use of hose alone." The Great Falls source would permit "a jet in the Capitol grounds of one hundred and twenty feet in height."[9]

The report was not all dry numbers. Meigs had a vision:

> The quantity of water to be advantageously used in fountains can be limited only by the supply. In a city of such long continued summer heats—the metropolis of a great country, *where assemble and suffer together, from dust and heat, the leading and most honored citizens...*—the supply of water used to cool the air, and to protect and preserve the health of its inhabitants, should be lavish. The founders of the city foresaw this necessity when they planned its broad and spacious avenues and its extensive public squares; not on the crowded model of a business city, but with reference to the future wants of a great metropolis—

leaving place for fountains and trees at every intersection of its main
avenues, and preparing streets, not for the passage of the busy throng
of merchants, but for the pomps and processions of a great capital.
[Emphasis supplied.][10]

Delivery "of the first necessary of life and health to the [city] inhabitants"
should not be left to a "bloated monopoly." "Water should be free as air,
and should always be supplied by the government."[11]

An option eliminated was pumping water from the Potomac near
Georgetown. Increased river pollution was anticipated: the water there
"flows back and forth, with the tide, over the extensive flats between
Georgetown and the Long Bridge [now the 14th Street Bridge], collecting
and retaining the sewage water of the cities; and, as these cities increase in
size, the water will become less and less fit for domestic use." The cost of
pumping was aptly described: "[t]he steam engine—an invaluable assistant where better means are wanting—is, at best, an eating sore, which
consumes the fuel paid for by taxation; and not to-day only, nor to-mor-
row, but forever." Pumping was contrasted with "lead[ing] the water in a
suitable channel, propelled by its own gravity, to reservoirs, whence it can
be drawn by pipes and distributed wherever wanted."[12]

The Great Falls option was for a conduit capacity capable of deliver-
ing over 67 million gallons each day. This was indeed a far-sighted approach at a time when the capacity needed for Washington was five million
gallons, and for New York close to 30 million gallons. This option was
described on the floor of the Senate as being on "a grand and magnificent
scale." It was criticized "as an attempt intended by its magnitude and
expense to emulate the regal splendor of the works of the old world." The
water to be supplied was one and one-half times what London was receiving and four times that for Paris, but only one-fifth of what Rome was
provided in A.D. 101.[13]

Montgomery Meigs did not think small in creating engineering designs or in expanding the Capitol. In 1897 the aqueduct was still adequate
for Washington but not with much margin. Currently many parts of the
aqueduct, as designed by Meigs, are still used to supply water to Washington. Meigs' confidence in his ability is reflected in the statement that
"in [1852] with money, any achievement of engineering was possible."[14]

His report is impressive—thoughtful and thorough. Congress was
satisfied—within a month of receiving the report it appropriated $100,000
in 1853 for the start of the project. Left for decision was which option
should be implemented—the new president, Franklin Pierce, went for the
grand scheme. Pierce, a veteran of the Mexican War, made former Mississippi Senator Jefferson Davis, a hero of that war, his secretary of war. Davis
and Meigs worked in complete harmony when it came to public projects
for the capital for the next seven years.[15]

To celebrate the start of the aqueduct, a ceremony was held in November 1853 at which President Pierce and others turned spades of dirt. The celebratory party came from Washington via passage boats on the Chesapeake and Ohio Canal. Meigs started off the ceremony by stating that "[o]f all the works which civilization and science enable man to construct, perhaps an aqueduct is the most useful, the most enduring." On this occasion he named the project the Washington Aqueduct. A name which Meigs thought would be a monument "fitter to [Washington] than obelisk or statue."[16]

In fact, the first spade of dirt was moved by Meigs in October 1853 in front of his assistants and some of the work force. His journal entry for that day shows how disappointed he was that no glory came his way from the Mexican War:

> Thus quietly and unostentatiously was commenced the great work. Which is destined I trust for the next thousand years to pour healthful water into the Capital of our union. May I live to complete it and connect my name imperishably with a work greater in its beneficial results than all the military glory of the Mexican War.[17]

Meigs, a man with strong religious beliefs, saw himself as an instrument in God's hand bringing "to millions yet unborn...health comfort and happiness." His efforts were appreciated by the people of Washington who presented him a silver tea kettle in the summer of 1854. When the kettle was put on public display he thought "public recognition of [his] authorship of the design for the Potomac aqueduct [would] be of service to [him.]" And "out of this reputation [he might] some day make more money than Uncle Sam pays to his servants." Public recognition was already coming his way—in January 1854 he was elected to be a member of the American Philosophical Society.[18]

As an army captain he was not well paid—$138.50 per month to support his family. His father helped out by giving him $300 per year. A continuing concern was the lack of savings to take care of his family if anything should happen to him.[19]

The Great Falls plan was for a nine-foot diameter conduit connecting a dam at Great Falls and a receiving reservoir at Dalecarlia near Georgetown and a distributing reservoir at Georgetown. The reservoirs were to provide storage and the settlement of the sediment before the water entered the Washington distribution system. The total distance between Great Falls and the Georgetown distribution reservoir is about 12 miles.[20]

One Meigs' thought did not hold up over time. In speaking of filtering the water from the Potomac, he said allowing it to settle "in extensive and capacious reservoirs [would give Washington a supply of] water unrivaled for purity and salubrity." In fact, until Washington constructed a filtration system some 50 years later, Washington's water was described in the newspapers as "murky," "brownish," and "not a drop fit to drink." Solace could be found in the knowledge that every other city taking water from rivers during this period were having the same problem, and large-scale filtration was not introduced into water systems in the United States until the turn of the century.[21]

An example of the thoroughness of the report is found in these observations about protecting the Capitol:

> The height at which the water of the Great Falls can be delivered in the Capitol, fourteen feet above the upper floor, is, I think, quite sufficient to secure the safety of the building, and of the invaluable collections therein contained; but should it be desired to have the power of pouring the water upon the roof itself, this can be done by a small turbine-wheel and force-pump, which...can be worked by water from the main.[22]

Amazingly, even though the aqueduct was not fully used until December 1863, it cost close to what Meigs estimated in 1853 ($2.4 million) if allowance is made for unavoidable cost increases resulting from Congress not appropriating funds for some of the 10-year period, and the requisite costs of closing down and starting up operations. Meigs anticipated, with adequate funding, the aqueduct would have been completed in three years.[23]

Not only were costs kept within bounds, there were two outstanding engineering accomplishments. To carry the conduit over the Cabin John Valley the Cabin John Bridge was constructed by use of "the longest masonry arch in the world," a record held for about 40 years. The arch has a span of 220 feet with a rise of $57^1/_4$ feet. The present tense is correct—the bridge is still in place carrying out its original function and also providing a single lane for car traffic.[24]

The 40-year record for Cabin John Bridge was a noteworthy segment in the engineering ability to arch over valleys, gorges, and rivers. Vaulted sewers with a 20-foot diameter date back to 600 B.C., and, by 62 B.C., engineers were capable of an 80-foot span. The Romans reached 142 feet as their best. Today, with the use of steel, the New River Gorge Bridge in West Virginia has the world's longest steel arch, 1,700 feet.[25]

The Cabin John Bridge may have been a challenge to Meigs' engineering abilities that he couldn't pass up. There is uncertainty as to whether the single span was more expensive than the use of six smaller arches as originally contemplated. A *National Geographic* article published after Meigs' death says the use of six 60-foot span arches would have cost $72,000 and that the single span cost $254,000. At the time Meigs made the decision to go with a single span he thought the relative costs were about the same.[26]

For many years the Cabin John Bridge was one of the things to see in the Washington area. Thousands of persons came to see it, including many engineers from foreign countries.[27] Meigs' pride in the bridge is reflected in the inscription carved on the east abutment:

UNION ARCH

Chief Engineer, Capt. Montgomery

C. Meigs, U.S. Corps of Engineers

Esto Perpetua

In fact, he got carried way on inscriptions and the like. An additional east abutment inscription reads:

M. C. MEIGS

CHIEF ENGINEER

WASHINGTON AQUEDUCT

A.D. 1859 FECIT

Fecit translates to "He made it." His name is found on the Great Falls gatehouse, waste-weirs, bridges, a culvert, and a sluice tower. At the distributing reservoir, the rise of each of 39 iron steps was composed of the letters "M. C. Meigs." Also stamped on many pieces of iron and brass was the inscription "Washington aqueduct, M. C. Meigs." He also designed elegant water hydrants with his name displayed.[28] When it looked like he might lose supervision of the aqueduct in 1858, because of conflicts with a new secretary of war, he had 24 copper plates made showing Captain Meigs as chief engineer and put some in masonry and under blocks of stone. He thought the plates would stay "clean and legible for centuries." Some of the plates also listed his assistants who were also named on an inscription stone at the Great Falls Gatehouse.[29]

Why would a person of his talents be so carried away with the need to inscribe his name? The answer probably lies within remarks he made at the ceremony of celebration in November 1853:

> The channels constructed by Pagan Emperors before the Christian era still continue to pour their healthful waters into decaying Rome. What other structure of those early days now continues to fulfil its original purpose?...the aqueduct, embalming in the gratitude of the people the name of its founder, still supplies health and life, and perpetuates his name after the lapse of eighteen hundred years.[30]

Although professionally 1853 was a satisfying year, it was punctuated with sadness. In September and October, eight-year-old Charles and two-year-old Vincent died from what Meigs described as "disease of the brain." The sadness was alleviated some by the birth of Louisa Rodgers (called Loulie) in August 1854. A daughter was born dead in 1856.[31]

An inscription not including Meigs' name is on the west abutment of the Cabin John Bridge reading, initially,

WASHINGTON AQUEDUCT
Begun A.D. 1853. President of the U. S.
Franklin Pierce Secretary of War
Jefferson Davis. Building A. D. 1861
President of the U.S. Abraham Lincoln
Secretary of War Simon Cameron

In June 1862, because of the War, supervision of the aqueduct was transferred from the War Department to the Department of the Interior. When the secretary of the interior was on an inspection trip of the aqueduct he was informed that "that d—d rebel Meigs has put Jeff Davis' name on the bridge." Secretary Caleb Smith ordered it removed. Lobbying by Southerners led President Theodore Roosevelt to order it replaced in 1908. Jefferson Davis thought the removal of his name "a great indignity" which was an effort to "eliminat[e] from history the part he had taken in construction of the bridge."[32]

The Cabin John Bridge was only one of the unusual engineering feats. It was also necessary to cross Rock Creek, and that bridge was equally novel. "Its essential features were two 48-inch cast iron pipes built in arch form with a 200-foot span and resting on masonry abutments." These pipes were "used to convey the entire city water supply, and also to support a street for many years." The pipes still function, but are covered by a reinforced concrete bridge completed in 1916 named the Montgomery Meigs Memorial Bridge.[33]

Water first passed through the entire aqueduct in December 1863. But, earlier, in January 1859, water flowed from the receiving reservoir filled from the Little Falls branch to create a water stream one hundred feet into the air at an elaborate fountain at the foot of Capitol Hill.[34] This occasioned a letter to Montgomery's father rejoicing at water arriving "for free use of the sick & well, rich & poor, gentle & simple, old & young for generation after generation, which will have come to rise up & call [Meigs] blessed."[35]

Meigs was never to have authority over the aqueduct again after Interior took over its supervision. But this did not keep him from giving advice. This started in 1863 and continued until the last year of his life. When Interior wanted to make certain changes he wrote to the secretary of the interior in August 1863 saying that if any changes were made in his plans he "anticipate[d] ill results—if not to the work, at least to the treasury." During the Civil War he found comfort in riding out to view the completed Cabin John Bridge.[36]

Chapter 5

Capitol Wings and Dome

"Here, sir, the people govern."
—Alexander Hamilton

The original planner of the city of Washington, Pierre L'Enfant, designated the top of Jenkins Hill as the site of the Congress House. Jenkins Hill, although only about 80 feet above the flat land to the west, has a commanding view of this land which extends a mile or two to the Potomac River. On this flat land, L'Enfant positioned the president's house (now the White House), the president's park (now the Ellipse), a grand avenue (now the Mall), and the location for an equestrian figure of George Washington (now occupied by the Washington Monument).[1]

L'Enfant was expected to design the Capitol, but refused to produce a plan with the explanation that he carried it "in his head." This was not adequate. L'Enfant was dismissed over this and other matters and a competition held for a design with a $500 prize and a city lot for the winner.[2]

William Thornton, an amateur architect from the British West Indies, won the contest with a Capitol featuring a center dome reminiscent of a Roman temple of the second century A.D., the Pantheon. George Washington laid the cornerstone on September 18, 1793. By the time the government moved to Washington City in 1800, only the north wing of the Capitol was completed. It was used to house both branches of Congress, the Supreme Court, the Library of Congress, and lesser courts.[3]

At the time of the War of 1812, the south wing had been completed, and repairs and changes to the north wing were under way. The British burned both in 1814. To this point no effort had been made to construct the center part of the Capitol which, according to the Thornton plan, was to contain the dome. Inclusion of a dome in the Capitol met with George Washington's favor: he wrote that it would "give beauty and grandeur to the pile; and might be useful for the reception of a Clock, Bell, &ca."[4]

Reconstruction of the partially burned north and south wings commenced under the leadership of Benjamin Latrobe, a London-trained architect. Latrobe found himself in disputes over costs and design, and left in 1817. His replacement was Charles Bulfinch, a Boston architect, who undertook repair of both wings as well as construction of the central, domed portion.[5]

Bulfinch was allowed to introduce his own ideas as to the central portion, but the contours of the wooden, copper-covered dome were set by President James Monroe and his secretary of state, John Quincy Adams. When Bulfinch left his job in 1830 the Capitol was finished. Fittingly, Bulfinch was the first American-born architect to work on the Capitol. The earliest known photograph of the Capitol taken about 1846, found in a California flea market, shows the Bulfinch dome, once described as looking like a washbowl turned upside down. Thornton, the original designer of the Capitol, thought the finished product to look ridiculous—reminding him of a "large sugar dish between two tea canisters."[6]

Growth in the number of senators and representatives with the addition of new states forced Congress to authorize an expansion of the Capitol. The Senate decided in 1850 to have a competition for the design of the expansion—the prize to again be $500 but no city lot. When one design could not be agreed upon, the prize money was split among the competitors. Congress then approved $100,000 to be spent toward the expansion, and authorized President Millard Fillmore to appoint an architect to execute such plan as the president approved.[7]

Thomas Ustick Walter, a prominent Philadelphia architect, and also a Whig like Fillmore, was appointed in June of 1851. Walter and Meigs were to have a bumpy relationship.[8]

Although the Senate suggested a design with detached wings on the north and south ends of the existing Capitol at right angles to its axis, President Fillmore did not feel bound by this since Congress had authorized him to approve the ultimate plan. The suggestion to connect the wings to the old structure by narrow corridors, ultimately adopted, was made by Fillmore's secretary of state, Daniel Webster. Walter took an oath to "discharge the duties of Architect to execute the plan adopted by the President for the extension of the Capitol" on June 11, 1851. The day before Walter took the oath, President Fillmore approved a plan described as an extension of "two wing buildings placed on the north and south of the old Capitol and 44 feet from it, but connected with the old building by corridors."[9]

In a gross sense, the exterior style used for the expansion was the pre-existing structure. The exterior was sensibly planned to match what was already in place. Neither the House nor Senate, which were not in session from March 14, 1851, to November 30, 1851, were consulted about the interior arrangements. This information was passed on in early 1852 after the construction was under way.[10]

A year into the construction, doubts were raised as to Walter's administrative abilities. In August 1852, the Senate formed a committee to look into abuses, bribery, or fraud. The committee's report considered alleged frauds respecting the Capitol extension. The committee concluded that "great irregularities, and gross abuses and frauds, have been practiced in the business of directing, supervising, and executing the work of the Capitol extension...."[11]

There was never any assertion that Walter was dishonest and he retained his position, albeit with different responsibilities at times, until the Capitol extension was close to completion in 1865. In March 1853 a new president, Democrat Franklin Pierce, directed that superintendence over the Capitol extension be transferred from the secretary of the interior to the secretary of war. Pierce said it was in the public interest to have the "general supervision and control of the whole work" in the hands of a competent military officer.[12]

Politically, whether fair to Walter or not, a transfer was needed. Comments on the Senate floor in 1856 by Senator James Pearce of Maryland indicate why this outcome was inevitable—the general subject under discussion was proposed legislation, with an exception for military superintendence over the Capitol extension, to preclude any military officer from acting as an architect or superintendent of any public construction except for military defense:

> Who does not recollect that, in 1852, and 1853, there were great clamors about the manner in which the extension of the Capitol was going on?...Committees and members of Congress themselves, assisted by architects and builders, went to work upon the walls with crow-bars and picks, to see if they had been properly laid. The architect was required to put larger stones on them and make various alterations, in order to give solidity to the structure. This was under one of the civil superintendents—a gentleman appointed...upon the recommendation of the President of the United States, Mr. Fillmore, and, no doubt, with entire confidence in his capacity and fidelity. We know what clamors there were not only about the want of solidity of the structure...but about infidelities in contracts. We know that the superintendent [not the architect Walter] was charged with being tainted with corruption in contracts; that he was charged with levying black mail, taking receipts for one sum when he paid out another; and we know that, under these circumstances, he resigned his office and quit the work.[13]

In early 1853, Meigs was in the right place at the right time. The new secretary of war, Jefferson Davis, and the new president were already reviewing his study for the Washington Aqueduct. They concluded Meigs was not only the man for running that job but also for straightening out the mess at the Capitol. On April 4, 1853, Meigs was directed "to take charge...of the public interests connected with the extension of the Capitol" and "to take such measures as may be necessary for the proper execution" of the work. The transfer of responsibility to Pierce's good friend

Jefferson Davis also made sense. Davis, as a senator in 1850, had spon-
sored the $100,000 appropriation which initiated the extension.[14]

With this background, a relatively smooth relationship between Meigs
and Walter is not surprising during the term of Davis as secretary of war.
Davis and Meigs were simpatico. Davis wanted a review of the Capitol
plans and Meigs was happy to oblige. Walter, kept on as architect with
Meigs' strong recommendation, was on thin ice.[15]

Davis directed that an examination be made "into the condition of
the foundation [as well as for Meigs to] minutely...inquire into the arrangements for warming, ventilating, speaking, and hearing." When "arrangements for ventilation and hearing were not found satisfactory,"
"modifications of the plans for the extension of the Capitol as proposed
by Captain Meigs" were approved. Meigs, a man of action, developed his
plans in sufficient time for a board of two respected scientists (A. D. Bache,
superintendent of the United States Coast Survey, and Joseph Henry, secretary of the Smithsonian) to tentatively approve them by June 24, 1853.[16]

A Meigs' trait was demonstrated with respect to the adopted plans
for acoustics. In 1856 Secretary Henry wrote a report on acoustics being
employed at the Smithsonian Castle. He said the basis for the Smithsonian
plans was studies made concerning the Capitol. The report was widely
distributed in a newspaper account and brought about letters from Meigs
to Henry and Bache pointing out that the plans for the Capitol acoustics
were "absolutely and solely" his (Meigs) and Henry's report accidently
did not give him (Meigs) the credit due. Meigs realized it was too late to
undo the reading of the misleading report by millions but wanted Henry
to set it straight in the official publication of the Smithsonian proceedings.
Meigs said he never wanted "to take anything belonging to others" and
was "jealous" of his own accomplishments since a "[r]eputation [was all
he had] any prospect of getting [from his efforts.]"[17]

To Walter's dismay, the 1853 changes were not minor. Walter had
designed the legislative chambers for each body to have exterior windows;
Meigs changed this so that the chambers were located in the middle of the
wings with no exterior windows. This change, although challenged from
time to time in Congress as giving up natural light and the ventilation
which the windows could afford, was followed.[18]

Meigs said the following about ventilation:

> The ventilation of so large a room...liable to frequent and great
> fluctuations in the number of persons within it, will require special
> provision. By supplying constantly a large quantity of pure air, at a
> moderate temperature, however, a perfect ventilation can be obtained.
> The only reliable mode of doing this is by using a fan or other blowing
> engine to supply the air, and by warming it as it enters, by pipes filled
> with moderately-heated water.[19]

The thoroughness with which Meigs approached problems is shown by the connection he perceived between pure air and the goal of good acoustics: "A pure atmosphere being favorable to the speaker's health and strength, will give him greater power of voice and more endurance; thus indirectly improving the hearing by strengthening the source of sound, and also by enabling the hearer to give his attention for a longer period unfatigued." Meigs was also worried about light from the windows blinding those speaking to the presiding officer.[20]

Great in theory, but not satisfactory to some of the members of the Senate. In 1856 Senator John P. Hale of New Hampshire said:

> I have thought that when the Infinite Creator of the world made the air for us to breathe, and spread it all around us, we had better take it the way He sends it to us. I think He understands the way to send it to us quite as well as the Secretary of War, who believes it had better be pumped up out of the cellar by a steam-engine.[21]

Four years later, after the new Senate wing was occupied, Senator Hale was still unhappy: "I understood the Senator from New York [William H. Seward] to say that this is the best legislative Hall in the world. If it is, I pity the rest of the world. I think it is the worst that ever I saw. I think it is the worst ventilated, and the worst contrived;....It is hot overhead and cold beneath, calculated to keep your feet cold and your head hot [and, in the opinion of another senator,] it is a great chance whether any man who was sworn in for six years on the 4th of March last will be alive at the end of his term, if we sit in it so long as we have done this session." So that congressmen could keep track of the temperature, Meigs "had thermometers made, each one bearing his name and rank"; he was accused of making a major mistake in having the thermometers calibrated to only go from "twenty-four degrees above zero" to "ninety degrees" since the temperatures in the chambers didn't always stay within those limits. Seward was not alone in his views; Kentucky Senator John J. Crittenden thought it "the very best public room [he] was ever in [in his] life."[22]

Part of the problem was caused by the conduct of the members of Congress. It was observed that "inlets in the floor were more or less contaminated by the refuse tobacco and spittle which had accumulated in them, and the air which came into the room was offensive from that cause." Frances Trollope, writing about the Capitol in the 1830s, said the senators looked like gentlemen, but "I would I could add they do not spit." Edgar Allen Poe was also observant: "If I were to drop my wallet on the floor of the Senate, I would not retrieve it without a gloved hand."[23]

Concerning Meigs' originally proposed changes to the design of the Capitol extension, changes approved by both President Pierce and Jefferson Davis, Meigs stated in his annual report for 1853 that Thomas Walter, an accomplished architect who prepared the implementing plans, was of the opinion that "the legislative halls [would be] better adapted to their main purpose as rooms for debate, [and] that the architectural beauty and the convenience of the buildings [would] be increased by the changes which [had] been made."[24]

If in fact Walter truly favored the changes, which required some tearing out of work he had already allowed to go forward, he was not so gracious in his thoughts after a new president and secretary of war came into office in March of 1857. When Congress convened in December 1857, the new chamber for the House of Representatives was ready for occupancy. Some, including Benjamin French, a former commissioner of public buildings, were not impressed:

> The idea of shutting up a thousand or two people in a kind of cellar; where none of God's direct light or air can come to them—where they are breathing *artificial* air, and seeing the secondary light, is one that does not jump with my notions of *living*.[25]

Walter pointed out that his original plan had called for no less than 50 windows. He went further. Writing to former Congressman Richard Stanton of Kentucky he appraised the color scheme, as to which he was not consulted, as "vulgar...the very worst I ever saw." In general, Walter favored restraint in styling whereas Meigs liked exuberance. Walter had specified that the walls should be plain and hung with paintings.[26]

Walter had no difficulty convincing Stanton who, while in Congress, forcefully expressed the view in June 1854 that Meigs was a "gentleman of exalted moral worth," but not "qualified for the intricate and elaborate architectural details of such work as the Capitol," and could not have carried on "[w]ithout the aid of the distinguished architect, Mr. Walter." In 1855 he said Walter should be in charge of the extension, and denounced the ruthless changes Meigs made in the original plans.[27]

Although Walter's relationship with Meigs during Jefferson Davis' time as secretary of war may have appeared relatively smooth on the surface, Walter very much supported Stanton's position that he, Walter, should be in charge. Writing in March 1855, he said, "Every possible influence has been brought to bear to keep these works out of the hands of the military," and, in December 1857, after Stanton was out of Congress, Walter wrote to him saying he was not forgotten—they had "pulled too long, and too pleasantly together in the cause of...taste and right" for that to happen.[28]

Neither Jefferson Davis nor Montgomery Meigs were ignorant of Walter's true attitude. Davis, who thought Walter was intriguing against Meigs and would assume credit rightly belonging to Meigs, on two occasions was ready to either change Walter's title, and make it absolutely clear as to who was in charge, or to discharge him, but was talked out of doing so by Meigs.[29]

Meigs had two reasons for wanting to keep Walter. First, speaking of the new wings, "Walter had designed the outside of the building, which was what the world would look upon, and that to Walter belonged this part of the building," and to change Walter's position might injure Meigs' reputation by the appearance that Meigs was trying to take credit for what was rightly Walter's. Although Meigs might not get all the credit he was due, the documents would show what he had done.[30]

Secondly, even though he knew Walter "would be governed by no delicacy and would [take all the credit] the world would allow him whether he deserved it or not," "[Walter] had done his duty to the best of his power, that he was very skilful...submissive and willing to be guided by [Meigs] in all things and the best assistant [he] could get, best for [his] own pleasure, best for the success of the work."[31]

Walter was submissive during Davis' four years as secretary of war only on the exterior. His internal feelings were expressed after Davis was out of office, and when it became apparent that Meigs and the new secretary of war were not getting along:

> [Written 10/12/57 to John Rice:] I am driven from morning to night and from night till morning in keeping up my designs for 15 draughtsmen...and if I stop one minute I shall get my shins broke— This is not as it should be—an artists brains should never by cudgelled—he should be the master of his own time, but under the reign that cannot be—Tyranny and despotism is the order of the day ....[32]

Although Jefferson Davis was back in Mississippi after March 1857, he still tried to influence what went on in Washington. An August 23, 1857, letter to Secretary of War John B. Floyd urged that Meigs be retained in charge of the Capitol work. Davis had heard he might be replaced. Not knowing what was behind such a possible change, Davis surmised, from his own experience, that it could be bottomed on either persons wanting contracts or of some architect wanting employment. Floyd was told that Meigs demonstrated "capacity zeal & integrity" which made him the right man for the job. His moral attributes had quieted much of the concern that was focused on the pre-Meigs' period.[33] Floyd, who, by this time, had a real dislike of Meigs, might have ignored this letter but for Jefferson Davis returning to Washington as a senator from Mississippi when Congress reconvened in December 1857.

Meigs lectured the public on colors in the Washington newspaper, the *National Intelligencer*, in December 1857:

> The decoration of the Representatives' Chamber has been...arranged by persons who have made the harmony and contrast of colors the study of their lives. The style is new in this country, where our public buildings generally, through the poverty of the public purse *or the perhaps greater poverty of the architect's taste*, starve in simple whitewash.

The rich and magnificent decoration, of the new Hall...when first seen, naturally excites surprise. The colors are so rich, so various, so intricate, so different from any thing seen before, that the impression is that it must be, what? "Gaudy?" But what is "gaudy?" Are the colors of the autumnal forests gaudy? Is there anything in this Hall more brilliant than the scarlet leafage of the gum or the maple, or the yellow of the oak and other trees?...

* * * * *

This is a great work. Let not the noisy babble of ignorance forestall public opinion upon its merits. [Emphasis supplied.][34]

Meigs, a recreational sketcher and watercolorist, wanted to put life into the building.

In the main, Meigs was vindicated in a letter from the Speaker of the House dated August 13, 1858:

[The new House chamber] has been occupied from December until the middle of June—seasons of the lowest and highest temperature of cold and heat; it has been occupied with crowded galleries and empty benches, by day and by night; and under all circumstances, in its acoustics, its ventilation, its heating, its lighting, and its conveniences for the comfort of members and the transaction of business, I consider it eminently successful....I presume there is no hall in the world, having so large a number of square feet within its walls, where the speaker is heard with so little effort on his part.

* * * * *

The arrangement for lighting the hall is admirable. Not a burner is seen, and yet such a flood of softened light is poured down through the stained glass ceiling of the hall that it was difficult to distinguish when the day ended and the night commenced.[35]

Meigs, and others, blamed the terrible acoustics of the old House chamber for difficulties that members without loud voices had in influencing legislation. Meigs' claim for credit for the excellent acoustics was disputed by Walter who said that his design had produced that result.[36]

Life in the old House chamber was hazardous. By comparison, Meigs found it remarkable "that no member of the House present in Washington died during the [1857–58] session [in the new House chamber]" even though the chamber was occupied for a record number of hours.[37]

When Congress went into session in December 1857, the new House chamber was occupied, and work was proceeding on the Senate wing and the installation of a new dome. Several of those competing in the plans for the Capitol extension in 1850 proposed replacing the old wooden dome.

Aesthetically the old dome did not fit into the enlarged Capitol. And, a fire in December 1851, which destroyed the Library of Congress portion of the Capitol, highlighted the danger posed by a wooden dome and pointed the way to a new, fireproof dome constructed of iron. The fire came close to encompassing the old dome which was considered a "nest of dry materials" inviting a fire. In addition, the old dome leaked.[38]

In May of 1854 Walter showed Meigs a sketch for a new dome which would be about one hundred feet higher than the old. In their discussions they considered St. Paul's in London which has a strong resemblance to the one ultimately built. After Congress convened in December, Meigs showed several congressmen the design for a new dome, suggested it might be built at once, and received encouragement. Walter was not anxious to have the new dome started thinking they had their hands full, but Meigs wanted "it done, for [he wished] to have the credit and the pleasure of building" it. Meigs even went further and made a design which he thought better than Walter's. Walter did not agree—an attitude Meigs attributed, at least in part, to Walter wanting all the credit.[39]

Meigs, who actively lobbied to get funds for the new dome, was abused in two newspaper articles printed in January 1855 praising Walter. In February, Congressman Richard Stanton offered an amendment to an appropriation for a new dome which would have provided that its construction be "under the direction of the architect." After Stanton withdrew this amendment, an appropriation of $100,000 was passed by a single vote in the House.[40]

The maneuvering for control wasn't over. Benjamin French, then the commissioner of public buildings, claimed the House bill would leave the money in his hands and that "Mr. Walter [would direct its use] like any other appropriation for the repairs of the old Capitol." Meigs was shocked. He didn't want the work put under the control of "Goths and Vandals." Considering that French later characterized the finished House chamber as "a kind of cellar," Meigs probably did not have warm feelings toward him.[41]

Senator James Pearce of Maryland agreed to straighten this out, and the bill, as passed by Congress, provided for the funds to be spent "under the direction of the President of the United States," but the design to be used was that of "Thomas U. Walter."[42] As to the design, Meigs told Pearce that

> [he] had been with Mr. Walter in making it, that it was drawn by Walter, that $9/10$ of it was his entirely; that he had changed some parts of it to suit [Meigs], particularly the lantern, but that the design was his almost entirely.[43]

Meigs viewed the new dome as "a great work the greatest in this country and excelled by few if any abroad." He saw it as "a great engineering work, and wanted to construct it so as "to reflect credit upon [his] corps & [the] National School [West Point]."[44]

Before physical work could start on the dome it was necessary to make the requisite construction plans. A significant contribution, attributed to Meigs, was the use of iron brackets to permit the peristyle of the dome (the 36 columns encircling the bottom drum of the dome) to extend 15 feet beyond the wall of the rotunda so as to avoid construction of an additional base. Meigs also overruled Walter, and adopted a plan of draftsman August Schoenborn, as to the point from which the curved iron trusses supporting the cupola (the semi-spherical part of the dome) would start on their way to the tholos (the lantern-like structure on which the Statue of Freedom rests).[45]

Schoenborn, who was Walter's chief architectural draftsman, presumably drew many of the exquisite plans carrying the signatures of both Walter and Meigs. Walter was himself skilled in producing carefully drawn and colored plans. However, preparing drawings was not a two-man undertaking. During the 1850s 20 draftsmen were employed.[46]

Although the dome could have been constructed of any fire-resistant material and been consistent with Congress' authorization, the choice of iron made sense from the standpoint of weight and cost. For example, each of the 36 columns in the peristyle would have weighed 23,000 pounds if made of marble, but only weighed 10,000 pounds when made of iron. To create the styling of an iron column was a one-time matter; once the form was created it was used repeatedly to mold columns. Whereas, each marble column required individual work.[47]

Use of iron throughout for the dome was a first. When, in December 1854, it looked like an appropriation for a new dome might be voted, Meigs noted in his journal that "[n]o dome of [such] magnitude...ha[d] ever been built except by years of toil." With the use of iron, and enough money, he thought the new dome could be built in months. Money, which came slowly starting with a $100,000 appropriation, a controversy about who was boss of the construction, and the Civil War caused completion of the dome to take several years.[48]

The year 1855 was taken up, insofar as the new dome was concerned, with drawing plans and building the scaffolding needed to dismantle the old dome and to permit the installation of a temporary covering over the Rotunda. The Bulfinch dome was removed while Congress was in recess from August 30 to December 1, 1856, and by that time the columns for the peristyle had been delivered. There was some continuity from the old to the new. Wood from the old dome was burned as fuel for the steam engines used in constructing the new. By the end of 1857 the new dome had proceeded to the point of having the peristyle well under way.[49]

At this time Walter's ill feelings toward Meigs boiled over. On December 31, 1857, Walter wrote to a willing listener, the secretary of war, John B. Floyd:

> [I have] permitted Capt. Meigs to have full sway in appropriating to himself the honors due me for more than four years without interposing a word in self defense. I have looked upon his desire for fame...as a very great weakness, and trusted to the world to do me ultimate justice.[50]

In this letter Walter was probably trying to salvage an effort made over the preceding months to have Meigs removed. It was no secret that Floyd and President James Buchanan were unhappy with Meigs who was not going to be a party to some of the patronage steps suggested by each of them. If they wanted to exercise patronage, not in the best interest of the public works under his charge, they needed to issue orders.[51]

Walter was supported by Pennsylvania politicians (in particular senator, and former governor, William Bigler, and former Congressman William H. Witte) and contractors presumably unhappy with Meigs. In September 1857 Walter wrote Meigs that he did not have an improper relationship with marble contractor John Rice, and, on the same day, sent Rice a copy of Meigs' letter to him (Walter) with an admonition that Rice "[m]ention this to nobody," and, in writing, to Meigs, to not "allude to anything said in it." Walter suggested that Rice "appoint an agent and [that Walter would] keep him in the right track." Rice was to "keep this strictly to [himself]."[52] Walter spoke differently to Rice than to Meigs. His closing lines to Meigs read:

> I shall...cut the matter short by refusing any further civilities, of any kind whatever, to Mr. Rice in reference to his business relations....I shall...cut loose Mr. Rice and his telegraphic dispatches, and refuse positively, ever again, to say a word to the clerks responsible to you in regard to Mr. Rice's affairs.[53]

During the months of July 1857 through June 1859 the firm of Rice, Baird & Heebner had a dispute going on with Meigs as to its obligation to furnish one hundred monolithic marble shafts—an arrangement carrying a sizeable price tag, circa $140,000. The letters between the firm and Meigs in the last half of 1857 and early 1858 were significantly contentious. In part, the failure to come to agreement was caused by John Rice's belief that he could get the contract altered.[54]

On October 2, 1857, Walter wrote Witte that he was looking "up certain documents" and Witte should "consider this confidential." In frequent letters to Rice, Walter complained of and disparaged Meigs. He was exultant on December 8 telling Rice *"the order was issued this morning* !!!"[55] The order, dated December 4, from Floyd to Meigs read in part:

> The vastly increased expenditure for the Capitol Extension beyond the original estimates, and the large sums you ask for the future, require that...you observe the following order:

No contract or order for any work upon the buildings under your
charge hereafter to be made for any alteration or work upon any plan
differing from the original plan adopted, nor is any change to be made
in the original plan, except upon a distinct proposition for such change
of plan, concurred in and approved by the architect and authorized by
the Department.[56]

On December 8 Walter wrote former Congressman Stanton that Meigs
had "come to the end of his rope." In a letter the next day to Rice, Walter
said he had heard that Meigs had resigned and suggested altering Rice's
contract. Walter misread his man—Meigs did not resign, and on December 22 Walter tells Rice that Meigs was "vain to an extent amounting to
insane" and a "black hearted scamp." This is to be contrasted to a more
conciliatory letter a few days before to a different person, and perhaps
when he thought Meigs had resigned: "I have not, in reality been much
interfered with, as far as it regards the forms and proprieties of my
work...all his [Meigs'] scientific investigations have remained to this day
uncommunicated to me."[57]

Meigs knew something was going on—he told Floyd on December
26 that he thought Walter was preparing a report attacking him, and that
he wanted a chance to respond if so. On December 30 Meigs had an unsatisfactory discussion with Floyd, leaving with the impression that Floyd
was "a man of no principle at all."[58]

With the new year, 1858, under way, Walter told Rice, in a "Confidential" letter, that Meigs "all the time, day and night [was] working on
the members" of Congress, and that "if W [presumably Witte] don't go to
work in earnest the jig is up." On January 21, in a "Not Official" letter to J.
B. Floyd, Walter suggested that another order similar to the one dated
December 4 covering painting, sculpture, and ornamentation at the Capitol be issued.[59]

Walter's problem was not with Floyd who would have liked nothing better than to be rid of Meigs. So much so that about this time he
probably blocked the appointment of Meigs' son, John Rodgers Meigs, to
West Point. In a letter dated December 16, 1857, Jefferson Davis called to
the attention of Floyd that John Meigs, being the son of an army officer,
was not eligible for an appointment from a congressional district, and,
therefore, would have to receive an "at large" appointment. Pointing out
that he was the grandson of Commodore John Rodgers and the son of
Captain Meigs, he urged his appointment. The letter was joined in by 11
other senators. Anyone not aware of the bad feelings between Meigs and
Floyd would have bet heavily on this appointment being made.[60]

President James Buchanan was being lobbied hard by Jefferson Davis,
as was Floyd, on Meigs' behalf. Davis, who was chairman of the Senate
Military Affairs Committee, at Meigs' request, on January 23, 1858, wrote
Floyd spelling out the relative positions of Meigs and Walter. Davis said

that Walter was not only Meigs' subordinate, he had only been retained in employment at Meigs' "generous solicitation." Davis, in February, told Buchanan that Walter ought to be removed.[61]

Walter knew he had crossed the Rubicon and, when Meigs moved his office from the Capitol to a nearby building in the winter of 1857–1858, expecting Walter to follow, Walter refused to do so. Walter stayed in the Capitol. This started a battle over control of the architectural drawings. Walter refused to transfer them to Meigs' office.[62] This struggle brought work on the new dome to a standstill. Construction of the north wing continued so that the Senate was able to occupy it in January 1859. As for the dome, Meigs put the blame for the delay on Floyd in his annual report for 1858, dated November 15, 1858:

> I should be pleased to be able to report a greater progress in this work, but the want of cordial co-operation on the part of the architect associated with me has much interfered with the studies and draw-ings of the work. As it appears to me, he has much mistaken his au-thority and his duty; and, as it was a matter which could be settled only by the department, I have awaited its decision.[63]

When it is observed that this report was addressed to Floyd, and destined to be in the documents sent by the president to Congress, it is apparent that Meigs was not one to back off from those in authority when he felt he was in the right.

Meigs tried hard in 1858 to get a decision from Buchanan and Floyd. On January 22, 1858, he gave Jefferson Davis copies of his and Walter's correspondence about custody of the drawings, asking that Davis see that the president and Floyd had copies. He also urged that the appropriation bill have language requiring construction to be according to "designs made under [Meigs'] direction and signed by" Meigs. Davis intended to see Buchanan to say it would be war if Meigs were removed.[64]

On January 30 Walter communicated to Meigs that he was never a subordinate.[65] This statement seems frivolous when compared to Walter's letters in September and October 1857 complaining of more than four years of despotism which he endured without a single complaint. Also, it does not square with what he wrote John Rice on September 4, 1858:

> [Meigs] holds that I am in a state of insubordination according to his letter of instructions (which is the fact) and until that letter is revoked he will live up to it—they are afraid to revoke that letter, hence all the difficulty.
>
> This question has become a very serious one, and I must either submit to M. send him the drawings as his underling and allow him to do what he pleases with them or I must retire—there is no other alter-native. I cannot justify myself before Congress or before the world if I hold on any longer....[66]

Meigs, in early 1858, as he had for most of 1857, was having continual run-ins with Floyd over contracts and employees for the Aqueduct.[67]
On January 20, 1858, he summed up this situation vis-a-vis Floyd:

> [Floyd] I do not believe likes much one who has stood in the way of
> many attempts to dispose of work and profits and contracts of the
> aqueduct for the advantage of his personal friends.[68]

Consequently, it rings true when Walter wrote his wife on August 10, 1858,
that he had seen Floyd who "seemed as much bent on sending Meigs
away as ever." This interview with Floyd emboldened Walter. On August
25 he wrote Meigs that he, Walter, had authority to give orders to contractors and foremen as "architect." Meigs immediately brought this to the
attention of Floyd by reading Floyd a draft letter that would make it clear
Walter did not have any such authority. At this meeting Floyd flew into a
passion, was mad about many items, and complained of Meigs giving
papers to the president.[69]

About two weeks later Meigs wrote Floyd outlining Walter's acts of
disobedience, and had a two-hour talk with him. Floyd said he intended
to keep Walter "in office to make designs which [Meigs] was to execute,"
and that "the skill and taste of Mr. Walter could not be spared." The following day Meigs wrote Floyd asking that the president be advised of
Meigs' "request for the dismissal of Mr. Walter." Meigs gave Senator Pearce
a copy of this request eight days later and Pearce told Buchanan of Meigs'
letter.[70]

The circuitous appeal to the president must have jarred Floyd; finally, in October 1858, he decided that Meigs should have the right to
"any and all drawings necessary to carry on the building under [Meigs']
charge." The order continued with the requirement for Meigs to report to
the War Department if any such drawings were not supplied, or, if the
drawings did not meet his approbation, to provide his plan of alteration
or modification.[71]

Meigs saw this as a way for him to be ignored, which was not acceptable. He immediately called on Walter for all drawings, a request he
did not expect Walter to comply with. Walter asked the secretary for clari-
fication of what was required, and, at the same time, offered to give up his
job if the secretary wanted Meigs to "control the architecture of the public
works." When Walter refused to deliver the drawings, Meigs told the secretary of the refusal. Floyd made it clear that Meigs was to only have the
drawings necessary to let the work go forward.[72]

Shortly before Meigs signed his annual report on November 15, 1858,
which cast blame for the lack of progress on the new dome on the War
Department, efforts were made by Davis to get the president to act. In
October 1858 Davis spoke to both Buchanan and Floyd. Floyd said Meigs

"had been disagreeable in some things" and would have been removed if he had anyone to put in his place. Davis told Buchanan that "for months past, there had been insubordination and disorganization unchecked....One ought to go."[73]

Following his annual report, Meigs tried, without success, to get Buchanan to act. In a meeting with Buchanan, Meigs who was also trying to get the West Point appointment for his son, John, that had been refused the prior year, delivered a letter to Buchanan. The letter did not succeed. The West Point appointment list came out in March 1859 without John's name on it.[74]

In June of 1859 Meigs learned that Floyd had blocked John's appointment to West Point, and took it up with Buchanan who told him to discuss it with Floyd. At this meeting Meigs asked the president, respecting the Walter-Meigs situation, "if it was right that the public should...suffer from the failure of the proper authorities to settle a question like this in dispute between two officers having the...charge of millions of the public money."[75]

Meeting with Floyd a few days later, Meigs, suppressing a strong distaste for having to go to Floyd, delivered a letter about John's appointment. Floyd accused Meigs of setting out "to thwart [Floyd] in everything," admitted opposing John's appointment, and said he was prepared to sacrifice "his position in the cabinet had the appointment been made." He was angry because Meigs had made the application to the president rather than to him. After Meigs mollified him that any failure in this regard was inadvertent, Floyd agreed that John would have an appointment if a vacancy should occur.[76]

John got the appointment in September when Buchanan personally gave it to Meigs with the hope that in the future, in dealing with Floyd, that Meigs "while expressing [his] opinions strongly and fully, [would] use some conciliatory language."[77]

Conciliatory language was not on Meigs' mind in 1859. In June he turned down a request of Colonel Rene DeRussy of the engineer department to delete or change a statement on a certificate of payment for an employee. Meigs had noted that the "man's services were useless" and that the secretary had ordered him to be paid. Meigs told DeRussy "there was nothing disrespectful in [this]. It merely stated the facts as they occurred. If there was anything wrong in the facts, that was the fault of the Secretary of War, not of Captain Meigs; that the order was a reprimand to [Meigs] which [he] could not send in willingly or in any way which could be construed as submission to it."[78]

One truce with Floyd occurred after John received his appointment to West Point. Meigs wrote Floyd thanking him for his help, and told John that he should save a copy of the letter to Floyd and keep in mind that, without Floyd's support, there would have been no appointment.[79]

In another effort to resolve the disputes with Walter, a Meigs' letter was addressed to Acting Secretary of War William Drinkard in August 1859. He was succinct as to what needed to be done: "When the drawings are restored and the disobedient and rebellious assistant dismissed, there will be no further difficulty." Drinkard did not budge—the drawings were to stay in Walter's office with use by Meigs when needed. Upon receiving this reply, Meigs excoriated Drinkard for speaking for the secretary: "I am as capable of understanding a written order of the Secretary as the chief clerk or Acting Secretary, and must act on my responsibility as an officer under orders as I understand them." Floyd supported his intimate friend Drinkard: "The conduct of Captain Meigs in thus interpolating the records in his possession with a paper manifesting such flagrant insubordination and containing language both disrespectful and insulting to his superiors is reprehensible in the highest degree."[80]

Meigs had the next to last word in his annual report on the dome for 1859. He substantially repeated language used in 1858: "I regret that I cannot report a greater progress. The obstacles referred to in my last annual report have prevented it, and a year has thus been lost." This report is dated October 26, 1859. On November 1, 1859, Floyd acted. Captain William B. Franklin was placed in charge of the Capitol extension and new dome.[81]

Buchanan bowed to Floyd's wishes. He thought Meigs had disobeyed an order, and was placed in a position of choosing between Floyd or Meigs.[82]

Meigs had support from many of those under his supervision. On December 5, 1859, they made public five resolutions referring to his integrity, moral purity, and courteous demeanor, and then presented him with a $875 silver tea service on January 10. The presentation speech observed that the inscriptions on the tea set might be defaced by time but nothing could take from the country's history that "Capt. Montgomery C. Meigs was a man." At the activities following the presentation a toast complimenting the chief architect and engineer of the Washington Aqueduct was made with "sparkling aqueduct water."[83]

After Meigs was relieved of his duties respecting the Capitol extension, Davis tried to have him written back in by Congress, and to have Walter written out. His sentiments toward Walter were clearly expressed in June of 1860:

> [A]fter the appointment of the late superintendent, Captain Meigs, the architect, became, in fact, a draughtsman. He made plans under Captain Meigs, who was both constructor and architect in fact, though he never took the name.

The effort, on both counts, came to naught.[84] But Floyd was not rid of Meigs who was still in charge of the Washington Aqueduct.

Chapter 6
Judging the Meigs-Walter Impasse

Undeniably, Meigs wanted recognition for important works. In the *Daily National Intelligencer* of May 21, 1858, he spoke of art at the Capitol. Referring to numerous unfinished panels and empty niches within the halls of the Capitol extension as calling out for paintings and statues, he stated they were there "due to the foresight and careful provision of Capt. Meigs, and of him alone."

Walter didn't agree with Meigs' ideas that once Walter's original dome design was brought to Meigs' attention "whatever credit or responsibility there [was] to be attached to the work" thereafter had to be shared; and that there was a "well established principle that the engineer who takes the responsibility of ordering a particular work, though he may not work out with his own hands its details, is entitled to the credit."[1]

Meigs had a military man's perspective on his relationship to Walter. Jefferson Davis made him responsible for the Capitol extension and new dome. A military superior will not tolerate insubordination. Hence, his statement that Walter was a "disobedient and rebellious assistant" who should be discharged. To him the relationship was clear. In May 1861 he wrote to Secretary of State William H. Seward "that it is no part of a soldier's duty to criticize the orders and policy of his commander"—unfortunately, Walter was not a soldier.[2]

Walter had his share of blemishes. He was also obsessed about having credit. When the House chamber was finished in 1857 he was eager to disassociate himself from features receiving sharp criticism (such as the interior location of the chamber), but to take credit for the excellent acoustics. It is specious to contend Meigs did not play an important part in designing the Capitol wings and at the same time censure him for the resulting House chamber. Walter's champion, Congressman Richard Stanton of Kentucky, described the changes Meigs made in Walter's original plans as "modif[ying], chang[ing], and revoluti oniz[ing]" all the exterior and interior details. Senator Solomon Foot of Vermont, a Walter fan, in 1862 said that Meigs "order[ed] the introduction into the plans of four grand stairways, to be constructed of fancy polished marble, and also the construction of a marble corridor, extending through the southern wing; and other material and expensive changes...."[3]

Walter's conduct, when it became apparent that Meigs was not getting along well with Floyd, was egregiously underhanded. Probably he was feeding information to the Pennsylvania politicians for use with Floyd to hopefully get rid of Meigs. His frequent letters to John Rice excoriating Meigs and urging Rice to help him gain ascendancy over the Capitol extension and new dome, plus what seemed to be a holding out of a hope of better times if he were in charge, does not appear proper. His admission to Rice that he was in fact being insubordinate, and needed to have the orders under which Meigs was acting changed, even though he had told Meigs that he had never been subordinate, reflects unworthy conduct.

Although both Meigs and Walter may have acted unreasonably, the most irresponsible in the impasse were Buchanan to a degree and Floyd for sure. Meigs and Walter wanted a decision albeit with different results. Each was dismayed at the lack of progress on the dome. These top officials owed it not only to the country but also to these two men to resolve the standoff.

Walter's hunger for proper recognition and to be out from under the Meigs' control was consistent with his efforts, starting as early as 1836, to have architects given professional respect. He was the first vice president of the American Institute of Architects (AIA) which was founded in 1857. Writing to an AIA officer in 1859 he said: "I have been in open war for more than a year contending for the dignity of our Profession against the assumptions and despotism of a military upstart who happens to have the power to annoy." Their age differences could have caused ill feelings— in 1859 Walter was 54 and Meigs 43. The disparity in their salaries (Meigs at $1,800 per year and Walter at $4,500) was acceptable to Meigs so long as his reputation was properly enhanced by the work, but to not give him proper credit took away what he thought his due.[4]

The years softened Meigs' attitude. When a claim by a C. F. Andrews was made in 1886 to be recognized as the originator of the design for the Capitol extension, Meigs wrote that "the extensions of the Capitol and the dome of the Capitol [are] great works of architecture whose external beauties [were] in great measure due to [Walter's] skill." As for his disputes with Walter, he saw them as "growing out of an involuntary association" and to be of "small consequence." After Walter's death he wrote the widow in 1890 saying: "Your husband was the first of American Architects & to this day No one has excelled him in power & taste & knowledge of his profession or Art...."[5]

The details about the dome show's that no one could claim to be the sole originator. In a building there are both interior and exterior appearances and the construction itself. It is clear that Walter came up with the original exterior appearance, albeit he was drawing upon what had gone before in domes constructed in Europe. Sir Christopher Wren, who designed St. Paul's Cathedral in London in the 17th century, if alive in 1860, might have claimed some credit. From a distance the Capitol dome looks much like St. Paul's. The exterior appearance went through a number of revisions as plans for construction went forward. It would be a difficult to apportion credit for changes to the original exterior appearance drawn by Walter, some of which were made possible by construction features undeniably associated with Meigs.[6]

Fortunately, the Capitol is such a magnificent and important structure that there is plenty of room for credit for Meigs, Walter, and Schoenborn.

Since the 1850s and 1860s Thomas Walter has fared better than Meigs in garnering credit for the Capitol extension, including a portrait outside the House restaurant. Writers or organizations interested in presenting the story of the Capitol have often been associated with either the Office of the Architect of the Capitol or the American Institute of Architects. For example, Glenn Brown, a Fellow of the American Institute of Architects, wrote a *History of the United States Capitol* in 1900 and 1902 which said Walter was "nominally subordinate to a Captain of engineers, who the reports show devoted the greater part of his time to the business of management and discussions on heating, ventilation, and acoustics." "Nominal control" Walter could probably have lived with, but strict control, which Meigs insisted upon, was the point of friction.[7]

Another illustration of Walter's contribution being exaggerated is found in a government document titled *The United States Capitol: A Brief Architectural History* published in 1990 to commemorate 200 years of the United States Congress. The Office of the Architect of the Capitol joined in the publication. Two quotes make the point that through surrogates Thomas Walter is being put on a pedestal: "Walter more than doubled the size of the Capitol" and a reference to the "Thomas U. Walter" wings. The same publication does a poor job in describing the months of antagonism between the two men. It speaks of "Meigs' overbearing arrogance clash[ing] with Walter's mild manner and professional self esteem." This description of Walter glosses over his underhanded actions and dissembling as to his existing de jure relationship with Meigs.[8]

Walter's connection with the Capitol came to an end in 1865, when most, but not all, of the work was done. For a person who gave so much of himself to the Capitol, it is regretful that he was treated shabbily after Lincoln's assassination. Lincoln was shot on April 14, 1865, and Vice President Andrew Johnson succeeded to the presidency the next day. On May 15 a new secretary of the interior, James Harlan, was in office.[9]

Two blows were aimed at Walter almost immediately. Without any prior consultation, Harlan advised Walter that he had canceled a contract Walter had made for the enlargement of the Library of Congress and put the enlargement under the authority of the commissioner of public buildings and grounds. A contemporaneous letter from the commissioner of public buildings and grounds included a Department of the Interior communication dated May 23 giving the commissioner "charge of all work on public buildings in the District of Columbia."[10]

Walter responded immediately on May 26 by resigning as "Architect of the United States Capitol Extension, the new Dome, the continuation of the Patent Office Building, the enlargement of the Library of Congress, and the extension of the Government Printing Office." In part the action was taken out of "self-respect."[11]

What prompted this sudden change of fortune? One explanation may be found in Andrew Johnson's attitude toward the Capitol extension while he was a senator. In 1858 he said he would "vote more cheerfully...to pull down" the Capitol extensions than for money to continue them. He was no happier in 1859 after the Senate moved into its new chamber; he referred to "the useless and wasteful extravagance of public money that has been incurred in the building of these two wings of the Capitol."[12]

Chapter 7
Capitol Embellishments

*"All this gorgeous painting, and these ceilings,
as far as my taste is concerned, are entirely discordant."*
—Senator James M. Mason of Virginia (1859)

*"I did not design this ornamentation. I do not pretend now to judge of it.
It pleases me; and I hope to sit here long enough to have my eye
cultivated to a higher taste, and to enjoy it more and more...."*
—Senator Jefferson Davis of Mississippi (1859)

Meigs not only rapidly rearranged the interior features of the Capitol wings, he also immediately set out to decide upon embellishments to the structures. He was detailed on March 29, 1853, to supervise and to "control...the whole works [erection of the wings]." Edward Everett, a former congressman, governor of Massachusetts, President Fillmore's last secretary of state, and, in July 1853 a United States senator, responded to a Meigs' inquiry as to "distinguished American artists...capable of designing and executing the works in sculpture contemplated for the enrichment of the pediments to the Capitol extension buildings." At some point between Walter's design for the wings approved by Fillmore on June 11, 1851, and Meigs' letter to Everett, the design was changed to have decorative triangular areas on the top of the eastern portion of the porches or porticoes of the wings.[1] These pediments match the pediment of the eastern entrance to the old Capitol.

Everett recommended Hiram Powers of Ohio and Thomas Crawford of New York, both experienced sculptors residing and working in Italy. Meigs' letters of August 1853 authorized by the secretary of war, Jefferson Davis, asked them for designs and cost estimates. Tracings for the Senate wing were sent to Powers and for the House wing to Crawford. Crawford responded favorably but Powers declined. Crawford's design was used for the Senate wing.[2]

Crawford made several significant contributions to the Capitol. Not only did he design and model the sculpture work for the Senate eastern

pediment titled Progress of Civilization and for statuary over the door-
way to the Senate wing titled Justice and History, he was also retained to
design the bronze doors today found on the eastern entries to the Senate
and House wings. An early death in 1857, at the age of 43, kept him from
completing work on the bronze doors, but his designs were followed.[3]

The grandest Crawford legacy is the 19.5-foot Statue of Freedom
which caps the dome. Crawford named the statue Armed Liberty, but the
official title adopted is Freedom. The statue, in the plaster form used for
making the mold for the bronze casting done by Clark Mills near
Bladensburg, Maryland, had a perilous, one-year journey from Rome to
Washington. The bark carrying it from Leghorn, Italy, sprung a leak and
was repaired in Gibraltar; then, in coming across the Atlantic, it passed
through heavy gales which resulted in more leaks and the need to jettison
some of the cargo. When the bark arrived in Bermuda it was not fit to
continue the trip, and the statue was shipped to New York with different
parts in different ships. The model did not reach Washington until March
1859.[4]

While secretary of war (March 1853–March 1857), Jefferson Davis
was actively involved in the work at the Capitol, including art work. Davis
was responsible for Crawford discarding his initial design of having Freedom wear a Liberty cap. Davis saw the Liberty cap as the "badge of the
freed slave," and not appropriate for "a people who were born free, and
would not be enslaved." Crawford substituted a helmet "the crest of which
is composed of an eagle's head, and a bold arrangement of feathers suggested by the costume of [American] Indian tribes." Meigs was not successful in getting Congress to require Freedom to be cast from captured
guns.[5]

Meigs, the amateur artist, had definite opinions. Specifically he told
Crawford that "too refined and intricate allegorical representations" were
to be avoided, and observed that the "naked Washington" sculpted by
Horatio Greenough, another American who had worked in Italy, had been
"unsparingly denounced." Meigs thought it natural for Crawford to like
his [Meigs'] ideas since he had given Crawford "the best order he ha[d]
ever had."[6]

The "naked Washington" refers to a 20-ton statue of a seated Washington bare from the waist up with the lower portion of the body covered
by a toga. A representative criticism was that of diarist Philip Hone: "Washington was too prudent and careful of his health to expose himself thus in
a climate so uncertain as ours, to say nothing of the indecency of such an
exposure—a subject on which he was known to be exceedingly fastidi-
ous." Today it is seen at the Smithsonian's National Museum of American
History on the Mall in Washington.[7]

Meigs knew, probably from common sense, but, if not, from the "naked Washington" experience, that any Capitol sculpture would be eyed

critically by many. His advice to Crawford was that the soldier figure for the pediment sculpture should have no resemblance to Washington so as to avoid critics thinking there was a failed likeness. Another suggestion was for Indian accessories to be true to life.[8]

A year after Meigs entered into the Capitol extension work, he set out his thinking on the use of the old Hall of the House of Representatives that would be vacated (February 8, 1854):

> I have proposed from the first to make the Hall of the House of Representatives a place for the public to congregate, and for the display of Works of Art....I hope that in time it will be furnished with statues, and I think that whenever the time may come to renovate it if it be committed to my charge, I will contrive to include in the appropriation for the purpose a sum to place proper pedestals between the columns and they will soon be occupied. It is on this principle that I have put so many niches in the wings.[9]

Congress approved such usage on July 2, 1864, and the space is now called Statuary Hall.[10]

A Meigs' letter dated April 24, 1854, demonstrates a mind open to change. He expressed skepticism about fresco painting on walls and ceilings, an approach later embraced. He said: "Michael Angelo's celebrated speech, that fresco alone was worthy of a man, and oil painting was only fit for women and children,...has doubtless done much to keep the repute of fresco at height, to which perhaps it has no right." The work of Constantino Brumidi changed his mind.[11]

The year 1855 brought two important commitments. One, Randolph Rogers was given a commission to do the bronze doors now used as the entryway to the Rotunda and referred to as the Columbus doors. Meigs and Jefferson Davis had similar tastes. Rogers made his proposal on May 24, 1855; on the same date, Meigs recommended its approval to Davis. On May 25 Davis approved.[12]

Second, Brumidi, an Italian artist came on to the scene in 1855. Depending on one's reaction to the Brumidi paintings completed between 1855 and 1880, his appearance was serendipity at its best or worst. Meigs thought of the Brumidi request to be employed as a "fortunate moment."[13]

An Italian by birth, he studied painting and painted in Italy until 1849 when political changes caused him to emigrate to the United States. Knowing of the construction of the Capitol extension, he thought it should have "a superior style of decoration in real fresco, like the palaces of Augustus and Nero, the baths of Titus and Livia at Rome, and the admired relics of the paintings at Herculaneum and Pompeii."[14]

When he approached Meigs, who Brumidi said "was always in earnest to emulate the example of majestic Roman grandeur," he was allowed, at his own cost, to paint a lunette in a room used as Meigs' office which later was assigned to the House Committee on Agriculture. At Meigs' suggestion the painting was of Cincinnatus, the Roman hero of the fifth century B.C., who left his farm to defend Rome.[15]

Meigs and Davis sought congressional approval by displaying the Brumidi fresco, together with colorful, encaustic floor tile later used throughout the two wings and which add so much decoration and color to the Senate wing today. The House replaced the tiles in its wing with marble in 1924. The Senate has retained its tiles and replaced worn ones from the source for the original ones, Minton, Hollins and Company in Stoke-on-Trent, England.[16]

The proposal was to use the tile instead of brick and sandstone, which floored the old Capitol, and paint for the walls and ceilings instead of whitewashing. The reaction to the Cincinnatus painting, probably the first real fresco (painting on wet plaster) in America, was favorable.[17]

Brumidi finished the room in 1855. A complementary picture, that is, The Calling of Putnam from the Plow to the Revolution, representing Israel Putnam leaving his farm to command the defense in the battle of Bunker Hill, opposed the Cincinnatus painting. Small, opposing panels, on the other walls, showed the use of the McCormick Reaper in contrast to cutting grain with a sickle. The ceiling was split into four sections each showing a different season of the year. The room not only displayed fresco painting, it also had ornate plaster work.[18]

Not unexpectedly, with more than two hundred House members and 60 senators, approval was not unanimous. Contrasting views were expressed in 1860 and 1858. In 1860 Congressman Samuel R. Curtis of Iowa viewed the "fresco work in the room of the Agricultural Committee" as beautiful. Congressman Owen Lovejoy of Illinois didn't think so in 1858:

> In place of [the Putnam picture] should have been the picture of a western plow, with its polished steel mold-board, with the hardy yeoman, with one hand resting on the plow-handle, and with the other holding a span of bays, with arched neck and neatly-trimmed harness. Pictures are symbols of ideas, and this would have told to the future the present mode of culture of free labor. At the opposite end, in the place of Cincinnatus and his plow, (the plow of two thousand years ago,) there should have been a negro slave, with untidy clothing, with a slouching gait, shuffling along by the side of a mule team, with ragged harness and rope traces, drawing a barrel of water on the forks of a tree. This would represent the idea of slave labor. Thus we should have a symbol of the two systems of labor now struggling for the ascendancy.[19]

Not only was Brumidi allowed to finish the Agriculture Room, for the next 25 years he painted numerous walls and ceilings in the Senate wing. The Brumidi corridor in the Senate is one of the more elegant tourist attractions in the Capitol today. The corridor is almost completely painted, walls and ceiling, in the Brumidi style. The Senate liked his work. When Meigs suspended work on the Capitol extension in 1862, Brumidi was allowed to continue to work by being put on the Senate payroll. Today, adjoining the corridor is a bust of Brumidi.[20]

Contemporary criticisms of Brumidi accurately described much of his work. Congressman Lovejoy said, of one fresco, "Over head we have pictures of Bacchus, Ceres, and so on surrounded with cupids, cherubs, etc., to the end of heathen mythology. All this we have, but not a single specimen of the valuable breeds of cattle, horses, sheep, etc., which are now found in the country." An 1860 Art Commission report characterized him as painting rooms "in the style of the 'Loggias of Raphael'," and "after the manner of the Baths of Titus." This was just what Meigs wanted. In his annual report for 1856 he speaks of the Senate Naval Committee room being decorated in a style "derived from the remains of ancient painting in the baths of Titus and the excavations of Pompeii." He liked this mixture with history—panels on the walls were filled with pictures of United States' naval battles.[21]

One of Brumidi's most admired contributions is the Apotheosis of George Washington painted above the eye of the dome during 1865–66. Walter, who negotiated with Brumidi for this work, was able to get a reduced price because of enhancement that would flow to Brumidi's reputation from such a magnificent painting. Brumidi virtually died in harness. In his 70s he was painting on the frieze that rims the inside of the dome. The frieze had been sketched by order of Meigs before the war with the object of representing the history of the country. A near fall from the scaffolding led him to take to his bed, and he died a few months later. At the time of Brumidi's death in 1880 only about one-third of the frieze was finished. Filippo Costaggini finished the painting using Brumidi's sketches in 1889.[22]

In trying to honor Meigs, Brumidi painted his likeness in the Apotheosis, but Meigs asked that it be painted out since he thought it might "cover him with ridicule."[23]

During the winter of 1854–55 Meigs had about one thousand people working on the extension, most of them marble carvers. Probably the most costly feature in the Capitol was the intricate carving on the caps for each marble, Corinthian column. That path was laid down by Benjamin H. Latrobe and urged by Thomas Jefferson. To carve each took a carver six months. The same intricacy is found in the numerous pilasters. Similar refinement is found in the Hall of Columns on the ground floor of the House wing except that tobacco leaves are used in the decoration instead of the more traditional foliage.[24]

All of this activity brought on criticism by Congressman Edward Ball of Ohio—on the floor of the House on May 26, 1856, he had this to say:

Are gentlemen aware that this Government has become an extensive manufacturer of statuary? It is even so. Just around the corner may be found two shops filled with Italian and German sculptors, busily engaged in manufacturing statuary to be placed in the east pediment of the two wings. This, too, is with no authority of law that I can find, unless under the general authority to construct the two wings to the main building. ...The statuary in question does not seem designed to commemorate any historical events or personages connected with this country—it seems to be a mere amateur collection, and therefore deserves no place in the National Capitol. The graven images have the likeness of nothing in the heavens above or the earth beneath—I beg pardon, however—one was pointed out to me as the wife of one of the foreign workmen. Yes, sir, we are to have this copy of a living original to adorn our Capitol.[25]

The House passed a resolution asking for information about the marble work connected with the erection of the wings, which Congressman Ball thought was being extravagantly handled, and respecting the sculptural adornment for the wings. Meigs gave a detailed response dated July 28, 1856, which was provided to the House through the secretary of war. Jefferson Davis made it clear that Congress was on notice that the Capitol wings were being constructed in a more extravagant manner than contemplated in the original plans. In part, he said:

[C]onsiderable expense has been incurred for the adornment of the Capitol, and in giving to the doors and windows greater durability and beauty than those of the main building. It was thought to be in accordance with a just national pride that the finish of the Capitol of the United States should be equal to the highest reach of art in our day, and that its durability might typify the perpetuity which the framers of the constitution designed our Union should possess. If these ends justify the expenditure which has been incurred, it is believed that the manner in which the work has been conducted must be approved. But if, in proceeding on that supposition, I have been mistaken, I have only to say that the adoption by Congress of the most ornamental style of architecture and costly material of construction has led to the misapprehension.[26]

Meigs explained: "If the object of Congress was to provide accommodations at the least expense, a plain brick building would have been the most appropriate. As they directed the erection of a white marble building, in the highest and richest style of architecture, I have supposed that the best and most durable construction was desirable."[27] Congress must have agreed. It appropriated the $750,000 sought by Meigs in 1856.[28]

Decoration of the new wings received renewed attention of Congress after the House moved into its new quarters in December 1857.

Understandably, Congress wanted to have control over what those decorations would be. It decided to stop further unilateral decisions by Meigs and the executive branch. This was done by establishing an Art Commission, a committee of distinguished artists not to exceed three in number, selected by the president, to screen proposed sculpture and paintings for subsequent decision by the congressional Joint Committee on the Library of Congress. No further funds were to be spent on art work, except for the designs by Crawford and Rogers already accepted.[29]

The Art Commission approach was suggested to Congress by a memorial of American artists. Over 120 artists signed on with Rembrandt Peale, a revered portraitist of leaders in the American Revolution, leading off. The theme was "buy American." American history should be illustrated, a task for which American artists were peculiarly qualified. The artists went further than Congress was willing to go. They wanted the Art Commission to "channel[] for...distribution...all appropriations to be made by Congress for art purposes, and [to] secure to artists an intelligent and unbiased adjudication upon the designs they may present for the embellishment of the national buildings." In other words, turn the decisions on art over to the Art Commission.[30]

Through the *Daily National Intelligencer* for May 22, 1858, Meigs took on complaints of the American artists over the use of foreign artists at the Capitol. He said foreign artists were mainly doing transitional decoration to later be replaced. Rather than leave the walls whitewashed, "the principal rooms [were] being decorated, not by historical pictures, not by artists, but, under the direction of an artist, by art workmen, by ornamental or decorative painters, by house-painters, grainers [painters imitating the grains of wood, stone, etc.], painters of ornamental marble, by scagliola workers [plasters imitating marble, granite, and the like], plasterers, gilders, &c." If American artists wanted to compete for those type jobs, they were welcome to do so.

The article pointed out a disadvantage to the Art Commission approach. "Common decency will demand of the proposed committee of artists...that they abstain from awarding commission to themselves; and thus...exclud[ing] from all chance of employment...the three most distinguished artists of the country."

Public comment on the art being put in the Capitol ran a full gamut. The *Crayon Art Journal* reported in July 1859 that "the cause of national Art ha[d] not had an impetus similar to that given to it by Captain Meigs since the organization of the government" which impetus was given "with excellent intentions and with...most beneficial results." Contrast this with a May 1859 article in the *New York Courier*: Meigs' "blunderings and stupidities have cost the country several million of dollars," resulting in "an indiscriminate collection of decorative trash."

The Art Commission had a short life. It made a report dated February 22, 1860, which concluded that the power given to the commission by Congress was not sufficient "to enable them to perform the duties contemplated in their appointment." Congress responded by deciding to abolish the commission but, at the same time, continued the restriction on the use of funds for paintings and sculpture in the Capitol extension.[31]

Meigs was undoubtedly pleased to have a defunct Art Commission. At the time of the commission report, he no longer was in charge of the Capitol extension, but the report had to rankle. The commission was not complimentary as to what had gone before. Viewing the halls of Congress as a place "where calm thought and unimpassioned reason are supposed to preside," it did not think "gaudy, inharmonious color" appropriate. Such color was "disturbing to thought."[32]

A House committee of five, which reported on the American artists' memorial in March 1859, was completely at odds with Meigs: "A plain coat or two of whitewash is better, in the opinion of this committee, for a temporary finish than 'tawdry and exuberant ornament with which many of the rooms and passages are being crowded.'"[33]

The House chamber and committee rooms were receiving more than plain whitewash. An Act of June 12, 1858, limiting the use of appropriated funds for "sculpture or paintings," did not stop Meigs. In his thinking, the limits on the use of funds did not keep him from decorating by painting and otherwise the walls and ceilings of the Capitol extension. Jefferson Davis expressed the same view in discussions in the Senate to which he returned after his tour as secretary of war. Davis explained how, in his view, Congress authorized the ongoing ornamentation:

> There is fresco painting in the committee room to which the Senator refers [the agriculture committee room]...because that room was prepared as a specimen to be submitted to Congress, and they were called upon by the then Secretary of War, being myself, to see whether or not they would have the other rooms completed in the same style, and they were told that if so, and if they would have the building floored with encaustic tiling, an additional sum of money would be required. An opinion was sought from Congress. It was not given by any vote, but it came to me in every other form that they wanted the building finished in the very highest order of modern art.[34]

Although it was too late to curtail Meigs in 1860, since he had been relieved of the responsibility for the Capitol extension and the new dome in November of 1859, the House proposed, and the appropriation statute included, a tightening of the limitation on the use of funds. The limitation went not just to "sculpture or paintings," which Meigs construed as "paintings" in the fine art sense, not decorative painting of the walls and the like, it also prohibited use of funds for "other works of illustrated art."[35]

Preceding the 1860 statute, Congressman John Cochrane of New York described the House as he saw it:

> Here, those who are engaged in debate encounter on every side the vermillion hue which excites the bull to the fight in Spain. ...[H]ow are we entertained here? The artists give us a piece of gilding here, a parcel of red there;....

* * * * *

> ...Italian taste has exhibited on every side of this Hall the vermillion hue of Italy, instead of the sober, sensible hue of American intellect.[36]

Not all House members were critical with what had taken place. Congressman Curtis of Iowa was emphatic:

> It is very easy to invent a popular criticism and find fault; but I would like to see some of these gentlemen who are so conversant with matters of taste and art to speak with the assurance of masters, bring forward some design, some specimen from their superior genius that they would themselves insert in place of that which they see around them....What, sir, can be more beautiful than the fresco work in the room of the Agricultural Committee? What more splendid than the fresco in some of the halls and passages around the Senate Chamber,...And in this Hall, where do you find room to criticize the combination of colors which you see around you? Some gentlemen think that it is too glaring; some that it is too much imbued with vermillion, and others that it is too much shaded with the yellow. Would they have it all brown, or all blue?...I believe that, among men of mind and of taste, all the work on this Capitol is susceptible of fair and honorable defense;....[37]

Senator William Seward of New York went to the nub of the controversy in 1858 when he expressed his approval of all the painting and ornamentation that had been completed and was going forward in the House and Senate chambers:

> If we discuss from now until the end of the session, I do not think we shall be able to agree in regard to the decoration of the Chambers of the two Houses. It is a matter of taste, and our tastes differ naturally, and differ in cultivation and habit....[38]

The point was demonstrated by Senator Sam Houston of Texas who criticized the statuary being prepared for the Senate pediment by saying in part:

> [T]here is an Indian woman, or squaw, to be more technical, seated on a slab of marble. That may be very well executed; but she has a little papoose in her arms and its little head is sticking out like a terrapin's,

without reclining gracefully on the arm. She has a blanket, or something, holding it up; and its little neck, without the least curve or grace, is very stiff, like an apple on a stick. Now, sir, think of it, that throughout all ages, as long as this Capitol shall stand, or this Union exist, which I hope is to be forever, that poor little Indian has to sustain a heavy head with that little neck....[39]

Jefferson Davis, not noted for his humor, responded to Houston by pointing out that this sculpture was the work of Thomas Crawford, the best American sculptor, who had since passed away. This led Houston to question if Crawford actually did the work being criticized before his death. Upon being assured that he had, Houston did not change his view but, on the other hand, wanted it clear that he did not intend to disparage Crawford, commenting that "[Houston's] friends and [his] enemies are to [him] alike when covered by the earth's dust—bearing no part of [his] animosity."[40]

At least at one point it is not likely that Houston considered Meigs an enemy. When Meigs called on him in 1854 he was treated cordially— Houston had served under a Meigs' relative, Return J. Meigs. Houston "was bitter against Walter." During the hour or so Meigs was with him and while other visitors came, Houston poured out "tobacco spit and Blasphemies in a mingled stream."[41]

Meigs, or any other person or body deciding upon art and sculpture for the Capitol, was subject to vehement denunciation from some quarter. Nonetheless Meigs acted upon his own judgment of what should be done, and many of his decisions have stood the test of time. Furthermore, decisions were made and actions taken. Without Meigs' drive, no statuary was put inside the eastern pediment of the House until 1916.[42]

Chapter 8

Orders to the Dry Tortugas

In September 1860 Captain Meigs was relieved of his Washington duties and ordered to proceed to Key West, Florida, en route to Fort Jefferson in the Dry Tortugas.[1] His frictionless relationship with the secretary of war ended abruptly with inauguration of President Buchanan on March 4, 1857, and the appointment of John B. Floyd as secretary of war. Chapter 5 details Meigs losing supervision over the Capitol extension and the dome construction in November 1859, a loss rooted in a hatred Floyd exhibited against an independent, no compromise Meigs. It took Floyd another year to strip him of the Washington Aqueduct.

Meigs had a bad start with Buchanan and Floyd. The day before Buchanan was inaugurated, Congress made an appropriation of $1,000,000 for the aqueduct. The day after the inauguration Meigs advertised for bids on contracts to spend some of this money. This was done without consulting either Buchanan or Floyd, something they didn't like.[2]

Meigs' action, in his eyes, was completely innocent. Work on the aqueduct between 1853 and 1857 went by fits and starts—no money was appropriated for new work for the years 1854 and 1856. In reporting on the aqueduct in September 1856, Meigs explained how the past appropriations of $600,000 had been used, and the additional costs and difficulties incurred because of the need to stop work when no funds for new work were made available in 1854 and 1856. To permit an efficient and expeditious completion of the project, he suggested that all of the remaining money be appropriated, or that $1,000,000 should be made available before the spring season of 1857 started. His haste in advertising for bids was to avoid wasting the best working months of the year.[3]

Not aware that his action had upset Floyd, he was frustrated when he had trouble meeting with the new secretary. He sensed trouble when the chief engineer, Brevet Brigadier General Joseph G. Totten, told him that Floyd was concerned about the "great amount [of work] under [Meigs'] direction." Totten tried to smooth out Meigs' relations with the new secretary by writing a letter of introduction to the secretary for Meigs to deliver.[4]

On May 5 Floyd told Meigs to open the bids for contracts and to send his opinion "to the Secretary and President for their approval." This ran counter to Meigs' advice that contracts should be left to him to "prevent [Floyd] offending...politicians who have come to get contracts by their political influence." This was a practice Meigs found offensive, but with which Buchanan and Floyd, a former governor of Virginia, had no problem.[5]

The secretary and Meigs had different ideas as to how the work should be done on the aqueduct. Floyd favored one or two large contracts with little work supervised by Meigs. Meigs preferred small contracts with much of the work done on a daily basis under his supervision. When Floyd wrote a letter dated June 4, 1857, directing Meigs to "furnish him with a statement showing in the most detailed manner the past and future condition and progress of the work" and, most significantly, a comparison of the amount of work done "under Captain Meigs by 'days-work' and that done by contract," Meigs quickly, in a long letter, laid out his modus operandi to head off an anticipated challenge as to how he had operated in the past.[6]

In brief, he acknowledged that government red tape was leading him to favor more and more doing work by contract.[7] However, giving contracts to the lowest bidder was not without problems:

> I am compelled, if I contract on advertisement, to give the work to the lowest bidder, whether responsible or not. Some of the [low] bidders...are, I know, irresponsible men, to whom, in any private work, I would not trust a dollar. Yet if they give...responsible security, they must have the contract, and we have inflicted upon us, as I have had before, an inefficient—perhaps a drunken, worthless vagabond, to cheat the laborer out of his wages and the United States out of its work, and to abuse and accuse the Engineer before Congress for tyrannical conduct in taking up the work, which, if left to stand, would in time, by its failure, have endangered both the Aqueduct and the canal.[8]

The tension between Floyd and Meigs is palpable in the closing language of the Meigs' letter:

> [The present] operation is the result of four years careful study and experience on my part. I am of course ready to devote my best energies to carry out any one which the Department may, on full consideration, determine to adopt; but if the system is changed and should not prove as satisfactory in the end as the present one, I ought not to be held responsible for it.
>
> I would have preferred discussing this matter in conversation with you, but I have been unable to obtain an interview.[9]

Floyd responded to the Meigs' letter with a curt note of July 3 "reminding the Captain that the information called for had not been furnished and directing him to comply with the order at the earliest practicable moment." Finally, on July 27, 1857, after receiving Meigs' report and after several good work months were gone, Floyd gave a go-ahead for days-work.[10]

Meigs' report for 1857 reflects the use of many contracts, generally awarded the lowest bidder, and day-work, that is, work on a daily basis arranged for directly by the supervising engineers. Washington summers were a problem: with "the advent of the hot months and the beginning of the sickly season on the line," it was difficult to get men to work; they "were scarce, hesitating to go upon the line, where they suffered from malarious diseases."[11]

Floyd's approval for the work to continue as in the past could have been influenced by the overreaching by a bidder wanting to do the whole job. Parties wanting a large contract may have sent an emissary to talk with Meigs' father, Dr. C. D. Meigs of Philadelphia, "in order to convince [Dr. Meigs] that his son was pursuing a course contrary to the wishes of the President and certain persons close to him." Dr. Meigs reported on this effort to his son, who immediately passed the information on to Buchanan.[12]

Apparently Buchanan confronted those reportedly behind the approach to Dr. Meigs, and they jumped on Captain Meigs with spirit. Meigs was not daunted and wrote a lengthy letter to the president dated July 3, 1857, responding to the attacks. The Meigs' explanation for writing the president was an article of war providing "that any officer who may receive a seducing proposition from an enemy and having the opportunity to do so does not within 24 hours make it known to his commanding officer shall suffer death, or such other punishment as may be inflicted by Court Martial."[13]

Meigs was tactful. He smoothly exonerated the president saying he had assumed the president's name had been misused by the person talking to Dr. Meigs. As for Lauman & Co., who he thought to be behind the talk with Dr. Meigs, he extended an olive branch—he said since "these gentlemen deny all knowledge of Mr. Thompson [the emissary]...their denial is sufficient. I hold no man occupying the station of a gentleman to be capable of deliberate falsehood."[14]

However, Meigs surmised, to the president, the attitude of the Lauman & Co. would have been most friendly to him if he had "'figured' them into a fat contract." They had bid such a high price that to readvertise wouldn't help them "unless they drive off competition by having the work put up in so large a *lot* as to make all the small fry hopeless of success, or by giving the impression that the work is not to be let fairly, but by political influence—which impression I have good reason to fear that their actions have already to some degree diffused."[15]

Floyd undoubtedly chafed at Meigs opposing his ideas in a large sense, but the real hatred probably grew out of their differences on smaller matters. On May 20 Floyd ordered Meigs to make a payment Meigs did not think was right; on June 8 Floyd told him to fire an employee who was a Know-Nothing; on September 4 Floyd wanted to allow reconsideration of some claims Meigs considered dead; on October 21 Meigs complained to Floyd about Floyd firing one man and appointing another without consulting Meigs; on November 16 Floyd insisted on being consulted about any orders over $2,000. Such actions by Floyd continued throughout his time with Meigs. As early as June 1857 Meigs wrote in his journal that "the Secretary is not up to his place;" and on October 13 "he is the smallest cabinet minister I have ever seen," and his attitude did not change—on November 6 is an entry that "Floyd is a man of no principle."[16] Meigs was not alone in this opinion. General Totten thought the same and was so irritated with Floyd that he asked for six months' leave.[17]

Meigs had a consistent approach. If he thought the secretary was wrong, he told him so. But, if ordered to take action, he did. The same rules were applied to the president when he suggested that Meigs employ a particular individual. Even though Buchanan agreed with Meigs' way of handling the wishes of his superiors, when Meigs failed to employ a person Buchanan had at least hinted he wanted employed, he was miffed.[18] Meigs got along better with Buchanan than with Floyd. Buchanan on a number of occasions said he respected Meigs and explained the difficulties between Meigs and Floyd as the clash of two strong wills.[19]

Matters were no better in 1858. In fact, they were exacerbated with the conflict that developed between Thomas Walter and Meigs and the obvious desire of Floyd to assign Meigs to other duties.

Frustration again occurred during the year 1859 for which Congress failed to appropriate any funds for the aqueduct. All but $2.05 of the money appropriated had been spent. Another $500,000 was wanted to complete it. By this time there was water flowing through water mains leading to various public buildings (navy yard, arsenal, observatory, patent office, post office, president's house, Departments of State, Treasury, War, and Navy). This was water caught in the receiving reservoir on the Little Falls Branch of the Potomac. During 1859 the water was used extensively.[20]

When Congress appropriated $500,000 on June 25, 1860, for the fiscal year ending June 30, 1861, it triggered the events leading to the relief of Meigs. Obtaining this appropriation was important to Meigs. Having lost his battle with Thomas Walter for control over the Capitol extension and installation of the new dome, this was his last responsibility on the level at which he had been operating for the past seven years.

Upon being relieved of supervision over the Capitol extension in November 1859, Meigs pushed members of Congress to look into Floyd's management of the War Department. Uncovered were instances of favoritism and incompetence. Floyd reciprocated by not asking for any funds for the aqueduct for fiscal year 1861 commencing July 1, 1860. Meigs countered by calling attention to the omission to Senator Jefferson Davis, and a $500,000 aqueduct appropriation was added to the War Department request. Fearful that merely getting the appropriation would not insure his position, Meigs suggested to Senator Robert Toombs of Georgia that a proviso be included that the money be expended by "the Chief Engineer of the Washington Aqueduct who shall be as heretofore an officer of the Corps of Engineers not below the rank of Captain and having experience in the design & construction of aqueducts." Congress more than adopted his suggestion.[21]

Specific language attached to the appropriation read:

> For the completion of the Washington aqueduct, five hundred thousand dollars, to be expended according to the plans and estimates of Captain Meigs, and under his superintendence....[22]

To specifically name Meigs in the law was opposed by some who saw it as an insult to the president and the secretary of war.[23]

A House considered hostile to Buchanan, and presumably not too worried about how the president would perceive Congress naming the person to supervise the work, was adamant about the work being under Meigs' supervision. One senator, after noting that several senators had made it a point to insure through the press and otherwise that the president and the secretary of war would know that at least some thought they were being insulted, was of the view that the president and secretary of war would not be so thin-skinned as to be offended. He was wrong.[24]

In approving the appropriation on June 25 Buchanan wrote Congress to advise that "he would order Captain Meigs to any other duty he might deem expedient." Floyd signed an order, dated July 17, making Captain H. W. Benham the chief engineer of the Washington Aqueduct—Meigs was to act as his disbursing officer and to "examine the works under construction from time to time...and [to] keep such general supervision of the work as to assure himself that they are being constructed according to [Meigs'] plans and estimates." "To aid Capt. Meigs in [his] duties he [was] authorized to employ a draughtsman, if necessary, and also a clerk."[25]

This order was designed to be technically consistent with Congress' appropriation and yet put Meigs in his proper place.

Understandably, Meigs was offended. A letter, several pages long, dated July 24, 1860, to Buchanan attacks the order:

> I am compelled to appeal to you to revise this order of the Secretary because it requires me to disburse public money contrary to law and attempts to put upon me a duty, which, while it is discreditable and derogatory to me as an officer, is out of the line of my immediate

profession, and one to which I am subject to be ordered, if at all, only
by special order of the President.[26]

Meigs, without directly accusing Floyd of improper intentions, laid the
seed for such speculation: "I understand from high authority that the Secretary of War expects the completion of the Aqueduct to cost a million—
and I assert on my responsibility as the Engineer who designed and
constructed it that without the grossest extravagance no such sum can be
expended upon it." As to the insult administered by the secretary, he says
"No Engineer Officer has ever before been required to act as a mere paying teller for another."[27]

Meigs' complaint about the special status of engineering officers was
grounded on an 1806 Act of Congress laying out the rules and articles for
governing the armies of the United States. Article 63 provided that the
"functions of the engineers being generally confined to the most elevated
branch of military science, they are not to assume, nor are they subject to
be ordered on any duty beyond the line of their immediate profession,
except by the special order of the President of the United States."[28]

Buchanan referred the letter to the attorney general, Jeremiah Sullivan
Black, for opinions on the legal ramifications in the Meigs' letter, and, on
August 4, 1860, forwarded the attorney general's opinion for Meigs' "guidance and direction." Black, a member of Meigs' church (St. John's Episco-
pal on Lafayette Square), found no illegality in Floyd's order, and included
the following:

> The words [Meigs] has used are not plain enough to justify the
> belief that he intended a threat of insubordination under the constitu-
> tional shelter of the legislature: and his reputation is too high to allow
> mere ambiguity of expression to be used against him. I do not permit
> myself to doubt that Captain Meigs will obey his orders without
> being put under the "strong pressure" of anything but his own sense
> of duty not as a "reluctant and unwilling instrument" but with the
> cheerfulness and alacrity which becomes an officer of his grade and
> character.[29]

Not so. Meigs went back to the president, but to no avail. Buchanan,
on August 13, 1860, said Meigs' appeal from the order of the secretary of
war

> was sanctioned neither by law nor practice; but even if this had been
> otherwise, it should have reached me through your superior officer
> according to the Army Regulations. From sincere good feeling to-
> ward yourself, I waived these objections referred your communica-
> tion to the Attorney General and transmitted you a copy of this
> opinion, "for your guidance and direction". This I understand to be
> an explicit order (though conveyed in the mildest language suitable
> to the occasion) from the "Commander-in-Chief of the Army and

Navy" to a captain of Engineers; and from your character as a soldier I have no doubt it has been promptly obeyed. In any event, however, it has ended all direct correspondence between us on this subject.[30]

There was no place else to go, so Meigs undertook to follow Floyd's order. But the engagement was not over. When Benham employed R. E. Whitlocke at $4 per day as an inspector of the aqueduct, Meigs refused to pay him saying

I, from some little experience upon the Aqueduct and knowledge of his [Whitlocke's] qualifications do not agree with you in that opinion [that it was in the interest of the government to employ Whitlocke] but believe that any such payment to him will be an improper use of the public money which by law is to be expended according to my plans and estimates and under my superintendence.[31]

Meigs knew the power of the purse. Earlier he told his father that his mind was "made up...not to pay 1 copper until [he was] satisfied that it is honestly & justly due according to law & to abide the result."[32]

He had a head-to-head conflict with Floyd over paying the cost of an aqueduct officer to go to Sandy Hook, New Jersey, on non-aqueduct business. He received different advice on this confrontation—some said he was not under any obligation to obey an illegal order of the secretary, and some that he had no right to question the legality of an order from the secretary of war. He decided to be true to the trust Congress had in him and follow the law, as he saw it, and, in the end, God would weigh his action. He was not concerned about being considered self-righteous, and was unwilling to bend even a little.[33]

Meigs' intransigence led to Floyd issuing an order on September 18, 1860, requiring Meigs to turn over all aqueduct matters to Benham and to proceed to Fort Jefferson, Florida, at the Dry Tortugas. The Dry Tortugas were the army's equivalent of Siberia—located roughly one thousand miles from Washington with communications limited to mail transported by ship to Key West on a semi-monthly schedule.[34]

Meigs could not resist getting in another shot—in the "Report of Operations on the Washington Aqueduct During the Month of September 1860" he said he had turned over the money in his hands to the Treasury, but since he

was ordered to proceed to a distant part of the country it would be, of course, impossible for [him] during this compelled absence to exercise that superintendence over the work and expenditures required by the law of 25th June, 1860, making the appropriation of $500,000 for completing the Washington Aqueduct according to the plans and estimates of Captain Meigs, to be exercised under his superintendence.

I also notified these [Treasury] officers that any bill, draft, requisition or warrant, paid during my absence would therefore be paid in direct violation of the law.

* * * * *

I understand that the work of the Aqueduct and the expenditures thereon are going on in defiance of the law of Congress, but I have no official information and can make at present no further reports upon this work.[35]

The stay in the Dry Tortugas was brief. Floyd resigned from office on December 29, 1860. Meigs was ordered back to Washington on January 28, 1861.

Captain Montgomery Meigs

In February 1858 Captain Meigs
bought a new uniform and had
his picture taken.

Massachusetts Commandery, Military Order
of the Loyal Legion and the US Army
Military History Institute

Cabin John Bridge

The Cabin John Bridge, with, at the time, the world's largest masonry span, finished
in the 1860s, remained an attraction into the early 1900s with an adjoining resort hotel.

Massachusetts Commandery, Military Order of the Loyal Legion and the US Army Military History Institute

Montgomery Meigs at Washington Aqueduct

Montgomery Meigs poses with large valves used in the Washington Aqueduct. The largest valve has "Capt. M. C. Meigs, Chief Engineer," cast into its body.

Aqueduct pipes crossing Rock Creek

Aesthetically, the arching aqueduct pipes across Rock Creek are pleasing, and pragmatically formed the support for a surface road across the creek.

The dome on the Capitol in 1848 (*top*) was in danger of fire, being of wood construction, and it also leaked. The drawing of the new dome as proposed in 1855 (*middle*) also shows pediments on the north and south wings. The pediments provided a platform for statuary almost immediately contemplated by Meigs when he was placed in charge of the Capitol extension in 1853. The proposed new dome bears a striking resemblance to the dome at St. Paul's in London (shown on the *bottom* in a World War II picture) designed by Sir Christopher Wren in the 17th century.

Library of Congress

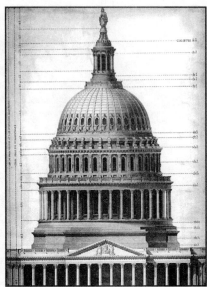

Dome proposed in 1855

Library of Congress

Dome planned in 1859

National Archives

The proposed 1855 dome (*left*) changed significantly between 1855 and 1859 (*right*). In part the flatter 1859 shape, which is what was built, was dictated by the size of the Statue of Freedom approved by Jefferson Davis and Montgomery Meigs. To keep the overall dimensions of the Capitol in harmony the lower parts of the dome were flattened. A wider peristyle (the bottom, columned part of the dome) also permitted this flattening to be acceptable. Meigs worried about the dome being too "steeple like," and the flattening avoided that.

Thomas U. Walter,
architect of the Capitol

National Archives

August G. Schoenborn,
head draftsman for the
Capitol extension

National Archives

Constantino Brumidi,
indefatigable decorator of
the Capitol

National Archives

Stalled dome construction, 1858–1859

Construction on the dome mostly stopped between January 1858 to November 1859 because of an impasse between Captain Meigs and Thomas Walter, the architect. Hence, when Congress convened in December 1858 and March 1859, it was apparent nothing was happening. Before Congress came back into session in December 1859, the impasse was broken by the secretary of war relieving Captain Meigs.

National Archives

Jefferson and Varina Davis

During the time no construction was going forth on the dome, Jefferson Davis was a member of the Senate and gave support to Meigs who, in 1855, when Davis was secretary of war, described him as "his superior and good friend." Varina Davis, shown here with her husband, had been a patient of Meigs' father in Philadelphia and, on at least one occasion, went to the opera with Louisa Meigs, Montgomery's wife.

Library of Congress

Brumidi paintings in Agriculture Room of the Capitol

Meigs' intentions, stylistically, for the Capitol are illustrated by the room to the right which was his office at the time he allowed Brumidi to paint the fresco picture, at the end of the room, showing the Calling of Cincinnatus from the Plow. The boy in the lower right corner of the painting was modeled on Meigs' son, Montie.

National Archives

Ornate Capitol staircase

National Archives

Bust of Flat-Mouth

National Archives

The ornate staircase was designed by Brumidi, whereas the bust of Flat-Mouth was done by Francis Vincenti who was doing other work at the Capitol.

Statue of Freedom

The Statue of Freedom, which tops off the Capitol dome, was the product of the American sculptor Thomas Crawford employed by Jefferson Davis and Meigs.

National Archives

Painting of Montgomery Meigs

The painting of Montgomery Meigs (*bottom*) has as a background two of his achievements—the Rock Creek Bridge for the Washington Aqueduct and the unfinished Capitol dome.

Courtesy Meserve-Kunhardt Collection

Chapter 9

Hiatus at the Dry Tortugas and Return to Washington

The presidential election in November 1860 changed the face of the nation. During the pre-election period Montgomery Meigs was on his way to his new post in the Dry Tortugas. Leaving Washington on October 22 he traveled through Lynchburg, Virginia; Knoxville, Tennessee; Columbus, Georgia; and Montgomery, Alabama, to Pensacola, Florida; thence to Key West and finally, on November 8, reached Fort Jefferson, harbor of the Dry Tortugas.[1]

The Meigs family, not unlike many other American families, was located in both the North and South. Montgomery was the oldest child in the family of Dr. Charles Meigs of Philadelphia—there were nine other children (seven brothers and two sisters). The fifth child, five years younger than Montgomery, was Henry who, in 1860, lived in Columbus, Georgia. He was both a business and slave owner. Montgomery visited with him and his family, arriving October 25.[2]

The visit had to be acrimonious. On November 12, 1860, Henry wrote to Montgomery stating the likelihood that South Carolina, Georgia, Alabama, Mississippi, Texas, and perhaps Louisiana would secede. He hit raw nerves by saying:

> The fanatic philosophy of the North—who have about as much knowledge of slavery as they have (aside from revelation) of the things of the upper & better world.[3]

A few days later Henry sought approval of his ideas from their father, complaining that Lincoln had been elected on slogans such as "Slavery a barbarism & a crime," "No labor without money wages." To force such beliefs on the South would redden the fields of the country with blood.[4]

To Montgomery slavery was a blot on humanity and against God's will. Henry's acceptance and practice of slavery was a barrier between the brothers which continued during and after the Civil War. The chasm was just as wide as to the right of states to secede. Henry, writing to Dr. Meigs before the election, said "The North has a constitutional right to

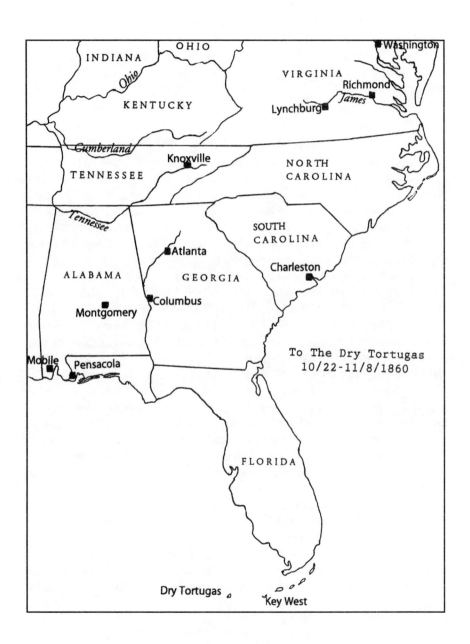

To The Dry Tortugas
10/22-11/8/1860

vote as she will. The South has a state right to refuse to abide by such a vote as will probably be cast. Right or not she will refuse. Elect a constitutional President and all will be well for the next four years," but to elect Lincoln would destroy the Union.[5]

Henry's passion is displayed in a letter to his father on December 24, 1860, about the reaction in Columbus of news of South Carolina's decision to secede:

> The news of the [Convention] action was received here with a brilliant illumination of the city, the firing of cannon rockets & fire works. Can a whole people be so deceived as you appear to think the South to be?[6]

Montgomery saw South Carolina's actions in a different light. When he found that South Carolina had interfered with the mail service to Key West and stopped his wife's letters, he reacted: "Pestilent South Carolina! What an object of ridicule in the eyes of the world. Filling the air with curses & resolutions. The clang of arms & drums & trumpets...."[7]

Montgomery was not surprised. A letter to General in Chief Winfield Scott dated November 10 reported on the hostility to the Union he observed on his trip—"the temper of the South is excited—is dangerous." His concern was about the relatively unmanned condition of the fortifications at Pensacola, Key West, and the Dry Tortugas. Both Fort Taylor (Key West) and Fort Jefferson (Dry Tortugas) were "at the mercy of a party which could be transported in a fishing smack." His advice was to put sufficient forces in the fortifications to discourage easy takeovers, but to screen the men put there to be sure of their loyalty to the Union.[8]

As Meigs was writing the election results were in. Lincoln was to be president without the benefit of votes from 10 of the 11 states that were to form the Confederate States of America. He received only one percent of the votes cast in Virginia. In the border states, which were to stay with the Union, Missouri, Kentucky, and Maryland, the percentages were 10, 1, and 3, respectively. The nation was decisively split ideologically, and was to be led by a president elected by a plurality of 40 percent of the votes.[9]

Lincoln's election started a domino reaction resulting in a de facto establishment of two countries at war with one another. Lincoln was inaugurated March 4, 1861. Much happened between his election and inauguration. Thirty-three states were in the Union at the time of his election. By the time of his inauguration seven states had seceded. South Carolina was first on December 20, 1860, Mississippi next on January 9, 1861. Before the March inauguration they were joined by Florida (1/10/61), Alabama (1/11/61), Georgia (1/19/61), Louisiana (1/26/61), and Texas (2/1/61).[10]

During these changes Captain Meigs worked diligently to protect a key United States property. Letters for help were sent in many directions. By mid-January he received a company of the Second Artillery. The addition to the society was appreciated: "officers of the army are to each other the most congenial companions. Even where they are not very bright there is a different mode of thought & feeling. Honorable aims without the eternal dollar peeping out and making discord as it so often does with others."[11]

A family crisis showing the Meigs' household thinking took place in November. Louisa Meigs received a report indicating John Meigs had accumulated 76 demerits, just 24 short of the 100 that could have led to his dismissal from West Point. She took John to task:

> I can scarcely tell you how pained I feel at this intelligence. I feel it deeply enough but it distresses me to think of your father's mortification. He has so much of a father's pride in your success and will be humiliated to learn that you are falling so far short of his expectations. He was never very anxious for you to go into the service and it was only on account of my oft repeated wish and your known desire to go to W. Point that he consented to use his influence for you.
>
> You know how distasteful it was, with what *loathing* even that he consented to ask the appointment of this Administration even compelling himself to ask the Sec[retary] of War to withdraw his opposition. Is this to be his reward? Is he to see you dismissed or if not, is he to see you take a standing so low in your class that it will always be a humiliation to his pride to see you in the Army.[12]

As of the first of February Fort Jefferson was sufficiently armed and manned to be safe. Meigs wrote the chairman of the Military Committee of the House of Representatives saying it was important to occupy several points about the harbor so that it could be held "against England & France." Also suggested was the building of a dry dock to repair the navy's ships rather than retaking the Navy Yard at Pensacola, Florida, which had been seized by Florida after it seceded.[13]

A return to Washington was never far from his mind. Floyd's order sending him from Washington was in his view "[a] bold, bald, violation of the law of Congress." With Congress back in session in December 1860 efforts were made to have him returned. An unflinching friend was Francis Preston Blair a Washington power since the presidency of Andrew Jackson. A combination of efforts by Blair, the affront to Congress's express requirement that Meigs supervise the expenditure of funds for the aqueduct, and the disgrace of Floyd, at least in the North, and his resignation from the cabinet at the end of December 1860 created a climate for his return.[14]

Learning that the Senate passed a resolution of inquiry as to the legality of the expenditures on the Washington Aqueduct, he thought he would soon be back in Washington. He was right. Orders dated January 28, 1861, and received February 12, instructed him to return immediately.

Physically back by February 20, 1861, he was put in charge of the Washington Aqueduct.[15]

Not only was he back, he was held in high regard. Joseph G. Totten, head of the Corps of Engineers, wrote to him on January 31:

> The Secretary of War [now Joseph Holt] and the Commanding General who have been made acquainted with all your proceedings and to whom the more important portions have been read have expressed high satisfaction at the zeal, activity, intelligence, and prudent forecast that have so strongly marked your course. In all this warm approval, you may assure yourself that the Engineer Department has entered feelingly and with pride.[16]

Meigs savored the disrespect with which Floyd left the cabinet. He was anxious to see the whole Buchanan administration out of power, writing in February 1861 to his father: "[O]ne month more rids us of this iniquitous, imbecility, traitorous, thievish administration." His hope was that the next administration would "deal moderately but strongly with the treason," in which case "all thinking men [would] rejoice at the delivery of the American republic from the shackles in which the arrogant overbearing south has so long held it bound."[17]

The phrase "fifth column" was used in World War II to represent persons and organizations in countries that would help an invader. Although the phrase was not used in 1860–61, there was a definite "fifth column" within the federal government. Illustrative of this in the army was the quartermaster general, Joseph Johnston, who joined the Confederacy immediately after Virginia seceded and was instrumental in the defeat of the Union at Bull Run, and Pierre Beauregard, who ordered the shots upon Fort Sumter, the superintendent of the U.S. Military Academy for a few days before he went south.[18]

The "fifth column" was prominently represented in Buchanan's cabinet—Secretary of State Lewis Cass highlighted the situation in speaking to his Assistant Secretary Trescot:

> I speak to Cobb [treasury secretary] and he tells me his is a Georgian; to Floyd, and he tells me he is a Virginian; to you and you tell me you are Carolinian. I am not a Michigander; I am a citizen of the United States. The laws of the United States bind you, as they bind me, individually.[19]

Union officials joining the Confederacy often violated oaths of allegiance to the United States, and many ignored the fact that their education and training at West Point or the Naval Academy was paid for by the Union. The acts of some went further and particularly angered Union officials. Lincoln's secretary of war, Simon Cameron, portrayed this in a report to Lincoln dated July 1, 1861:

Revenue steamers have been deliberately betrayed by their commanders.... [Various] Government arsenals...the ordnance depot at San An-
tonio and all other Government works in Texas, which served as the
depots of immense stores of arms and ammunition, have been surrendered by the commanders or seized by disloyal hands. [A number of
Forts]...have been successively stolen from the Government or betrayed
by their commanding officers. [Various] custom houses...containing
vast amounts of Government funds, have been treacherously appropriated to sustain the cause of rebellion. In like manner [several] branch
mints...have been illegally seized, in defiance of every principle of common honesty and of honor.[20]

Undoubtedly the loss of property was not as important in the conduct of
the war as was the loss of trained and experienced military personnel.

An estimate of the loss to the army officer corps of 1,108 before the
war was 313 and, of course, many of the famous leaders of the Confederate army were former U.S. officers (Beauregard, Joseph E. Johnston, Lee,
Longstreet, Stuart, Albert Sydney Johnston). Defection of naval officers
was 373 out of 1,554. Those joining the Confederacy thought they were
meeting their obligations to their states. Most, but not all, regular army
enlistees remained loyal to the North.[21]

Regardless of how one looks at these acts in a gross sense, the conduct of Floyd needs to be judged separately. He was a Virginian receiving
letters like this one dated November 24, 1860, from the master armorer,
Virginia State Armory:

I desire that the honorable Secretary issue an order to the superin-
tendents of the Springfield and Harper's Ferry armories to give the
master armorer of Virginia State Armory...every facility they may need
in said armories, at the same time not interfering with the legitimate
business of the armory.

I desire to get all the assistance we can from the national armories
before our much-honored and esteemed Secretary of War vacates his
office, for I have no hopes of any assistance after a Black Republican
takes possession of the War Department.[22]

After Lincoln's election (November 6, 1860), private sales of 17,500
muskets were made, by order of Floyd, to the states of Alabama, Mississippi, Louisiana, and Virginia.[23]

A firestorm of criticism arose against Floyd when it was discovered
he gave an order on December 20, 1860, for the transfer of over 120 cannon to United States forts in Mississippi and Texas from a Pittsburgh arsenal. These canon "were at the time considered equal, if not superior, to
any cannon in the world." Later investigation showed the forts, which
were under construction, were not close to the time they would need the
cannon. After Floyd resigned his order was countermanded.[24]

In the South Floyd's acts were viewed positively. He was credited with the transfer of "115,000 improved muskets and rifles from the Springfield armory and Watervliet arsenal to different arsenals [in] the South," and with blunting the desire of Winfield Scott to reinforce military installations in the South.[25]

Why Floyd resigned from office is stated differently—Buchanan said it was in response to his request dated December 23, 1860, for his resignation because of the so-called "Floyd Acceptances," and Floyd said it was because Buchanan went back on his word in not forcing Major Robert Anderson, of Fort Sumter, to go back to Fort Moultrie in Charleston after Anderson withdrew from Moultrie to Sumter. The "Floyd Acceptance" scandal developed rapidly in the last days of 1860.[26]

In brief it had to do with the unauthorized removal of $870,000 in Indian Trust Bonds from the Department of the Interior facilitated by Floyd's unauthorized issuance of "acceptances," that is, agreements for the War Department to pay money. There was never evidence that Floyd benefited from his acts, but the House committee investigating the matter, after Floyd left office, characterized his administration, in this instance, as "deplet[ing] the public treasury and [debasing] public virtue."[27]

On arriving back in Washington, Meigs proceeded with zeal to straighten out the wrongs he thought had been perpetrated on him and his character. Some revenge was taken against Captain Benham and Lieutenant Morton, who had charge of the aqueduct in Meigs' absence, and had their names inscribed on an arch of the Cabin John Bridge. Meigs had their names cut out and his substituted. Morton was dispatched to the Dry Tortugas.[28]

Meigs did not only want back the Washington Aqueduct. He wanted, and got, superintendence over the Capitol extension and the new dome. He thought Captain William B. Franklin, who Floyd put in charge in November 1859, should have

> gone to Secretary Holt & said Sir against my protest that it was unjust to Capt Meigs I was compelled by positive orders from Mr. Floyd to relieve him of the charge of certain great public works on which he had lavished years of faithful labor. I was compelled to tolerate dishonest men as agents upon the public works. I early learned that the architect was a man unreliable in word and act. I ask as simple justice [that] Meigs...be restored and that the order state it to be done at my request.

To Meigs this was the only way for Franklin "to save him[self] from the stain which attaches from this time forth to all who have been protected & promoted [by] Floyd."[29]

When Franklin didn't act, after waiting four days, on February 25 Meigs wrote Franklin explaining why he needed to be back in charge:

Personally I don't desire the labor and the responsibility of the public buildings, but no man has reputation enough to be able to throw away any of it....

The vindication of public justice the vindication of myself from attacks published officially & to be effectually answered in no other way, the interest and credit of the administration of Mr. Buchanan & of Mr. Holt require that I should be restored to the position from which the intrigues of corrupt men removed me.

I have always held a firm conviction that with or without effort on my part if God spared my life I should place the Statue of American Freedom upon the Dome of the Capitol and having a firm faith in the justice of God and in his providence which rules all things great & small for good I believe that I shall yet do this.

"*Finis Coronat Opus*"

To this end I invite your cooperation.[30]

Franklin saw the situation differently, and responded in writing the next day:

The wrongs inflicted upon yourself were...the acts of Mr. Floyd.... [Y]ou must certainly be aware of the fact that no respectable man believes the assertions made by him and that your character as a gentleman and as a man of ability is and always has been far above any assault from him.

* * * * *

I was placed in charge of these works by a dishonest Secretary of War, and great injustice was done you by that act. I remain in charge of them only long enough for you to get back from Tortugas under orders from an honest Secretary of War and am then relieved from duty and you are put back in your old place. Will not the inference be plain to everybody...that I am only retained in the place so long as the dishonest administration lasts and that I am dismissed as soon as you are at hand to fill the place.

I do not believe that any man's reputation can bear such a blow, and I can not consent to cooperate with you in inflicting such injustice upon myself.[31]

Franklin added that if he did not retain his present job he would be placed entirely on the shelf since there was no other work he could go to. Besides, Meigs already had enough "work & responsibility [through] the Aqueduct."

Meigs found a solution to the two endangered reputations. He insisted on being restored and Secretary Holt agreed. Holt, a good friend of Meigs' relative, Return Jonathan Meigs III, was well disposed to help. He had "little sympathy" for the transfer when he knew little about it, and "none" when fully informed. Franklin's concern was met by appointment to a newly vacant position to superintend construction of the new Treasury Building and custom houses and post offices throughout the country.[32]

Although angry with Buchanan, Meigs saw him as a beaten man. Commenting on his appearance after he paid his respects: "His haggard face has cadaverous complexion his hollow eye his tottering gait tell a fruitful tale of the savages of the place....Poor weak unhappy old man....[N]o one who looks at him can feel emotion more harsh than pity & history will make him the subject of analysis & dissection." And, in his journal after bidding Buchanan farewell at the end of his presidency: "He is to be pitied, for, though weak and unfit for his place, I believe that so far as his weak character, honesty and policy went, he wished to save his country from disunion."[33]

But pity was not what he had in mind for Thomas Walter. Walter decided to face facts and went to call on Meigs. According to Walter, Meigs' reaction was to "look[] daggers at [Walter], [give] a grunt, gnash[] his teeth and turn[] his head away." Later, on March 2, armed with an order from Holt restoring him completely to the power held while Jefferson Davis was secretary of war, Meigs wrote to Walter: "I have the honor to inform you that your services are dispensed with from this date."[34]

Walter did not retreat. He reminded Meigs that Walter's "connection with the public works...depends upon the will of the Pres[ident] of the United States & is in no way at your disposal as your letter assumes."[35]

At this point the political trump card of Holt was gone. Meigs' abortive effort to fire Walter occurred in the last few days of the Buchanan administration. When Lincoln came into office a new secretary of war was appointed and confirmed. Simon Cameron, who in 1859 considered Meigs an autocrat, and a former Senate colleague of Senator Bigler who had worked to have Meigs relieved in 1857, overruled Meigs and instructed him not to interfere with Walter "in the performance of his official duties until the Pres[ident] decide[d] the question of his continuance." However, later, after Meigs talked with Francis Preston Blair about the situation, Cameron agreed to support Meigs—Walter was to be his subordinate but should be permitted to draw his pay.[36]

With typical tenacity Meigs appealed to Cameron. The appeal did not carry the weight he hoped for since he relied in part on orders he had received from Jefferson Davis who, as temporary president of the Confederacy, was not a favorite with the incoming administration.[37]

The Meigs-Walter battle was overtaken by events. With the start of the Civil War, work on the Capitol extension and the new dome, except for continuing fresco work by Brumidi and a mural by E. Leutze, was suspended. The suspension left material lying around on the ground—the marble was being damaged by nature. The painted iron for the new dome was being damaged by

> the hog, goat, and geese nuisance now suffered to triumph over all law...hogs can not be kept out of the Capitol enclosure and have done much damage to the newly painted iron lying in front of the Capitol ready for the new dome—so much that it is necessary to renew the painting where it has been rubbed off or discolored by the hogs, at more expense than all the hogs are worth.[38]

Congress decided to transfer responsibility for the Capitol work from the secretary of war to the secretary of the interior (4/16/62), and two months later the aqueduct followed. The job of taking charge of the Capitol extension and the new dome went to Walter who thought the cheapest way to protect the Capitol was to proceed vigorously to finish it. Congress agreed.[39]

The new dome was topped off with the Statue of Freedom on December 2, 1863. At the moment of installation there was a 35-gun salute from Capitol Hill, a salute for each state in the Union including those that had seceded, which was answered by 12 forts surrounding the city. Meigs saw none of this—he was in Tennessee where he had been present for the battle of Chattanooga.[40]

Chapter 10
Forts Sumter and Pickens

President Buchanan had reason to look old. He was near 70, a lame-duck president with a cabinet about evenly divided between men from the South and North. The Union was fragile. Before the presidential election of 1860, many of the Southern states let it be known that they would secede if Lincoln, who headed what they considered a "sectional party," was elected.[1]

Buchanan's Annual Message to Congress delivered December 3, 1860, said little to discourage secession. Included in the opening words was the statement that "[t]he long-continued and intemperate interference of the Northern people with the question of slavery in the Southern States has at length produced its natural effects." Like Pilate, he washed his hands of any responsibility. As he saw it, the president was required to enforce the laws, but, as was then the case in South Carolina, where all the agents of the United States had resigned, it was not practical to do so. No laws passed by Congress were found to give him authority to make war on a seceding state, and he discharged his duty by "submit[ting] to Congress the whole question in all its bearings." Gratuitously, he threw in that the Constitution did not "delegate[] to Congress the power to coerce a State into submission which is attempting to withdraw or has actually withdrawn from the [Union]."[2]

A meeting between Buchanan and members of the South Carolina congressional delegation on December 8 led to a misunderstanding which inflamed feelings in South Carolina. The congressional delegation had the impression that Buchanan would not send any reinforcements to Fort Sumter in the Charleston harbor, or transfer forces from Fort Moultrie, also in Charleston, to Sumter. In return for this guarantee, South Carolina would make no effort to take forts in Charleston by force. When Major Robert Anderson, in charge of the Charleston forts, on the day after Christmas, transferred his troops of about 75 men from Moultrie to Sumter, the Carolinians felt betrayed. In their view, they could take on national umbrage since they had seceded on December 20, and had authorized a delegation to proceed to Washington to negotiate "for the delivery of the forts, magazines, light-houses, and other real estate, with their appurtenances, within the limits of South Carolina" before Anderson had moved to Sumter.[3]

When the Washington delegation learned of Anderson's action, they urged on Buchanan "the immediate withdrawal of the troops from the harbor of Charleston." The president made a December 31 response to the South Carolina representatives, who he did not accept as having any official capacity, denying any agreement at the December 8 meeting. The president restated what was included in his message to Congress of December 3; namely, "any attempt...to expel the United States" from United States' property in South Carolina would be met with defensive action.[4]

The verbal exchange became nasty. The South Carolinians said that "By [Buchanan's] course [he had] probably rendered civil war inevitable. Be it so. If [he chose] to force this issue...the State of South Carolina will accept it, and relying upon Him who is the God of Justice as well as the God of Hosts, will endeavor to perform the great duty which lies before her, hopefully, bravely, and thoroughly."[5]

On December 30, Lieutenant General Winfield Scott, general in chief of the army, asked permission of the president to secretly, that is, without the knowledge of the War Department, reinforce Sumter with men, weapons, and subsistence stores. Permission was granted. The reinforcements, carried by the *Star of the West*, an unarmed, steam side-wheeler, chartered for the trip and flying the United States' flag, were not landed at Sumter because of shelling by South Carolina forces on January 9, 1861.[6]

No further efforts were made to reinforce Sumter before Lincoln was inaugurated. Lincoln faced a dilemma:

> Within [the States that had seceded prior to March 4, 1861] all the forts, arsenals, dock-yards, custom-houses, and the like...had been seized, and were held in open hostility to [the] government, excepting only Forts Pickens, Taylor, and Jefferson, on and near the Florida coast, and Fort Sumter, in Charleston harbor, South Carolina....
>
> The forts remaining in the possession of the federal government in and near [the seceding] States were either besieged or menaced by warlike preparations,...Fort Sumter was nearly surrounded by well-protected hostile batteries, with guns equal in quality to the best of its own, and outnumbering the latter as perhaps ten to one.[7]

On the fifth of March Lincoln learned from a February 28 letter of Anderson that Sumter could not be held "with a force of less than twenty thousand good and well-disciplined men," and that, according to Scott, no such "sufficient force was then at the control of the government, or could be raised and brought to the ground" before the fort ran out of food. Faced with the probable necessity of giving up Sumter, Lincoln decided that Fort Pickens near Pensacola, Florida, should be reinforced to dispel any impression that the United States was recognizing secession as a fait accompli.[8]

Lincoln's order for troops to land at Pickens went awry. Scott passed it on but, as Lincoln learned about April 6, the officer commanding the vessel on which the troops were embarked "refused to land the troops" because of "some *quasi* armistice of the late administration." Scott was aware of the "armistice" agreed to by Buchanan embracing the Charleston and Pensacola harbors but may have not brought it to Lincoln's attention under the belief that the "armistice" terminated with the end of the Buchanan presidency.[9]

Lincoln did not want the secession movement to grow any larger. He faced a delicate situation. A provisional government for the Confederate States of America was established on February 7, 1861, and a provisional president, Jefferson Davis, was elected on February 9. Although the seceding states were large in number, the population was not too large:

> White: 2.6 million
> Slave: <u>2.3 million</u>
> Total: 4.9 million

out of a national population of 31.4 million. To fire on secessionists was not what he wanted to happen. But he did not want to leave the impression secession was to be tolerated.[10]

March 29 was an eventful day for Meigs. On that date Lincoln decided that preparations to help Sumter should be undertaken. The secretary of war was to cooperate with the secretary of navy in the preparation of an expedition to be ready to sail as early as April 6. Meigs was taken by Secretary of State William H. Seward to talk to the president about Pickens.[11]

Seward favored evacuating Sumter and, in informal exchanges with representatives of the Confederate government, indicated this was likely to happen. However, he supported, as did all of the cabinet, protecting Pickens and wanted the president to hear from someone young enough to ride a horse in the field as compared to Scott and Totten (in command of the Corps of Engineers) who were too old (74 and 72 respectively) to do so. Although Seward did not try to influence Meigs as to what he should tell the president, he told him "some officers of higher rank...were indisposed to advise active measures to relieve posts in danger." As to Sumter, Meigs told the president its relief was a matter for the navy and volunteered to find "young naval officers then in Washington who would gladly, if authorized, undertake to attempt it."[12]

Meigs told the president that Pickens, located on an island offshore from Pensacola, Florida, could be held "if the Navy had done its duty and not lost it already." He was familiar with Pickens, having passed it on his way to the Dry Tortugas, and knew it could be taken by a boat attack from the mainland by a few men. His plan to relieve Pickens was to "[s]end a ship of war immediately under sealed orders to enter the harbor and prevent boat expeditions" and to add troops to the small garrison at Pickens. He told the president that "Providence [had] supplied the man and the means." Lieutenant David Porter, U.S. Navy, was in Washington, and the warship *"Powhatan* had just returned from a foreign cruise." Lincoln was told "the strictest secrecy was indispensable," not because Meigs had "suspicion of any body in high station," but because "ordinary business of the Executive Department brings every paper under the eye of more than one person."[13]

To the president's inquiry as to whether Meigs could go to Florida and take general command of the Florida forts still in United States' hands (Taylor at Key West, Jefferson at the Dry Tortugas, and Pickens at Pensacola), Meigs explained that an officer of higher rank would be required since majors were already there. Politician Seward saw no problem with this, and said Meigs should be promoted, and urged Lincoln to put Meigs in charge. Lincoln said he would consider it for a day or two.[14]

Prior to the March 29 meeting Lincoln was "given a cold shock" by Scott who "did not think that Pickens ought to be held." Scott counseled, on March 15, that both Sumter and Pickens be evacuated to soothe the Southern slave states that had not yet seceded.[15]

The next Meigs heard of the matter was on Easter Sunday, March 31. As he was preparing for morning church, Scott's military secretary, Lieutenant Colonel Erasmus D. Keyes, called on him. Earlier Keyes had been sent by Scott to explain to Seward the difficulties of landing artillery on Pickens. Seward was not interested in hearing about the difficulties, and asked Keyes to find Meigs and bring him back to Seward forthwith. Keyes and Meigs were before Seward about 10 minutes later and received peremptory directions: "I wish you two gentlemen to make a plan to reinforce Fort Pickens, see General Scott, and bring your plan to the Executive Mansion at 3 o'clock this afternoon." They did as directed, except for seeing Scott, and upon arrival at the Executive Mansion found the president and Seward expecting them.[16]

Keyes was reluctant to tell the president his portion of the plan, dealing with artillery, because he had not shown it to Scott. Meigs was not deterred and went forward and explained his plan which dealt with engineering requirements. Keyes then explained his ideas, and they were told by Lincoln to tell Scott that he wanted their plans carried out unless Scott saw reasons that they shouldn't be. When told the president wanted to hold Pickens, notwithstanding his recommendation that Pickens be evacuated, Scott responded by quoting the great Frederick: "When the King commands, all things are possible." He approved the Keyes-Meigs plans.[17]

On April 1 Scott appointed Colonel Harvey Brown to be in charge of the expedition which was to reinforce and hold Pickens. Meigs was to accompany the expedition as engineer but to return to Washington once the army was established. Meigs and Keyes spent April 1 writing orders for the president's signature and brought into the picture Lieutenant David D. Porter to handle the navy's requirements.[18]

Secrecy had a high priority. Meigs did not tell his wife Louisa—to do so would "violate a trust." All she knew was that he was going to New York and his large trunk was to be packed with clothes to last some weeks. Porter told the president that Secretary of the Navy Gideon Welles was surrounded by many not loyal to the Union, and, if the orders came through the normal channels, the South would be alerted and Pickens taken. Seward assured Lincoln that he would take care of the fact that Welles was being ignored. At one point, Porter suggested cutting telegraph lines around Washington.[19]

Lincoln signed orders, dated April 1, directing Porter to proceed to New York and "take command of the steamer *Powhatan*, or any other United States steamer ready for sea which he may deem most fit for the service to which he [had] been assigned by confidential instructions." A separate order to Commandant Andrew H. Foote at the New York Navy Yard directed that the *Powhatan* be made ready to go to sea at the earliest possible moment.[20]

Colonels Brown and Keyes left for New York on April 2, and Meigs followed the next day. Meigs took with him $10,000 in funds, which Lincoln directed Seward to provide from Secret Service funds, to assist in arranging the expedition. An April 2 order signed by Lincoln relieved Captain Samuel Mercer from command of the *Powhatan*. The orders concerning the *Powhatan* bypassed the Navy Department but Welles did become aware, without details, that some secret operation was under way.[21]

When Porter tried to gain command of the *Powhatan*, the lack of orders from the Navy Department in the usual form created a problem. Finally, after considerable discussion, Porter was able to convince Foote that the order signed by Lincoln should be followed without alerting the Navy Department in Washington. This may have been a particularly difficult decision for Foote since he and Welles had been classmates at Cheshire Academy. The feat of persuasion also involved convincing one who had, "long before the war, when commanding the United States fleet of three vessels in Chinese waters,...converted every officer and man in the fleet to the principles of temperance, and had every one of them sign the pledge." For navy men to take the pledge, at a time when the navy gave grog rations to sailors, speaks well of Foote's steadfastness.[22]

At this point an unintended consequence of not including Welles was felt. Before the *Powhatan* got under way, on the evening of April 5, a telegram arrived in New York from Welles directing that the *Powhatan* be detained. On that date Welles directed the captain of the *Powhatan*, Samuel Mercer, to take charge of a naval force of the *Powhatan* and three other steamers to participate in an expedition to provision Sumter.[23] This caused Meigs to go into action the next day. His journal for April 6 reads:

Had to go to the Navy Yard to endeavor to save the *Powhatan*. This did twice, and I succeeded in taking her though written orders from Secretary of Navy to send her to help reinforce Sumter on the 11th were in the yard. I took the ground that Capt. Mercer had been relieved by orders signed by President, that she was promised to our expedition, was a necessary and most important part of it, and that no man, secretary or other, had a right to take her, and that the secretary could not do it as I was by the President made responsible and told not to let even the Secretary of the Navy know that this expedition was going on. They gave her up to us and Porter sailed about noon. He was seen going down the harbor at 3 P.M.[24]

The struggle was not over. Meigs telegraphed Seward to tell him of the mix-up and complaining of Welles' interference. Seward took the message to Welles on the night of April 6. This set off a dispute which was presented to Lincoln that night. Lincoln did not realize that the *Powhatan* had been assigned to the Sumter expedition, but, once convinced, he rejected Seward's arguments that the *Powhatan* should be allowed to proceed to Pickens. Seward was told to telegraph New York without delay. The message read: "Deliver up the *Powhatan* at once to Captain Mercer" and was signed Seward.[25]

Foote, probably shocked, acted to undo the situation. A fast tug caught the *Powhatan* and the message was delivered, but Porter elected to ignore it. Porter's reply was: "Have received confidential orders from the President, and shall obey them." On he sailed to Pickens. Meigs thought only Lincoln, Seward, Colonel Brown, Keyes, Porter, and he knew the *Powhatan's* destination.[26]

Meigs sailed early in the morning of April 7 aboard the steamship *Atlantic* together with Colonel Brown and about 400 persons connected with the expedition. Another ship, the *Illinois*, left the next day with additional men and supplies.[27]

As it turned out, the *Powhatan* was not needed at Pickens. Meigs' rationale for the *Powhatan* was to have it enter Pensacola harbor to prevent any landing of hostile forces from the mainland on Santa Rosa Island, the tip of which was occupied by Pickens. Even though the *Powhatan* left New York some 12 hours before the *Atlantic*, the *Atlantic* unknowingly passed it at sea and arrived at Pickens on April 16, a day before the *Powhatan*. And, even before the *Atlantic* arrived, the force Lincoln had directed Scott to have landed in mid-March had already been convinced that no armistice should stop them and went ashore on April 12.[28]

Consequently when the *Powhatan* arrived the morning of April 17, Colonel Brown did not want her to enter the harbor for fear of setting off

a confrontation with the provisional Confederate army forces on the mainland. Meigs, knowing that Porter's orders came from the president, and
his character to be such that "no man on earth could stop Porter bent on
an act of desperate gallantry & devotion," was afraid Porter could not be
stopped from entering the harbor.[29] Notwithstanding, Meigs asked the
commander of the *Wyandotte*, which he was aboard when informed of
Brown's wishes, to place his vessel across the path of the *Powhatan* and to
send a message to Porter that Meigs wanted to talk with him. Porter took
steps to pass by the *Wyandotte*, and felt like running her over, but eventually stopped and agreed with Brown.[30]

On April 20 the *Illinois* arrived. After all the men and supplies were
off-loaded from the *Atlantic*, she left, with Meigs aboard, to return to New
York on the 23rd. About one thousand men were garrisoned in the fort
and four navy vessels, with a combined complement of another one thousand men, were anchored nearby. The provisional Confederate forces on
the mainland, under command of Brigadier General Braxton Bragg, a West
Point graduate who had left the army in 1856, numbered from five to
seven thousand.[31]

Before Meigs departed, on the 23rd, he heard shots fired from the
Confederate positions and, even though it turned out that they were not
directed to Pickens, they led him to ponder the start of a civil war:

> It gave me a very grave feeling....The opening of a civil war is not a
> thing lightly to be seen & though I saw my duty plainly in reinforcing
> this beleaguered fortress & rescuing my countrymen shut up here from
> the hands and the power of rebels & traitors I could not [see] the open-
> ing of the fire without great regret. It must soon come however & God
> protect the right. I believe that we are on the right side.[32]

In fact the war started about 10 days before at Sumter which Meigs learned
had surrendered "as a military necessity" from "newspaper slips" Bragg
sent to Pickens.[33]

The political importance of taking a stand at Pickens was less than
that perceived when the expedition was approved on April 1, and the
evacuation of Sumter was still a possible course. About April 4 the president resolved to hold Sumter. As he explained to Congress, after it was
discovered Pickens had not been reinforced pursuant to Scott's orders of
March 12 and that Sumter would run out of food about April 8:

> To now re-enforce Fort Pickens, before a crisis would be reached at
> Fort Sumter, was impossible—rendered so by the near exhaustion of
> provisions in the latter-named fort. [As a] precaution...the government
> had...commenced preparing an expedition...to relieve Fort Sumter,
> which expedition was intended to be ultimately used, or not, accord-
> ing to circumstances. The strongest anticipated case for using it was
> now presented; and it was resolved to send it forward. As had been

intended...it was also resolved to notice the governor of South Carolina, that he might expect an attempt would be made to provision the fort; and that, if the attempt should not be resisted, there would be no effort to throw in men, arms, or ammunition, without further notice, or in case of an attack upon the fort.[34]

The message to Governor Francis W. Pickens, which reached him on April 8, set off a chain of events leading to war. On April 10, 1861, Brigadier General Pierre G. T. Beauregard, commanding the Provisional Army of the Confederate States at Charleston, was authorized by the Confederate government in Montgomery, Alabama, to demand the evacuation of Sumter, and, if the demand was refused, to "proceed, in such manner as [he] may determine, to reduce it." On April 11 Major Anderson refused Beauregard's demand to evacuate, but orally indicated the fort would be starved out within days.[35] When asked to clarify the "starved out" statement, Anderson wrote:

> I will, if provided with the proper and necessary means of transportation, evacuate Fort Sumter by noon on the 15th instant, and...in the mean time [will not] fire[] upon your forces unless compelled to do so by some hostile act against this fort or the flag of my Government by forces under your command...should I not receive prior to that time controlling instructions from my Government or additional supplies.[36]

Jefferson Davis did not consider this any guarantee of evacuation since it was known a relieving force was expected at Charleston any time. Anderson was advised on April 12 at 3:20 A.M. that Sumter would be fired upon within one hour. At 4:30 A.M. on April 12 Beauregard opened fire on Sumter. Sumter surrendered April 13 and was evacuated the next day.[37]

As Lincoln saw this, Sumter "was attacked and bombarded to its fall, without even awaiting the arrival of the provisioning expedition:"

> [T]he assault upon, and reduction of, Fort Sumter was, in no sense, a matter of self defence on the part of the assailants. They well knew that the garrison in the fort could, by no possibility, commit aggression upon them....They knew that this government desired to keep the garrison in the fort, not to assail them, but merely to maintain visible possession, and thus to preserve the Union from actual and immediate dissolution—trusting...to time, discussion, and the ballot-box, for final adjustment; and they assailed, and reduced the fort, for precisely the reverse object—to drive out the visible authority of the federal Union, and thus force it to immediate dissolution.[38]

Jefferson Davis, of course, saw it differently:

> The disingenuous rant of demagogues about "firing on the flag"...will be impotent in impartial history to relieve the Federal Government from the responsibility of the assault made by sending a hostile fleet

against the harbor of Charleston, to cooperate with the menacing garrison of Fort Sumter. After the assault was made by the hostile descent of the fleet, the reduction of Fort Sumter was a measure of defense rendered absolutely and immediately necessary.

* * * * *

Mr. Lincoln well knew that, if the brave men of the garrison were hungry, they had only him and his trusted advisers to thank for it. *They had been kept for months in a place where they ought not to have been.*...[Emphasis supplied.][39]

The niceties of who started the war were lost on the public North and South. The rest of the Confederate states seceded (Virginia [4/17/61], Arkansas [5/6/61], Tennessee [5/6/61], and North Carolina [5/20/61]) almost doubling the Confederacy population by adding another 2.9 million whites and 1.2 million slaves. At the same time the North was caught up in a desire to put the seceding states in their place.[40]

Militarily, concern about Pickens was not misplaced. As of April 30 the Confederate War Department still intended to take it. As it developed, Pickens remained in Union hands throughout the war. The danger of attack waned after Bragg was called upon to send part of his infantry to Virginia at the end of May. As Meigs speculated, after learning about Sumter, the next focus in the conflict was around Washington.[41]

Chapter 11

A New Army—A New Quartermaster General

During Meigs' Pickens-trip from New York to Florida and back (April 7–May 1), momentous events took place. Lincoln's reaction to Sumter's fall was immediate. On April 15, he issued a proclamation calling for 75,000 militia and set a session of Congress to start on July 4. The express job for the militia was to "suppress [the combination of the seceded states] and to cause the laws to be duly executed." The militia were to serve for three months.[1]

Although Lincoln and others referred to the "seceding States," the legal status of the Confederate States was an ideological barrier between Lincoln and Jefferson Davis. Davis saw the Confederate States as a separate nation formed by the exercise of their right to withdraw from the United States. Lincoln saw them as rebelling states advocating a view of the U.S. Constitution which, if true, would doom the United States—withdrawal of states whenever they wanted to wasn't consistent with a union of states. Lincoln's message to Congress on July 4, 1861, made it clear that, in his opinion, use of the adjective "seceding" merely sugar-coated the phrase "rebelling States."[2]

A telling reaction to Lincoln's call for the militia was a Virginia Convention vote on April 17 to secede. Virginia immediately prepared for war. Robert E. Lee followed Virginia into secession and was made commander in chief of Virginia forces on April 22. On the same date, the quartermaster general of the U.S. Army, another Virginian, Joseph E. Johnston, resigned to take up arms for the Confederacy. Anticipating that Virginia would be the focal point of combat, Jefferson Davis moved the Confederate capital from Montgomery, Alabama, to Richmond.[3]

The defection of West Point graduates, Jefferson Davis, Lee, and Johnston, was high treason to Meigs:

> No man who ever took the oath to support the Constitution as an officer of our army or navy a graduate of West Point a member of Congress or Cabinet & who has since actively engaged in rebellion in any

civil or military station should escape without loss of all his goods & civil rights & expatriation. The leaders should be put formally out of the way if possible by sentence of death executed if ever caught.[4]

Within days of Virginia's vote to secede, Washington was cut off from the states sending troops to the capital. On April 19 there was a riot in Baltimore and an attack on Massachusetts troops passing through the city. At least four soldiers and nine civilians were killed. The Maryland governor and the mayor of Baltimore reacted by asking the Baltimore and Ohio and the Northern Central railroads to send no more troops through Maryland. Municipal bridges were taken down at the direction of Baltimore officials, and railroad bridges by others. On April 21 the Baltimore police cut down telegraph poles and wires leading from Baltimore to the North.[5]

Rumors were rampant in Washington. One fear was that the Confederate army would seize Washington. Anyone knowing that the Confederate secretary of war, L. P. Walker, told a crowd in Montgomery about April 15 that the Confederate flag "will, before the 1st of May, float over the dome of the Old Capitol in Washington," did not take such speculation lightly. Secretary of State Seward was told on April 5, 1861, that one of the Confederacy's commissioners sent to negotiate with the United States asserted "that within sixty days the Government of the Confederate States would embrace [Washington] and all the states north as far as New York." The *Richmond Examiner* spoke of Washington as "[t]hat filthy cage of unclean birds [which] must and will assuredly be purified by fire."[6]

The Confederacy had the muscle to try to back up the threats. On April 29 the Confederacy had 19,000 men in the field and 16,000 more on the way to Virginia. By comparison, the regular army of the United States of about 16,000 troops was spread all across the country.[7] General Scott took steps to protect the capital. His meager forces were rapidly augmented as militia, responding to Lincoln's April 15 proclamation, were able to reach Washington. By April 29 Scott thought sufficient troops had reached the city to protect it.[8]

Cessation of troop transportation through Baltimore impelled Benjamin F. Butler, a New England politician who wrangled a commission as brigadier general in the Massachusetts militia, to "seize[] the Annapolis and Elk Ridge Railroad, a subsidiary of the Baltimore and Ohio," so that troops could effect an entry from Annapolis into Washington. Annapolis could be reached by ship from Philadelphia, New York, and New England, as well as from Perryville, Maryland, which could be reached by rail from the North. The Baltimore problem was solved by federal troops taking possession of the city early in May.[9]

Davis called the Confederate Congress back into session on April 29, and told it that Lincoln's call for the militia was a "declaration of war."

During that session, all of the laws necessary to allow the Confederacy to prosecute a war were passed. Among the authorizations, Davis was to "use the whole land and naval force to meet the necessities of the war thus commenced." The Confederacy had taken earlier steps, in February and March, to create an army of more than one hundred thousand. To take advantage of those officers in the United States Army who wanted to come over to the Confederacy, they were to enter the Army of the Confederate States with the same ranks as they had in the United States Army.[10]

Before leaving Pickens, Meigs knew about the surrender of Sumter, the Virginia Convention vote for secession, and seizure of the Navy Yard in Norfolk. Bragg supplied the news. He was afraid Washington might be lost before he got back, but, nonetheless, envisioned "a bright future in which this great land under a strong & united Government will at length again be free & happy, when traitors will have received due punishment for their crimes & the sin of slavery wiped out by the hands of an avenging God."[11]

Meigs landed in New York on May 1 and, via Annapolis, Maryland, reached Washington on May 3. Patriotic ardor in New York was apparent. "Broadway looked like a peach orchard in full blossom all red & white with the star spangled banner which flew from every window & door." Meigs found the "free States to be in a tumult of enthusiasm caused by the attack on Sumter & the fact...that slavery [was] doomed."[12]

When reaching Washington he immediately went to the State Department to report to Seward, and then on to see the president and most of the cabinet. Over the next few days he had an intimation from Secretary of the Treasury Salmon P. Chase that he might be used in connection with the new army organization. Seward told him that he would be used as a general, and Postmaster General Montgomery Blair asked if he would take a major general promotion. Blair was trying to get him placed in command of the army.[13]

The attitude of Meigs was that the "[o]ffice should seek the man not man the office." Notwithstanding, he was disappointed when Seward told him on May 10 that the cabinet had agreed on making him a colonel. This was quite a come down from earlier suggestions by Seward, Chase, and Blair that he might be made a general and put in command of the army.[14]

He couldn't help but compare how high other West Point graduates had been placed. George B. McClellan, who graduated six years after he did, a major general in command of the West for the Union. Beauregard and Bragg, the first younger than Meigs, and the second in his West Point class, made generals for the South. As he saw it

> [t]o be made a Col[onel] of a marching regiment is to give up my profession in which I may be useful, to become a Col[onel] a position which can be filled by hundreds better than by me. No room for brains & some fighting fellow is enough, while if I retain my position as Capt of

Engineers I should probably be Chief Engineer of any forward movement & would be of some use to the country and a better chance of distinction.

When Seward was told this on May 14 he seemed disappointed.[15]

Seward on May 10 asked Meigs for his views on conducting the war. These were turned over to Seward on May 13, and later read by Seward to the president. Just as he had been able to do in connection with the Washington Aqueduct and the Capitol extension, Meigs was capable of, in a short time, formulating a comprehensive plan for a major undertaking. What follows is a summary of what he wrote:

> The South intended to wage an "aggressive war...to withdraw" from the Union. "Their people [were] warlike [and] trained to the use of arms," bore a hatred of the Northern people and probably were "sincerely persuaded that they [had] a just cause." "The City of Washington [was] the great object of attack for the South." It was full of spies—"[m]en in high official positions [were] open sympathizers with the rebels &...walk the streets see everything & report all to the enemy whom they hail as friends."
>
> The North needed to preserve its territory to retain a place among nations. Arlington Heights in Virginia, overlooking the Potomac and opposite the Executive Mansion, posed special problems. If the North were to take the heights it would precipitate immediate conflict with troops in Virginia, a fight which the North was not ready to handle. On the other hand, the North could not afford to let the Confederacy take over the heights which were 2.24 miles from the President's House—to do so could result in awaking some morning to "a discharge of artillery aimed at the Executive Mansion, to find the bridges all burnt &...facing skillfully planted batteries served by 10 to 80,000 men."
>
> Washington's communications were threatened by a conquered city (Baltimore) behind it and "a disaffected province [Maryland] through which...communications [were] constant[ly in] peril" of being disrupted by "a single nail or a single bolt or spike." The Potomac could easily be closed by batteries overlooking it.
>
> How should the North extricate itself from this situation? Troops must be concentrated in Washington in such numbers as to discourage any effort to take it. A camp should be established at Chambersburg, Pennsylvania, large enough for not less "than 40,000 men" to be drilled and transformed into a usable army capable of "marching into the enemy's country." Similar bodies of men should be assembled at Boston, New York, and Philadelphia. "The point to strike should be determined by circumstances" and not "decided upon until the moment of striking." Otherwise the government could not keep the point of attack a secret.

By keeping the South in doubt as to where it will be attacked, it would be forced "to hold large forces at their principal ports ready to resist attacks. This will exhaust them." The blockade of Southern ports, which Lincoln announced on April 19, "will soon distress them & in the end be the most effective mode of disgusting them with the war."

In the West, no flotilla could make it down the Mississippi. "Operations in the direction of N[ew] Orleans must...be conducted by land." "Certain points in K[entucky] where R[ail] R[oads] meet must be occupied by [Union] forces...with or without consent of K[entucky]." Care must be taken to not let Pickens be lost.

In short, "a policy defensive in the main, offensive only so far as to occupy important positions in the border states...to keep the...battle...out of the sight of Washington and offensive also by the threats of the assembled armies held at important strategic points on the border & at the great seaports will be the policy most tending to a solution."

"A thorough strangling & smothering of [the] nest of traitors [would] be the most effective the least costly the best policy.... It will leave the least hostile feeling after the contest is over & yet will put in position to go on & subjugate the South if that sad necessity arises."[16]

As for timing, Meigs said it would be a mistake to march "a small army ill provided with wagons bridges horses artillery & provisions [into] the states of Virginia Kentucky or Tennessee." The North was not prepared to do so. It had no generals to lead the armies. The armies would be made up of "new men—they must be made soldiers."[17]

In addition to written views outlined above, Meigs wrote out his ideas on slavery that were read to Seward since he did not desire to commit them to a paper record. He thought the time might come when the North would call on the slaves to revolt against their masters.[18]

The go-slow approach reflected in the Meigs' analysis did not accord with those of Postmaster General Blair, a Meigs' supporter. Because of this, when Lincoln wanted it shown to Blair, Seward asked Meigs if that was agreeable. Meigs agreed on condition that Blair know they were prepared at the request of Seward. Later that evening, Blair told Meigs it would ruin the country to delay—it would give time for the South to consolidate the rebellion.[19]

Blair also told Meigs that he had scolded Seward for cheapening Meigs by offering him a colonelcy, and that it looked as if Meigs would have to take the position of quartermaster general. Blair's change from talking of Meigs as the head of the army to being quartermaster general may have been caused by their differences on how soon the army should move. Blair wrote a note to the president on Meigs' views, with which he did not agree, but did not blame Meigs, saying to the president that Meigs was a soldier, not a politician.[20]

On May 17 Meigs was promoted to colonel of a marching regiment, but was led to understand it was but a step to a higher position. Although Blair was confident that Meigs would be made quartermaster general by May 30 this did not happen, and Meigs was ordered, by Secretary of War Simon Cameron, to lead another expedition to Fort Pickens. The roadblock to the quartermaster general appointment was Cameron. Lincoln asked Scott to use his influence to overcome Cameron's objection to making Meigs quartermaster general and said about Meigs: "I do not know one who combines the qualities of masculine intellect, learning, and experience of the right sort, and physical power of labor and endurance, so well as he." Meigs was an impressive-looking man, six feet one inches in height weighing two hundred pounds.[21]

It is something of a mystery as to why Cameron was reluctant to have Meigs as quartermaster general. Perhaps Cameron had his own candidate. Or it may have been the Pickens episode. At the time he learned Meigs was acting, respecting Pickens, without Cameron's knowledge, he was ready to court-martial him, but this anger must have subsided as Cameron learned of Lincoln's involvement. Or his notion that Meigs was an autocrat, dating from the Walter-Meigs confrontation, may have given him second thoughts as to what type working relationship they would have. Also he did not like the fact that Meigs, before going to Pickens in April, had written suggesting that if he did not return from Pickens, his family should be paid something for the years of work performed on the Capitol—this disclosure seemed to irritate Cameron at a cabinet meeting. Remembering that Meigs was paid $1,800 per year during the time Thomas Walter was being paid $4,500 per year, and that in 1858 when his oldest son, John, applied to President Buchanan for an appointment to West Point he said that his father's "pay [was] not sufficient to allow him to give [John] such an education as [John] thought [he could] make good use of," that letter was not out of line. As early as 1854 Meigs observed that he was paying watchmen at the Capitol more than he, who was in charge of all the work there, was paid.[22]

Meigs had a solid relationship with Seward, but the egos of Scott and Cameron, largely ignored concerning the Pickens expedition, were offended. Erasmus Keyes suffered. Scott fired him from his staff and refused to see him on his return from Pickens. As far as Meigs was concerned, he had no animus against Scott—he found him "hearty, [with] true loyalty and fidelity to his oath as an officer of the Army of the *United States*." Cameron told Keyes that, if he had been involved, he would have sent neither Keyes nor Meigs. At one point Cameron expressed to Meigs concern about his temper.[23]

During the time of uncertainty, Colonel Meigs was willing to leave his future in the hands of others: he wrote that "God only knows what is best for my usefulness and safety—for what I am fitted and He will not, I trust, put me into any position which I cannot fill with credit."[24]

But, in the end, Meigs had the most important support, that of Lincoln. At one point Meigs wrote in his journal that "[t]hey had better make me Q. M. Gen'l than to keep up the present already rotten system.... I fear that I am growing ambitious. I thought I desired only to be useful." He was appointed quartermaster general on June 13, 1861, with the rank of brigadier general dating from May 14.[25]

What type man had Lincoln appointed? An important Meigs' supporter, the old Blair, that is, Francis Preston, who, nearing 70, had been a power in Washington since the presidency of Andrew Jackson and a principal organizer of the Republican party, wrote to Cameron on June 2 recommending Meigs as quartermaster general describing his qualifications as

> energy, industry, knowledge of the wants of an army—his zeal in the cause our army is about to vindicate—above all his well known probity, punctuality & strong common sense in dealing with men, fit him for the service. His manner of doing business would put to utter discredit all suspicions of foul speculations in the transactions managed by him, which are so much urged to disparage even the most honest administration.[26]

There is no question but what the zeal was there. His wife wrote her mother saying that Montgomery's "soul seems on fire with indignation at the treason of those wicked men who have laid the deep plot to overthrow our Government and destroy the most noble fabric of freedom the world has ever seen....He looks so dreadfully stern when he talks of the rebellion that I do not like to look at him but he does not look more stern and relentless than he feels." Meigs saw this as "a great & holy war. God is with us. Who shall be against us." The war would "hasten[] by a few years the deaths of certain thousands of men, the mourning of widows and orphans. All must die all must mourn in time."[27]

Although the new quartermaster general had some reservations about Scott, who did "not tolerate original independent thinking" and was operating with a small staff "of some half dozen not distinguished officers," he noted that Scott had "never failed never retreated never lost a campaign" and trust had to be put in him "for the present."[28]

Much happened while Meigs was functioning as a captain and a colonel. A May 3 presidential proclamation called for volunteers to serve at least for three years, and for a 23,000-man increase to the regular army. On May 23 Virginia's general population ratified the Virginia Convention's ordinance of secession. The United States took aggressive action against Virginia. About midnight, on May 23–24, troops passed the Meigs' house "down 14th street with no music, every bayonet [gleaming] brightly in the moonbeams." Arlington Heights, including Robert E. Lee's home, and Alexandria, Virginia, diagonally opposite Washington and a busy Potomac

River port, were occupied. Lee's home was converted into an army head-quarter. Meigs thought none of the politicians of the South were patriots "unless Davis may be one, and he is led away by his mad ambition to do that which I am sure his conscience rejects."[29]

Troops organized in Ohio and Indiana, under overall command of Major General George B. McClellan, entered northwestern Virginia and, after a few small battles in May through July, gained possession of what was to later become West Virginia. Control of this area was important to the North since a major railroad link to the West (Ohio, Indiana, Illinois, and Missouri), the Baltimore and Ohio Railroad, ran through it. McClellan, a West Point graduate who, in 1861, was president of a railroad, was put in charge of the quota of troops raised by Ohio and, in turn, given a commission as major general in the regular army and assigned to command the Department of Ohio.[30]

McClellan was not one to understate his accomplishments. He described to his troops what had happened as the "annihila[tion of] two armies, commanded by educated and experienced soldiers, intrenched in mountain fastnesses." McClellan, hailed in the North as a young Napoleon, was shortly catapulted into command of the North's largest army.[31]

As of July 1, 1861, the North had 230,000 men either under arms or committed to join the army. In the main, they were located on the northern border of Virginia. Simon Cameron's hope was that the South would be cowed by the creation of a large army. As quartermaster general, Meigs saw himself as a major player. He wrote his father that a major general commands a corps; a lieutenant general commands the whole army; but the quartermaster general supplies the means of moving that army and his command extends from the Atlantic to the Pacific, from the Lakes to the Gulf, and, in doing so, was in "second place not in military rank but in actual real influence over the war."[32]

A person with Meigs' drive and efficiency was needed badly. When Francis Preston Blair saw him on his third day in office, Meigs "had on a busy look."

Orders were going out for horses and wagons and tents. Wagons and horses were flowing into Washington. Concerning any allegations that the United States was buying broken-down horses, it was not possible to avoid some bad ones when two thousand horses were being bought in a week. Just then "any horse [was] worth...more than none." He was working to get the right men to work with him "but like good war horses they [were] hard to find." With the demands on his time, he still had time to ride out to look at Cabin John Bridge before giving the order to strike the center support.[33]

He advised Cameron that factories in the U.S. needed to be put to work making rifled muskets, and that the Ordnance Department had to be ordered to decide which projectiles should be adopted—"time is of more importance than the best, the second best being good enough for practical purposes no doubt." The nature of the war was such that he found in one case "that a sudden demand from the [Confederacy] had taken all [the] horses [needed from an area]."[34]

Two personnel decisions were made within a week of his assuming office. He would continue a practice he had always followed—no employment of kith and kin. When Montgomery's younger brother (Samuel Emlen) joined the army in December 1861, although commissioned as a quartermaster, he was purposefully kept from the Washington office of the quartermaster general. Secondly, care was needed so as not to interfere with the decisions of field quartermasters as to who they select to help handle funds intrusted to the quartermaster.[35]

Chapter 12

Bull Run

Getting volunteers to join the army was not a problem in either the South or North. Secretary Cameron reported to the president on July 1, 1861, that one of his problems was "to keep down the proportions of the Army and to prevent it from swelling beyond the actual force required." Lincoln told Congress on July 1 that "[o]ne of the greatest perplexities [was] to avoid receiving troops faster than [they could be] provide[d] for." Lincoln thought the confrontation could be "a short and a decisive one," and, in his July 4, 1861, message to Congress, asked for an army of at least 400,000 and $400,000,000. Congress did him 100,000 better as to men, authorizing an army of 500,000 on July 22, 1861.[1]

In his new position, Meigs was part of the councils of war held by Lincoln and his cabinet and high-ranking officers in June. On June 25 Scott reported 66,000 men available. Confederate Major General Pierre G. T. Beauregard had 26,000 at Manassas Junction, about 28 miles south and west of Washington. The pluses and cons, according to the quartermaster general, were:

> Ours are the better armed, equipped and paid troops. They [the Confederates] are out of money, no pay, little food, badly clothed but are men of greater experience in the use of arms, longer drill, though not so amenable to discipline. On the whole ours are the best, but all are raw. We have less artillery than they and almost no cavalry. The raw troops are liable to sudden panic....[2]

Expeditions into Virginia using the York or James Rivers, by way of Aquia Creek, or by a route direct from Washington to Richmond were all touched upon but nothing determined.[3]

Meigs worried about weapons for the new soldiers. When he found out from Cameron that nothing was being done about gun carriages for a recent order of three hundred guns, he told him "some one must take the risk of being blamed, must act, and get guns, materials of war." In July, finding that Congress had not appropriated enough money for guns, he took steps to get $10 million appropriated, and saw to it that an agent was standing by in New York to sail to Europe to buy guns once the money was available.[4]

At a council of war meeting on June 29, Scott suggested "blockading the Mississippi by a line of posts, and remaining inactive [in the Washington area.]" Meigs, when called upon, said

> that [he] did not think [they] would ever end this war without beating the rebels; that they had come near us. We were, according to Gen. Scott's information...stronger than they, better prepared, our troops better contented, better clothed, better fed, better paid, better armed.... [I]t was better to whip them here than to go far into an unhealthy country to fight them, and to fight far from our supplies, to spend our money among enemies instead of our friends. To make the fight in Virginia was cheaper and better as the case [then] stood.[5]

A movement from Washington, "as soon as the army could be got ready, and the transportation provided," was decided upon. Meigs wanted the march to start on Monday, July 8. One good battle would break the back of the rebellion, so thought Meigs.[6]

Arrangements for an advance by Brigadier General Irvin McDowell resulted in a lot of scrambling. On July 6 the Washington depot was "blocked up with cars loaded with horses, mules, wagons, ambulances, etc." The city looked as if it had been raining horses and wagons. The scheduled march date of July 8 had to be postponed because enough transport was not yet available. On July 16 McDowell moved out with 30,000 men. Beauregard, a West Point classmate of McDowell and his immediate adversary, was thought to have 25,000, and the Confederates had 15 or 18,000 more in the Winchester area which might attempt to join Beauregard—if so, Major General Robert Patterson, approaching 70 years, with 23,000 men located near Harpers Ferry, was "under orders to follow him."[7]

After a month in office Meigs was rightly proud—he had collected "the means of moving forward...30,000 men...succeeded in getting large amounts of rifled guns ordered...and got the President to change his orders in regard to the mustering of cavalry by which the U.S. [paid] for the purchases of the horses, instead of the volunteers." The last encouraged formation of cavalry which had not theretofore occurred. Having done some good, he felt "as though [he] ought to be at the head of one of [the] moving armies."[8]

The advancement of McDowell's army was not favored by Scott who had an overall plan, referred to disparagingly by the press as the Scott Anaconda plan. In essence, he would cut the South off by a naval blockade and take control of the Mississippi River. He knew the plan to be weak politically, but saw "the great danger [to the North was] the impatience of [its] patriotic and loyal Union friends [who] urge instant and vigorous action...."[9]

Public pressure for action was compelling. Horace Greeley's *New York Tribune* cried out "Forward to Richmond." The movement was motivated, in part, by the fact that the Confederate Congress was due to convene in Richmond on July 20 and the three month members of the Union army would be eligible to go home soon.[10]

McDowell moved slowly—on the third day, July 18, contact was made with the Confederate army situated behind a small stream, Bull Run. McDowell used up July 19 and 20 in scouting. This delay in his attack, which took place on July 21, permitted Beauregard time to ask the Confederate government in Richmond for help from the 10,000 troops under command of General Joseph E. Johnston, the former Union quartermaster general, located in the Shenandoah Valley near Winchester, Virginia. By a rapid transfer, using the Manassas Gap Railroad, Johnston moved his forces to bolster Beauregard.[11]

Louisa Meigs, in a letter to her mother, described what happened.

I cannot recollect whether I informed you of John's departure for Virginia.... I knew nothing of his determination until he came riding up to the door on Thursday morning of last week [July 18] and told me that he had asked and received permission of his father to join Major Hunt's battery. I felt a pained shocked sensation when he told me of it. [Note: John Rodgers Meigs was on furlough from West Point. Major Hunt's battery had gone with Montgomery Meigs to Fort Pickens and returned in time for the Bull Run battle.[12]] He said he felt it his duty to offer his services to the Country—that he had for two years been educated at the expense of the Govt and would be ashamed to return to W. Point without having made some effort to be useful at a time when the Country needed all her soldiers. What could I say....

I felt that it was the prompting of a nature the stirring of his blood which comes from a patriotic race.... but I felt a very motherly and womanish sinking at the heart nevertheless. I had been all the time congratulating myself that he would not be allowed...to go into service at this time. He went off full of excitement. The night he left us his father...assist[ed] him to arm himself—buckling on his sword pistol arranging his telescope slinging it over his shoulder etc....

On Sunday morning [July 21] an attack was anticipated...and Mont[gomery] who had seemed uneasy and anxious the evening before told me after breakfast that he had determined to go up to the scene of action. It gave me the heart ache to hear him say so, but I felt that it was useless to say a word.... All Sunday the City was filled with rumors. On Sunday afternoon, news came of the success of our army.... About 12 at night [I learned] our army...was retreating panic stricken before the rebels.

You may be sure there was no sleep or repose for me.... About 4 o'clock I threw myself upon the bed and was roused from a doze by hearing my dear husband's voice down stairs.... His voice was so cheery that I hoped we had been deceived in regard to the reports we had heard.

It was too true and Monts cheerfulness only arose from his invincible spirit and the fortitude which can make him endure adversity like prosperity with a serene composure....

* * * * *

When Mont came in on Monday morning he could tell me nothing about John. He...had not seen or heard of him.... About 8 o'clock a horseman came galloping to the door. It was John—black with dust & smoke he rushed into his father's room—threw himself down by his father who was asleep and exclaiming Father the army is completely routed. We have fallen back to Fairfax and Major Hunt does not want to stir an inch further.

He had come home on his own responsibility to report to General Scott & to get fresh horses for the batteries. He said he must go back immediately, that they were expecting an attack of the Cavalry.... He laughed when I told him that I would not consent to let him go back. You may imagine what a relief it was to hear his father say after a visit to General Scott that he was ordered not to return to the Army [which] would fall back to Arlington Heights.

That Monday was a sad day. The rain poured down unceasingly all day. The ambulances were passing our house and the poor weary foot sore soldiers tramped along....[13]

Reaction to the defeat at Bull Run was fast. Heads rolled. McDowell was reduced to a division commander, Patterson was mustered out of service, and, unfortunately for the North, was relieved by a political general, Nathaniel P. Banks, former governor of Massachusetts, who ended up losing enough supplies in the Shenandoah Valley to be known in the Confederate ranks as Commissary Banks. Political generals sometimes worked out, but Banks, who was "studying military works" in May of 1861, had few successes.[14]

Even though the casualties on both sides were relatively even (Union: 460 killed, 1,124 wounded, 1,312 missing—total 2,896; Confederates: 387 killed, 1,582 wounded, 13 missing—total 1,982), the reverse was enough for Horace Greeley to change his tune—he thought it now time for a negotiated peace.[15]

Meigs participated in Bull Run only as a witness. He left home at 11 A.M., returned by 3 A.M., briefed the president, and was back home by 4 A.M. During this time he covered over 60 miles—about 25 by carriage and 35 on horseback. For 15 or 20 minutes he was located where musket fire and shells were in the air. For the first time he heard the hurtling of hostile shells. The sound was very different from the scream of round shot. Afterward he looked back and commented on how calm he had been, and that, in time, he might find a place in a contested field. Both Union and Confederate, he thought, fought gallantly.[16]

The day after the battle he was back in his office with a confident air. Although disheartened, he was sure of ultimate success. He salvaged what he could from the Bull Run battlefield. Long trains of wagons were sent out (albeit it wasn't easy to get men willing to drive the wagons), and 175 four-horse wagonloads were saved. Of four hundred wagons which had been supplied the army, all but 13 were saved.[17]

Cadet Meigs received high marks from Major Hunt:

> On the death of Lieutenant Craig, Cadet Meigs performed his duties until the close of the action with spirit and intelligence, and was very useful, after the affair was over, in conveying orders, observing the enemy, and rallying our troops.[18]

Secretary Cameron offered a commission to Cadet Meigs, but the decision was made for him to finish at West Point. Cameron wrote him on December 15, 1861, lauding his gallant conduct.[19]

Nine days after the battle, in a letter to his father, Meigs said McDowell was a "good, brave, commonplace fat man" who no one in the army would have picked to lead—he was appointed through Secretary Chase's influence. Elsewhere, McDowell is described as "squarely and powerfully built." McDowell was replaced by General George B. McClellan, summoned the day after the battle, from the Department of Ohio, to take charge of the defeated and demoralized Army of the Potomac.[20]

Chapter 13

Problems in the West—1861

One week's experience...is sufficient to prove that everything here [in St. Louis] is in complete chaos. The most astonishing orders and contracts for supplies of all kinds have been made and large amounts purport to have been received, but there is nothing to show that they have ever been properly issued, and they cannot now be found. [Major General Henry Halleck reporting in November 1861.][1]

Missouri and Kentucky were states of major concern to Lincoln in April 1861. They did not have large slave populations—Missouri, 115,000 out of a population of 1.2 million (10 percent); and Kentucky, 225,000 out of a population of 1.2 million (19 percent), compared to an average of almost 40 percent for the states which ended up in the Confederacy. Nonetheless, they had ardent supporters for secession. Missouri Governor Claiborne Jackson characterized Lincoln's April 1861 call for 75,000 militia as "illegal, unconstitutional, and revolutionary in its object, inhuman and diabolical."[2]

In St. Louis and Louisville, with populations of 161,000 and 68,000, respectively, they contained the eighth and twelfth largest cities in the country. But, most important of all was their relationship to two major rivers, the Mississippi and the Ohio. If the South had control of the Mississippi River up to St. Louis, or could block its use by the North at that point, and controlled the southern bank of the Ohio River which separates Kentucky from Illinois, Indiana, and Ohio, the North's ability to bring the war into the Confederacy would have been decreased.[3]

Aggressive action of U.S. Army Captain Nathaniel Lyon, the commandant of the federal arsenal in St. Louis, and Congressman Francis P. Blair, Jr., who organized a force of Missouri Home Guards, kept the federal arsenal in Union hands. Troops loyal to the Union, under Lyon's command, on May 10, 1861, surrounded and disbanded Missouri militia loyal to Governor Jackson who favored secession.[4]

When Brigadier General William Harney, in command of the Union's Department of the West, returned to St. Louis from a trip to Washington, he made an effort to reconcile the two forces. Francis Blair, who thought forceful action was required, arranged for Harney to be relieved on May 31 and for Lyon to be put in charge. Lyon, who was promoted to brigadier general, almost immediately marched on Missouri's capital, Jefferson City, about one hundred miles up the Missouri River from St. Louis, which was occupied without difficulty. Next, near Boonville, Missouri (roughly 40 miles north of Jefferson City on the Missouri River), the first shooting confrontation of relatively large bodies of armed men (two thousand Union and 1,300 Confederate) occurred. Lyon prevailed there on June 17, but later, on August 10, lost the battle of Wilson's Creek (in southwest Missouri) and his life in a Union attack of about five thousand on a Confederate army of about 12,000.[5]

Before the Wilson's Creek battle, Lyon was superseded in command of the Department of the West by John Fremont who embittered his supporters, the Blair family (that is, the Blair brothers, Montgomery, the postmaster general, and Francis, and the patriarch, Francis Preston Blair), by not providing Lyon additional troops at Wilson's Creek.[6]

Lincoln commissioned John Fremont as a major general in the regular army on July 3, 1861, and made him head of the Department of the West, that part of the United States between the Mississippi River and the Rocky Mountains and Illinois. According to Fremont, Lincoln gave him *carte blanche*. This was a mistake. Fremont had never administered a large army, and was much in the swashbuckler type.[7]

Fremont, a national figure, made numerous explorations of the western territories of the United States before the Civil War, gaining the title The Pathfinder, played a prominent role in the United States taking California from Mexico in 1847, and had short stints as governor of California and as its United States senator. Supporting most of his expeditions was the powerful senator from Missouri, Thomas Hart Benton, whose daughter, Jessie Benton Fremont, was Fremont's wife.[8]

Many of the expeditions he headed as an officer in the U.S. Army Topographical Corps. After being convicted of mutiny concerning actions in California, by a court-martial in November 1847–January 1848, and, in an outrage at his conviction, he resigned from the army. A zealous abolitionist, he was the Republican presidential candidate in 1856, and lost to Buchanan.[9]

Fremont's vision, one shared by Lincoln, Winfield Scott, and Meigs, was for the North to gain control of the Mississippi River. A first step was for Fremont to firmly control the state of Missouri, a hotbed of secessionist activity.[10]

Although Fremont may have looked like the ideal leader for Missouri, his shortcomings quickly came to the surface. He crossed swords with Lincoln about one month after his arrival in St. Louis on July 25. On August 30 he placed Missouri under martial law, and proclaimed that property held by those in rebellion against the United States, including slaves, was confiscated and the slaves declared free. He overstepped on the slave question. Lincoln, not wanting to unnecessarily offend the border states, asked Fremont to withdraw that part of the declaration—Fremont refused and dispatched his wife to Washington to confer with Lincoln, which she did. Jessie Fremont not only restated the refusal of her husband to back down, she even threatened he might establish a separate nation in the Mississippi Valley. Not persuaded, Lincoln ordered the withdrawal of the emancipation part of the order and that was done. But Fremont, in an act of effrontery, had two hundred copies of his unchanged proclamation distributed after Lincoln ordered that it be modified.[11]

Fremont complained about a lack of support by the Quartermaster Department. On August 28 Meigs wrote to Francis P. Blair, Jr., in St. Louis, who had written his brother, the postmaster general, about Fremont's assertions. Meigs summarized how supplies could be acquired without delay, but made it clear that the responsibility for deciding to shortcut the system, or to pay high prices, would rest with Fremont as the commanding general. Meigs said he had a duty to speak up when it appeared the prices being paid were probably too high. However, he realized there were instances where a general may decide to buy at a high price. His example was

> If General Fremont orders Captain Turnley *to pay $1,000 for an ax*, Captain Turnley will be supported by [the Quartermaster] Department in obeying. The propriety of such a payment, however, will be between General Fremont and the Government.
>
> The general is charged with *saving the country*. The country will be very careful to approve his measures, and will judge his mistakes, if any, very tenderly if successful.[12]

Had Meigs had known the degree to which army regulations and statutes were being disregarded, he would have realized more than a letter was needed.

Unfortunately for Fremont and the Quartermaster Department, Major Justus McKinstry, a West Point graduate and the regular army quartermaster in St. Louis, was not an honest, upright man, nor was Captain R. B. Hatch who Fremont appointed as assistant quartermaster at Cairo, Illinois. The House Government Contracts Committee warned about July 1862 that no "vouchers bearing the name of R. B. Hatch...should be paid without a thorough investigation." In January 1862 Hatch was arrested by Brigadier General Ulysses S. Grant who was headquartered in Cairo. Hatch, at times, purchased at one price and billed the government for a higher price, and sold to the government horses and mules captured from the Confederates.[13]

Reports from St. Louis were not good. Francis P. Blair, Jr., wrote his brother on September 1, 1861, that Fremont should be relieved. He wrote his sister that Jessie Fremont had "set up Court in St Louis in Louis Napoleon fashion" and that Fremont's "Italian attaches [took] precedence & exclud[ed]...leading men from the presence & counsels of Fremont" while "soldiers wander[ed] the streets drunk." Lincoln wrote a letter, dated September 9, to Major General David Hunter asking him to assist Fremont. Lincoln said Fremont's "cardinal mistake [was] that he isolates himself, & allows nobody to see him; and by which he does not know what is going on in the very matter he is dealing with."[14]

Montgomery Blair and Meigs were sent to St. Louis to inspect conditions and to deliver Lincoln's message to Hunter.[15] They arrived in St. Louis on September 12 and found much wrong—in his journal Meigs wrote:

> [C]alled with Blair upon Gen. Fremont; we found him living in state with body-guards sentinels etc. ...Fremont is building fortifications about the City at extravagant cost. He has built more gun-boats than directed. He is buying tents of bad patterns...at prices fixed by himself—not by the proper purchasing officers. The impression among the regular officers is that he is incapable, and that he is looking not to the Country but to the Presidency; he is thought to be a man of no principle.
>
> The rebels are killing and ravaging the Union men throughout the state; great distress and alarm prevail; in St. Louis the leading people of the state complain that they cannot see him; he does not encourage them to form regiments for defence, but keeps his eye fixed upon Cairo and the expedition down the Mississippi, while he leaves the state unprotected. Some talk of his intending to set off—like Aaron Burr— for himself with an independent empire. He lives in great style in a fine house....A general atmosphere of distrust and suspicion pervades the place; none of the regular officers seemed to think him honest....[16]

On returning to Washington on September 18, Meigs and Blair reported to the president and cabinet. Montgomery Blair was particularly indignant since Fremont had arrested his brother, Francis, for writing letters to Washington about conditions in St. Louis.[17]

Meigs was not impressed with McKinstry, who was promoted from major in the regular army to brigadier general U.S. Volunteers on September 2, 1861. McKinstry "talk[ed] rapidly but [did] not give the impression of truth." Dissatisfied with McKinstry, Fremont asked that he be replaced, and Meigs made an important and lasting choice by sending a classmate, and an experienced quartermaster, Major Robert Allen, to St. Louis to relieve McKinstry.[18]

Meigs had to guard against favoritism, a failing extending to Lincoln. On September 10 Lincoln wrote a note of introduction for a James L.

Lamb of Springfield, Illinois, to McKinstry saying that he, Lincoln, would "be pleased, if consistent with the public good, that [McKinstry would] make purchases of him of any army supplies needed."[19]

Shortly after Allen arrived, Secretary Cameron and Adjutant General Lorenzo Thomas were in St. Louis, and Allen sought guidance. His letter captures the chaotic conditions:

> Is it competent for every member of the staff of Maj. Gen. John C. Fremont to issue orders in the name of the general, directed to me, and involving an expenditure of money?

> * * * * *

> Accounts involving hundreds of thousands of dollars have been presented to me within the few days I have been here, informal, irregular, and not authorized by law or regulations.[20]

Three days prior to his letter of October 11, Allen telegraphed Meigs that "unless the wanton, reckless expenditures in this command are not arrested by a stronger arm than mine, the Quartermaster's Dept. will be wrecked in Missouri along with Gen. Fremont." Meigs antidote for reckless spending was, whenever feasible, to have public notice of and bidding for government contracts. This gave the public confidence, allowed for competition, and disclosed sources not previously known.[21]

While Cameron and Thomas were in St. Louis, Fremont's excesses were curtailed. On October 14 Thomas wrote to him that any money currently in the hands of disbursing officers should only be used to pay current expenses of his army—debts were to only be paid after they were "properly examined and sent to Washington for settlement." All contracts were "to be made by the disbursing officers." As for those given commissions by Fremont, they would not be paid until their appointments were approved by Lincoln. Construction of field works around St. Louis and barracks being erected near Fremont's St. Louis quarters was to be discontinued.[22]

Thomas, in his report of the October 1861 trip, had little good to say about Fremont: "The opinion entertained by gentlemen who have approached and observed him is that he is more fond of the pomp than of the stern realities of war; that his mind is incapable of fixed attention or strong concentration; that by his mismanagement of affairs since his arrival in Missouri the State has almost been lost, and that if he is continued in command, the worst results may be anticipated."[23]

Cameron and Thomas arrived back in Washington on October 21 and, on October 24, Lincoln signed a letter to Brigadier General Samuel Curtis, a West Point graduate and former Iowa congressman at a camp near St. Louis, enclosing a Winfield Scott order relieving Fremont by Major General David Hunter. Fremont was not to be relieved if "in personal command, [by that time had] fought and won a battle, or shall then be actually in a battle, or shall then be in the immediate presence of the enemy in expectation of a battle." When Fremont was reached, none of these conditions existed, and he was duly relieved on November 2.[24]

McKinstry was arrested on November 13, 1861, tried by general court-martial and dismissed from the service. His relief, Major Robert Allen, as chief quartermaster for the Mississippi Valley, was a Meigs' stalwart throughout the war.[25]

The Washington quartermaster office cannot be blamed for these activities. Fremont acted so much outside the regular system that quite a time delay occurred before Washington became aware of the fraud, corruption, and misuse of public funds. As of August 28, Meigs was pledging full support for meeting Fremont's needs. Shortly thereafter, Meigs got a sample of what was going on.[26]

A J. E. Reeside was appointed inspector of horses for the western department and ordered by Fremont to go to Cincinnati. Reeside was so pleased with his arrangement with the Department of the West that he wanted to get a like deal with the Department of the East. His request came to Meigs' attention.[27]

On September 3, 1861, Meigs wrote to Cameron telling him that someone other than a quartermaster had hired Reeside and was paying him a commission of two and one-half percent of the price to inspect horses. Meigs calculated that for the 20,000 horses to be acquired for the Army of the Potomac for artillery and transportation during the next six or so weeks, Reeside would, "were he able to perform the duty," be paid $60,000. Not a bad wage at a time when the assistant secretary of war was paid $3,000 per annum. Meigs wanted nothing to do with Reeside, nor with the Union Defense Committee at Chicago which Fremont had appointed to acquire supplies for him—Meigs got Cameron's approval to have "all [Union Defense Committee] contracts...examined by some Government officer before [they were] executed."[28]

The Congressional Government Contracts Committee, although not liking the commission paid to Reeside, gave him credit for not passing bad horses on to the army. Unfortunately, another inspector in Cincinnati had no qualms about this, and approved many of the horses Reeside turned down. Reeside was out for all he could get. He also had a contract to inspect harness. Cameron canceled all Reeside contracts.[29]

The Union armies needed, in a hurry, many horses and mules. The Department of the West was not alone in having loose practices. A blatant example was an order made in October 1861 for one thousand horses bought in Pittsburgh, Pennsylvania, to be shipped to Springfield, Illinois. As it developed, during a stopover in Chicago for one lot of 252 horses, the quartermaster questioned their value and called for a board of inspection.

The board's report, rejecting all but 27 of the horses, was a map of ills which horse "flesh is heir to:"

> The causes for rejection are specified as being blind, swenied, spavined, stiff shoulder, split hoof, curbed legs, stoven shoulder, glanders, distemper, curb-spavined, ring-boned, deformed back, stiff neck, gash on the head, shroup shoulder, big knee, wind-broken, cut feet, hoof-bound, deranged hip, stock-legged, besides being too old, and too young, and too small, and of the wrong sex.[30]

Fremont's profligate spending came at a poor time. Meigs wrote Major Allen on October 4 that he was having $500,000 sent to the Department of the West Quartermaster's Department, but that it had to be used judiciously. At that time the calls for money on the treasury were exceeding its daily receipts and heavy debts were being incurred—Secretary Chase told the heads of the bureaus that "it would be necessary to spread the payments for equipping, organizing, and raising [the] army over a longer time."[31]

Major General David Hunter was left in command of the Department of the West for only weeks. The department was renamed the Department of Missouri, and Major General Henry Halleck took over command. Under Halleck's overall command, Brigadier General Samuel Curtis won the battle of Pea Ridge in March 1862, where 11,000 Union men faced 16,000 Southerners. This victory, in northwest Arkansas, kept Missouri clearly in Union hands, albeit with a lot of guerrilla and raider warfare throughout the war, until Major General Sterling Price and a Confederate army invaded Missouri in 1864.[32]

It is a testament to Fremont's stature and influence that he was given the command of the newly established Mountain Department, in general an area east of a north-south line through Knoxville, Tennessee, and to the west of the westward boundary of the Department of the Potomac, in March 1862. When then Secretary of War Edwin Stanton was urged to give Fremont another command he said he would give him a chance—his maxim was "the tools to him that can handle them." Sadly, Fremont could not handle the tools.[33]

Chapter 14

The New Secretary of War Goes to Russia

Simon Cameron, the new secretary of war, was a politician. And, like Buchanan and Floyd, was not geared to scrupulous regard for traditional army procedures, nor, as it turned out, was Lincoln. Predictably, the new quartermaster general, who had been through four years of that attitude with John Floyd, didn't intend to bend his standards. He made this clear. A message handed to Cameron in August 1861, read:

> The enclosed note from the President & yourself "recommends" the purchase of eastern mules at a price of $8 per head higher than is to be paid for many thousands now collecting in Kentucky.
>
> There are two objections to this purchase. One is the higher price which it will be difficult to explain....
>
> The other is that the [quartermaster general] has refused a great many mules offered at 118 to $120 on the ground that enough were already ordered to this army.
>
> These gentlemen unless I can tell them that I act by order of my superiors will suspect me of bad faith.
>
> If political considerations connected with the situation of Kentucky induce the President & yourself to direct this purchase it should be plainly ordered not left to my discretion.
>
> These are considerations for you not for me & I will cheerfully obey any orders on the subject.[1]

The responsibilities of the Quartermaster Department during the war were to

> provid[e] means for transportation by land and water for all the troops and for all the material of war. It furnishes the horses for artillery and cavalry, and the horses and mules of the wagon trains; provides and supplies tents, camp and garrison equipage, forage, lumber, and all materials for camps and for shelter of the troops. It builds barracks, hospitals, and store-houses; provides wagons and ambulances, harness,

except for cavalry and artillery horses; builds or charters ships and steamers, docks and wharves; constructs and repairs roads, railroads, and their bridges; clothes the Army, and is charged generally with the payment of all expenses attending military operations not assigned by law or regulation to some other department.[2]

Quartermasters shared responsibilities with the Ordnance Department, which procured and issued arms and ammunition, the Subsistence Department, which supplied provisions, and the Medical Department, which acquired medical and hospital stores, by transporting and distributing this property at "the camps, upon the march, and [at] the battle-field."[3]

When Meigs took office, much of the transportation function was in civilian hands as the result of actions by Cameron and the president who faced unprecedented transportation demands after Fort Sumter fell. Lincoln explained the situation in a message to the Senate and House dated May 26, 1862:

> [Shortly after Fort Sumter fell] all the roads and avenues to this city were obstructed, and the capital was put into the condition of a siege. The mails in every direction were stopped and the lines of telegraph cut off by the insurgents, and military and naval forces which had been called out by the government for the defense of Washington were prevented from reaching the city by organized and combined treasonable resistance in the State of Maryland.... It became necessary for me to choose whether, using only the existing means...I should let the government fall at once into ruin, or whether, availing myself of the broader powers conferred by the Constitution in cases of insurrection, I would make an effort to save it with all its blessing for the present age and for posterity.[4]

Lincoln and Cameron acted to save the government.

Regular channels to meet the under siege problem of May 1861 were not adequate. As stated by Lincoln, "[S]everal departments of the government...contained so large a number of disloyal persons that it would have been impossible to provide safely through official agents only for the performance of the duties" which were "confided to citizens favorably known for their ability, loyalty, and patriotism."[5]

Cameron asked John Tucker, a successful Pennsylvania businessman, to come to Washington to help, and Tucker was made general agent of transportation for the War Department on May 8, 1861. The quartermaster general, and other bureau chiefs requiring transportation, were to turn to Tucker.[6] Earlier, on April 29, 1861, Cameron put Thomas A. Scott, a vice president of the Pennsylvania Central Railroad, in charge of "railroads and telegraphs" to overcome the blockage at Baltimore of Washington's communications with the North. Later, Cameron put Scott in charge of "all the Government railways and telegraphs or those appropriated for Government use," first as superintendent of railroad transportation, until August 1861 when he was appointed assistant secretary of war and carried on the same, and additional duties.[7]

The arrangement between Cameron and Tucker was a strange one. As of January 4, 1862, even though he had acted as "general agent of transportation for the War Department" since May 8, 1861, there was no agreement as to the compensation he was to receive, he resided in Philadelphia, and still held, and was performing, his jobs as president of three railroad companies.[8]

Tucker's job was not an easy one. The crisis caused by the Baltimore blockage, which started April 20, was still in effect when he first arrived, and there was an ongoing need for ships to transport troops and supplies to Annapolis so that a rail connection to Washington could be used for the remainder of the trip. The Baltimore problem was permanently solved when Union troops took control of the city on May 13, 1861, but the demand for ships was not lessened. Lincoln's proclamations of April 19 and 27 establishing a blockade of the Confederacy's 3,500-mile coastline set in motion naval purchases of ocean-going vessels, and expeditions designed to seize important points on the South's coastline needed them as well.[9]

Important seagoing operations were carried out during 1861 and the early months of 1862. In August 1861 ships from Fort Monroe, Virginia, located opposite Norfolk and which was held throughout the war by the North, took troops to the Hatteras Inlet in North Carolina which subdued the forts there. From August into November 1861 plans were made and acted on to capture Port Royal and Hilton Head Island in South Carolina.[10] During October through December 1861 ships were gathered for an expedition under Brigadier General Ambrose Burnside which took Roanoke Island, New Berne, North Carolina, and other points important for an effective blockade of the North Carolina coastline. This occurred in the months of February through April 1862.[11]

Meigs' attitude toward Tucker in January 1862, when he testified before the House Government Contracts Committee, was that he had "done his duty faithfully and honestly; but at the same time, [Meigs had] not the means of knowing certainly whether he ha[d] or not." The committee's report, released about July 1862, said that "the government...suffered more injustice in the purchase, and especially in the charter, of vessels than in reference to any other subject of public expenditures."[12]

The committee was harsh in its remarks about Tucker. It was "unable to ascertain" what qualified him to be the "general transport agent of the War Department." The committee put a resolution before the House where "the practice of employing irresponsible parties, having no official connection with the Government, in the performance of public duties which may be properly performed by regular officers of the Government" was abhorred. The House agreed.[13]

Railroads were of utmost importance in the war. Meigs said a "railroad is an engine of war more powerful than a battery of artillery." Railroads "supplied [the] armies, and...enabled them to move and accomplish in weeks what without them would have required years, or would have been impossible."[14]

In putting Thomas Scott in charge of railroads Cameron selected a person well qualified for the job, but one who created a suspicion of a raid on the treasury. Scott was a political supporter of Cameron. His connection with the Pennsylvania Central, and the fact that Cameron had an ownership interest in the Northern Central Railroad, as did the Pennsylvania Central, and that these roads were employed to carry troops and materials through Pennsylvania on their way to Washington, caused the committee to make the polemical statement that employing Scott "was a grave *mistake*, if not an act of intentional fraud on the part of the late Secretary of War." Meigs saw it otherwise—he found Scott to be a "man of force and ability" who volunteered and whose "knowledge capacity & energy was of great value."[15]

The committee never charged Scott with acting immorally, but thought it unwise to subject a public officer to unnecessary temptation. The main complaint was that Scott, "exercising a power which in reality belonged by law to the quartermaster general, issued" an order to the quartermaster general regulating the compensation to be paid to railroads. This order dated July 12, 1861, set rates much higher than the committee thought appropriate. When Meigs first saw the order, he had the impression it set out bargain rates about 33 1/3 percent less than ordinary tariffs.[16]

In calling the tariff outrageous and indefensible, the committee said it fixed the price for the government to transport freights "at least 33 1/3 per cent [higher than the] prices paid by private parties for like transportation." Exacerbating the committee's outrage was the fact that Scott's railroad, the Pennsylvania Central, reported in February 1862 an increase in earnings of over 40 percent in relation to a like earlier period. The earnings of the Northern Central railroad, in which Cameron had an ownership interest, a brother-in-law as president, and a family member as vice president, more than doubled.[17]

Both Cameron and Scott denied that the July 12, 1861, order was designed to set anything but maximum rates above which quartermasters should not go. Meigs and the other quartermasters did not understand it that way—they thought it set the rates to be charged. To get the message in the July 12 order to all the quartermasters around the country, Meigs used the newspaper press. The misunderstanding was discovered sometime between October and December 1861 and quartermasters then advised to treat the specified rates as upper limits. The language of the order, particularly that saying "please observe the following as a general basis," was at best ambiguous. Probably the military mind set came into play; it is not common to use the word "please" in a military order.[18]

The House committee investigating government contracts uncovered enough fraud, corruption, inattention, and favoritism to make Cameron's continuance as secretary of war undesirable. He was replaced in January 1862 and appointed minister to Russia. Cameron also threatened the president's efforts to hold on to the border states by urging in his annual report for 1861 that slaves be used as soldiers. In the half year Meigs worked with Cameron he developed warm feelings toward him and made a point of calling on him and thanking him for his kindness and confidence. His assessment of Cameron was that he "mean[t] well but [was] weak and infirm of purpose."[19]

Chapter 15

Challenges in Supplying an Expanding Army

The Union army didn't do much fighting in 1861, but that didn't stop it from requiring uniforms, shelter, and the other necessary articles furnished by the Quartermaster Department. In addition to taking care of the men, quartermasters had to provide the horses, mules, and wagons that gave the army mobility. The magnitude of the job was proportional to an increase in numbers from 16,000 before the war to roughly five hundred thousand by 1862.[1] Not only did the quartermaster general have to figure out where to get these needed supplies, he had to worry about how to pay for them and be sure the money was spent wisely.

When Congress came into session on July 4, 1861, it rapidly turned its attention to the "hue and cry in the country about corruption." Disappointed contractors were telling stories of fraud. Contracting officers were reportedly making contracts for more than necessary so that they could get a kickback. The legislative answer was twofold. First, a committee was appointed in the House to look into contracts made without advertising, and into whether middlemen were profiting from government contracts. And second, a bill passed in the House and Senate put detailed requirements on those within the government making contracts.[2]

Meigs opposed the legislation, the thrust of which was to require contracting officers to put all contracts in writing—it was not required that all contracts be advertised, but that the contracts be reduced to writing whether advertised or not. Copies of contracts were to be filed with the Department of the Interior.[3]

Meigs' experience and acquaintance with Congress paid off. After the bill passed both the House and Senate, he wrote a letter to Senator Henry Wilson of Massachusetts with a preface that he knew "the responsibility attaching to any Government officer who ventures to argue against a bill whose object is stated as the prevention of frauds," nonetheless the consequences could be to yield to the Southern rebels:

[Such] regulations as this bill imposes starved the British army with cold and hunger, while ship loads of stores...lay till they perished in Balaklava bay.

...[O]rders are sent by telegraph. Contracts are thus made with persons a thousand miles away. If we are to trammel every purchase with new conditions of writing, of record, of affidavit, no human brain will be capable of conducting the business of the great supply departments of the Army.

The Quartermaster's department contains many officers who are, in this time of public extremity, taxed to the limit of their energies in providing the means of moving the Army—wagons, horses, mules, forage, tools, tents, and clothing, for the thousands who are actually suffering for want of it.

If, in addition to these duties, they are called upon to record in writing every verbal contract; to put it upon a certain piece of printed paper of a certain shape; to go before a magistrate and take in every case a certain oath; delay, irresolution, inefficiency, will take the place of promptness and energy; suffering, discontent, and defeat, will attend our armies.

All expeditions which should be secret will be made known to the public, and the life and strength of military operation will be gone.[4]

Meigs was persuasive, and the bill was tabled in the Senate by a vote of 26 to 9. Wilson was told: "Some confidence must be reposed in human agents. The officers of the Government endeavor to do their duty. If a dishonest man finds a place among them, no mere forms and certificates of record will prevent his stealing. The greater the fraud the more perfect the papers."[5]

Meigs had to be proud of the statements of confidence in him expressed during the debate on the proposed legislation. For example, Senator Ira Harris of New York said:

If there has been one appointment in the executive department of the Government which has met the emphatic approbation of the public, it is the appointment of General Meigs at the head of the Quartermaster's department; and he has in this communication [opposing the legislation] shown a fearlessness and fidelity which is admirable.[6]

Clothing the thousands of new recruits was an immediate problem. In August, after Bull Run, the governors were ordered to send regiments to Washington "whether provided with equipments or uniforms or not." The prewar army relied on a clothing depot at Philadelphia to make uniforms. Eight days after his appointment Meigs decided that Philadelphia, in addition to operating at full capacity, should buy and inspect material to be furnished to contract makers. This would, according to Meigs, "give employment to many large, well-organized establishments whose business had been cut off by war and whose workers were suffering." He also asked the U.S. Legation in Paris to order in France complete equipment for 10,000 men.[7]

With a best price objective, Meigs retained approval of large contracts in Washington, and, to keep competition at a high level, wanted to use many small contracts. Although he always had in mind the advantage of competition, the size of the demand in 1861 caused him shortly to change his mind as to using large contracts. And, facing up to reality, in July 1861, any contract that appeared reasonable was accepted, and "materials manufactured for the ordinary clothing of the people" were purchased. This resulted in some Union soldiers being dressed in gray, black, or brown uniforms.[8]

After Union troops fired upon their own in thickly wooded fields, orders were issued that only uniforms of light or dark blue color should be worn. Criticism of the quality of the material and the use of colors other than blue was met by Meigs' observation that the troops were clothed and the sight of "sentinels walking post about the capital of the United States in freezing weather in their drawers, without trousers or overcoats" addressed.[9]

To meet the clothing demand, additional clothing depots were established at New York, Boston, Cincinnati, Louisville, Indianapolis, St. Louis, Detroit, and Springfield, Illinois. Making uniforms required a lot of labor. Even though the sewing machine was invented in the 1840s by Elias Howe and improved upon by Isaac Merrit Singer, the army thought "hand sewn garments were...more durable." As many as 10,000 women worked at the Philadelphia depot. "Men's shirts, which took over fourteen hours to make by hand, could be done [by sewing machines] in little over an hour."[10]

The domestic supply for heavy woolen blankets routinely issued to soldiers was never adequate during the war. On October 1, 1861, the quartermaster general put out a call to the public for help:

> The troops in the field need Blankets. The supply in the country is exhausted....
>
> To relieve pressing necessities, contributions are invited from the surplus stores of families.

* * * * *

> To such as have Blankets which they can spare, but cannot afford to give, the full market value of suitable Blankets...will be paid.[11]

When a call for six hundred thousand more men was put out after the losses on the Peninsula campaign (May–July 1862), the War Department advised volunteers and draftees to bring their own blankets so as to "avoid much discomfort."[12] To help out, waterproof, or gum, blankets were issued. They had a slit in them so that they could be used as ponchos, and eyelet holes to permit their use as a one man tent.[13]

Civil War troops moved from time to time by rail and ship, but, in the main, armies walked. Putting shoes on the soldiers was expensive. In the first year of the war, about 5 million pairs of shoes were bought for the Union men of which about 3 million had been worn out. Each soldier was allowed four pairs of shoes a year and probably still needed an additional pair.[14]

The House Government Contracts Committee wanted the Quartermaster Department to save about 75 cents per pair by buying pegged shoes (those using wooden pegs to attach the uppers to the soles) instead of hand-sewn ones. The soldiers would not be any worse off, and the treasury would benefit. Meigs disagreed. He thought the hand-sewn shoes gave the soldier more comfort and lasted longer. There would be fewer blisters which disabled soldiers who then required special care. Meigs eventually came around to the point of buying some pegged shoes, and also, as the war progressed, bought machine-sewn shoes.[15]

For fiscal year 1862 (July 1861–June 1862) the Quartermaster Department was responsible for $176 million dollars—about one-half of all the money provided to the army for that year. About one-fourth of this amount (some $41 million) had been studied in the quartermaster general's office by November 1862—most of the money, of the amount studied, went to

Forage	$ 3 million
Cavalry and artillery horses	$ 6 million
Transportation	$ 15 million
Clothing, camp and garrison equipage	$ 13 million[16]

The cost of supplying an army headed for more than a half million was staggering by comparison to any prior federal expenditures. When Edwin M. Stanton took over from Cameron on January 15, 1862, Meigs told him the "department [was] heavily in debt for transportation and clothing, and [found] itself unable to pay promptly for the supplies, even of forage indispensable to maintain its position in face of the enemy." Not only was the department in debt, its appropriations were exhausted and had been much exceeded. Stanton did not flinch. Meigs was pressed to spend more.[17]

Congress was advised in November 1861 of a $29 million estimated deficiency in the appropriation supposed to last until July 1, 1862, whereas, as of January 28, 1862, "floating debt" of the department already exceeded that amount. Meigs was not apologetic about the inaccuracy of the earlier estimate: "We have no experience of the cost and contingencies of carrying on war on a great scale, and it is beyond any human foresight to estimate it with accuracy."[18]

Concerning the treasury not paying for supplies which were purchased with the understanding that cash would be paid, but it was not, Meigs told the deputy quartermaster general in New York:

> Many other injustices are the result of this war, and great as this is, it is one of the least; so long as there are found merchants, manufacturers, or capitalists who will take the risk of supplying this department with clothing or other indispensable stores for the defense of the country, we must continue to exert ourselves to obtain them.[19]

Meigs' solution to the uncertainty surrounding appropriation estimates was for Congress to place in the hands of the president $100 million to be used for unforeseen exigencies. A consequence of such a step would be to "give greater confidence and security to those who have heretofore and may hereafter give to the Government their manufactures, their goods, or their services in the firm confidence that the country will see them repaid."[20]

Getting the money appropriated was just the start. Secretary of the Treasury Salmon P. Chase had to raise it. Lincoln's message to Congress of December 3, 1861, was confident. He opined "that the expenditures made necessary by the rebellion [were] not beyond the resources of the loyal people." But, by January 10, 1862, Lincoln moaned to Meigs that "Chase has no money and he tells me he can raise no more."[21]

Chase found a way. He started paying the government's debts to both its soldiers and suppliers with "fiat" money; that is, paper money with no backing other than the requirement that the general public accept the money for transactions.[22] A combination of "fiat" money, increased taxes and import duties, and government bonds and notes which paid interest and were ultimately redeemable by the government was how the North financed the war—its national debt rose dramatically, starting with about $65 million before the war to

July 1, 1861	$ 91 million
July 1, 1862	$ 524 million
July 1, 1863	$ 1,120 million
July 1, 1864	$ 1,816 million
July 1, 1865	$ 2,678 million[23]

The "fiat" money had great benefits from the treasury's standpoint. Chase told Congress in December 1862 that "circulation of United States notes constitutes practically a loan from the people to their government without interest." Printing money has a one-time benefit of creating government wealth which never has to be paid back to anyone—a certain level of money must always be in circulation. "Fiat" money was only a boon so long as it was readily accepted as currency among the public. If too much was issued, it would have the fate of money issued during the Revolutionary War, it would "not be worth a Continental."[24]

Horses and mules were the fossil fuel engines of the Civil War. Instead of petroleum they were fed hay and grain, commonly referred to as forage. Keeping the armies supplied with the animals and required forage was probably the most challenging requirement of the Quartermaster Department. The easiest way to get the animals was to take them from the enemy; the same for forage.

In the early days of the war in Northern Virginia the taking of horses from Virginians was not allowed. Meigs wrote Stanton in April 1862 decrying the "leaving [of] disloyal people in possession of horses fit for military service" while the army marches on foot or is "supplied with horses to be drawn from the loyal people of loyal States" which are acquired by "promises to pay." Stanton agreed and authorized Major General Nathaniel P. Banks, then commanding in the Shenandoah Valley of Virginia, "to require a military contribution of not less that 1,500 horses" from the territory he occupied. Lincoln had no problem with this—in May 1862 he told Major General John Fremont, then in command of the Mountain Department (mostly West Virginia and eastern Tennessee), "to purchase...or take [400 horses] wherever or however [he could] get them." The procedure was to give receipts for horses seized.[25]

Until experience could be gained, and time was not forcing quick action, Meigs recognized shortcuts had to be taken. When Major General Robert Patterson, who was in charge of troops at Harpers Ferry prior to the battle of Bull Run, wanted horses and his quartermaster was thoroughly inspecting and rejecting horses, Meigs advised that a military movement could not be delayed so that only first-class horses were obtained—"a horse that will do a month's work, may in certain cases be worth his weight in silver."[26]

Next to chartering ships, in the first 12 months of the war the most fertile ground for foul use of the government was the need for horses and mules. In fiscal year 1862 (July 1, 1861–June 30, 1862) the United States acquired 109,789 horses and 83,620 mules—if only an average of $100 per animal was paid, the total would have been over $19 million. The typical cost was about $120. A lot of money but a necessity.[27]

Supposedly, Lincoln, on being told that the Confederates had captured a Union general and some mules, expressed more concern about the mules than the general. Lincoln explained that he could make another general in five minutes, but "those mules cost...two hundred dollars apiece."[28]

The amount of forage required during the last years of the war was about 2.5 million bushels of grain and 50,000 tons of hay per month. On average, each day a horse required 14 pounds of hay and 12 pounds of oats, corn, or barley—a mule needed the same amount of hay, but only nine pounds of grain. Since a soldier could get by on three pounds of food a day, the logistics of keeping animals fed was the tougher job. For a wagon pulled by four horses, each day of travel required 104 pounds of forage. Since such a wagon, on good roads, could be loaded with 2,800 pounds, if the trip did not get to a new source of forage sooner than 10 days, close to half the load would be the forage for the horses.[29]

Lincoln warned against having "a thousand wagons doing nothing but hauling forage to feed the animals that draw them."[30]

There was a need for many quartermasters—Meigs lacked "officers of experience and knowledge."[31] Charles A. Dana, who made a number of inspection trips for Stanton, before and after being made an assistant secretary of war, reported on conditions in Cairo, Illinois, in 1861 and early 1862:

> The quartermaster's department at Cairo had been organized hastily, and the demands upon it had increased rapidly. Much of the business had been done by green volunteer officers who did not understand the technical duties of making out military requisitions and returns. The result was that the accounts were in great confusion, and hysterical newspapers were charging the department with fraud and corruption.[32]

Considering that Dana found that "illiterateness [was] a general characteristic of [General Ulysses S.] Grant's staff, and in fact of Grant's generals & regimental officers of all ranks," it wasn't that easy to find good quartermasters. Without much success, both in his 1861 and 1862 annual reports, Meigs tried to get assistance from Congress in holding on to experienced quartermasters. Many valuable quartermaster officers had been drawn into other branches by "promo[tions] to higher rank, and [he] hope[d], though [he] doubt[ed] it, to higher usefulness in the organization of the vast force of regulars and volunteers called into the service." For those officers that remained he wanted "such increase of rank and emolument as w[ould] place them more nearly on a level with their late companions who have accepted promotion and been transferred to positions of higher rank, but whose duties are less laborious and difficult." Stanton's answer was that "no duty of a soldier is unimportant or less than honorable," implying that the quartermaster officers should not place so much importance on rank.[33]

The lack of a rank structure, where most of the field quartermasters were captains, resulted, in Meigs' words, to "no more organization than you have in a flock of sheep or goats." He wanted a hierarchical organization headed by a major general followed by two brigadier generals, four colonels, eight lieutenant colonels, twenty-four majors, and forty-eight captains. This would create a chain of responsibility. It wasn't until 1864 that he was able to get Congress to go along with some of his ideas. Prior to 1864 and after, important quartermasters were given higher rank by assigning them to the staff of commanding generals as aides-de-camp, and promotions were also given by commissions in the volunteers and brevets for distinguished service.[34]

The 1864 law reorganized the headquarters office. Meigs remained a brigadier general but was authorized nine colonels to head nine divisions; for example, the first division was responsible for providing animals for the armies, the second handled clothing and equipage, etc. Meigs also sought increases in civilian clerks and employees for the quartermaster general's office. After starting with 13 in June 1861, in 1863 the number increased to 213, and by 1865 was at 591. For the first time, the department employed women as copyists.[35]

Chapter 16

River Campaigns—Tennessee Invaded

Writing in about 1884 John Fremont felt that events had vindicated actions he took in Missouri between July and November 1861. One action listed was the preparation of gunboats, which work was countermanded as a "useless extravagance." Without entering into any debate as to whether Fremont's actions concerning gunboats were prudent, there is no question but what gunboats played a major role in the battles along the western rivers in 1862.[1]

Brigadier General Lewis Wallace, who fought under Brigadier General Ulysses S. Grant's command in the battle for Fort Donelson, succinctly states the importance of the Tennessee River for Union advances in the West:

> It is of little moment now who first enunciated the idea of attacking the rebellion by way of the Tennessee River; most likely the conception was simultaneous with many minds. The trend of the river; its navigability for large steamers; its offer of a highway to the rear of the Confederate hosts in Kentucky and the State of Tennessee; its silent suggestion of a secure passage into the heart of the belligerent land...; its many advantages as a line of supply and of general communication, must have been discerned by every military student who, in the summer of 1861, gave himself to the most cursory examination of the map.[2]

The Confederates anticipating Union efforts to use the Tennessee and Cumberland Rivers, built two forts, Henry and Donelson, near the rivers' points of entry into the Ohio River. Gunboats built in the area were important instruments used by Grant to capture both of these forts in February 1862.[3]

Major General George B. McClellan suggested a need for gunboats in May 1861. He thought they would help troops occupying Cairo, Illinois, which is at the mouth of the Ohio River where it empties into the Mississippi. McClellan was not alone in thinking there was a need for gunboats. Attorney General Edward Bates, a Missourian, arranged for his friend James Eads of St. Louis to come to Washington to meet with naval officials about how the Mississippi could be blockaded at Cairo. Eads suggested use of "floating batteries," or gunboats, in conjunction with shore batteries; he also envisioned their use against Confederate shore positions.[4]

When Eads' ideas were presented in writing to the navy, Secretary of the Navy Gideon Welles bucked them to the army, saying "the subject more properly" belongs there. However, the navy was willing to supply crews and armaments as needed, and Welles directed Commander John Rodgers, U.S. Navy, to report to McClellan, who was in command of the Department of the Ohio. Since the navy was only going to supply men and armament, the Quartermaster Department of the army was to supply the boats themselves.[5]

The initial thinking was that three boats would be needed to block the South from using the Mississippi and Ohio Rivers above Cairo. Rodgers, Meigs' brother-in-law, found three sidewheelers (*Conestoga, Lexington,* and *A.O. Tyler*) which he thought could be converted, but not into ironclads, and was given the go ahead by Meigs. Rodgers' task was enlarged by work going forward in Washington in the War and Navy Departments to design additional boats to be built specifically with the intent of supporting the western armies. The initial design was turned over to Rodgers in June, modified, and by mid-July Meigs approved specifications, and there was advertising for bids to build the new gunboats. These were to be ironclads. Eads came in with the low bid and received a contract for seven gunboats to be delivered to Cairo by October 10, 1861.[6]

Meigs' family link with the gunboats was severed in September 1861. Commander Rodgers was relieved, at Fremont's request, by Captain Andrew Hull Foote formerly of the New York Navy Yard. Louisa Meigs thought her brother acted "with grave dignity" in not making a row and that the government was fortunate in assigning Foote, "a splendid officer and more than that a high toned gentleman & a sincere Christian." Foote had a lot to supervise. The three redesigned woodclad boats were operational, and seven ironclads were being built by Eads. In addition, Fremont, who arrived in St. Louis in late July 1861, as Commander Rodgers' superior, ordered the conversion of two river steamers (*submarine No. 7* renamed the *Benton,* and the *New Era*) into ironclads and for the construction of 38 mortar boats. In Fremont style, some of this was done without War Department authorization.[7]

The mortar boats were "rafts or blocks of solid timber of sufficient burden to carry...upon the deck of each one thirteen-inch sea-coast mortar"—vessels, without motive power, to be used to attack shoreline fortifications.[8]

Meigs was caught between the Washington establishment and Fremont on how appropriated funds should be spent. Congress appropriated

$1 million for "gunboats on the western rivers" in July 1861. Meigs was directed to spend these funds to construct seven gunboats designed by the navy. To meet pressing demands of Fremont, Meigs used some of this money to build Fremont's fleet of mortar boats and to convert two river steamboats into gunboats. The diversion of funds resulted in Eads being unable to meet the October 1861 contract delivery date, and, in fact, Eads' gunboats, which were not finished until January 1862, were not fully paid for at the time they went into battle at Forts Henry and Donelson. After Fremont was relieved, Meigs explained the situation, and Congress appropriated another million dollars in December 1861 for "gunboats on the Western Rivers."[9]

The misdirection of the appropriated funds had nothing to do with Meigs' evaluation of the need for the gunboats. He thought the gunboats so important that he "begged [Montgomery Blair on September 3, 1861] to get [Fremont] to order 15-inch guns from Pittsburg for [them.] [Meigs said] that the boats can empty any battery the enemy can make with such guns. [Meigs] advise[d] that [Fremont] contract for them directly...telling the contractor [Fremont would] direct [his] ordnance officer to pay for them." Meigs probably gave this advice before he learned that Fremont was going around the Quartermaster Department at will.[10]

By mid-January 1862 Foote accepted nine ironclads for the army: seven new ironclad gunboats (*St. Louis, Carondelet, Louisville, Pittsburg, Mound City, Cincinnati,* and *Cairo*), and two steamers converted to ironclads (*Essex* and *Benton*). The mortar boats were not completed. After Fremont was relieved in November 1861, and Halleck took over, construction of the mortar boats stopped. Construction started again, in January 1862, when Lincoln intervened; they were finished early in March.[11]

The river navy was put to use. Grant and Foote were ordered at the end of January to proceed against Henry, which fell to the gunboats' shelling alone, and then Grant proceeded to march on Donelson. The gunboats took quite a battering at Donelson but still helped the ground forces to take the fort. These victories opened the Tennessee all the way to Florence, Alabama, the end of navigation from the west because of Muscle Shoals, and the Cumberland River to Nashville, Tennessee. General Albert Sydney Johnston, the Confederate commander, was forced to retreat, first from Bowling Green, Kentucky, and then from Nashville because of the threat to the rear of his army.[12]

Meigs' old adversary, John B. Floyd, was one of the generals at Donelson. After Donelson fell, Jefferson Davis removed him from command for "failing to ask for reinforcements, for not evacuating sooner, and for abandoning command to [Brigadier General Simon] Buckner and escaping with his own troops." Floyd never played a major role after that, even though the Virginia assembly made him a major general, and died in ill health in August 1863.[13]

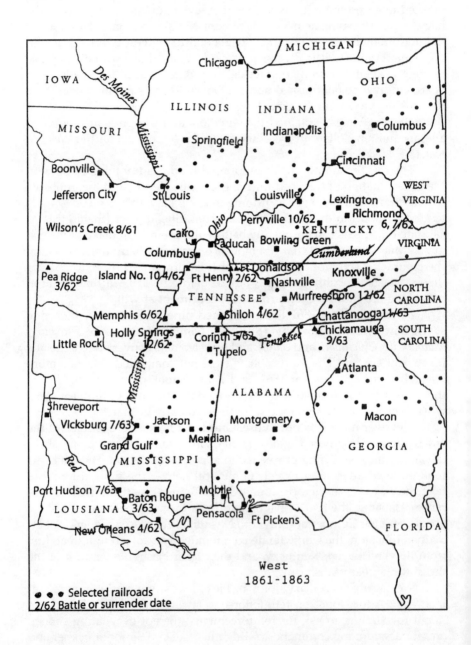

IOWA

Des Moines

MICHIGAN

Chicago

ILLINOIS

INDIANA

OHIO

MISSOURI

Springfield

Indianapolis

Columbus

Mississippi

Cincinnati

Boonville

WEST
VIRGINIA

Jefferson City

St Louis

Louisville

Lexington

Richmond
6, 7/62

Wilson's Creek 8/61

Cairo

Ohio

Perryville 10/62

KENTUCKY

Columbus

Paducah

Bowling Green

Cumberland

VIRGINIA

Pea Ridge
3/62

Island No. 10 4/62

Ft Henry 2/62

Ft Donaldson

Nashville

Knoxville

NORTH
CAROLINA

TENNESSEE

Murfreesboro 12/62

Memphis 6/62

Shiloh 4/62

Chattanooga 11/63

Tennessee

Little Rock

Holly Springs
12/62

Corinth 5/62

Chickamauga
9/63

SOUTH
CAROLINA

Tupelo

Atlanta

Shreveport

ALABAMA

Vicksburg 7/63

Jackson

Montgomery

Macon

Grand Gulf

Meridian

GEORGIA

Red

MISSISSIPPI

Port Hudson 7/63

Mobile

LOUSIANA

Baton Rouge
3/63

Pensacola

Ft Pickens

FLORIDA

New Orleans 4/62

West
1861–1863

● ● ● Selected railroads
2/62 Battle or surrender date

Before the Army of the Potomac engaged the Confederate armies in Virginia in the summer of 1862, and after Albert Sydney Johnston retreated in the West, Meigs was pleased with what had happened and optimistic about the future. He reviewed the Union's accomplishments: control of over 156,000 square miles of which, at the start, the Confederates "had at least an equal hold with [the North] & entire possession of a great part"— Maryland, western Virginia, Kentucky, half of Tennessee, Missouri, and part of North Carolina, an area inhabited by three million people. The war was being prosecuted on a grand scale. A front of attack of one thousand miles; an army in the field of 670,000. Although optimistic, he refused to speculate, even after the U.S. flag was raised in New Orleans on April 29, 1862, whether the war would be over in 1862 or 1863—saying he was no prophet.[14]

In early 1862 the economic noose around the South was tightening. Much of the coastal area was controlled by the North. Hatteras Inlet (North Carolina), Port Royal Entrance (South Carolina), and Ship Island (Mississippi) were taken in 1861, and Fort Pulaski, opposite Savannah, Georgia, in April 1862; other key points on the Gulf coast were seized in early 1862 (Apalachicola, Florida, and Pass Christian, Mississippi), and New Orleans in April 1862.[15]

Grant proceeded south down the Tennessee River and was engaged by Johnston at the battle of Shiloh on April 6 and 7, 1862. The Shiloh battle was close to a draw, but the Union advance to that point, and a short time later to Corinth, Mississippi, together with aggressive use of gunboats on the Mississippi, led successively to the abandonment of former Confederate strongholds at Columbus, Kentucky (March 2), Island No. 10 near New Madrid, Missouri (April 7), Fort Pillow some 40 miles above Memphis (June 3), and finally Memphis on June 6. Even though Captain David Farragut's fleet took New Orleans in April 1862, and attacked up the Mississippi River, neither Farragut nor Grant were able to gain control of the Confederate batteries overlooking the river at Vicksburg, Mississippi. Consequently, throughout 1862, the Confederacy had access to its states lying west of the Mississippi River.[16]

Notwithstanding the gunboat contributions to land advances, Meigs thought they should be handled by the navy. This was accomplished on July 16, 1862, when the president approved a bill to transfer the river navy to the Navy Department. Command went to acting Rear Admiral David Dixon Porter, Farragut's foster brother, and Meigs' collaborator in holding Fort Pickens in 1861.[17]

Staying under the War Department was the "ram fleet." Ramming with oar-driven galleys was an ancient wartime tactic for ships. This tactic came to prominence when, on March 8, 1862, the Confederate ironclad, the *Merrimack* (renamed the *Virginia*) sank the Union wooden sloop-of-war the *Cumberland* by ramming at Hampton Roads, Virginia,

together with inflicting heavy damage on other wooden ships in the blockading Union fleet. Washington was fearful that the *Virginia* would run
amuck. But, fortunately for the North, it fought a standoff battle with the
Union ironclad, the *Monitor*, the next day.[18]

Following the *Monitor-Merrimack* battle, Meigs suggested to Stanton
that a longtime advocate of rams, Charles Ellet, be asked to construct vessels on the western rivers. Ellet, commissioned a colonel, was authorized
by Halleck to purchase vessels for conversion to rams, payments to be
made by the Quartermaster Department. Meigs was urged to hurry the
completion of the ram conversions after the South, on May 10, used steamers, converted to rams, to sink two ironclads which were part of the ships
attacking Confederate Fort Pillow.[19]

An Ellet belief that gunfire was not a sound way for one ship to fight
another, because of the inaccuracy of gunfire when one moving vessel
was shooting at another moving vessel, led him to put no guns on the
steamers converted to rams. Ellet's group of rams were significantly involved in the battle of Memphis, on June 6, at which the Federal fleet
defeated that of the Confederates. Ellet was mortally wounded by a pistol
ball during the Memphis battle. Command of the ram fleet went to his
brother, Alfred.[20]

Chapter 17
The Peninsula Campaign

After the July battle of Bull Run, 1861 was essentially a year of quiet war. The South was content to wait and see, and the North, particularly in the East, confined the war to its parade fields and combined navy-army expeditions to effectuate the blockade. The North excelled in military pomp and ceremony.

When called upon to take command of the Army of the Potomac after Bull Run, Major General George B. McClellan was 34 years old. A West Point graduate and veteran of the Mexican War, who left the army in 1857 with the rank of captain, before the war he was a railroad president living in Cincinnati, Ohio. His military exploits, albeit minor in scope in what is now West Virginia as head of the Department of the Ohio with the rank of major general, led to his being called the Young Napoleon.[1]

With McClellan at the head of the Army of the Potomac, Meigs thought that between them they were running the government—McClellan in the field and Meigs in the cabinet. Whatever Meigs asked of the cabinet he received. At this time Meigs was going to his office "booted & spurred ready to take horse & gallop over the river in case an engagement should break out in the course of the morning." To him, the Confederates had a great opportunity to take Washington after Bull Run. So great that he moved his family out of Washington to Germantown, Maryland, about 25 miles from Washington.[2]

McClellan started out with much favor, putting discipline and élan back into the Army of the Potomac. By December the Northern forces had, with incremental steps, advanced sufficiently for the "rebels [to be] out of sight & sound of [Washington]."[3]

He was the object of much adulation in November 1861, when 75-year-old General in Chief Winfield Scott, a hero of the War of 1812 (brevetted a major general at age 29) and the Mexican War, the head of the army since 1841, the first lieutenant general of the army since George Washington, and a presidential candidate of the Whig party in 1852, resigned as general in chief. McClellan, who was instrumental in bringing about the resignation by backbiting and disrespectful conduct, took his place—a change Meigs thought overdue. But it wasn't long before a chorus of complaints was heard about his failure to use the fine army he had reorganized. Military parades were common fare around Washington after McClellan took charge, but little fighting.[4]

Fundamental to McClellan's refusal to march against the Confederates, positioned around Manassas, was his belief that they were "not less than 150,000 strong, well drilled and equipped, ably commanded, and strongly intrenched" with four hundred guns. In December 1861 Meigs told Congress he could not "disbelieve" that the Rebels had one hundred thousand men facing McClellan. In writing to his father on the subject, Meigs explained how difficult it is to estimate large numbers of men. In fact there were only about 63,000 facing the Army of the Potomac in northern Virginia, about 45,000 of whom were at Manassas.[5]

When questioned by the Joint Committee on the Conduct of the War in December 1861, and asked when the Army of the Potomac would be taking to the field, Meigs didn't know McClellan's intentions. His philosophy was to "avoid[] asking anybody, who was responsible, what his intentions were" thinking that if such a person "chose to tell [him], [he] was willing to hear them." He assumed McClellan would "move whenever, in his opinion, his army is ready."[6]

Meigs did not envy McClellan. He told his father that the "stake [was] so great [in a battle in front of Washington] that without almost certainty of success a commander would not be justified in fighting a battle." When it appeared the administration might want to put him in command of an army he did not encourage them—"too much rested upon success & [he] might fail." This was a heady time for Meigs—one press story said: "Quartermaster General Meigs is admirably managing the thieves and plunder mongers who infest Washington.... The great thief Floyd removed him because he could not mold him to suit his plundering propensities but he has nothing to fear from this Administration."[7]

As 1861 came to an end, Meigs seemed to have some doubts as to McClellan's adequacy for his job as general in chief. He told the committee on the Conduct of the War:

> I take it for granted that General McClellan is equal to his position; I hope that he is. A great commander does not arise more than once in a century, and we have yet to prove whether General McClellan, or anybody in this country, has the elements of a great commander.[8]

Meigs had his eye on the cost of warfare. He told the committee the "expenses of the armies are very exhausting on both sides. It is terrible to us; it must be worse to them. Our paper is at par; theirs is at forty per cent discount, and, therefore, their expenses must be greatly increased."[9]

Reflecting some 20 years after the war about this period he summed up what was happening from his point of view: "McClellan seemed to have no sufficient appreciation of the fact that an American soldier costs his country $1,000 a year, whether merely drilling, or engaged with the enemy. He seemed satisfied, with two hundred thousand men in his army, to rest quiet and drill and review them; to ride the picket line occasionally."[10]

Lincoln was exasperated. On January 10, 1862, he entered the quartermaster general's new office in the Winder Building, near the president's house, and asked Meigs:

> General what shall I do? The people are impatient; Chase has no money and he tells me he can raise no more; the General of the Army has typhoid fever. The bottom is out of the tub. What shall I do?[11]

Meigs' advice was that if McClellan had typhoid fever he might be laid up for six weeks, and Lincoln had better call together those who might have to lead if the enemy should attack. Lincoln did this but, when a group gathered on January 12, he dismissed those in attendance saying McClellan was better and would be able to attend a meeting the next day.[12]

At the meeting held on January 13, McClellan did not speak up as to his plans. Meigs, who attended both meetings, urged McClellan to say something to the president. McClellan demurred saying he could not move against the Confederates at Manassas because they were too strong—had approximately 175,000 men, and if he were to tell the president his plans they would be in the *New York Herald* the next day. McClellan finally suggested that Major General Don Carlos Buell's troops advance in Kentucky. The impression left with Meigs was that "McClellan would prefer to send forward any other troops than those under his present command."[13]

The War Department was energized on January 20, 1862, when Edwin Stanton took over as secretary of war. Right or wrong, Stanton was not one to live with a status quo—physically he was "short thick set," at 47 years energetic, honest, excitable, brusque, irascible, self-confident, and decisive with a suspicious temperament.[14]

Lincoln's friends, aware that Stanton, as a lead attorney in litigation in 1859, had been rude and insulting to Lincoln, an associate counsel, were surprised at the appointment. To those advising against one with Stanton's "impulsiveness," Lincoln said: "Well, we may have to treat him as they are sometimes obliged to treat a Methodist minister I know of out West. He gets wrought up to so high a pitch of excitement in his prayers and exhortations that they are obliged to put bricks in his pockets to keep him down. We may be obliged to treat Stanton the same way, but I guess we will let him jump awhile first."[15]

As seen by an outsider, Elizabeth Blair Lee (who lived across the street from the White House in one of the Blair-Lee houses), Stanton was "ever so prostrate that one can scarce approach old Abe" without giving him a shove. However, Stanton was anything but prostrate with others.[16]

Lincoln had had enough. It was time to end McClellan's "dashing through the streets like a small earthquake-in-new uniform" with a "glittering staff."[17] With Stanton's full agreement, on January 27 Lincoln issued General War Order No. 1 calling for a general movement of land and naval forces on February 22 (Washington's Birthday). On January 31, in the Special War Order No. 1, Lincoln ordered that the Army of the Potomac "be formed into an expedition for the immediate object of seizing and occupying a point upon the railroad southwestward of what is known as Manassas Junction" with the expedition to move before or on February 22. At least in part, these orders were instigated by Lincoln's fear that a failure to act could result in a failure of the government because of its enormous debt and the possibility of foreign intervention.[18]

McClellan was forced to come forth with his plan. A move against the Confederate army at Manassas, even if successful, he thought would merely cause the enemy to move south and prepare for another battle at another location. He wanted to end the war by capturing Richmond in short order. The Army of the Potomac should go by ship down either the Potomac (at the time he was writing Confederate batteries had effectively blocked transportation on the Potomac to and from Washington) or from Annapolis, Maryland (which borders the Chesapeake Bay) to land at Urbana, Virginia, located on the Rappahannock River. From Urbana it was but a one-day march to West Point, Virginia, which fronted the York River. From West Point, Richmond could be reached by a two-day march.[19]

Lincoln had to decide between the advice of those wanting a direct assault (McDowell and Meigs among others) and those supporting McClellan's plan.[20]

On February 27, John Tucker, who Stanton had made an assistant secretary of war, was directed "to procure at once the necessary steamers and sailing craft" to move the Army of the Potomac. He informed Meigs of the decision, and Meigs detailed Captain Henry C. Hodges to help Tucker in the chartering and Colonel Rufus Ingalls to see to the embarkation of the troops. By March 13 Meigs was able to report the transports were ready.[21]

Even though Lincoln acquiesced in McClellan's plan, he and Stanton were not content to stand by idly. Several significant events occurred which bothered McClellan. Lincoln, throughout the war, worried about the capital being seized, and particularly so in March 1862. Notwithstanding, he wanted the Army of the Potomac to do something. After agreeing to McClellan's plan, President Lincoln issued General War Order No. 3, on March 8, which addressed each of these concerns.

First: any change in the base of operations would include leaving "in and about Washington such a force as, in the opinion of the General-in-Chief and the commanders of army corps, [would] leave [Washington] entirely secure"; second: no more than 50,000 troops would be moved from in front of Washington until the enemy's batteries blocking use of the Potomac were removed; and third: if a move was made down the Chesapeake Bay it should commence no later than March 18.[22]

The day of the president's order, the Confederate ironclad, the C.S.S. *Virginia*, referred to here by her former name, the *Merrimack*, threw Washington into a panic. By attacking and sinking wooden men-of-war in Hampton Roads at Norfolk, Virginia, she created the specter of a neutralization of the Federal navy, which was necessary for the Peninsula campaign and the blockade. Stanton feared that the *Merrimack* would come up the Potomac and shell Washington. Meigs was concerned that she could sink the transports assembled at Annapolis to take the Army of the Potomac south.[23]

Reactions to the *Merrimack's* one-day success were quick. With the president's approval, and in the presence of Stanton, McClellan, Meigs, and the commandant of the Washington Navy Yard, John Dahlgren, decided at 2 P.M. on March 9 to block the Potomac River by sinking some filled "canal-boats and other craft" in the channel. By 5:30 P.M. Meigs arranged for 16 canal-boats, loaded with stones, to be towed with an order that they "be sunk if necessary."[24]

Writing from the Executive Mansion, Meigs told Ingalls, the quartermaster at Annapolis, that if the *Merrimack* should "attempt anything at Annapolis,...the best defense would be an attack by a number of swift steamers, full of men, who should board her by a sudden rush, fire down through her hatches or grated deck, and throw cartridges, grenades, or shells down her smoke-pipes; sacrifice the steamers in order to take the *Merrimac[k]*." Thrown in as encouragement was the statement that "Promotion, ample reward, awaits whoever takes or destroys her."[25]

The panic subsided when word reached Washington the night of March 9 and the next day that a Federal ironclad, the U.S.S. *Monitor*, held its own against the *Merrimack* in a battle on March 9. Secretary of the Navy Gideon Welles had long known the *Merrimack* was being modified as an ironclad, and a contract was let for the *Monitor* in October 1861. Fortuitously, the *Monitor* was under tow on her way to Hampton Roads from New York City on March 8.[26]

Uncertainty as to whether the *Merrimack* would continue to be a threat kept Meigs and Dahlgren busy planning on blocking the Potomac—they would have 12 hours' notice from Fort Monroe if the *Merrimack* were to try to go up the Chesapeake Bay to the Potomac. Meigs was a prudent man—he did not propose to trust the safety of Washington "to the strength of a single screw-bolt in the *Monitor's* new machinery." The novelty of the *Monitor*, essentially a "revolving gun-tower," which the Confederates described as a "Yankee cheese-box on a raft," dictated caution. The *Monitor*, manned by 12 officers and a crew of 45, was only 172 feet long and 41 $^1/_2$ feet wide with little depth between its deck and the water surface.[27]

Consistent with his concern about Washington's safety, and the requirement that a military consensus guarantee this, on March 8 Lincoln had also issued General War Order No. 2, organizing the Army of the Potomac into corps and the leader of each corps was named. McClellan was not alerted that the order would be issued, and did not approve of it. This was indeed a peculiar way to operate—to reorganize the commanding general's army without warning to the extent of even deciding who would lead the various elements.[28]

McClellan favored the corps arrangement, but only after senior officers had shown on the field of battle the capability of handling such high commands. During this period, McClellan said that "there were very few men who could command and manoeuvre 100,000 men but that he believed he could do this."[29]

McClellan was able to talk Stanton into holding off on forming the corps so that he could march on Manassas to confirm information received about March 9 that the Rebels had abandoned their line in northern Virginia and along the upper and lower Potomac. He found that General Joseph Johnston had retreated behind the Rappahannock and Rapidan Rivers some 30 miles south of his old line, and closer to Richmond. Johnston made this move so his army could be better positioned to counter whatever route the Army of the Potomac took toward Richmond.[30]

Johnston's retreat from Manassas to Fredericksburg caused McClellan to alter his plans to a backup he had proposed to Lincoln, namely, to land the troops at Fortress Monroe opposite Norfolk, which was in Union hands, and march up the Peninsula between the James and York Rivers to Richmond, a distance of some 75 miles. Johnston's ability to threaten any landings at Urbana, which was on the Rappahannock, necessitated the change.[31]

Before embarking on a movement which would take his army to Fort Monroe by ships, McClellan had to decide if the *Merrimack* was a threat. On March 13 Assistant Secretary of the Navy Gustavius V. Fox told him the "*Monitor* is more than a match for the *Merrimac[k]*, but she might be disabled in the next encounter." However, the navy assured him he would be able to use the York River without any concern about the *Merrimack*. To keep the *Merrimack* confined to Hampton Roads and the James River, the navy had seven steamers ready to act as rams near Fort Monroe if the *Merrimack* tried to enter Chesapeake Bay.[32]

Another surprise for McClellan was in the General War Order No. 3 of March 11, 1862. McClellan was relieved of any duties other than to be in command of the Department of the Potomac. New departments were established—the Department of the Mississippi swept in the departments of Henry Halleck (Missouri), David Hunter (Kansas), and Don Carlos Buell (Ohio) into one command, that of Halleck; and the Mountain Department, comprising the area between the Department of the Potomac and the Department of the Mississippi, was placed under General Fremont. The department heads were to report directly to Secretary of War Stanton.[33]

More was to come. After the troops started embarking at Alexandria (March 17), the Potomac River becoming available when Johnston retreated, the army was reduced by 20,000 men which McClellan had counted on (from 155,000 to 135,000). McClellan objected vehemently. Meigs had no sympathy: McClellan "disobeyed the express command of the President, founded on the opinions of the officers commanding [McClellan's] corps" in not leaving for the protection of Washington the number of troops considered necessary for its defense.[34]

The situation became worse from McClellan's standpoint. On March 23 Major General Thomas J. ("Stonewall") Jackson, with 3,500 men, attacked a superior Union force (nine thousand) at Kernstown, Virginia, a few miles south of Winchester. Although the Union won tactically (718 casualties to 590), it lost strategically. Lincoln decided to hold back more men from joining McClellan on the Peninsula.[35]

The forces in northern Virginia were reorganized. Two additional departments were established. The I Corps of the Army of the Potomac under Major General Irvin McDowell, which had been scheduled to go to Monroe, was taken away from McClellan and put in a new Department of the Rappahannock, which included Washington, commanded by McDowell. A new Department of the Shenandoah was placed under the command of Major General Nathaniel Banks. The I Corps had about 43,000 troops, and this brought McClellan's forces down to around 92,000.[36]

Meigs was concerned about the independent commands not having an overall military commander to coordinate actions of the various armies. Stanton, to whom all military commands were reporting, tried to get military guidance from a war board made up of the heads of various army bureaus, including Meigs. The board only functioned formally for a few months, but during these months Meigs was brought into discussions on operational matters. He and other members of the war board either reported on, or were consulted by the president, on the need to keep forces back to protect the capital.[37]

Salt was added to McClellan's wounds when Stanton closed the recruiting stations on April 3. The order struck Meigs like a thunderclap, but he thought it useless to speak—the "idea had got into official brains that [the North] had plenty of men too many men." Stanton's naivete of the real world of armies and their attrition from sickness, desertions, death, and wounds had to be unsettling. In May, McClellan was losing three hundred men a day—the sick, wounded, or those just worn out. "The swamp & mud & rains of the Chickahominy [were] as fatal as the balls of buckshot of the rebels."[38]

By McClellan's calculations he actually had about 85,000 when he started moving up the Peninsula, and only 67,000 of those could be committed to fight. Once McClellan was established on the Peninsula, he moved at a snail's pace. On April 29 Meigs expressed regret that the army had gone there. He never favored splitting the army as McClellan did. A few days later he worried that Jefferson Davis may be gathering "his hosts...in behind Fredericksburg to make [a] dash at the...lines before Washington."[39]

A letter to John Forsyth Meigs, Montgomery's brother, before McClellan made any significant movement up the Peninsula set out the quartermaster general's thinking. A march from Aquia Creek, about 10 miles northeast of Fredericksburg, to Richmond was one day shorter than from Fort Monroe, would have been over high, rolling, dry country, compared to swampy land found on the Peninsula, and supported by a railroad. Any fortifications between Aquia Creek and Richmond could be bypassed, whereas the advance up the Peninsula had to overcome a narrow point six miles wide which could be easily fortified by the Rebels and only carried by an assault with great loss. Furthermore, it took a month to transport the army to Monroe at a cost of millions. Why did McClellan go there? He offered no explanation but said "[l]et him answer by success."[40]

Meigs, in the 1880s, summed up McClellan's cautious movements by quoting French Marshall Marmont's observation of most generals: "They prepare for battle with intelligence and skill; but then hesitation commences." "A battle is such a chance medley, success depends on so many chances, that the General doubts and hesitates till the favorable moment is lost before he makes up his mind to give the word."[41]

McClellan's method of battle at the first objective, Yorktown, was to put it under siege, and Yorktown was abandoned by the Rebels on May 3, after a siege of about one month. Sieges are not without cost. The post-Peninsula report of Brigadier General John G. Barnard, chief engineer of the Army of the Potomac, who had many criticisms of McClellan's generalship, said:

> Our troops toiled a month in the trenches or lay in the swamps of the Warwick [River]. We lost few men by the siege, but disease took a fearful hold of the army, and toil and hardship, unredeemed by the excitement of combat, impaired the *morale*. We did not carry with us from Yorktown so good an army as we took there.[42]

McClellan proceeded up the Peninsula, and the retreating Confederates abandoned Williamsburg on May 5.[43]

The advance toward Richmond was not easy for the army's chief quartermaster, Brigadier General Stewart Van Vliet. Road conditions did not make it feasible to keep the army supplied overland. Consequently, adequate wharves were needed at points on the York River—this was accomplished by "throwing...barges and canal-boats ashore at high water and bridging them over." Tons of food and supplies were required daily. "One hundred thousand men [ate] up 150 wagon loads of subsistence daily."[44]

By May 16 the advance proceeded so that a supply depot was established at the landing of the White House plantation, owned by a Lee and, at the time, occupied by Robert E. Lee's wife and a daughter. Large vessels could navigate the Pamunkey River, a tributary of the York River, to that point, and a railroad ran from White House to Richmond, factors making it an ideal depot.[45]

George Washington courted the widow Martha Custis at White House. Although the home of Washington's period had been replaced, McClellan treated the residence reverently. About a month later, McClellan chivalrously delivered Mrs. Lee and daughter through the lines to her husband. Mrs. Lee left a note on the door reading:

Northern soldiers who profess to reverence the name of Washington, forbear to desecrate the home of his early married life, the property of his wife, and now the home of her descendants.—A granddaughter of Mrs. Washington.

Later, when the White House supply depot was abandoned, the residence was, without authority, burned.[46]

McClellan's attitude toward the South was much different from that of Meigs. An officer, after paying two dollars to one of the Negroes at White House to shoot one of the pigs on the plantation, was placed under arrest and confined to his tent. Only after a written apology to McClellan was he released. McClellan had issued an order against marauding. Horses, cattle, and hogs were to be scrupulously respected.[47]

Contrast this with Meigs upbraiding a cavalry colonel for returning from a foray through northern Virginia without enough horses to mount his men. Meigs asked, "Are there no horses in the Shenandoah [Valley] why did you not help yourself at the expense of the rebels." He reasoned that "to expect [the quartermaster general] to buy horses from Minnesota paying for them [with] promises on paper & transport them to Strasburg [Virginia] which was full of horses was impressing the horses of loyal citizens in a loyal state in order to spare those of rebels in a disloyal state." Not many horses, cattle, and hogs on the Peninsula would have been spared if Meigs controlled the situation.[48]

On May 18 Stanton advised that McDowell would advance from Fredericksburg to join with McClellan's attack on Richmond. By that time Joseph Johnston had relocated his army so as to oppose McClellan's threat to Richmond.[49]

Writing in the 1880s, McClellan attributed his failure to take Richmond to the May 18 order. It caused him to split his army to be on each side of the Chickahominy River, so as to be in a position to join up with

McDowell. His preference was to move his line of attack so as to rely on the James River where he could easily get reinforcements by water. But, instead, he had to hold to the York River.[50]

Use of the James River became possible when the threat from the *Virginia* (formerly the *Merrimack*) was lifted. Lincoln, Stanton, and Chase were at Fortress Monroe early in May and, while there, mounted a successful attack on Norfolk. As a consequence, the Confederates destroyed the *Virginia* on May 11. When the mayor of Norfolk told a gathering of townspeople that the Confederate government had decided Norfolk was to be abandoned, and "they must yield to authority," the crowd "gave three cheers for President Davis...and...three groans for Lincoln."[51]

If blame is to be attached for the May 18 order, Meigs must take some responsibility. There was no general in chief at this time. The various army field commanders were reporting to a lawyer, Stanton, who reported to a lawyer, Lincoln. Of necessity they were relying on professional soldiers in Washington. The orders to McClellan and McDowell for the juncture were in Meigs' handwriting and were decided upon in consultation between the president, Joseph Totten (the 73-year-old chief of engineers), James Ripley (the 67-year-old chief of ordnance), Joseph Taylor (commissary general of subsistence who entered the army in 1813), and Meigs.[52]

Stonewall Jackson again took up the cudgel in the Shenandoah Valley and delayed implementation of the May 18 order. He attacked and defeated Banks at Winchester (May 25). This sent Banks north across the Potomac. At first it was thought Jackson was marching toward Washington, and a force was collected near Warrenton to intercept him.[53]

When it was determined that Jackson was lingering in the Winchester area, Lincoln and Stanton saw an opportunity to trap him. Meigs had in mind as soon as McClellan had landed that the Union forces in the Shenandoah Valley might have to come at Richmond from the west so as to squeeze the Rebel army protecting it.[54] But first this required handling Jackson.

Jackson stayed in that area to accumulate and remove the stores and wagons captured from Banks; this was the engagement that resulted in Banks being referred to thereafter by the Confederates as "Commissary" Banks. Fremont, in charge of the Mountain Department, with troops located west of the Valley, and McDowell, who was east of the Valley, were ordered to cut Jackson off from going south from Winchester. Banks was to move against his rear as he retreated (south) up the Valley.[55]

Meigs wrote his father on May 28 that "if the generals commanding our troops show the energy which belongs to their statures Jackson will find a strong net around him. Where meshes will be too close I trust for him to slip through & whose cords will be too strong to break." This was a busy time for the quartermaster general. With telegrams coming in and being sent out all hours of the night, at times he would sleep on a couch at the War Department.[56]

Jackson was not one to slip through a net; he blasted it. On June 8 and 9, caught between two Federal forces, Fremont on the west and Brigadier General James Shield's detachment from McDowell's Department of the Rappahannock to the east, he fought them seriatim and caused them to retreat. With about 16,000 men Jackson avoided capture by an inadequately coordinated 40,000. He made off with a double train of wagons seven miles long. Meigs faulted McDowell and Banks for not generating any enthusiasm from the men in their commands.[57]

Jackson avoided the trap by long marches—a record 35 miles in one day. He had the advantage of a macadamized road in the Valley, but the 646 miles his army marched over 48 days (starting with the March 23 attack at Kernstown) justified the description given his army as "foot cavalry." Not only was he marching, he was fighting major and minor engagements—Kernstown (3/23), McDowell (5/8), Front Royal (5/23), Winchester (5/24, 25), Cross Keys (6/8), and Port Republic (6/9).[58]

Richmond may have been saved. McClellan essentially stayed in place for the last two weeks of May. He positioned himself for the anticipated joinder with McDowell. That juncture never happened.[59]

Johnston, leading the Army of Northern Virginia, attacked him on May 31. The battle of Fair Oaks (also called Seven Pines) was over on June 1 with McClellan holding his ground. However, of greater consequence to the war was the wounding of Johnston and the appointment of Robert E. Lee as the ground commander. The fact that Johnston attacked McClellan instead of vice versa led Meigs to "begin to doubt whether they are not right who say McClellan never did & never will give an order for attack." No other major attack on either side was launched until the end of June. Idleness did not stop deaths from illness—typhoid was a big killer. At the White House depot "twenty men worked day and night turning out hundreds of pine box [coffins]."[60]

A thunderbolt hit Stanton. The casualty reports from the battles of Shiloh in the west (April 6–7), Winchester in the Valley, and at Fair Oaks made Stanton realize he had made a big mistake. Recruiting stations were reopened on June 6.[61]

Washington was galvanized into action to get more troops to McClellan; the plan was still for McDowell to join McClellan. Around June 25 McClellan had his army in a position so that he could attack Richmond; his picket lines were within four miles of the city. Unfortunately for McClellan, Lee used the time after Fair Oaks preparing to attack. Brigadier General James ("Jeb") Stuart, dispatched to scout the location of Federal forces, ended up riding completely around McClellan's army. This disgusted Meigs. As Stuart went close by the White House depot he burned

wagons loaded with grain and coffee—in all, some 30 acres of wagons were destroyed.[62]

About mid-June McClellan thought the Confederacy might be interested in a truce and a peace conference. He put out feelers without consulting Lincoln or Stanton. On learning this Stanton exploded at McClellan: "Officers bearing flags of truce in respect to the exchange of prisoners...[should not discuss] the general subject of the existing contest."[63]

Before McClellan could get his attack started, he became convinced that Stonewall Jackson had come from the Shenandoah Valley and was about to hit him on his flank. The situation as McClellan saw it was

> [that he had] not more than 75,000 men for battle. The enemy, with a force larger than this, the strong defenses of Richmond close at hand in his rear, was free to strike on either flank.

Accordingly, he decided "to carry into effect the long-considered plan of abandoning the Pamunkey and taking up the line of the James"; that is, to move his army from the right side of the Peninsula to the left as one looks up the Peninsula towards Richmond. McClellan estimated the Rebel forces facing him to number two hundred thousand after Jackson's arrival. The truth was that after Jackson arrived from the Shenandoah Valley, the Confederates had between 80,000 and 90,000. Based on "present for duty equipped" Union reports, McClellan had about 105,000.[64]

From the quartermaster's standpoint this was a demanding decision. The major base of supplies was White House Landing at the mouth of the Pamunkey. The new base of supplies was to be some 20 miles across the Peninsula. The positioning of the army during this change was controlled by the need to protect the "immense trains that were...moved virtually by a single road." The wagon train, if spread on a single road, was not far from 40 miles long. Also moved was a herd of 2,500 beef cattle. Although the trains made it to the James, large volumes of supplies and ammunition were abandoned or destroyed en route.[65]

Lee aided McClellan's decision by aggressively attacking. In a series of battles, the Union army retreated, or as McClellan said, changed its base of operations, to the James River. The battles, Mechanicsville (June 26), Gaines' Mill (June 27), Savage's Station (June 29), Glendale (June 30) and Malvern Hill (July 1), resulted in heavy casualties on both sides. The immediate threat to Richmond was over, and the Army of the Potomac moved down the James River about 8 miles below Malvern Hill to a new base of supply, Harrison's Landing.[66]

Union Chaplain Stewart captured something of the feel of those on the battlefield at Malvern Hill:

> Two hundred pieces of artillery were belching forth their awful thunders and scattering solid shot, shells, and canister among the rebels. ... Nor were *they*, the meantime, idle. Bold and unflinching, they opened

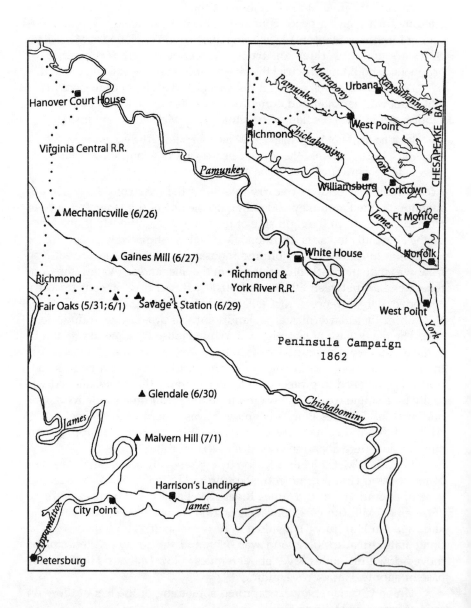

on us. ... At first their balls, shells, and canister flew and whizzed and screamed and burst over our heads, or fell beyond, yet soon obtaining such accuracy of range as to make each one feel that between him and death there might be but a moment. Yonder, a cannonball tore through the ranks, dashing to pieces one, two, or three soldiers. There, a horse and rider were knocked down together. Here, a shell exploded, tearing off the head of one, the arm of a second, and leg of a third.[67]

As the dawn broke the day after the Malvern Hill battle, a Rebel colonel described the scene:

> Our ears had been filled with agonizing cries from thousands before the fog was lifted, but now our eyes saw an appalling spectacle upon the slopes down to the woodlands half a mile away. Over five thousand dead and wounded men were on the ground in every attitude of distress. A third of them were dead or dying, but enough were alive and moving to give the field a singular crawling effect. The different stages of the ebbing tide are often marked by the lines of flotsam and jetsam left along the seashore. So here could be seen three distinct lines of dead and wounded marking the last front of three Confederate charges of the night before. Groups of men, some mounted, were groping about the field.[68]

McClellan had major mood swings. While the battle of Malvern Hill was in progress he wired Stanton: "We are hard pressed by superior numbers. I fear I shall be forced to abandon my material to save my men under cover of the gunboats. ...If none of us escape, we shall at least have done honor to the country. I shall do my best to save the army. Send more gunboats." A few days later his chief of staff and father-in-law, Brigadier General Randolph B. Marcy, brought a letter to Lincoln asking for "much over than much less than 100,000 men" so Richmond could be taken. Marcy upset Lincoln and Stanton when he said that McClellan might have to capitulate if he did not get the troops.[69]

By July 7 McClellan's spirits were up sufficiently for him to give Lincoln advice—"the Union must be preserved"; the war "should be conducted upon the highest principles known to Christian civilization"; "[n]either confiscation of property, political executions of persons, territorial organization of States, or forcible abolition of slavery should be contemplated for a moment." In the letter McClellan argued for a commander in chief of the army, not for himself, necessarily, and closed with a heroic flourish about the possibility that he was "on the brink of eternity."[70]

As for the transfer of the army from the Pamunkey-York River base to the James River, Meigs called its description as a "change of base" to be "[an] euphonious amendment of title." Another euphonious phrase for retreats used in the Civil War was "retrograde movements." Casualtywise the Union had the best of the so-called Seven Days' battles, but the threat to Richmond was lifted.

	Union	Confederates
Killed	1,734	3,286
Wounded	8,062	15,909
Captured or missing	6,053	940
	15,849	20,135 [71]

The Meigs' reaction was set out in a letter to his father dated July 8:

We have had a terrible reverse on the Peninsula. One which I have feared from the moment I learned that it was determined to move the army to that cul de sac.

Believe nothing you hear against the President & Secretary as responsible for this disaster. The true cause is the false military move which placed an army in a narrow peninsula where it was easily checked by inferior forces until the gathering hordes of a barbarous people driven by a wide sweeping conscription enforced by a merciless military despotism...overwhelm[ed] our gallant freemen decimated...by malaria & mud & storms & toil.

This is not time however for...criticism....

If the administration has erred it has been by permitting Gen. McClellan to adopt a false line of operations & by not appreciating the immense waste of men attending such operations as we have carried on during this campaign.

* * * * *

God punishes us for our sins.[72]

President James Buchanan and his cabinet

President James Buchanan's Cabinet with the president in the *center*. Viewing the picture, those who went with the Confederacy are Jacob Thompson (Interior), *seated to the far left*; John B. Floyd (War), *seated on the left* near Buchanan; and Howell Cobb (Treasury), *standing to the right* of Buchanan. The other cabinet members were Lewis Cass (State), *standing to the left*; Joseph Holt, *standing at the far right*; and Jeremiah Black (Attorney General), *seated far right*; and Isaac Toucey, *seated to the left* of Black.

Library of Congress

Abraham Lincoln and his cabinet at the time of Emancipation Proclamation

President Abraham Lincoln's Cabinet at the time of the Emancipation Proclamation (January 1863). From *left to right:* Stanton (War), Chase (Treasury), Lincoln, Welles (Navy), Seward, seated, (State), Smith (Interior), Blair (Postmaster General), and Bates (Attorney General).

Massachusetts Commandery, Military Order of the Loyal Legion and the US Army Military History Institute

THE FIRST BULL RUN COMBATANTS

Irvin McDowell (West Point, 1838)

Library of Congress

Pierre G. T. Beauregard (West Point, 1838)

National Archives

Joseph E. Johnston (West Point, 1829)

National Archives

"Beanpole and cornstalk" bridge

"Beanpole and cornstalk" type bridge built in four and one-half days across the Chattahoochee River which was needed to support Sherman's advance to Atlanta in 1864. This description was first applied by Lincoln after seeing a similar bridge built by Herman Haupt in 1862.

Library of Congress

Thomas A. Scott

Scott, vice president of the Pennsylvania Central Railroad, was in charge of government railroads and telegraphs for the first 12 months of the war.

Library of Congress

Daniel A. McCallum

McCallum was director of all the military railroads (those constructed or seized by the government) for most of the war.

Library of Congress

Herman A. Haupt

Haupt ran the railroads in the field, with McCallum, a good friend, running them from Washington, for the period April 1862 to September 1863.

Library of Congress

With these experienced railroad men running the railroads, the quartermaster general was primarily concerned with contracts for service, which Meigs insisted be made only by quartermaster officers, and with keeping the quartermasters out of the way of the actual running of the railroads. In general, railroads and telegraphs were left in the hands of their owners but were subject to being seized by the president if needed for the public safety.

Eads class gunboat used on Western rivers

John Rodgers,
Montgomery Meigs' brother-in-law

A navy captain and later commodore, he was involved in early construction of Western riverboats.

Flag Officer Andrew H. Foote

Foote was in command of gunboats on the Western rivers during battles for Forts Henry and Donaldson.

Lincoln and his military leaders

Left to right: Admiral Farragut, Generals Sherman, Thomas, Meade, Grant, Hooker, Sheridan, and Hancock.

Massachusetts Commandery, Military Order of the Loyal Legion and the US Army Military History Institute

George B. McClellan

McClellan was Robert E. Lee's adversary at the Seven Days' battles and Antietam.

National Archives

Robert E. Lee

Lee opposed George B. McClellan at the Seven Days' battles and Antietam.

Library of Congress

Henry W. Halleck, key officer in Second Bull Run

Although a Washington fixture from July 1862 on, he did not fulfill expectations as general in chief.

Library of Congress

John Pope, key officer in Second Bull Run

His policy of treating Southern supporters in occupied Virginia harshly angered Lee.

Library of Congress

Valley Pike

The Valley Pike, shown some 20 years after the war, was an important part of the marches of Stonewall Jackson.
Massachusetts Commandery, Military Order of the Loyal Legion and the US Army Military History Institute

Thomas J. ("Stonewall") Jackson

Jackson marched his army more than 640 miles up and down the Shenandoah Valley in the first six months of 1862 disrupting Union plans to take Richmond.
Massachusetts Commandery, Military Order of the Loyal Legion and the US Army Military History Institute

Burnside Bridge

The Burnside Bridge over which Ambrose Burnside threw repeated attacks to dislodge the Rebels on the hill on the opposite side during the battle of Antietam in September 1862.

Massachusetts Commandery, Military Order of the Loyal Legion and the US Army Military History Institute

Stone wall on Marye's Heights

The road behind the stone wall on Marye's Heights at Fredericksburg where Burnside repeatedly threw troops, with staggering losses and no success, in December 1862.

Massachusetts Commandery, Military Order of the Loyal Legion and the US Army Military History Institute

Ambrose E. Burnside

His belief in November 1862 that he was not competent to command the Army of the Potomac was proved correct at Fredericksburg in December 1862.

Library of Congress

William B. Franklin

Franklin commanded a division at Fredericksburg, and tried to put blame for the Union defeat on those who failed to have the pontoon bridges ready before the battle. Franklin, a prewar engineer, as was Meigs, relieved Captain Meigs of being in charge of the Capitol extension and new dome in 1859, and was in turn relieved by Meigs in early 1860.

Library of Congress

William S. Rosecrans

A prewar army engineer for years corresponding with similar service by Montgomery Meigs, Rosecrans gave Meigs a bad time over supplying his infantry with mounts.

Library of Congress

Horse depot, Giesborough Point

Providing horses and mules was a big part of the quartermaster's job. One effort to economize was the use of depots where the animals were kept and unserviceable animals nursed back to a healthy state. Giesborough Point, constructed in Washington in late 1863, could handle 30,000 animals.

Library of Congress

The War Department Building (*top*) during the Civil War, located just west of the White House together with an adjoining Navy Department Building, was torn down in the 1870s to make room for the State, War and Navy Building (now the old Executive Office Building). When it was torn down, Meigs had the columns (*shown above*) taken to Arlington cemetery for use in entry gates. The quartermaster general's office at the start of the war was across the street, west of the War Department, in the Winder Building which is still in use today. When more room was needed, the quartermaster general moved to the Corcoran Art Building (*bottom*), located immediately north of the War Department, across Pennsylvania Avenue—this is now the Renwick Museum. A couple of years after the war the building was returned to Mr. Corcoran.

National Archives

National Archives

Grant crosses the Rapidan

Grant crossed the Rapidan River to head toward Richmond in May 1864. This picture (*top*) captures part of his many miles of wagon trains making the crossing. Ulysses S. Grant (*below left*), who was then general in chief of the Union forces, traveled with the Army of the Potomac under the command of George Meade (*center below*). The officer to the *right below* is Rufus Ingalls, chief quartermaster of the Army of the Potomac from the time it left the Peninsula in mid-1862 to the end of the war. In 1882 he became quartermaster general.

Massachusetts Commandery, Military Order of the Loyal Legion and the US Army Military History Institute

Ulysses S. Grant

Massachusetts Commandery, Military Order of the Loyal Legion and the US Army Military History Institute

George Meade

Library of Congress

Rufus Ingalls

Massachusetts Commandery, Military Order of the Loyal Legion and the US Army Military History Institute

MONTGOMERY MEIGS WAS BLESSED WITH MANY OUTSTANDING OFFICERS. AS A GOOD ADMINISTRATOR, HE LET THEM DO THEIR JOB.

Stewart Van Vliet (West Point, 1840), chief quartermaster of the Army of the Potomac during the Peninsula campaign; thereafter chief quartermaster in New York City

National Archives

Langdon C. Easton (West Point, 1838), Sherman's chief quartermaster in 1864-1865

Massachusetts Commandery, Military Order of the Loyal Legion and the US Army Military History Institute

Lewis B. Parsons (no prewar connection), chief of rail and river transportation first in the West and later out of Washington

National Archives

Parked wagon train at Brandy Station

Large wagon trains were the norm with Civil War armies. These are parked at Brandy Station, Virginia, in May 1863.

Massachusetts Commandery, Military Order of the Loyal Legion and the US Army Military History Institute

Corduroyed road crossing a creek

A lot of trees were consumed in corduroying roads and bridging over creeks.

Massachusetts Commandery, Military Order of the Loyal Legion and the US Army Military History Institute

Dock at Belle Plain

Rufus Ingalls, chief quartermaster of the Army of the Potomac, spoke of the "flying depots" used by quartermasters as Grant pushed south in 1864. Two are shown here: Belle Plain (*above*) is on the Potomac close to Fredericksburg, and, Port Royal (*below*) is on the Rappahannock, a short way downstream from Fredericksburg.

Dock at Port Royal

William Tecumseh Sherman
Library of Congress

George H. Thomas,
the "Rock of Chickamauga"
Library of Congress

Each one of these generals led armies in important battles shortly before and shortly after the presidential election of November 1864. An unanswerable question is whether Hood, by aggressively attacking Sherman outside Atlanta, causing the city to fall before the election, produced an elation in the North instrumental in Lincoln's win.

Hood surely shortened the war by aggressively fighting and advancing to the outskirts of Nashville only to see his army crumble when Thomas came out of his defensive positions to attack with superior numbers.

John Bell Hood

Massachusetts Commandery,
Military Order of the Loyal Legion
and the US Army Military History Institute

White House landing

Two more "flying depots." Above is White House, used by McClellan in the Peninsula campaign of 1862, and by Grant in 1864. Below is City Point, the ultimate in Civil War supply depots. The traffic at City Point, which was on the James River, averaged 40 steamboats, 75 sail vessels, and 100 barges each day.

City Point

Union wagon train passing through Petersburg

The end for Lee's army was close at hand as this Union wagon train went through the streets of Petersburg.

Three quartermasters who performed admirably for the quartermaster general are shown below.

Daniel H. Rucker	*Robert Allen*	*James L. Donaldson*
In command of the quartermaster depot Washington, 1861–1867.	*(West Point, 1836)*	*(West Point, 1836)*
	Chief Quartermaster Department of Missouri and Mississippi Valley 1861–1866.	Chief Quartermaster of New Mexico, Middle Department, and Department of the Cumberland 1858–1865.

As military governor of Tennessee
in 1864 he supervised construction
of the Nashville & North Western
Railroad, recommended by Meigs
as a way to get more supplies to
Nashville in a hurry.

Reviewing stand at Grand Parade

In the reviewing stand for the Grand Parade in May 1865 President Johnson is
positioned in the *center*, and Meigs on the first row to the *right*.

Chapter 18

Bull Run Again and Antietam

The Seven Days' battles and Jackson's success in the Valley resulted in the appointment of a general in chief, Henry Halleck, who assumed that position on July 23, 1862, and the consolidation of northern Virginia forces under Major General John Pope, as of June 27, as the Army of Virginia. Each had been successful in the West.

After McClellan had his Peninsula army back in a safe position, at Harrison's Landing on the James River, he thought he could take Richmond if supplied a fresh infusion of troops. At first he wanted one hundred thousand reinforcements, but later agreed to try for a victory with 20,000 more.[1]

Meigs was glad he did not have to make the decision as to what should be done with the Army of the Potomac.[2] Nonetheless, he laid out his thinking to his father:

> There is much in favor of hurling it upon Richmond & were it under an active enterprising dashing leader who kept heart amid disasters...I incline to think that this would be the true policy. But McClellan has not shown himself of this nature. He has never attacked. He has never followed up an advantage. He has always believed the enemy stronger than himself, has promised to be ready when this or that reinforcement should reach him & when it came has still stopped & waited....
> "If 100,000 men were to be sent to him tomorrow he would be delighted & in the highest spirits but the next day he would hear & believe that 200,000 had joined the rebels in Richmond...."

* * * * *

...I fear...that the young general overwhelmed with the responsibility of knowing that another repulse would almost ruin his army & would greatly injure our cause would hesitate & halt in his advance & substitute for the rush of victorious assault the slow trench of the engineer.

* * * * *

...One principle much influences me. It is that it is always (almost)
best to abandon an error than to endeavor to patch repair...it.

It was wrong to go to Yorktown. The effect of this blunder remains.[3]

From the relatively safe position at Harrison's Landing McClellan
wrote the new general in chief, on August 4, the day after Halleck told
him his army was to be withdrawn, that to call the Army of the Potomac
back to northern Virginia would be a "fatal blow." It would have a "terribly depressing effect upon the people of the North, and the strong probability that it would influence foreign powers to recognize [the
Confederacy]." Then, doing something he said he had never done before
in his life, he "entreated[ed] that this order [directing the withdrawal of
the Army of the Potomac from the Peninsula] be rescinded."[4]

His entreaty fell on deaf ears. He was hoisted on his own petard.
Halleck explained to him that, if the Rebel army was two hundred thousand, as McClellan thought, and was being reinforced, there was great
danger of it falling in separate actions on Pope's army of 40,000 protecting
Washington and McClellan's army of 90,000. The Union forces needed to
be reunited. Deprecatorily, Halleck wrote: "I have not inquired, and do
not wish to know, by whose advice or for what reasons the Army of the
Potomac was separated into two parts, with the enemy between them. I
must take things as I find them." He assured McClellan that he had been
objective. Immediately on his arrival in Washington, around July 23, he
was advised "by high officers, in whose judgment [he] had great confidence, to make the [withdrawal] order immediately." In all likelihood
Meigs was one of the high officers. Meigs and Halleck were old acquain-
tances. Meigs accompanied Halleck on a July 25 trip to McClellan's camp
to talk with McClellan before the decision was made, and undoubtedly
stiffened Halleck's resolve.[5]

Meigs' 1880s assessment of the decision to withdraw the army was
that it took Grant, "the greatest soldier of the war," almost a year and a
loss of 60,000 men to take Richmond, and "McClellan, with a defeated
army, could not have done better."[6]

Either McClellan dragged his feet in getting the Army of the Potomac
back to the Washington area, or had a severe attitude problem. The order
to withdraw was given on August 3—on August 4 McClellan writes to
Halleck that he was "convinced that the order to withdraw this army to
Aquia Creek [near Fredericksburg] [would] prove disastrous."[7]

Halleck is back to McClellan by noon of August 4 saying the "President expects that the instructions...sent...with his approval will be carried
out with all possible dispatch," and that Meigs was "sending to Fort Monroe all the transportation he [could] collect." By August 9 the need for
speed was even greater. Halleck to McClellan: "I am of the opinion that
the enemy is massing his forces in front of Generals Pope and Burnside,
and that he expects to rush them and move forward to the Potomac. You

must send re-enforcements instantly to Aquia Creek. Considering the amount of transportation at your disposal, your delay is not satisfactory." Halleck had recalled some of Burnside's troops from North Carolina to complement the Army of Virginia.[8]

Even this did not move McClellan—he told Halleck that "Colonel Ingalls [his chief quartermaster] ha[d] more than once informed the Quartermaster-General of the condition of [the] water transportation." On August 12 Halleck telegraphed back that Meigs informed him "that nearly every available steam vessel in the country is now under [McClellan's] control."[9] Halleck must have thrown up his hands when McClellan sent a dispatch on August 12 saying:

> It is not possible for any one to place this army where you wish it, ready to move, in less than a month. If Washington is in danger now this army can scarcely arrive in time to save it. It is in much better position to do so from here than from Aquia.[10]

Finally, on August 14, McClellan told Halleck his orders would be obeyed, and from that point on the movement of the army from Harrison's Landing was rapidly completed around August 17, and by the 20th all of the army was ready to embark at Yorktown, Fort Monroe, and Newport News.[11]

During the time McClellan was resisting his orders to return to Washington, Lee was acting. Even before McClellan received orders to remove his army from the Peninsula, Lee sent Stonewall Jackson to guard against Pope. Once McClellan started removing men and supplies from Harrison's Landing, Lee rapidly marched the bulk of his army to join with Jackson. Lee wanted to attack Pope before the Army of the Potomac could be relocated in the Washington area.[12]

As early as August 18 Pope was being pressed by Lee and crossed over to the north bank of the Rappahannock River. With an army of about 50,000, Pope wanted reinforcements. Two days later, skirmishing was engaged in along the Rappahannock, and as well on August 21. As fast as the Army of the Potomac arrived back at Aquia Creek and Alexandria, Virginia, units were hurried into Pope's Army of Virginia.[13]

McClellan and staff were at Aquia on August 24, and he respectfully reported for orders. He was left in limbo with his army being absorbed into Pope's. McClellan, although not removed from command, was "in the position of a man temporarily out of work."[14]

On August 25 Jackson moved north of the Rappahannock and Pope, finding himself outflanked, on August 27, retreated from the Rappahannock toward Manassas. Over the next three days Pope, with a force of about 75,000, was out-generaled by Lee and his army of about 50,000. Though beaten, Pope's army was not routed. It fell back into Washington's prepared entrenchments.[15]

The losses for the period August 27 through September 2 were markedly in favor of the Confederates:

	Union	Confederates
Killed	1,724	1,481
Wounded	8,372	7,627
Missing	5,958	89
	16,054	9,197 [16]

Nonetheless, Lee was in a precarious position. With a weakened army, he was operating from an extended supply line and confronting a Union army, close to its supply line, with many more men than he had. Writing to Jefferson Davis on September 3, Lee said:

> The Army is not properly equipped for an invasion of an enemy's territory. It lacks much of the material of war, is feeble in transportation, the animals being much reduced, and the men are poorly provided with clothes, and in thousands of instances are destitute of shoes.[17]

Common sense would have Lee relocate to a safer position and rest his army.

But this was not Lee's style, and instead, on September 3, he circled to the west of Washington and headed north. He was looking to end the war. His plan was to cut the North in half by breaching the Chesapeake and Ohio Canal, and the Baltimore and Ohio and Pennsylvania Railroads—the Union could, then, only get reinforcements from the west via a slow northern route. With this isolation of the East from the West, Lee could turn on Philadelphia, Baltimore, or Washington and hopefully force the North to recognize the Confederacy and agree to an end of the war.[18]

Pope had several explanations for his bad showing, one of which was a lack of support by McClellan. McClellan opened himself up to such an allegation when he suggested as an alternative to trying to support Pope that "Pope [be left] to get out of his scrape, and [we] at once use all our means to make the capital perfectly safe."[19]

As Pope's retreat produced concern about the safety of the capital, and the streets of Washington were clogged with stragglers, McClellan was asked to take over the Washington defenses. And, when the immediate threat to Washington ceased, with Lee marching toward Maryland, McClellan was at the head of the Army of the Potomac going to head off Lee.[20]

Lincoln thought McClellan had acted despicably in not giving Pope the support needed, and contributed to Lee's victory at Second Bull Run. Nonetheless, he recognized two McClellan strengths making him best for the overall command. McClellan was without a doubt a preeminent organizer—he could be relied upon to get the army back into shape, and, secondly, the army liked him. There is uncertainty as to the extent to which Halleck favored putting McClellan back in command. Halleck told Congress that Lincoln made the decision, but Lincoln said Halleck had recommended the action. Stanton and most of the cabinet were against it.[21]

Halleck was probably correct. After all, Lincoln was the commander in chief, and also, Halleck, in Lincoln's words, "shrunk from responsibility wherever it was possible" after Pope was defeated. From that time on he was more of a chief clerk to Lincoln and Stanton than a general in chief.[22]

Notwithstanding all the problems Washington had had with McClellan, Meigs advised that he be given command of the united armies when he returned from the Peninsula. His support for McClellan was based on the adulation of the Army of the Potomac for him, and the lack of anyone worthier.[23]

However, Meigs, at the same time he was approving the placement of McClellan at the head of the army, complained of the pace at which McClellan moved northwestward out of Washington to confront Lee. So did Lincoln who thought McClellan had the "slows." The army moved 45 miles over good roads in seven days, a march which should have been made in three days. The tardiness kept McClellan from attacking Lee's army in detail while it was scattered, part at Harpers Ferry, part at Hagerstown, and parts at Williamsport or Martinsburg.[24]

Meigs was not reluctant to give McClellan advice. As the Army of the Potomac moved northwest out of Washington there was a shortage of wagons to transport supplies requisitioned from the Washington depot. Meigs wrote:

> I believe there are with the army under your command not less than 6,000 wagons, drawn by 30,000 animals, and yet such is the confusion that it is impossible this morning to send out at once the supplies called for by your requisition....[R]egiments ordered to march...should [not] be allowed in all more than one wagon to 80 men, including officers.
>
> The extra wagons, now filled with officers' baggage, should be emptied, and the officers compelled to move without this unnecessary load.
>
> None but the stringent authority of the commander of the army can carry out this reform, and, until it is done, the army will not be a movable one, and will not be effective. Colonel Ingalls, your chief quartermaster, armed with full power from you, could, if here, in a few days reduce to order this confusion, which is now wasting the Treasury and the means of transportation collected here. The wagons and teams having once been issued to your army, I have not the power to organize them, as orders from me in relation to them interfere with your authority.[25]

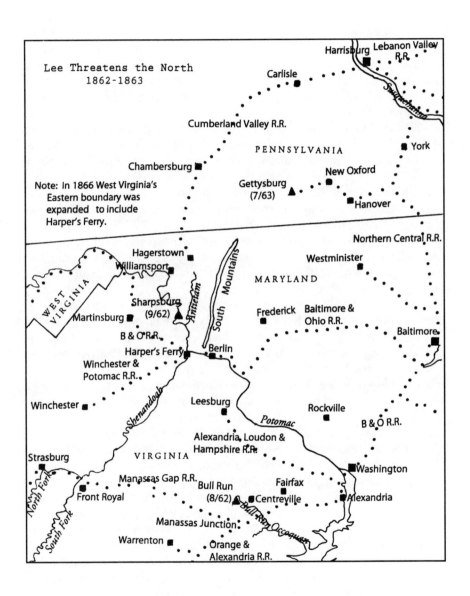

Lee Threatens the North
1862-1863

Note: In 1866 West Virginia's
Eastern boundary was
expanded to include
Harper's Ferry.

Harrisburg   Lebanon Valley R.R.
Carlisle
Cumberland Valley R.R.
PENNSYLVANIA
York
Chambersburg
New Oxford
Gettysburg
(7/63)
Hanover

Northern Central R.R.
Hagerstown
Williamsport
Westminister
MARYLAND
WEST VIRGINIA
Sharpsburg
(9/62)
Martinsburg
Frederick   Baltimore &
Ohio R.R.
Baltimore
B & O R.R.
Harper's Ferry   Berlin
Winchester &
Potomac R.R.
Winchester
Leesburg   Rockville
Potomac   B & O R.R.
Alexandria, Loudon &
Hampshire R.R.
VIRGINIA
Strasburg
Washington
Manassas Gap R.R.   Fairfax
Bull Run
Front Royal   (8/62)   Centreville   Alexandria
Manassas Junction
Warrenton   Orange &
Alexandria R.R.

A gruesome record was set when Lee and McClellan went head-to-head at Antietam Creek, near Sharpsburg, Maryland, just across the Maryland line, about 55 miles up the Potomac River from Washington, on September 17. The bloodiest single day of the Civil War was the result. In one day there were combined casualties of 26,000 (North: 2,010 killed, 9,416 wounded, and 1,043 missing; the South, 2,700 killed, 9,024 wounded, and about 2,000 missing). Although the casualties are roughly equal, Lee's army was only about 40,000 strong at the start whereas the North had a force of over 75,000—the impact to Lee's army, as a whole, was almost twice that on the Union.[26]

Following the conclusion of the first day's fighting at Antietam, McClellan decided he would not resume his attack the next day because of heavy losses, disorganization, and the expected arrival of 15,000 fresh troops. The second morning after the battle, as he was preparing to renew his offensive, he found that Lee had abandoned his position and was moving back across the Potomac River into Virginia. Lee was able to do this without McClellan doing him any serious injury.[27]

After the battle of Antietam, Meigs softened his complaint about McClellan's slow march. He told his father "[t]here may [have been] good reasons for slowness"; there are "many ifs...in all speculations upon military events after or before the facts," and that he found no fault. However, sparks were soon to fly between McClellan and Meigs. In anticipation of moving the main supply depot for the Army of the Potomac from Frederick and Hagerstown, Maryland, both of which were on railroad lines, to Harpers Ferry, Virginia, which was on the Baltimore & Ohio Railroad and the Chesapeake & Ohio Canal which followed the Potomac River northwest from Washington, McClellan's chief quartermaster, Rufus Ingalls, told Meigs of the expected move and that McClellan wanted the canal repaired. Meigs responded that with the southern bank of the Potomac in Rebel hands the canal was subject to artillery fire and could not be repaired. McClellan was incensed—message to Halleck: repair of canal "indispensably necessary for ulterior military operations" and, as for Meigs' response, "I do not require suggestions of this kind."[28]

McClellan's Antietam success removed him from political criticism only for a short time. Why, Lincoln and Halleck wanted to know, was he not pursuing the retreating Lee? Over 15 to 20,000 men in the Army of the Potomac saw no fighting at Antietam and could be used on attack.[29]

Ten days after the battle, McClellan wrote Halleck that he intended "to hold the enemy about as it now is, rendering Harper's Ferry secure, and watching the river closely, intending to attack the enemy should he attempt to cross to this side [that is, to the Maryland side of the Potomac]." McClellan also said "it [was] absolutely necessary to send new regiments at once to the old corps for purposes of instruction, and that the old regiments be filled at once."[30]

This is not what Lincoln had in mind. Lincoln visited the army around October 1 and, upon his return to Washington, had Halleck wire McClellan on October 6 that the "President directs that you cross the Potomac and give battle to the enemy or drive him south. Your army must move now while the roads are good." Halleck wrote McClellan on October 7 that the "country is becoming very impatient at the want of activity of your army, and we must push it on."[31]

McClellan was not an easy person to push. Lincoln suggested two possible lines of operation—one, to keep McClellan's army between Washington and Lee, and two, a move up the Shenandoah Valley, that is, push south. In the first case 30,000 men could be supplied as reinforcements, and in the second, 12,000 to 15,000. By telegraph, McClellan elected the Shenandoah line, in part because this would protect Maryland and Pennsylvania, but then said little would be accomplished by that move. Because he did not have "sufficient means of transportation to enable [the army] to advance more than 20 or 35 miles beyond a railroad or canal terminus," if Lee retreated beyond Winchester McClellan would not be able to pursue him. However, McClellan would fight Lee if Lee remained at Winchester.[32]

In the same letter, dated October 7, McClellan gave reasons why he could not move immediately:

[T]he first, fifth, and sixth corps [were not] in readiness to move from their present camps. They need shoes and other indispensable articles of clothing, as well as shelter tents, &c.[33]

On October 13 McClellan had not moved. In a October 13 report to Halleck about Rebel Jeb Stuart riding completely around the Army of the Potomac a few days earlier, McClellan credited Stuart's accomplishment with "the deficiency of [McClellan's] cavalry" and the need for "a sufficient number of horses to remount every dismounted cavalry soldier within the shortest possible time." Absent an adequate supply, he would be "constantly exposed to rebel cavalry raids."[34]

Meigs was impliedly taken to task for not supplying McClellan. Stanton, not a person to mince words, in forwarding McClellan's complaint said the quartermaster general for a long time had had unrestricted authority to supply cavalry horses and wanted to know what had been done. Meigs' report was that McClellan's army, including that in front of Washington, had received 8,754 horses between September 1 and October 11. This was an average of 1,459 horses per week over a six-week period rather than an average of 150 horses per week as McClellan had stated.[35]

Stanton also asked what could be done to alleviate the problem. Meigs had definite thoughts on this—he found "the number of horses disabled and broken down [to be] alarming." Causes of this lay in "the management of horses in the army," which is a question of discipline beyond the control of the Quartermaster Department. "Discipline can be enforced only through the military commander. The galloping of orderlies and cavalry without necessity wears out the horses more than their proper service in campaign. Orders have been repeatedly issued to prevent this in the streets of [Washington], but they are not enforced."[36]

In Meigs' view, "[u]pon the efficiency of the animals depend the precision, rapidity, and success of...marches, and thence of all...military operations," and "[e]very commander, from the highest to the lowest in rank, from the commander of an army to the chief of the smallest detachment to which a wagon is attached, has a direct interest in the condition of the stock." Another problem, which Stanton undoubtedly was well aware of, was that the horses were being purchased on credit. This at a time when the Quartermaster Department had over $11 million in unpaid requisitions pending for payment in the treasury. Preserving the government's credit was important to keep prices from rising. Notwithstanding, what had gone before, Meigs stood ready, if McClellan said precisely the number of horses needed by a particular date, to procure them, if possible.[37]

Lincoln was indeed a patient man. On October 13 he wrote McClellan a restrained letter considering the circumstances. He pointed out that McClellan was being overcautious, a trait Lincoln had discussed with him earlier. As for the need to be close to a railroad terminal, Lincoln said Lee, while at Winchester, was twice the distance from a railroad terminal as would be McClellan. Lincoln saw no danger if Lee should decide to go back into Pennsylvania—his supply lines would be completely at the mercy of McClellan, and McClellan could pursue and ruin him.[38]

Lincoln called to McClellan's attention that he, Lincoln, had preferred a line of operation for the Army of the Potomac which would interpose it between Lee and the capital, and that, if that were done, McClellan would be closer to Richmond than Lee and could hopefully beat Lee in a race to get there. If this course were taken, and Lee elected to stay at Winchester, that is, neither moving north or south, McClellan should fight him there. A battle at Winchester would be one where Lee bears the "wastage" of being away from his base of supply, a definite advantage to McClellan. Lincoln went to lengths to explain to McClellan that which surely was clear to him: all the way from Winchester to Richmond, McClellan would have good supply lines over turnpikes, railroads, or water.[39]

Lincoln's letter, to the layman, has compelling reasoning, but he was not ready to impose that reasoning on McClellan. The letter closes with the sentence: "This letter is in no sense an order."[40]

When Lincoln received a McClellan letter of October 17 responding to his of October 13, he must have thought this was one arrogant general. McClellan sent the bearer of the president's letter back to Washington without anything other than an acknowledgment and the statement that he would give the president's views "the fullest and most unprejudiced consideration, and that it [was McClellan's] intention to advance the moment [his] men [were] shod, and [his] cavalry...sufficiently renovated to be available." Remember, this was 11 days after Lincoln had Halleck telegraph McClellan: "The President directs that you cross the Potomac and give battle to the enemy or drive him south" and 10 days after the general in chief told him "The country is becoming impatient at the want of activity of your army, and we must push it on."[41]

McClellan continued to have reasons why he couldn't move. He needed horses, shoes, and other articles of clothing, and at this point he laid blame on "the want of proper action [by] the quartermaster's department."[42] This accusation resulted in Stanton writing to Halleck on October 27 asking the following questions:

1. "To whom...requisitions for supplies to the [McClellan] army have been made...and whether any requisition [had] been made upon the Secretary of War,"

2. "[W]hether there [had] been any neglect or delay, by any department or bureau, in filling the requisitions for supplies...and...the condition of [McClellan's] army, as compared with other armies, in respect to supplies,"

3. "At what date, after the battle of Antietam, the orders to advance against the enemy were given to General McClellan, and how often have they been repeated,"

4. "Whether...there [had] been any want in the [McClellan] army...of shoes, clothing, arms, or other equipment or supplies, that ought to have prevented its advance against the enemy when the order was given," and

5. "How long was it after the orders to advance were given...before [McClellan] informed [Halleck] that any shoes or clothing were wanted."[43]

At this point Meigs was very much in the controversy. The next day Halleck responded: "No requisitions had been made on the secretary of war; requisitions went through the normal channels. McClellan had telegraphed on several occasions as to deficiencies, and, when checks were made, except in one instance, the "requisitions had been immediately filled." He knew of no neglect or delay "in issuing all supplies asked for by General McClellan, or...his staff."[44]

Halleck flatly contradicted McClellan:

From all the information I can obtain, I am of the opinion that the requisitions from that army have been filled more promptly, and that the men, as a general rule, have been better supplied than our armies operating in the west....In fine, I believe that no armies in the world, while in campaign, have been more promptly or better supplied than ours.[45]

Meigs, of course, agreed with Halleck. He told his father in a letter dated October 26:

Ten days ago I was assured that every requisition for clothing & such supplies from the army on the upper Potomac had been filled. Within the last three days came in new requisitions sufficient to do...thirty thousand men....

The stores are being pushed off as fast they can be shipped & moved. We had them on hand either here or in Philadelphia or New York. The consumption is enormous.

* * * * *

Forty eight thousand pairs of boots & shoes have been rec[eived] by the Army of the Potomac since the battle of Antietam & 35,000 more are on there way to them.

The complaint that the army must wait for such supplies is not true. It has been kept well supplied but it of course requires continuous issues. Of 150,000 men many wear out their shoes every day. Many tear their coats or pantaloons daily & as supplies of clothing & food must be continually poured into Philadelphia or New York so must they into such a camp.

* * * * *

I think the miserable error of last fall has been repeated & that the opportunity offered during the last six weeks is lost. Lost opportunities! Oh suffering Nation how long will you bear with this waste of your blood.[46]

Meigs was a "can-do" man. Answering a message from Ingalls in which Ingalls says he did not want to be drawn into controversy, Meigs told him:

the Quartermaster-General would regard it as a great misfortune, if not a great crime, to have any controversy grow up between it, or its officers, and the generals commanding armies. It is its duty to assist them, by every means under its control, in making and keeping their commands efficient. The Quartermaster-General desires to accomplish this, and will not allow any controversy to arise. All the late correspondence on this subject has been with the intention and desire to get the facts necessary for the efficient support and assistance of the general commanding, and to remove any defects or difficulties in the way of prompt and sufficient supply of all that this army needs, and though one of General McClellan's letters bore rather hardly upon the Department, his telegram of later date relieved it from all accusation.[47]

Ingalls undoubtedly put his finger on much of the problem when he told Meigs on October 26 that "an army will never move if it waits until all the different commanders report that they are ready and want no more supplies."[48]

Being a "can-do" quartermaster general did not mean relinquishing authority to decide what the army needed. When Ingalls asked for "water proof horse blankets for...cavalry, artillery, and even wagon horses," he was rebuffed by Meigs saying regulations did not provide for such and that he "doubt[ed] very much the propriety of encumbering [an] overloaded cavalry with one thousand heavy horse-covers to a regiment."[49]

When McClellan went too far in his battle with Washington isn't clear, but a message to Lincoln of October 26, in which he condescendingly said he was sure Lincoln, in commenting on Jeb Stuart's Rebel cavalry efforts, did not intend to "do injustice to the excellent officers and men" of the Union cavalry, must have contributed. He seems to have reached the point where he would not accept any criticism from Washington, and would obey orders only when ready to do so. Getting the army in motion on October 28 did not save him.[50]

McClellan exceeded Lincoln's tolerance level, and was relieved as head of the Army of the Potomac on November 7. In his place went Major General Ambrose Burnside who did not think he was competent to command such a large force. Burnside was right. Burnside, a "wholly good patriotic brave & modest & generous" man "shrunk from the responsibility" which Meigs agreed was one difficult for "any man [to] covet." On hearing of the change, Lee said he regretted McClellan leaving since he understood him so well, and was fearful the Union would make "changes till they find someone" who Lee didn't understand.[51]

The patience Lincoln showed to McClellan, in Meigs' assessment, was the result of Lincoln's "personal kindness & goodness [and] his hatred to give pain." He saw Lincoln, at this time, as "simply a man of respectable ability no education honest brave good tempered kind hearted with considerable firmness which however generously yields too often to his kindness."[52]

Meigs thought McClellan's downfall came from his "swell[ing] up, out[growing] advice, be[coming] pompous, and want[ing] to be surrounded by courtiers, aides, and retinues." From a military perspective he "[c]ommanded from the rear instead of the front" and was "always afraid that if he should actually get into a fight some of his men, if not himself, might get hurt." The "swelling up" started almost from the minute McClellan hit Washington in July 1861. On July 27 he wrote his wife: "By some strange operation of magic I seem to have become the center of power. I receive letters often alluding to the presidency, dictatorship, etc. *I would cheerfully take the dictatorship* and lay down my life when the country is saved!"[53]

Burnside took over an army of 100,000 men, 36,000 animals, 4,000 wagons, and about 300 pieces of artillery.[54] He was fighting, as Meigs saw it, a people suffering under a military tyranny driven like sheep from their farms herded together in armies & marched till they drop by the wayside pushed forward at the point of the bayonet to attack & murder their fellow citizens who meet them without hate without revenge & give water & kindest attention to their wounded.[55]

Burnside was satisfied that he had enough men—there was a limit to the number of men that could be marched and handled.[56]

Antietam had a major impact on slavery. Piecemeal action had already been taken—the First Confiscation Act of August 6, 1861, freed slaves "employed in hostile service against the United States." Following the Union setbacks on the Peninsula, the Second Confiscation Act was signed (7/17/62) which, among other matters, provided that those found guilty by a court of treason or of assisting the rebellion could have their slaves declared free. And, almost at the very start of the war, slaves escaping into Union lines were treated as "contrabands," i.e., enemy property subject to seizure, who were put to work.[57]

Lincoln tried out a draft of an Emancipation Proclamation on his cabinet on July 22, 1862—in part it would free slaves in the states of the Confederacy as of January 1, 1863. Seward proposed, and Lincoln agreed, to postpone any Emancipation Proclamation until there was a Union victory. Antietam provided the victory. On September 22 Lincoln issued a preliminary Emancipation Proclamation. Meigs thought the proclamation was something "thinking men must have foreseen since the first gun was fired."[58]

Meigs and the secretary of war generally saw things alike. Prior to the issuance of the secretary of war's annual report at the end of 1862, Meigs furnished some ideas as to the slave population of the South. Most of his observations were inserted verbatim into the annual report. In brief, he thought the slaves in areas occupied by the Union should be organized to take advantage of the slaves' ability to raise crops. To so use them freed the North of the need to raise and transport food and forage for the troops and animals. This would be done by turning over to them the land which had been "vacated by the original proprietors deeply involved in the crimes of treason and rebellion." Two advantageous results would follow: the slaves would not be tempted to emigrate to the North, and the power and influence formerly accorded landowners over the population of the South because of their wealth and property would be blunted.[59]

On January 1, 1863, the Emancipation Proclamation was signed, and the portions of the Confederacy affected delineated—all of the rebellious states except for parts of Louisiana and Virginia. Additional language was added to that in the preliminary proclamation; in part, freed slaves were enjoined "to abstain from all violence, unless in necessary self-defense." Those freed, of suitable condition, would be received into the armed service of the United States. And, in fact, at the end of the war more than 10 percent of the Union armed forces were made up of black men.[60]

Meigs had long anticipated the use of freed slaves or revolting slaves as a Union weapon. In November 1862 he told his father of a company of 64 black soldiers going on a foray in Georgia and coming back 156 in number having given arms to those joining them. He speculated that if 64,000 were sent out they might come back as 150,000. The use of black troops was a "dark & threatening cloud which will burst in a tempest overthrowing Jeff Davis & his white 'nation.'"[61]

Jefferson Davis, in his message to the Confederate Congress dated January 12, 1863, thought the admonition to slaves to "abstain from all violence, unless in necessary self-defense" was designed for a contrary result—it encouraged "a general assassination of [the slaves'] masters." He proposed that the Confederacy strike back. He wanted to "deliver to the several State authorities all commissioned officers of the United States that may hereafter be captured by our forces in any of the States embraced in the proclamation, that they may be dealt with in accordance with the laws of those States providing for the punishment of criminals engaged in exciting servile insurrection." So long as the North had many Confederate officers in their hands this proposition was nothing more than bluster just as was Davis' threat to hang Major General Benjamin Butler, if captured, because of alleged atrocities occurring in his administration of captured New Orleans.[62]

The Emancipation Proclamation was not warmly received throughout the North. Illinois' state legislature resolved on January 7, 1863:

> [T]he emancipation proclamation...is as unwarrantable in military as in civil law; a gigantic usurpation, at once converting the war, professedly commenced by the administration for the vindication of the authority of the constitution, into the crusade for the sudden, unconditional and violent liberation of 3,000,000 negro slaves; a result which would not only be a total subversion of the Federal Union but a revolution in the social organization of the Southern States...the present and far-reaching consequences of which to both races cannot be contemplated without the most dismal foreboding of horror and dismay. The proclamation invites servile insurrection as an element in this emancipation crusade—a means of warfare, the inhumanity and diabolism of which are without example in civilized warfare, and which we denounce, and which the civilized world will denounce, as an ineffaceable disgrace to the American people.[63]

Illinois had earlier, in response to Grant's advance into the South, put into its constitution a prohibition against Negroes immigrating into the state. To some extent the issuance of the preliminary Emancipation Proclamation in September may have influenced the November 1862 congressional elections which almost took away control of the House from the Republicans.[64]

Chapter 19
1862–1863—In the West

In the West, Fremont had been removed (November 1861), and Missouri was protected from a major Southern incursion by the battle of Pea Ridge in northwest Arkansas (March 1862). Major General Henry Halleck, who relieved Fremont, wanted to join the Union forces commanded by himself and Major General Don Carlos Buell for a push down the Tennessee and Cumberland Rivers into the heart of the Confederacy. Halleck's concept was opposed by Buell, in command of the Department of the Ohio, who was headquartered in Louisville, Kentucky. Buell wanted to proceed separately south along the Louisville and Nashville Railroad to Nashville.[1]

Brigadier General Ulysses S. Grant's victories at Forts Henry and Donelson in February 1862 opened up the Tennessee and Cumberland Rivers giving credibility to Halleck's plan. But, at the same time, it allowed Buell to follow through on his approach. Grant threatened the west flank and rear of General Albert Sydney Johnston's army causing him to change the northern-most Confederate defensive line from one extending from Columbus, Kentucky, on the Mississippi River, to Bowling Green, Kentucky, to a line going from Memphis to Chattanooga, Tennessee, between which the Memphis and Charleston Railroad ran. This withdrawal yielded to the Union most of Tennessee.[2]

As Johnston abandoned Bowling Green and Nashville, Tennessee, Buell marched his army from Louisville to Nashville. In February 1862 Stanton, exasperated by the lack of offensive action by either McClellan or Buell, was inclined to put Halleck in charge of all forces in the West. This happened on March 11, 1862; Lincoln relieved McClellan as general in chief, and put Halleck in charge of all forces west of a north-south line through Knoxville, Tennessee.[3]

Grant, having moved south on the Tennessee River after the fall of Henry and Donelson, was situated at Pittsburg Landing, near the Tennessee-Mississippi state boundary, with about 43,000 troops in mid-March

1862, waiting to be joined by Buell's army of a like number coming from Nashville. The next objective was Corinth, Mississippi, Johnston's major base after his retreat from Kentucky and Tennessee. At Corinth important rail junctions connected the Mississippi Valley, the Gulf Coast, and the eastern Confederate states.[4]

Johnston, with slightly more men than Grant, wanted to fight Grant before Buell joined him. Consequently, he struck Grant on April 6 for the battle of Shiloh (or Pittsburg Landing). By a close margin, given by the timely arrival of some of Buell's forces, Grant was able to hold on, and the next day, with additional troops from Buell, he launched a counterattack that defeated the Confederates. The Rebel loss was exacerbated by a fatal wound to Johnston. Casualties were high on both sides and shocked the country, North and South. Grant, with a combined force of about 62,000, after some of Buell's forces joined with him, had 1,754 killed, 8,408 wounded, and 2,885 missing, a total of 13,047 casualties. Major General Pierre Beauregard, who took over with the death of Johnston, only had about 40,000 men, of whom, 1,723 were killed, 8,012 wounded, and 959 were missing for a total of 10,694.[5]

Criticism settled on Grant for the battle of Shiloh since his army had been surprised by Johnston's April 6 attack. Halleck demoted Grant and proceeded to take to the field after Shiloh; he ponderously moved combined forces (the Armies of the Tennessee (Grant), the Ohio (Buell), and the Mississippi (Pope)) toward Corinth, some 20 miles southwest of Shiloh.[6] He arrived in front of Corinth on May 25 ready to bombard the city when Beauregard, who had only been able to muster about 53,000 men, compared to Halleck's 110,000, decided to retreat to Tupelo, Mississippi, about 52 miles south of Corinth on the Mobile and Ohio Railroad.[7]

Halleck's accomplishment was good enough to have him named general in chief on July 11, 1862, and transferred to Washington after McClellan's Army of the Potomac was forced by Lee into the small enclave at Harrison's Landing on the Peninsula. A by-product was the elevation of Ulysses S. Grant to part of Halleck's old command—he took charge of the Armies of the Tennessee and the Mississippi. Major General John Pope was also transferred to the East following the advance on Corinth and ended up in command of the Army of Virginia.[8]

When Meigs bragged to his father that he would not be wedded to one of the Union armies, he was correct. Supplies were needed as badly by the western establishment, over one hundred thousand strong, as they were by the Army of the Potomac with well over one hundred thousand. Likewise, demands were being made for supplies for Union forces located around the perimeter of the Confederacy. The feats of the quartermasters to keep everyone happy, or reasonably so, are on the same high level as those of the industrial and agrarian bases of the North to provide the supplies. When compared with how the South had to scrape and search for minimal supplies, the accomplishments of the Southern armies, without the first-class logistical support Meigs supplied, must be admired.

Not only the Eastern armies swelled the casualty lists in the last half of 1862. The West did its part.

After Beauregard's retreat to Tupelo, Mississippi, in May, the South had to decide what to do. It needed an initiative. In the preceding nine months Kentucky had gone with the Union, much of Tennessee was conquered, minor incursions were made into the northern parts of Mississippi and Alabama, and New Orleans was gone.

When Beauregard became ill, command of all Southern forces between Virginia and the Mississippi River was given over to General Braxton Bragg. This occurred in mid-July 1862. The forces headquartered in Tupelo had been increased by bringing scattered units into its sway, and, by the end of June, Bragg had about 45,000 men under arms. The more than one hundred thousand Yankees to the north of Tupelo made an advance in that direction unappealing.[9]

Bragg's initiative was a reactive one. The North wanted Chattanooga and nearby Cleveland, Tennessee, both important railroad junctions about two hundred miles east of Corinth. On June 11 Halleck released Buell and the Army of the Ohio to move along the Memphis and Charleston Railroad which ran through Corinth to Chattanooga and beyond. The objectives were Chattanooga and Cleveland. Bragg decided to hold these places.[10]

On June 27 he transferred a division from Tupelo to Chattanooga, and, as the North reduced its army at Corinth, Bragg decided to race Buell for control of Chattanooga. Buell lost the race, albeit he started well before Bragg, because Buell was ordered to repair the railroad as he proceeded. Southern marauders tore up the track about as fast as it was repaired. Starting over a month later, Bragg was able to get significant parts of his army to Chattanooga first by using working railroads running from Tupelo to Mobile, Alabama, from Mobile to Atlanta, Georgia, and from Atlanta to Chattanooga—a rail distance of 776 miles compared to a "as the crow flies" of about two hundred miles.[11]

Bragg's objective, beyond Chattanooga, was to cooperate with Major General Edmund Kirby Smith's force of about 14,000. Smith was located at Knoxville, Tennessee. Smith and Bragg met in Chattanooga on July 31 and decided to make a movement into mid-Tennessee—in fact, their advance went further and turned into an invasion of mid-Kentucky. Smith had to deal with the fact that the Union held the Cumberland Gap, almost due north of Knoxville, which it had occupied on June 18. Eventually Smith decided to circle around Cumberland Gap, and to march toward Lexington, Kentucky. En route Smith fought and won a battle at Richmond, Kentucky, on August 8, and established his headquarters at Lexington.[12]

This may have been the strongest overall military position of the Confederacy during the war. Lee and Jackson were about to raise havoc with the Army of Virginia, already having stopped the Army of the Potomac in front of Richmond. But the South was using up its manpower, and the North had much more to call upon.

Buell, supposing Bragg's objective was Nashville, stationed his army so as to protect it. But, after the battle at Richmond, seeing the likely objective as Louisville, Kentucky, he hurried his army to that point. Buell was right. Bragg was headed toward Louisville. The two armies clashed on October 8, 1862, at Perryville, Kentucky, some 60 miles south and east of Louisville. A disappointment to both Smith and Bragg was the failure of Kentucky men to rally to their colors. Smith summed up the problem for Bragg: "The Kentuckians are slow and backward in rallying to our standard. Their hearts are evidently with us, but their blue-grass and fat cattle are against us."[13]

Bragg had about half the strength of the Union forces at Perryville, and, even though his casualties were less overall, the invasion of Kentucky was blunted, and Bragg and Smith returned to Tennessee.[14]

A few days before the Perryville battle, Rebel forces attacked the Union army at Corinth hoping to force it back into, and hopefully, out of western Tennessee. The combating generals were Major General William Rosecrans for the North and Major General Earl Van Dorn for the South. The forces were almost equal, around 23,000 each, and the losses were not much different. Rosecrans was able to hold his ground, so the end result of the October 3–4 fight was to keep the status quo at Corinth. Meigs attributed this result to efforts to fortify Corinth. He believed that the North was deficient in not fortifying "all important points," and that care should be taken to fortify significant railroad junctions.[15]

It wasn't enough for Union generals to win battles in the fall of 1862. For not pursuing Bragg and Smith aggressively, Buell was relieved October 24 and ultimately left the army. Rosecrans was given command of the newly designated Army of the Cumberland. Meigs looked for an improvement from the West Point graduate who had labored in the Corps of Engineers for several years before resigning his commission in 1854. He saw Rosecrans as a prudent and daring leader who would move with deliberate promptitude.[16]

Bragg's retreat took him to Murfreesboro, about 30 miles south of Nashville. Rosecrans made Nashville his supply base and challenged Bragg on December 31 with an army of about 41,000 compared to Bragg's 35,000. On the first day's fighting, the Confederates administered a drubbing to the Union, but Rosecrans stayed the course, renewed the battle on January 2, 1863, and forced Bragg to retreat. The battle of Stone's River (or Murfreesboro) cost each side dearly. Bragg's casualties were 12,000 and Rosecrans' 13,000. Meigs thought Rosecrans should be awarded $5,000 a year for life for the victory—such recognition could give incentive to other generals to act with similar vigor. Congress was too prone to pick "out faults & imperfections," and to do nothing to "strengthen & encourage."[17]

Later, when Halleck and Stanton proposed to give a major generalship, U.S. Army, to either Rosecrans or Grant, depending on who first had an important victory, Rosecrans wrote, and angered Washington, that this was an auction of military honors. Congress took an action more in keeping with Meigs' idea by giving him a "Thanks of Congress" joint resolution.[18]

Rosecrans, who Meigs outranked in the regular army, now, as a major general of volunteers in charge of a large Union army, irritated the quartermaster general. On January 14, 1863, Rosecrans wrote to Halleck saying he "must have cavalry or mounted infantry." With his mounted infantry he intended to "drive the rebel cavalry to the wall." So far so good, but then Rosecrans crossed the line; he asked Halleck to "authorize the purchase of saddles and horses," a request that should have been made of the quartermaster general. The same day the same request was made of Stanton who was also told that Rosecrans had to have "some light-draught transports, with bullet-proof boilers and pilot-houses immediately."[19]

This wasn't bad enough, it also developed that Stanton had authorized Rosecrans to mount some infantry regiments. Meigs accepted the fact that Stanton could do anything that he desired, but also wanted to let him know that coordination and use of channels was important. He got this across in a letter of January 14 to Stanton saying that he, Meigs, was "ignorant of the existence of a law authorizing the mounting of infantry in a public emergency" and asked for copies "of the authority to General Rosecrans to mount infantry, and for the Quartermaster's Department to supply the horses."[20]

Not wanting Stanton to miss the point, Meigs went on to say that he assumed Rosecrans had "made, as usual, his requisitions or orders upon the officers of the quartermaster's department...in the West" since none had been made on Meigs' office. Stressing the importance of going through the Quartermaster Department, Meigs said that if, as it appeared, five thousand horses were needed, it would "require some time to collect and forward [them], especially as the Department [was] largely in debt." He also, on the same day, asked Rosecrans upon whom requisitions had been made. Rosecrans' reply was to ask for more—he now wanted horses to mount about eight thousand infantry.[21]

Rosecrans also dismissed a quartermaster general suggestion. Meigs told him on January 15 the steps being taken to get him eight thousand horses, which would require some time, and suggested he might "seize [some] in the field of [his] operations," and asked why the infantry could not be transported in "wagons for forced marches to intercept cavalry."

Rosecrans came right back: no wagons to spare and in the narrow roads where he was they couldn't travel across the country even though they "[w]ould do well on Pennsylvania avenue."[22]

With efficiency Meigs addressed the request for bullet-proof transports. Stanton, probably after receiving Meigs' letter of January 14, referred Rosecrans request to Meigs asking that "measures be taken to provide such transports as rapidly as possible." After conferring with the navy, Meigs did not think this was something for the army to do. The navy didn't want the War Department to take iron plating for use on transports at a time when it was attempting to complete armoring gunboats. Stanton was advised on January 19 of the steps taken by Meigs. Rosecrans was told that he should "communicate with [the] naval commander at Cairo, and ask convoy for supply vessels," and the quartermasters in St. Louis and Louisville were told to protect the boilers and machinery on transports with coal and the pilothouse by bales of hay, sacks of grain or earth, and to not let any transports travel the Cumberland River without naval convoy. On operational matters, it was Meigs turn to be dismissive to Rosecrans: "Transports cannot contend with [the Rebel] forces," "[g]unboats alone can carry them through safely."[23]

Meigs' assessment of Rosecrans as one who would move with "deliberate promptitude" was, in part, borne out. He was so deliberate that he incurred the wrath of Washington. For about six months (January–June 1863) he sat opposite Bragg who was positioned near Shelbyville, Tennessee (about 20 miles south of Murfreesboro) and drained the U.S. Treasury without doing anything. Meigs was probably happy Congress had not voted him $5,000.

During this six months Rosecrans had acrimonious relations with Washington. With Halleck it was about the auction of a major generalship, and with Meigs it mainly had to do with horses. Rosecrans complained about the quality of horses he was getting. Meigs said the answer was to have good inspectors to be sure the horses purchased met specifications or, maybe, to "hang one or two bogus and bribing contractors." When the quality of the horses was improved by a good inspector, Rosecrans found he did not get horses fast enough. After several messages back and forth Meigs wrote him on May 1, 1863:

It is difficult to provide as many horses as you demand....

...You say the mounted rebels outnumber you five to one, and this I do not take to be a careless expression, for I find it repeatedly used in your dispatches to the General-in-Chief and to myself. Have they 60,000 mounted men? How do they find food for them?...I cannot but think you are mistaken in your estimate....

You report to General Halleck that you have received, since December 1, [1862,] 18,450 horses and 14,607 mules....Is not this a large supply?...The animals cost, by the time they reached you, nearly

$4,000,000....You...report that one-fourth or one-third of the horses on hand are worn out. Now, all this, it seems to me, shows that the horses are not properly treated. They are either overworked, or underfed, or neglected and abused....

...With great deference to your experience, would not the less costly mode of defending your communications from the rebel cavalry be to give them some occupation in protecting their own? One thousand cavalry behind an army will give full occupation to 10,000 in pursuit....Our armies have been ridden round time and again; our trains captured, bridges burned, communications cut, and we never succeed in destroying or capturing the force which does the damage, and never will except by fortunate accident....

The main body of the cavalry should, it seems to me, be thrown upon the rear of the enemy, to live upon the country, cut his communications, and harass the country generally; take every horse seen, good or bad; shoot all those that cannot follow, and thus put the rebels to straits while mounting your own men.

* * * * *

...Our armies, it appears to me, are encamped too much in mass....Look at the Army of the Potomac—a solid, inactive mass of men and animals for the last five months. How it has taxed the country to supply it! It has drawn nothing from the country it occupies, except wood.

* * * * *

Compel your cavalry officers to see that their horses are groomed; put them in some place where they can get forage, near the railroad, or send them to your rear to graze and eat corn. When in good order, start them, a thousand at a time, for the rebels' communications, with orders never to move off a walk unless they see an enemy before or behind them; to travel only so far in a day as not to fatigue their horses; never to camp in the place in which sunset found them, and to rest in a good pasture during the heat of the day;...never to pass a bridge without burning it, a telegraph wire without cutting it, a horse without stealing or shooting it, a guerrilla without capturing him, or a negro without explaining the President's proclamation to him. Let them go any way so that it is to the rear of the enemy, and return by the most improbable routes, generally aiming to go entirely round the enemy, and you will put Johnston and Bragg into such a state of excitement that they will attack or retreat to relieve themselves; they will not be able to lie still.

...[Your] long inactivity tells severely upon the resources of the country. The rebels will never be conquered by waiting in their front....[R]ely more upon infantry and less upon cavalry, which in this whole war has not decided the fate of a single battle rising above a skirmish, which taxes the resources of the country, and of which we have now afoot a larger animal strength than any nation on earth. We have over one hundred and twenty-six regiments of cavalry, and they have killed ten times as many horses for us as for the rebels.[24]

Rosecrans thanked Meigs for the letter, even though it had a number of errors, including the claim of the largest animal strength on earth—Russia had 80,000 regular cavalry. Finally, near the end of June through July Rosecrans advanced and maneuvered to get Bragg south of the Tennessee River.[25]

The creative thinking found in Meigs' letter makes one wonder how he would have performed as a general in the field. His ideas on choosing and handling cavalry horses were shortly after his letter adopted by the formation of a separate Cavalry Bureau and the promulgation of orders as to how the horses were to be handled. This happened on July 28, 1863.[26]

Purchases of cavalry horses were to continue to be made by quartermasters assigned to the bureau, but inspections of the horses were to be made by cavalry officers. A large, new depot in Washington (Giesborough Point) was hastily constructed by the efforts of five thousand men late in 1863. The depot was able to handle 30,000 horses by early 1864, and the bureau needed 1,500 men to run it. At the depot unserviceable horses were nurtured back to serviceable condition. Another large depot for 10,000 to 12,000 horses was in St. Louis, and temporary accommodations for four thousand to five thousand were to be established in the Indiana-Ohio area. The Cavalry Bureau also had depots in Greenville, Louisiana, Nashville, Harrisburg, Pennsylvania, and Wilmington, Delaware.[27]

An objective of the bureau was to have "greater care and more judicious management on the part of cavalry officers." The bureau was to estimate the funds it would need, but the quartermaster general had final authority on the amount allowed.[28]

Chapter 20

Fredericksburg

At the battle of Fredericksburg, Virginia (December 11–13, 1862), Major General Ambrose Burnside unrelentingly hurled infantry against Confederates lined up behind a stone wall along a sunken road at the base of Marye's Heights, a ridge above the city. The Confederate position was well covered by Confederate artillery located on ground above the road. The Union army suffered fearsome losses. Its casualties were 1,284 killed, 9,600 wounded, and 1,769 missing; the Confederates had 595 killed, 4,061 wounded, and 653 missing. Comparatively, the Union casualties totaled 12,653 and the Confederates 5,309.[1]

Burnside's stubbornness in not giving up on carrying the stone wall can be traced back to the success he had at Antietam in gaining control over an important bridge by repeatedly sending troops against well-situated Rebel positions. Before the battle of Fredericksburg he spoke with bravado to Meigs:

> Burnside says...he has met the rebel troops & has always found the troops of the loyal states drive them...& he has no fears in attacking in meeting them again. That which he most apprehends is their refusing to meet him.
>
> At Antietam...he watched the rebels & saw them move from a strong position when attacked by his regiments some wildly & in panic while had they stood bravely to their posts they ought to have repulsed his attack.[2]

Fredericksburg was a major victory for Lee's 73,000 Army of Northern Virginia which repulsed a Federal force of 114,000. But, in the long run, it was another significant drain upon the South's manpower.[3]

The congressional Committee on the Conduct of the War did not wait long to inquire into the defeat. A given from all the testimony was that Fredericksburg and the heights behind it, which was the line of Lee's dispositions, could have been occupied easily if Burnside had made his attack earlier. Major General William B. Franklin, who commanded a unit at Fredericksburg, stated: "This whole disaster...resulted from the delay in the arrival of the pontoon bridges." He continued, "[W]hoever is responsible for that delay is responsible for all the disasters which...followed." This was the same Franklin Meigs forced to give up supervision over the Capitol extension and dome. Meigs was one of the suspects.[4]

When Burnside took over command of the Army of the Potomac, it was located around Warrenton, Virginia, facing Lee's Army of Northern Virginia which was near Culpeper, Virginia, about 20 miles south and west of Warrenton. McClellan's intentions had been to proceed toward Culpeper. Meigs thought McClellan was on the right track and favored "a march to the South along the eastern base of the Blue Ridge. Keeping between the rebels & Washington was the true & effective movement. One which could by threatening to out flank Lee compel him either to give battle run for Richmond or cross into Maryland. If he gave battle [the North] had a good prospect of beating & destroying him. If he ran for Richmond [the North] held the shortest route. If he crossed into M[aryland] his fate was sealed."[5]

Burnside, with Lincoln's approval, changed the line of attack. He would take Fredericksburg which was on a rail line (the Richmond, Fredericksburg, and Potomac) almost due north by 50 miles from Richmond. An army at Fredericksburg could be supplied from Washington over surface roads leading to Washington and by water with a discharge point at Aquia Creek about 10 miles from Fredericksburg.[6]

Indigenous supplies around Warrenton were small. The armies of Pope, Lee, and Jackson had exhausted the forage. Meigs foresaw starvation in the region during the winter—"Starvation well deserved," he thought. The Army of the Potomac required five hundred tons a day, that is, one hundred carloads of food and forage daily.[7]

To reach Fredericksburg pontoons enough for two bridges were needed for passage of the Army of the Potomac from the north to the south side of the Rappahannock River. Burnside thought he had discussed this need with Halleck and Meigs at a meeting on the night of the 11th or 12th of November. Burnside sent telegrams to Washington covering the needs for his plan, including pontoon bridges, and supposed Washington would follow through. Washington followed through but not fast enough to have the pontoons at Fredericksburg when the first, large part of Burnside's army, under command of Major General Edwin V. Sumner, arrived on November 17.[8]

The pontoons did not arrive until November 22 or 23. The failure to occupy Fredericksburg and the ridges behind it before that time allowed Lee to take possession of both. It wasn't until December 11 that Burnside decided to proceed against Lee's army. With some difficulty, the pontoon bridges were positioned across the river and the army was able to take possession of Fredericksburg, but it was the attacks against Lee's army holding Marye's Heights that led to its defeat, and ultimate retreat back to the other side of the Rappahannock River on December 13.[9]

To place the blame for the Federal defeat on whoever was responsible for the pontoon bridges not being in Fredericksburg at an earlier date is not reasonable. After all, battlefield commanders must adjust their plans to changing events on a daily basis. Burnside must be blamed for what happened at Fredericksburg. He could have changed his plans and gone around Lee's well-fortified positions, or he could have recognized, during the battle, the impregnability of Marye's Heights. Burnside's decision to not change his plans is all the more mysterious when a letter he wrote to Halleck's chief of staff (Brigadier General George W. Cullum) dated November 22, 1862, is reviewed. In part he said:

> I must, in honesty and candor, say that I cannot feel that the move indicated in my plan of operations will be successful after two very important parts of the plan have not been carried out [delay in pontoons and in arrangements for provisions], no matter for what reason.[10]

The problem of the pontoons was publicly recognized about two weeks before Burnside attacked. Before the 30th of November the *New York Times* ran an article blaming the quartermaster general for not having the pontoons at Falmouth (on the north bank of the Rappahannock opposite Fredericksburg) when the Army of the Potomac arrived there. On November 30 Meigs explained to his father why he was not at fault:

> It would have hardly been wise of those in charge of the [pontoon] train to send it to Falmouth while [it] was held by the rebels before the army drove them out.
>
> Knowing that pontoons would be needed I directed the Q[uartermaster] to furnish a steamer to tow the boats down to Aquia & thus relieve the wagon train of this weight & the Engineer troop took the wagons & horses by a land march. The pontoons [in the Quartermaster] transports got there long before the wagons whose transit was delayed.
>
> None in authority will complain of the [Quartermaster Department]—on the contrary Gen B[urnside] has taken pains to express his entire contentment with the work of the Corps which probably has never been exceeded in vigor activity & success. So he told me yesterday.[11]

And, in another letter to his father dated December 7, on the same subject, he said:

> The public mind is disturbed...& goes in any groove prepared for it—for a time. It seeks some one to whom to attach the blame for delay at Falmouth. I have done my full duty in the premises....
>
> The [Quartermaster Department] does so much for the army that it is apt to be blamed if anything goes wrong but it does not march

pontoon wagon trains or artillery batteries or cavalry regiments & when they fail to reach their destination moving by land in the appointed time the [Quartermaster] is not responsible—but the commanders are.[12]

Notwithstanding the mix-up with the pontoons, Meigs still wanted the attack pushed forward telling his father "[p]ush on the columns Burnside while the northern breeze blows fresh & keen." He thought the cold weather might be demoralizing the Southern troops—he envisioned them as being "so starved with cold as to be as helpless as rattlesnakes at this season."[13]

Any bad press Meigs received may have been instigated by sutlers rankled by restraints placed on their vessels blocking the banks of the Potomac at Aquia which were in use by the army for supplying its provisions and forage. Not less than 150 to two hundred sutlers followed the Army of the Potomac. If permitted to do so, they would have had one hundred vessels offloading at Aquia Creek and nearby Belle Plain in a space hardly large enough for debarking regular quartermaster and commissary supplies.[14]

Sutlers had an important function, something akin to modern post exchanges, but could not come into a blockaded port without a permit issued by the Quartermaster Department. In addition to hampering needed operations at the debarkation points, there was the possibility the trade would be with the Rebels instead of the Yankees if the sutlers were not closely watched. Sutlers at times would arrange to have their "wagons, horses, and goods...captured and the sutler or driver paroled, with the southern value of the articles in his pockets [so as to be able] to repeat the operation." Another sutler practice was, "with aid or connivance of troops, [to] send North captured and stolen horses."[15]

In discouraging Burnside from allowing the sutlers to go to Belle Plain, Meigs laid out the drawbacks but concluded that if Burnside wanted the permits granted they would be. Sutlers were not held in high regard by quartermasters—one said, "It is always safe to reverse the rule of common law, and adjudge a sutler guilty until he prove his innocence." Confiscation from sutlers of unauthorized goods was common. Probably the ultimate in chicanery attributed to sutlers was to collude with Rebels to get sutler goods transported by the army captured and then to make a claim against the United States for indemnification for goods lost.[16]

In testimony before the Committee on the Conduct of the War Meigs gave some insight into how he operated. Referring to a telegram from Burnside's chief quartermaster asking that supplies be loaded on railroad cars and located so as to match the march of the army from Warrenton to Fredericksburg, he said, "[A]s [was his] habit [he] wrote on the back of that telegram...to give the [necessary] orders." Copies of the telegram were sent

> to the principal agents of the supply departments, to the commissary general, in regard to commissary stores, and to the chief quartermaster of this depot, whose duty it [was] to provide quartermaster's stores,

and provide the transportation for them, and to those who had charge of the repairing and running of the military railroads—General [Herman] Haupt and Colonel [Daniel] McCallum.... [He] knew the matter was in good hands, and...took it for granted that all proper preparations had already been made; and...learned on inquiry that they were ready.[17]

After the standoff at Fredericksburg, Meigs was worried. He wanted to tell Burnside things "which neither the newspapers, nor, [he] fear[ed], anybody in [Burnside's] army [was] likely to utter."[18] On December 30 he wrote him that the demands on the treasury and the increasing price of hay and grain could result in a failure of supply—"Should this happen, [Burnside's] army would be obliged to retire, and the animals would be dispersed in search of food." This was a prelude to his urging Burnside to make use of his army at the present time:

> General Halleck tells me that you believe your numbers are greater than the enemy's, and yet the army waits!...There are few men who are capable of taking the responsibility of bringing on such a great conflict as a battle between two such armies as oppose each other at Fredericksburg....Upon the commander, to whom all the glory of success will attach, must rest the responsibility of deciding the plan of campaign. Every day weakens your army; every good day lost is a golden opportunity in the career of our country—lost forever. Exhaustion steals over the country. Confidence and hope are dying....I begin to doubt the possibility of maintaining the contest beyond this winter, unless the popular heart is encouraged by victory on the Rappahannock.
>
> The Treasury fails not only to pay the troops, but to pay for the hire of the vessels and laborers employed in supplying them, and for the forage bought for your cavalry, artillery, and trains. Suppose the army broken up for want of rations and forage, what a prospect for the country!

* * * * *

> ...[W]hat is needed is a great and overwhelming defeat and destruction of [the Rebel] army. Such a victory would be of incalculable value. It would place upon your head the wreath of immortal glory. It would place your name at the side of Washington....

* * * * *

> It seems to me that the army should move boldly up the Rappahannock, cross the river, aim for a point on the railroad between the rebels and Richmond, and send forward cavalry and light troops to break up the road and intercept retreat....The result would be with

the God of battles, in whose keeping we believe our cause to rest....If any other movement promises greater or readier results, let it be adopted; but rest at Falmouth is death to our nation—is defeat, border warfare, hollow truce, barbarism, ruin for ages, chaos!...

The gallantry of the attack at Fredericksburg made amends for its ill success, and soldiers were not discouraged by it.[19]

Meigs' pessimism was based on reality. Secretary Chase made his annual report on the state of the treasury on December 4, 1862. The war was costing about $1.25 million per secular day, and revenue was about one-tenth of that amount. Chase did not think many more greenbacks should be placed in circulation—too much currency could cause "inflation of prices, increase of expenditures, augmentation of debt, and, ultimately disastrous defeat of the very purposes sought to be attained by it."[20]

Meigs passed on some further advice to Burnside. In an effort to reduce the strain on the national treasury, he wanted Burnside to forage the "country between the Potomac and Rappahannock," that is, the peninsula extending southeast from Fredericksburg. More than eight hundred square miles of generally fertile land could, perhaps, support 10,000 men and their animals. Not only would the national treasury benefit, it would also take a source of supplies from the Rebels. Meigs thought Union control over this land could be accomplished with a small force. He would take "large supplies of grain, of forage, of tobacco, of cattle, and of horses, for the support of [the Union] army" from "loyal owners by payment, and from rebels by seizure, and receipts payable after the war, on proof of loyal conduct."[21]

Burnside did not give up fighting Lee. The Army of the Potomac moved up the Rappahannock River on January 19, with the objective of going around Lee's left. The first day saw two divisions near the planned ford some 10 miles above Fredericksburg. Then the elements turned against Burnside. Rain started and continued for two days. His army was stopped by the mud:

An indescribable chaos of pontoons, wagons, and artillery encumbered the road down to the river—supply wagons upset by the roadside, artillery stalled in the mud, ammunition trains mired by the way. Horses and mules dropped dead, exhausted with the effort to move their loads through the hideous medium. One hundred and fifty dead animals, many of them buried in the liquid muck, were counted in the course of a morning's ride.[22]

The so-called "mud march" was over and the Army of the Potomac worked its way back to winter quarters opposite Fredericksburg.[23]

Meigs concluded the "war [was] gradually assuming the aspect of a long one, to be settled by exhaustion, and [that] every pressure [the North could] put upon a rebel is so much toward the end."[24]

The men in the ranks were not happy. One officer said "Little Mac would never have dreamed of hurling men against such a stronghold" only to have the response, "O, no, Little Mac would have kept you ditching till the ditches were your grave. He did not know when to order his army forward into the works of the enemy, and Burnside did not know when to call them back from inevitable disaster."[25]

There was, in Meigs' opinion, a downside to merely maneuvering with the Army of the Potomac so as to force Lee back to Richmond. Lee in Richmond could only be whipped by "cutting off [his] supplies" and thus forcing him to come out and fight. There was also an advantage in fighting Lee closer to Washington—the nearer the battle was to the Union base of supplies "the worse for [Lee] & the better for [the Army of the Potomac]."[26]

December 1862, and January 1863, were sad months for the men of armies on both sides. The battles of Stone's River (Murfreesboro), Tennessee, and Fredericksburg, Virginia, resulted in combined casualties of 43,000 without any significant change in the relative positions of the armies. But the South, with less than one-fourth the manpower pool of the North, could not stand the manpower attrition, as could the North.

Chapter 21
God's Will and More Bloodshed

The start of the new year in 1863 found Jefferson Davis in a belligerent mood. After a visit to the Confederate armies in the field, he spoke to a crowd on January 5 in Richmond. Characterizing Virginia's soil as being consecrated in blood of Confederate warriors, he said it called for "vengeance against the insensate foe of religion as well as of humanity." Their fight was not "against a manly foe," but rather against "the offscourings of the earth." To him the Union had "so utterly disgraced [itself] that if the question was proposed...whether you would combine with hyenas or Yankees, I trust every Virginian would say: 'Give me the hyenas.'"[1]

In his message to the Confederate Congress dated January 12, 1863, Davis acknowledged that there had been "frightful carnage on both sides," but drew the conclusion that the Confederacy had shown "the impossibility of subjugating a people determined to be free." He expected the war to be over during 1863.[2]

At the other capital, Lincoln had much over which to be despondent. Burnside had been aggressive as Lincoln wanted, but recklessly so. Vicksburg had not been taken so as to allow the Mississippi River to be used as a road of commerce for the North and as a barrier between Arkansas, Louisiana, and Texas and the other Confederate states. The signing of the Emancipation Proclamation was causing a schism in the North—the peace Democrats did not want to fight a war over slavery.

Meigs wrote privately to Lincoln that "[e]xhaustion steals over the country. Confidence and hope are dying.... The slumber of the army since [the attack at Fredericksburg] is eating into the vitals of the nation. As day after day has gone, my heart has sunk and I see greater peril to our nationality in the present condition of affairs than I have seen at any time during the struggle." From the quartermaster's standpoint a large army "consumes the treasure & blood & life of the country as rapidly when still as when moving & when still as it does not act upon the enemy we have no compensation for the waste." It was like having 10 men to work in your garden and having them lie abed all day—many times worse when it is a large army abed for months.[3]

To his father Meigs put on a more optimistic face: "[S]o long as our territory is clear of the enemy the North has no cause to complain of the progress of the war or to be discouraged.... [T]hroughout the South there is suffering for luxuries & even necessaries. Property & wealth are destroyed & as the great planters lose their property their money they must lose their influence. All these things [are] enfeebling [and] exhausting...the southern people who though they have borne up wonderfully must at length give up the contest."[4]

Meigs was upset that the Senate had not approved a bill passed in the House to increase the number of quartermasters—this was analogous to the biblical injunction, "[m]ake your bricks without straw say the Egyptians." Also there was a lack of recognition of the importance to the country of experienced quartermasters—higher rank and pay should be given such men. Congress gave some relief by adding 94 clerks, 30 copyists, and 6 laborers to Meigs' Washington office, each to be paid $600 per annum.[5]

Public reaction to battlefield losses had hardened. Meigs observed that a "battle is less to the public mind [in December 1862] than a skirmish was a year ago." A loss of a thousand men provoked less comment than formerly a loss of 10 did. But the death and mutilation of thousands preyed upon the minds of Lincoln and Meigs. Both North and South sought the help of God in their struggle.[6]

Lincoln's meditation on the subject posed the question as to why God should allow such suffering to go on:

> The will of God prevails. In great contests each party claims to act in accordance with the will of God. Both may be, and one must be, wrong.... In the present civil war it is quite possible that God's purpose is something different from the purpose of either party.... I am almost ready to say that this is probably true; that God wills this contest, and wills that it shall not end yet.[7]

Near the end of the war, Lincoln was still puzzled. In his Second Inaugural Address on March 4, 1865, he said it was "strange that any men should dare to ask a just God's assistance in wringing their bread from the sweat of other men's faces; but let us judge not, that we be not judged."[8]

Meigs, in a Christmas Day letter (1861), expressed his rationalization of what God was doing:

> To what does [the Almighty] intend to bring us can it be his purpose to chastise us for grievous indifference to the rights of the four millions of the oppressed who now groan under the lash. Our fathers looked upon them with pity looked to their ultimate release from bondage. We have been consenting to the southern masters policy which has been to perpetuate their bondage & extend the area directed to it.[9]

Following the failure at Fredericksburg, he told his mother "We suffer now for our sins & this generation is expiating the crimes of its fathers & its own." And, after a later defeat, to his father: "God does not intend to give us peace again until we expiate our crime against the sins of slavery until the last shackle is stricken from the wrist of the black man."[10]

On the other side, Robert E. Lee in August 1863, perhaps motivated by remorse from his losses at Gettysburg, told his men:

Soldiers! we have sinned against Almighty God. We have forgotten His signal mercies, and have cultivated a revengeful, haughty, and boastful spirit. We have not remembered that the defenders of a just cause should be pure in His eyes; that "our times are in His hands," and we have relied too much on our own arms for the achievement of our independence. God is our only refuge and our strength. Let us humble ourselves before Him. Let us confess our many sins, and beseech Him to give us a higher courage, a purer patriotism, and more determined will; that He will convert the hearts of our enemies; that He will hasten the time when war, with its sorrows and sufferings, shall cease, and that He will give us a name and place among the nations of the earth.[11]

What Meigs knew well was how to deal with Washington politics. On the floor of the Senate on January 15, 1863, the institution of West Point was attacked because of the 820 West Point-educated officers in the army at the start of the war approximately two hundred, "out of sympathy with treason," went South.[12] Senator James H. Lane of Kansas accused Meigs of being disloyal. Senator Henry Wilson of Massachusetts told Lane that Meigs was as loyal as Lane and declared:

A question has been raised here in regard to the loyalty of General Meigs, and why? It is said that he was Jeff Davis's friend, and Jeff Davis was his patron. I do not think there is anything in that. Jefferson Davis stood by General Meigs when John B. Floyd undertook to crush him. Floyd was not only a traitor but a thief, and left the Government only when there seemed nothing more for him to steal. Davis was not a thief, but a traitor to the country. I do not think any of us ever accused Jeff Davis of being connected dishonorably with money affairs, or, in the ordinary matters of legislation, to be a corrupt man; but we knew that Floyd was partial and corrupt. In the controversy which General Meigs had with Floyd, he was sustained by Jefferson Davis. He was also sustained by nearly all of us on this side of the Chamber. As to the loyalty of General Meigs, I do not think there is a man in America who has a right to question it.

General Meigs was among the first men engaged in this war who declared it to be the true policy of the Government to organize the black men of the South for military purposes. More than a year ago he expressed to me, in the strongest language, his conviction that it was the duty of the Government to use the black men of the South for the country—for military purposes.[13]

On seeing this exchange in the *Congressional Globe* Meigs rushed a letter over to Wilson:

I thank you for your remarks in the Senate.

* * * * *

...Senators forget the obligation of their high station when they allow themselves to be made, in the Senate, the mouthpiece of loose accusations against public officers.

* * * * *

Those who have published these accusations or suspicions in the Senate should present to the President the grounds upon which they rest them, or stand before the world subject to the condemnation of all patriotic, of all honorable men.

The Rebels, though so many of their leaders are blackened with broken oaths, have wit enough not to undermine their cause by public defamation or slander of their chief officers.[14]

Meigs was being put through what in the 1950s was called McCarthyism; the victim of unsupported allegations of treason. Some senators thought his letter should not be read on the floor of the Senate since he was lecturing or insulting them, some thought he was entitled to have his say. Because of the objections to reading the letter, which was read in part, the remainder was not read. Meigs sent it to newspapers which published it throughout the country.[15]

The attack on West Point may have had some merit, but overall West Point-educated officers, who in January 1863 made up about eight hundred out of 34,000 officers in the Union army, reflected glory on the institution. Many famous leaders, North and South, were West Point graduates—Meade (class of 1835), Meigs (1836), Hooker (1837), Halleck (1839), Thomas (1840), Pope (1842), Rosecrans (1842), Grant (1843), Sherman (1846), McClellan (1846), Burnside (1847), Sheridan (1853), Jefferson Davis (1828), Lee (1829), Joseph Johnston (1829), Bragg (1837), Pemberton (1837), Beauregard (1838), Longstreet (1842), Pickett (1846), and Stuart (1854). As in everything else, the North had many more West Point graduates to rely on than did the South.[16]

Of course, being a West Point graduate did not guarantee competence—witness the case of Napoleon Bonaparte Buford (1827) who Grant noticed to be nominated for major general in February 1863. Of Buford, Grant wrote to Lincoln: "He could scarsely make a respectable Hospital nurse if put in petticoats, and certain[ly] is unfit for any other Military position. He has always been a dead weight to carry becoming more burthensome with his increased rank."[17]

Meigs younger brother, Emlen, with whom he had a close relationship, who, at around age 33, was commissioned and assigned as a quartermaster in St. Louis, decided to resign his commission in April 1863. Although Montgomery was disappointed, he told his father that Emlen had "made some sacrifice to serve his country" and that he would "say no more to [Emlen] on [the] subject." Emlen had fallen in love and was separated from his fiancée.[18]

Anger was reserved for brother Henry who, in Montgomery's eyes, married a Southern cotton factory heiress who separated Henry "from his friends & family & [made] him false to his country's rights & interests." In May 1863 he told his father he wanted nothing to do with the correspondence his father tried to carry on with Henry.[19]

The Washington routine for Meigs was one of quiet work—little time for anything else. On occasion, confinement to an office and lack of exercise caused him to become discouraged. The city had become so accustomed to war that the ups and downs of the armies were taken without great emotion. No longer were Rebel flags flown within sight of the Capitol—no longer could Rebel guns be heard from the hills about Washington.[20]

The Meigs household was missing its sons, John was in his last year at West Point and was to graduate at the top of his class, the other son, Montgomery (Montie—age 16), was attending school in Philadelphia because a suitable school did not exist in Washington, and had at home two daughters, Mary, age 19, whose close friend had lost her husband at Antietam, and Louisa (Loulie—age 8) who was pampered and spoiled as the youngest family member.[21]

Mrs. Meigs' (Louisa) naval brother, Captain John Rodgers, added luster to the Rodgers' family name by leading an unsuccessful naval attack on Charleston harbor in April 1863—his ship, the ironclad *Weehawken*, took 53 hits from Forts Sumter and Moultrie. Other ships sent in by Rear Admiral Samuel Francis Du Pont also took a large number of hits, and this led Du Pont to conclude Charleston could not be tamed by the navy alone. Two months later Rodgers met and vanquished the Rebel ironclad *Atlanta*—for this the president and Congress commended him and he was promoted to commodore.[22]

Washington in the summer of 1863 was not a pleasant city. The "heat & dust & foul air...contaminated with 10,000 worn out & 10,000 good horses," was reason enough for Louisa Meigs and her daughters to go visit elsewhere.[23]

Burnside's mismanagement of the Army of the Potomac brought on a brash, colorful Major General Joseph Hooker as the new leader. A leader who Meigs saw as brave and ambitious, but no Napoleon. Hooker molded the army back into a confident, potent weapon. Lincoln worried that Hooker was bragging too much about the "perfect" plans he was going to apply to Lee. He thought the "hen is the wisest of all of the animal creation, because she never cackles until the egg is laid."[24]

Hooker was ready to make his mark at the end of April 1863. A substantial part of his 124,000-man army moved from in front of Fredericksburg westward, up the Rappahannock River, to allow him to circle around Lee's left flank. A large force remained at and below Fredericksburg, so as to create confusion over his intentions and also to strike Lee from the side and rear if he moved up the river to confront Hooker's major move. The plan was similar to what Burnside had in mind and tried to execute back in January only to be bogged down in mud. A plan much like what Meigs had urged on Burnside and passed on to Hooker.[25]

Lee followed up the river and, after Hooker had his army across the Rappahannock, was positioned to meet him. With some 60,000 men, he could not afford to let Hooker maneuver his 134,000 at will. Surprisingly, Hooker went into a defensive position. The night of May 1 Lee and Stonewall Jackson agreed upon the most successful tactical move of the war. Jackson was to take a force of about 26,000 men, march across the front of Hooker's forces, and strike Hooker's right flank. This required a march of 16 miles along back roads. Lee demonstrated in front of Hooker with about 21,000 men.[26]

Hooker missed a chance to demolish Lee's army which was split into three sections—Jackson's 26,000, Lee's 21,000, and the remainder in the Fredericksburg area. He misinterpreted Jackson's march as that of a fleeing army, and started pursuing its rear. Jackson, reaching a position to attack, did so on the afternoon of May 2. He drove Hooker's right flank back for over two miles before he had to stop to reorganize. After dark, Jackson was mortally wounded by fire from his own soldiers while reconnoitering in front of his line to plan for the next day's attack.[27]

Somewhere in the conflict, Hooker lost his bold confidence, and, after some heavy fighting on May 5, retreated back across the Rappahannock even though he still held a roughly two to one advantage over Lee. Federal casualties at Chancellorsville and from related actions totaled 17,287—1,606 killed, 9,762 wounded, and 5,919 missing; Lee had 1,665 killed, 9,081 wounded, and 2,018 missing, that is, a total of 12,764. The trouble was that 12,764 casualties was a much bigger bite out of an army of 61,000, than was the 17,287 Union casualties out of an army of over 130,000. And, in Lee's thinking, the mortal wound suffered by Stonewall Jackson was a terrible loss for the South.[28]

Meigs recognized the positive in Chancellorsville. The missed opportunities were not to be dwelt upon—they were past. And, in fact, the army was stronger after the battle than before—it was more seasoned. Relatively the North was stronger and was steadily gaining in the war of attrition. In Meigs' words, the "maniac is powerful & huge but he bleeds constantly & no new drops supply those wasting daily." He saw the anomaly of the "victims of war [who] die perhaps a few months or a few years only earlier than if they had [stayed] at home," and the fact that the world goes on. "Those whose business is not to fight have as much time, to live to eat, to enjoy the sunshine & the air as though their brothers were not in [a] daily battle front."[29]

He did not blame the troops of German heritage on Hooker's right flank who failed to hold against Jackson's attack. "Most men will run away when they are convinced that they cannot stay & the Germans appear[ed] to have been caught off their guard & to have run away before they had time to consider the situation."[30]

Meigs always worried about the size of the armies' wagon trains. He liked Napoleon's opinion of five hundred wagons for 40,000 men (approximately 12 wagons per one thousand men), and in October 1862, drafted a general order on the subject which was issued. Over time the Army of the Potomac had wagon-creep. At Harrison's Landing in 1862 there were 26 wagons per one thousand men, at Antietam 29 for one thousand, and in 1864, when Grant marched south, 33 for one thousand. The comparison with Napoleon was unfair—Napoleon was marching rapidly over cultivated country which afforded good forage—conditions not often existing for the Army of the Potomac.[31]

When Meigs learned that Hooker's army fought at Chancellorsville over an eight-day period "carrying with it all necessary supplies" and no baggage trains, he was excited. He thought, if true, the "whole character of the war" was changed much to the Union's advantage. He immediately contacted Hooker's chief quartermaster, Rufus Ingalls, and chief of staff, Daniel Butterfield. Elimination of the drag of large wagon trains, by use of what the French called "flying columns," was the subject of a paper Meigs had circulated in January 1862.[32]

Ingalls and Butterfield confirmed the "flying column" approach, but Ingalls dampened the enthusiasm somewhat. Although each soldier starts out adequately supplied, that could change rapidly. "When men become heated or fatigued, they...throw away such articles as are not imperatively needed." And when they go into action, the impulse of soldiers "to throw off all impediments...is almost irresistible." The reality was that large wagon trains should not be too far away when a battle was being fought. Carrying eight days' rations worked best when the troops were marching and not fighting.[33]

To Meigs a major flaw in the North's efforts was the lack of an overall military commander. The "Pres[ident] & the Sec[retary] of War & the General in Chief [were] a sort of advisory administrative body of ministers & the Gen[erals] such as Rosecrans Hooker Grant & Banks [did] what their special characters enable them to do with the means furnished them." An unsatisfactory arrangement. A Napoleon was needed but none was in sight.[34]

Chapter 22

1863—The South Is Sundered

More than a month after Chancellorsville, Hooker had done nothing to use the Army of the Potomac. Meigs speculated that Lee would go on the offensive. Lee could "be pardoned for despising so inactive an opponent" superior in numbers. He bemoaned the trials of the soldiers of the Army of the Potomac who had "fought bravely...[only to be] despoiled of the glory & the advantages of victory by the acts of their commanders."[1]

In anticipation that Lee might raid Maryland, Hooker proposed that, in such a case, he march on Richmond and deal the "rebellion a mortal blow." Lincoln did not think this a good idea—Lee's army was his objective, not Richmond, and if Lee should not move, Hooker should "fret him and fret him." Lincoln did not want to exchange Washington for Richmond.[2]

Hooker had a McClellan-type reaction, and said, "[I]f he could not carry out his own plans, others must give orders, and if disaster ensued his skirts would be clear, or words to that effect." When this attitude was reported to the nominal General in Chief Halleck, who later let it be known that Hooker had always reported directly to the president, Halleck apparently took the information to the president who telegraphed Hooker to clear up any misunderstandings—Halleck was in overall command, would give the orders, and Hooker would obey.[3]

Jefferson Davis' decision to invade the North was not easily reached. Vicksburg, Mississippi, was being threatened by Grant from its rear. For Vicksburg to fall would be catastrophic for the South. Davis discussed two approaches to saving Vicksburg with his cabinet and Lee on May 16 and 17, 1863. One was to strip men from Lee's army and send them west to augment the force under General Joseph P. Johnston who had been ordered to break the siege—something he reported could not be done without more men. Lee proposed an alternative approach: invade the North, hopefully get food for his army and animals, stimulate dissatisfaction with the war, and maybe even get European recognition of the

Confederacy. The increasing disparity in manpower required bold action. Some of Davis' cabinet thought such an invasion would cause Grant to withdraw from Vicksburg.[4]

In hindsight, Davis may have made a colossal error in not sending troops to save Vicksburg. The win at Chancellorsville would probably have bought time in the East. But time was fast running out at Vicksburg.

During the period June 16–24 Lee crossed the Potomac several miles northwest of the Antietam battlefield and headed for Pennsylvania. Hooker marched so as to protect Washington from attack at the head of an army which Meigs considered to be "the most perfectly equipped army of its size that ever took the field." Having Hooker in command was the president's decision and no responsibility of the quartermaster general. On June 27 the command changed—Hooker telegraphed that he could not comply with the orders received and "earnestly request[ed] that [he] may at once be relieved." The president acted the same day. Three days before one of the most important battles of the war, Major General George G. Meade took over the Army of the Potomac.[5]

Looking ahead, Meigs told the Army of the Potomac's chief quartermaster, Colonel Rufus Ingalls, to not burn 126 railroad cars that had been used to take supplies from Aquia landing to Fredericksburg. The cars were to be dumped in shallow water where they could be retrieved if Aquia was later used.[6]

An encounter between the two armies, although not critical to the ultimate showdown, created a record. The largest cavalry battle of the war took place at Brandy Station, Virginia, near Culpeper. More than 20,000 horsemen met one another. A discouraging sign for the South was the ability of the Union cavalrymen to hold their own with those from the South. Meigs found the spirit and confidence of the Union cavalry to be increased.[7]

The cavalry was the glamour service in the Civil War. Charging forth astride a noble horse beat marching shoulder to shoulder into artillery grapeshot and infantry musket vollies. Not only was it glamorous, it was relatively safe. A common taunt was "whoever saw a dead cavalryman." After 10-plus hours of cavalrymen charging one another, the North ended with 866 casualties, only 81 of whom were killed, and the South had 523 casualties.[8]

Something resembling panic set in when it became clear that Lee was moving to cross the Potomac. Pittsburgh dug trenches, New York sent 10,000 militia to Harrisburg, and Lincoln called for one hundred thousand emergency volunteers from Pennsylvania, Ohio, Maryland, and West Virginia. Pennsylvania got Stanton's agreement for the Quartermaster Department to provide uniforms for Pennsylvania's emergency troops. Meigs observed that Harrisburg was a rich area and "should place its resources at the disposal of the commanding general." The Harrisburg quartermaster was told to "not allow speculative prices. With the approval of the Commanding General" prices should be fixed and supplies compelled.[9]

Pennsylvania was the land of plenty for the Confederates. Horses, cattle, grain, and whatever else the Rebels wanted were taken but usually paid for with worthless Confederate money. Union Major General Abner Doubleday describes an instance of payback. When Confederate Brigadier General Albert G. Jenkins complained of thefts of horses from his men and demanded payment, the town of Chambersburg readily paid up with Confederate money.[10]

After Meade took over from Hooker, an unintended battle came about at Gettysburg by an escalation of a chance encounter between segments of the two armies. The Union army had a force in Gettysburg to secure control of the joinder of several roads at that point. Confederate forces, looking for a supply of shoes reported to be in Gettysburg, met up with and fought these Union forces. One thing led to another, and a bloodletting between a Union army of about 83,000 and Confederates numbering about 75,000 took place on July 1–3. Lee, fighting a well-positioned, entrenched Union army, made the same mistake Burnside made at Fredericksburg; repeated, unsuccessful efforts were made to dislodge the Yankees. The final unsuccessful effort, a charge by 12,000 soldiers, half of whom were led by Confederate Major General George Pickett, fell back, leaving half of their numbers on the field, and the battle of Gettysburg was essentially over. The cost: Union—3,155 dead, 14,529 wounded, 5,365 missing (23,049 total); Confederacy—2,592 dead, 12,709 wounded, 5,150 missing (20,451 total). Lee also had a qualitative cost—five generals dead, three captured, and eight wounded.[11]

After the war Lee expressed a positive view of Gettysburg:

> Its loss was occasioned by a combination of circumstances. It was commenced in the absence of correct intelligence.... [I]t would have been gained could one determined and united blow have been delivered by our whole line. As it was, victory trembled in the balance for three days, and the battle resulted in the infliction of as great an amount of injury as was received and in frustrating the Federal campaign for the season.[12]

Meade seemed to agree that the battle could have easily gone the other way.[13]

Spirits were high in Washington. Meigs reported to his father that the "rebels are in full retreat" and that Lee faced a destroyed pontoon bridge across the Potomac River which was rising. Ingalls told Meigs that "[f]ive thousand good cavalry horses...would give great additional results to [the] important victory." Lincoln told Halleck to be sure Meade's intent was "to prevent [Lee] crossing [the Potomac] and to destroy him."[14]

Meigs did all he could to get horses to the army. The railroads were asked to take extraordinary steps to transport the needed horses. On July 6 he had converging on Frederick, Maryland, five thousand fresh horses coming from Washington, Boston, New York, Philadelphia, Baltimore, Harrisburg, Indianapolis, Detroit, and Chicago—horses already purchased and "held in reserve at various points" for such a need. At the same time, Meigs ordered two officers to Gettysburg to "collect all property left by both armies."[15]

Nine days after the battle of Gettysburg Lee was still north of the Potomac which, from recent rains, was expected for a day or two to be a roaring flood. Meigs saw Lee as being trapped and likely to "fight desperately" like a cornered rat. Meigs never underestimated the fighting qualities of Lee's army—after Antietam, in the context of how Lee might be maneuvered into another battle, he observed: "Lee would be compelled to fight. A thing by the way which the rebels have seldom shown hesitation about." And then, after Meade let Lee get back across the Potomac on July 13 without another major battle: "That rebel army fights so hard that every time it is touched it is like touching a hot iron. Whoever touches it gets hurt."[16]

When Halleck wrote Meade on July 14 saying that "the escape of Lee's army without another battle has created great dissatisfaction in the mind of the President," Meade asked to be "immediately relieved from command." By the 28th of July Halleck framed and sent a soothing letter to Meade—the gist of the letter was that what was felt was "disappointment," rather than "dissatisfaction"—Meade was able to join in that sentiment.[17]

Despite Lee's escape, a letter from Jefferson Davis to Lee showed that the manpower pinch was hurting the South. According to Meigs, the letter showed that troops were needed everywhere, and Davis had none to send. Since the Rebels had violated their agreement to exchange prisoners by detaining Union officers, Meigs saw no obligation to release theirs. The "exchange of prisoners [was] a great evil" for the North, but a policy demanded by the people.[18]

Lee was able to retreat back into Virginia without any aggressive pursuit by Meade. Again, another hard-fought, costly battle, which essentially left matters as they had been before, but for the attrition of manpower on both sides. In the North the heavy casualties were starting to build sentiment for settling the war politically, and, in the South, the casualties were making it virtually impossible for the South to do anything other than dig in and defend its remaining territory.

The South suffered another calamitous failure in July. On the Fourth, Vicksburg fell. On July 7 one hundred guns were fired in Washington for its surrender.[19]

In Grant's opinion, gaining control of the Mississippi River was the turning point of the war. An examination of a map tells one why. Cotton country, Mississippi, Alabama, and Georgia, was great for raising revenue, that is, if there hadn't been a blockade, but it was not good at feeding armed forces of around four hundred thousand men. The trans-Mississippi states of Texas and Louisiana could give a lot of sustenance, so long as the Mississippi River was not a wall against the flow of food to the other warring parts of the country. In prewar days the South "depended on the North & upon Tennessee & Kentucky for a very large portion of [its] food," and these sources had to be replaced. Davis, in a proclamation of April 1863, tried to make the east of the Mississippi part of the Confederacy more self-sufficient. He wanted "fields [to] be devoted exclusively to the production of corn, oats, beans, peas, potatoes, and other food for man and beast; let corn be sown...for fodder in immediate proximity to railroads, rivers, and canals."[20]

To the North the river provided an outlet for the production of northwest states, such as Iowa, Illinois, Indiana, and Ohio, to the eastern markets of the Union and to foreign customers. The rail connections between these states and the East were being monopolized by the military. After the Emancipation Proclamation, it was important to accomplish something to mollify the unhappy elements in these states.

In November 1862 Grant was in charge of the Department of the Tennessee. A Confederate attempt to drive him back up the Mississippi River by attacking Corinth, Mississippi, in October 1862 failed. Grant turned his attention to Vicksburg.[21]

Grant's initial intention was to attack Vicksburg over a land route east of the river. He was thwarted when his supply lines in western Tennessee were cut by Confederate Brigadier General Nathan Bedford Forrest and 2,500 men during December 1862. The crowning blow was delivered by Major General Earl Van Dorn who, in December 1862, destroyed Grant's advance supply base at Holly Springs, Mississippi, which held over a million dollars in supplies. Meigs was aghast at the failure to fortify Holy Springs so that it could not be captured after an hour's siege.[22]

Vicksburg occupied bluffs high above the river. During the winter of 1862–1863 Grant tried a number of approaches to take it. Most of them involved approaching Vicksburg from the north on the east side of the river. Most involved prodigious efforts at constructing or clearing waterways, and all were without success. It wasn't until March 1863 that a successful plan was put in motion. Grant marched his army down the west side of the Mississippi to get below Vicksburg, and had Rear Admiral David Porter's fleet run south past the Vicksburg bluffs to aid his army to cross to the eastern bank of the river.[23]

All was well so far, but to cross the river and approach Vicksburg from the south meant cutting away from the army's supply lines. Grant decided to take the risk, and, on April 30, made an unopposed landing about 30 miles down river from Vicksburg. To draw attention from his army, Grant ordered two diversionary operations. First, Major General William T. Sherman made a faint at Vicksburg by attacking bluffs north of the city, and second, Colonel Benjamin Grierson led a cavalry force of 1,700 through the full length of Mississippi, starting about the middle of its northern boundary and proceeding through the middle of the state and then turning to the west to end in Baton Rouge, Louisiana, which was in Union hands. This trip lasted from April 17 to May 2.[24]

With 44,000 men Grant marched on Jackson, Mississippi, the state capital, near 40 miles due east of Vicksburg with which it was connected by the Southern Mississippi Railroad. The capital, defended by a relatively small force, was overrun on May 14. As Grant turned to march on Vicksburg, he was met by some of Lieutenant General John Pemberton's Vicksburg garrison, and a hard-fought battle took place on May 16. Pemberton was unable to stop Grant's advance, and by May 19 Grant was in position to assault the city. After a failed assault on May 22, he settled in for what resulted in a six-week siege of the city which surrendered on July 4—Pemberton's army consisted of roughly 30,000 men. The siege caused close to double the casualties for the North (4,910) to 2,872 for the South, but, of course, to the victor went the captives.[25]

Undoubtedly to Meigs' pleasure, Grant used the ultimate "flying column" technique. Over 20 days, starting without a wagon train, his army marched two hundred miles and collected wagons and supplies from the land through which it moved. A daring, successful campaign.[26]

Most of the 30,000 Confederate captives were paroled. Grant explained this as a way of "leav[ing] troops and transports ready for immediate service." Grant was eager to keep the pressure on the Rebels. He wanted to proceed to take Mobile, Alabama, and approach the Confederate Army of Tennessee (which was then in Tennessee) from the rear. General in Chief Halleck did not agree and took from Grant most of his army, and placed him in a defensive position with what was left. Complete control of the Mississippi was achieved five days after Vicksburg fell when the Southern forces at Port Hudson surrendered to Major General Nathaniel Banks. Banks paroled about six thousand enlisted personnel so as to not encumber his army with their care.[27]

Meigs enjoyed Mississippi's plight—a state of "special malignity" was trembling and faltering. The Rebel armies had practically abandoned it. He thought the plotters of the war "must begin to feel the horrors of defeat & approaching punishment." The North was no longer hearing of "festivities of the Richmond court." As for Charleston, which was being slowly advanced upon, he would, if in command after it was taken, "plow up its foundations & sow them with salt."[28]

He expressed anger toward Jefferson Davis who accused the Union of "cruelty & outrage." Accusations Davis knew to not be true, and made only "to excite anew the hatred which the political leaders & intriguers of the South had nursed until it exploded [into the] rebellion." Davis was not being spared by political leaders in the South. In December 1863 Governor Zebulon B. Vance of North Carolina importuned him to negotiate with the enemy. Only in this way would sources of discontent in North Carolina be quieted. The best he got from Davis was a long letter pointing out the intransigence of the North with respect to the sine qua non for settlement with the Confederacy, namely, that the Confederacy be "left alone."[29]

After Gettysburg and Vicksburg, Meigs told his father the "intolerable heat & the preparations for holding what ha[d] been gained cause[d] the armies to be still." He likened the situation to that of the anaconda after swallowing its prey—the armies were "going through the sluggish process of digestion." He saw hope for the ultimate mending of the country in the fraternization among the men of the competing armies after Vicksburg fell. He foresaw a future with the slaves and white peasantry of the South "[f]reed from the damnation of the aristocratic slaveholding class."[30]

In an August 1863 appraisal of the military situation for Seward he stated: "The rebels are a gallant people and will make a stern [?] resistance but it is exhaustion of men and money that finally terminates all modern wars, and in their case that exhaustion rapidly approaches[.]"[31]

The death of Louisa Meigs' cousin, George W. Rodgers, fleet captain and commander of the *Katskill,* caused Meigs to look philosophically at what was happening:

> Another hero has gone to rest before Charleston....
>
> And so goes on the work: one after another, the nations dearest jewels are laid upon the alter of sacrifice...Will God allow this sacred blood to be poured out upon the ground & not accept it as an expiation of the national sins; not call the authors of this bloodshed this strife this war against humanity, against the Christian brotherhood of our race to a strict account!
>
> *   *   *   *   *
>
> If the Almighty denies to use us for the humbling of the infidel emperor & his attendant soldiers He will in his own good time bring it about....
>
> Man can but live a short space on this earth. Let him do his duty & at his death comes to him the end of the world the judgment. His absence will not lose the great cause which is in the hands of his country men who are in the hands of the Almighty.

*   *   *   *   *

...[O]ur country men & our sons go in the cause of duty merrily to the slaughter. When laying in hospital, they utter no complaint.... The wounded suffer in body but are glad in heart & the maimed & scarred carry on their bodies the certificates of good conduct which compensate them for suffering & mutilation.[32]

He had some concern about Louis Napoleon of France placing his agent Maximilian in power in Mexico. But he had no doubt that in the longer term France would not pose a problem for the United States' southern border:

...[W]hen in forty years we number perhaps 60 perhaps 100 millions will any European monarch or emperor venture to [have an] intrusive seat in this continent?

* * * * *

40 years is little in the life of a nation, & whenever the proper time comes he will regard the warning, or if not a million of men will tie his adherents neck & heels & fling them into the Gulf.

* * * * *

I see a great future before us. Two fresh & vigorous nations are in the East, & the other in the West. Russia will rule the eastern as we shall rule the western continent & England & France having done their work must take their positions as subject vassal nations.[33]

On the manpower front the North was benefitting from Negro soldiers and laborers, some 82,000 in number. Meigs told his father "[t]he formation of negro regiments [was going] on & soon the Mississippi [River would] be held wherever a gun [could] be planted with well fortified negro garrisons."[34]

The South needed some good news in the fall of 1863, and it got it from northern Georgia. Major General Rosecrans and the Union Army of the Cumberland, with superior numbers, and deft maneuvering, advanced from central Tennessee to Chattanooga, near the Georgia border, over the period June 23 to September 9. At the same time, Major General Burnside and the Army of the Ohio moved down from Lexington, Kentucky, and captured Knoxville, Tennessee, in eastern Tennessee, on September 2.[35]

General Braxton Bragg, and the Army of Tennessee, with inferior numbers, did not dig in to force a battle at Chattanooga. But, as Rosecrans continued into northern Georgia, Bragg went on the offensive at Chickamauga Creek a few miles south of Chattanooga. The comparative army sizes swung to Bragg's advantage when Lee sent him a corps commanded by Lieutenant General James Longstreet which traveled some 843 miles by rail from Richmond, Virginia. The battle of Chickamauga was between a Northern army of 58,000 and a Southern one of 66,000.[36]

On September 19 and 20 Bragg attacked, and, but for the stubborn resistance of Major General George H. Thomas' command, would have routed Rosecrans' army. Thomas got the title the Rock of Chickamauga, and Rosecrans got the chance to settle his forces behind defensive lines at Chattanooga which bordered the Tennessee River.[37]

Chapter 23

The Quartermaster General Takes to the Field

Few families in the North matched that of Mary Todd Lincoln for relatives supporting the Confederacy. Four out of five brothers joined the Confederacy, three of whom died in the war. She had four sisters, three of whom were spouses of Rebels. When her brother-in-law, Confederate Brigadier General Ben Hardin Helm, died at Chickamauga, his widow stayed for a time with the Lincolns in the White House. Lincoln critics referred to Mrs. Lincoln as "two-thirds slavery and the other third secesh." As battle lines changed, families would find themselves on the wrong side of the line. After Chickamauga Rosecrans approved the passage of about 30 families through his lines since they had family members in the Confederate army.[1]

On September 22, later to be president, Major General James A. Garfield, Rosecrans' chief of staff, telegraphed Stanton that Rosecrans "could hold out at least ten days where he was," but there was a need for more men and supplies. Before the battle of Chickamauga, General in Chief Halleck, in early September, learned that Lee was sending reinforcements to Bragg and ordered Grant to send additional forces to Rosecrans. Consequently, when the urgent need for men at Chattanooga arose, three divisions under Major General William Tecumseh Sherman were on the road from Vicksburg via Memphis—they did not reach Chattanooga until mid-November in large part because they were trying to make the Memphis and Charleston Railroad, which ran from Memphis to Chattanooga, operational and had periodic fights with Confederate forces.[2]

After conflicting views were expressed at Washington meetings, on September 23 it was decided to send the XI and XII Corps of the Army of the Potomac, under Major General Joseph Hooker's command, to reinforce Rosecrans.[3]

By chance, Meigs was in the West when the Chattanooga crisis arose visiting the principal armies and supply depots west of the Allegheny Mountains so that he could issue such orders for the Quartermaster Department as might be necessary to correct "abuses and errors, and for promoting efficiency and economy in its operations." Among the alleged abuses was the delivery at Louisville of "two-year-old mules instead of three-year-old" as called for by contract. Stanton delivered news of the Louisville abuses to Meigs by telegram in a customary brusque manner: "You will take measures to investigate the matter promptly and to prevent the fraud, and bring the perpetrators to justice."[4]

Before Meigs became involved in the Chattanooga crisis, he and Stanton curtailed action by Major General Ambrose Burnside who had command of the Army of the Ohio. Burnside ordered the construction of lengthy railroad connections in Kentucky and impressment of eight thousand Negroes—supplies and payment were to be provided by the quartermasters and commissaries. He was told this was illegal, and the expenditures would not be approved or paid.[5]

While in Pittsburgh, on September 20, Meigs received a dispatch from Stanton telling him of the battle at Chickamauga and ordering him to go to Rosecrans' headquarters with all speed. Meigs immediately arranged for the forwarding of one thousand horses from Indianapolis, Indiana, and for the purchase of another one thousand to refit the cavalry and artillery of the Army of the Cumberland.[6]

On September 24, the day after the decision to send Hooker west, Stanton called on Meigs to report on the capacity of the railroads from Louisville to Nashville to transport troops, and to augment that capacity to the utmost extent over the next five days. Colonel Thomas Scott, who had resigned as assistant secretary of war in June 1862, was asked to help in this emergency, and was on his way to Louisville to try to increase the capacity. Military control was assumed over the needed railroads.[7]

An immediate reaction was a Meigs' recommendation for the construction of a railroad (Nashville & North Western) from Nashville westward to the Tennessee River—when completed, this took pressure off the railroad line from Louisville to Nashville. Since Louisville was located on the Ohio River, troops and supplies could be sent by boat from Louisville to the terminal of the Nashville & North Western Railroad on the Tennessee River and thence over the 75-mile line to Nashville. Anticipating approval, Meigs ordered iron necessary for the road to be dug up from the ground where it had been buried to hide it from Rebel raiders. The approval came, and Andrew Johnson, then military governor of Tennessee and later Lincoln's vice president, was put in charge of the construction.[8]

Meigs arrived in Chattanooga on September 25. During the trip he discovered the value of corn. "A few ears husked gave to each of [the horses in his party] a satisfactory meal & one large ear [parched] with a little salt made a fair lunch for five." At Chattanooga Rosecrans was entrenched and posed a threat to Georgia and Alabama, but supplying the army was a difficult problem needing to be solved. The magnificent wagon train of the Army of the Cumberland was still intact with "forage and subsistence for some time" in the wagons. This situation changed rapidly.[9]

Lincoln was skeptical about Hooker arriving at Chattanooga in time to help, but an outstanding feat of coordination among the involved railroads brought off a transfer over nearly 1,200 miles of some 20,000 men in about nine days.[10] By October 2, elements of Hooker's command reached Bridgeport, Alabama, the Union supply depot, about 40 miles downstream from Chattanooga, and on the railroad route between Nashville and Chattanooga, but not before the supply line from Bridgeport was struck by Rebel cavalry, several thousand strong. About 350 wagons were burned, 520 mules shot, and the rest carried off. When this happened Meigs asked Stanton to forward Hooker's wagon trains with dispatch.[11]

The manpower imbalance between Rosecrans and Bragg was remedied with the arrival of Hooker's men, but, without his wagon train and horses for artillery, Hooker was tied to the end of the railroad, i.e., to Bridgeport. Stanton responded to Meigs' message. Between October 4 and 7 the quartermasters shipped from Washington:

> 411 six-mule teams (a total of over 2,400 mules)
> 150 four-horse teams (a total of 600 horses)
> 150 two-horse ambulances (requiring 300 horses)

together with harness, wagon-masters, and drivers.[12]

The supply situation continued to disintegrate. Since Bragg's army had broken Rosecrans' direct line of supply from Bridgeport to Chattanooga (a distance of approximately 28 miles by rail or road and longer by the Tennessee River), a 60-mile circuitous road involving some "very steep, narrow, and rough" terrain was used.[13]

For a time this road was usable, during a period when "corn which remained standing upon...abandoned plantations...supplied some forage to the animals and some food to the men of the [wagon] trains." But, with rains starting early in October, the road became virtually impassable—added to road deterioration were attacks by Rebel cavalry on the wagon trains. In mid-October, when teams made it through from the railroad terminal to Chattanooga it took about 10 days.[14]

Without a line of supply, the Army of the Cumberland was doomed. Meigs reported that "animals of the [wagon] train, starved to death, lined the roadsides, the horses of the artillery died at the picket ropes or were sent to the rear when reduced to disability in the hope of recuperating them when forage could be obtained." It was not only getting from Bridgeport to Chattanooga that was a problem.[15]

The rail connection between Nashville, the focal point for supplies and men coming from the North, and Bridgeport was in poor condition. Constructed with light rail it was worn down from use by Bragg's army when it was located southeast of Nashville. Between poor rails and the efforts of the Confederates to make the line unusable, not enough supplies were coming from Nashville to Bridgeport to feed the army at Chattanooga.[16]

Rosecrans' conduct was unusual—it denied the gravity of his situation. On October 3, the day Meigs reported to Stanton that the enemy's cavalry had struck Rosecrans' supply line, Rosecrans suggested to Lincoln a grand strategy—an offer of "general amnesty to all officers and soldiers in the rebellion," an act Rosecrans thought would give the North "moral strength, and weaken [the South] very much." His grand scale thinking, at a time when he had immediate pressing problems, is reminiscent of McClellan giving Lincoln his views on non-military matters after the Seven Days' battles pushed McClellan's army down the Peninsula.[17]

On October 5 Meigs' report to Stanton reflects a deteriorating situation. Chattanooga was being shelled from Lookout Mountain and Missionary Ridge—Meigs estimated the guns were from two and a half to three miles away. Bragg also controlled the channel of the Tennessee River at the base of Lookout Mountain.[18]

On October 9 Meigs told Stanton there was danger to the continued existence of the Army of the Cumberland. "Forage grows scarce. Many horses are unserviceable and some have died.... If the artillery and ammunition horses give out the army cannot move." Meigs recognized a mistake was made in not "sending to Bridgeport grain in abundance as soon as the army retired to" Chattanooga, and directed that grain be accumulated in both Bridgeport and Nashville. Of course, getting it to Bridgeport only helped Hooker, it did nothing for the animals at Chattanooga. Furthermore, Rosecrans' troops were on meager rations.[19]

Stanton was not only receiving on-the-spot reports from Meigs. Charles A. Dana, an assistant secretary of war and a Stanton outpost with the Army of the Cumberland, found Rosecrans to be a "dazed and mazy commander" who "could not perceive the catastrophe that was close upon [the Army of the Cumberland], nor fix his mind upon the means of preventing it."[20]

Stanton ordered Meigs to return to Washington about October 10 but, on the 16th, changed his mind and told him to stay—there was a need for a "controlling and regulating mind" in the West.[21]

After receiving Stanton's message of October 16 Meigs went into action. He advised Stanton on October 16 that Hooker should get control of the river, "at least as far as the rebel batteries on Lookout Mountain [would] permit," to within five or six miles of Chattanooga. Also, Hooker should repair the road to Chattanooga so that "full supplies of rations and forage" could be gotten to Chattanooga by wagon trains. At the same time Meigs got this message to Hooker who passed it on to Rosecrans.[22]

Meigs met with Stanton and Grant in Louisville on October 17. Stanton delivered orders to Grant putting him in charge of a new Military

Division of the Mississippi which included all the forces in the Departments of the Ohio, Cumberland and Tennessee. Sherman was to head the Department of the Tennessee and Rosecrans, at Grant's choice, was relieved by the Rock of Chickamauga, Major General George H. Thomas. Burnside continued with Ohio. Meigs found Grant to be "unassuming unpretending perfectly *true*—straight forward," and said he would succeed.[23]

To Stanton nothing was as important as the movements in the West, and he told Meigs to establish his headquarters there "for nearer & personal attention to the work." Stanton had no instructions other than for Meigs "to use [his] discretion [to] help this thing through & he would put his name at the foot of a sheet of paper & [Meigs could] write over it what he would." This put in Meigs' hands "the fullest powers &...money & means of war."[24]

Grant, realizing the gravity of the situation, ordered Sherman to get to Chattanooga as soon as possible. This message reached Sherman on October 27 by messenger who floated down the Tennessee River and over the Muscle Shoals which blocked navigation up the Tennessee River for about 20 miles between Eastport, Mississippi, and Florence, Alabama.[25]

On October 20 Rear Admiral David Porter reported to Secretary of the Navy Welles on rising rivers and that Meigs knew that gunboats could convoy up both the Cumberland and Tennessee Rivers. Meigs asked Thomas Scott, who was running the trains out of Louisville, to get "hay, mules, cavalry, and artillery horses" to Nashville by using the Ohio and Cumberland Rivers.[26]

Supplying and reinforcing the Army of the Cumberland was accomplished in steps. The first goal was to assemble at Louisville what was going forward to Nashville by water and train. Nashville could, in relative safety, be reached by boats on the Ohio and Cumberland Rivers when the river levels permitted. This added to what went by rail from Louisville and permitted an early accumulation at Nashville that would, if successfully delivered at Chattanooga, take care of the supply problem.

The next steps were the most difficult. The rail line from Nashville to Bridgeport was constantly in danger of being cut, and an even larger problem was to get supplies from Bridgeport to Chattanooga.

Grant, with whom Meigs was traveling, arrived at Chattanooga October 23. On the trip they "saw many dead mules & horses by the way side" and met "many wagons with animals ready to drop from fatigue & want of proper food."[27] Grant hastily approved a plan proposed by Thomas and his chief engineer, Brigadier General William Farrar ("Baldy") Smith, to get more supplies to the troops. The plan, which worked, was to float soldiers down the Tennessee River at night, past Lookout Mountain, so that a bridgehead could be secured on the south bank of the Tennessee. The Confederates only lightly manned this area (Brown's Ferry) and were surprised by the landing. The bridgehead, once a bridge was constructed across the Tennessee, was part of a good wagon road eight miles long going from a point down river (Kelley's Ferry), which could receive ships from Bridgeport, to Chattanooga.[28]

At the same time (October 26–27), Hooker marched toward Chattanooga from the west to position himself west of Lookout Mountain so as to protect this path to Chattanooga. The route, called the "cracker line" by the troops, was beyond the ready reach of the menacing Southern army.[29]

Longstreet's troops unsuccessfully attacked Hooker the night of October 28–29, and the effectiveness of the siege of Chattanooga was greatly reduced.[30] Meigs looked over the battle area the next day and saw

> 30 brave fellows buried with head boards by their comrades & near by was a grave marked "One Reb Unknown" upon the stake bearing this inscription was placed a grey felt hat...showing where the bullet had found its way into & out of his brains.[31]

By November 2, Grant was able to report to Halleck that steamboats were regularly going from Bridgeport to Kelley's Ferry. Coal was abundant in the area as fuel. Meigs sent for coal miners to work the mines, and arranged for additional mines to be opened. The people in the Chattanooga area, who Meigs described as "simple & uncultivated ignorant but kindly," had divided loyalties. In general those living in the mountains favored the North and those in the valley split in their sentiments.[32]

Meigs worked to increase the number of steamboats at Bridgeport, and soon found that by working up some rapids they could get practically to Chattanooga and save the eight-mile wagon trip. He was also active in building fortifications and bridges. Charles Dana told Stanton that Meigs' services were invaluable.[33]

Even though the Army of the Cumberland was no longer endangered from a lack of food and supplies, the army was crippled by the loss of over 10,000 animals during the time it had subsisted, to a degree, from the supplies transported over the old road. The surviving animals were on the verge of death. Meigs reported to Stanton on October 25 that the "animals with this army will now nearly all need three months' rest to become serviceable. They should be returned to Louisville for this purpose. Hard work, exposure, short grain, and no long fodder have almost destroyed them."[34]

Once the Bridgeport to Chattanooga bottleneck was overcome, attention was directed to getting supplies and animals from Nashville to Bridgeport. The recovery at Chattanooga was slow. Meigs told Stanton on November 16 that he was at Bridgeport with ten days' rations on hand but forage was still short; he suggested, and Grant ordered, the cavalry to relocate so it could forage for itself rather than rely on the railroad. Work went forward to re-lay the rails from Nashville south. As of November 21

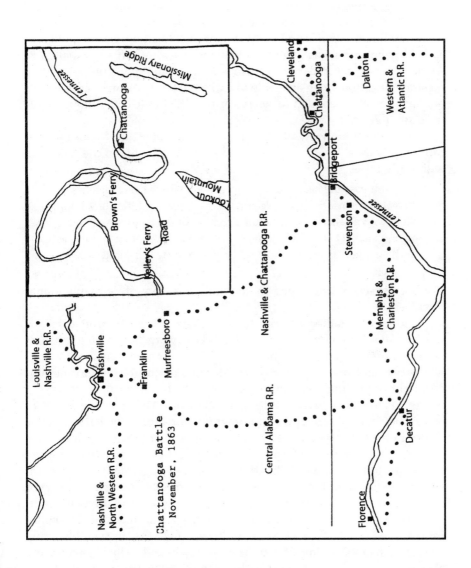

Chattanooga Battle
November, 1863

Grant found that the Army of the Cumberland was not in shape to move—to get artillery from place to place it had to borrow horses from Sherman's army.[35]

Meigs found being in the field energizing—the countryside was beautiful and picturesque, and he found himself enjoying the "relief from the weary monotony of office labor." He likened it to a hunting excursion. In early November he was living in a tent and enjoying soft autumnal days. As the nights grew colder he "had to sew up a blanket & stuff it with hay no straw or cotton being available to make [his] bed warmer [since he did not have] blankets enough to sleep warm in [his] little cot without a mattress any longer."[36]

The nighttime view of "mountains illuminated...by [thousands of] camp fires" were a continual feast to his eyes.[37] The life in the field was without luxuries:

> You pass the headquarters of a general whose battle victories or defeats have insured him a place in history & see him sitting on a camp stool with no state & no furniture except a cot & a valise living on the plainest fare. On our table & the quartermaster general ought to be as well supplied as most is now set out with bread & soup & meat & potatoes.[38]

The bucolic scene was sullied by the odor and sight of decaying animal carcasses.[39]

He told his father that he did not believe a letter to brother Henry could be sent through the lines, and he did not want "anything to do with correspondence with him. He has taken his post with rebellion & civil war. I only hope that the advances of our army may catch him & send him north out of the infamous companionship which has corrupted his good nature." Later, when he was at Ringold, Georgia, in a house which was to be evacuated, on the chance that it might be forwarded, he left a note for Henry in the drawer of a washstand telling of their father's welfare.[40]

John B. Anderson, a former superintendent of transportation for the Louisville and Nashville Railroad, who Stanton appointed to be general superintendent of military railroads south of the Ohio River at the start of the Chattanooga crisis (September 28), did not reason and act as the military leaders thought he should. The generals would have quickly bankrupted a railroad in time of peace, but they knew the urgency of acting, even at high costs, in time of war. Anderson worked hard to overcome the obstacles starting with the crisis, but came under fire from Grant and Sherman in mid-November. Sherman said there was a lack of work on the Nashville to Decatur Railroad, a second avenue from Nashville to Bridgeport, and Grant relieved Anderson from work on that line and told him to concentrate on the Nashville to Bridgeport line. Meigs took personal control over Anderson and work on the lines from Nashville.[41]

Meigs acted to get more locomotives and rolling stock. Grant, on November 19, approved giving priority to building engines Meigs had ordered. Thirty-one new engines were expected between November 22 and the end of December. Meigs directed that one thousand tons of railroad iron be sent to Anderson from Washington and had rails removed from a lateral line off the Nashville to Bridgeport line.[42]

Grant waited for Sherman's troops, which arrived at Bridgeport on November 15, before mounting an offensive. Meigs ordered 20,000 muleshoes and 10,000 horseshoes be supplied to Sherman during the trip to Chattanooga. Bragg, as a result of sending General Longstreet off to eastern Tennessee with 15,000 men on November 4, and another two brigades on the eve of Grant's offensive, and of the reinforcements to the Union Army of the Cumberland, only had about two-thirds the number of men as did Grant (70,000 to 46,200). But he occupied wonderful defensive positions. He held Lookout Mountain to the southwest of Chattanooga, and Missionary Ridge, a five hundred-foot escarpment, running northeasterly in front of Chattanooga which terminated near the Tennessee River. Chattanooga, with the Tennessee River to its back, was partially encircled by an army looking down on it.[43]

Grant's battle plan was for Hooker to proceed from the Lookout Mountain area on the southerly end of Bragg's line (Bragg's left flank), Thomas to attack Bragg's center, and Sherman to strike the Confederate right flank. Within three days (November 23–25) Grant took the high ground from Bragg who retreated back into Georgia. Bragg's defeat cost him his command, taken over a short time later by General Joseph Johnston.[44]

Meigs was witness to the battle of Chattanooga, a remarkable engagement in that most aspects were within view of Grant's headquarters where Meigs was mainly located. The face of Missionary Ridge was nearly denuded, except for many oaks, the other trees being cut for camp fires.[45]

The day after the battle he sent Stanton an unofficial dispatch describing what happened. Stanton gave it to the newspapers.[46] As reported:

> On the 23d...General Grant ordered a demonstration against Mission[ary] Ridge, to develop the force holding it. The troops marched out [and] advanced in line of battle, as if on parade....
>
> As the line advanced, preceded by skirmishers, and at 2 p.m., reached [the Union's] picket lines, they opened a rattling volley upon the rebel pickets, which replied and ran into their advanced line of rifle-pits....
>
> * * * * *
>
> ...At 3 p.m., the important advanced position of Orchard Knob and the lines right and left were in [the Union's] possession, and arrangements were ordered for holding them during the night.

The next day at daylight General Sherman had 5,000 men across the Tennessee, established on its south bank [thereby threatening Bragg's right flank.]...

Skirmishing and cannonading continued all day on the [Union] left and center. General Hooker scaled the slopes of Lookout Mountain [on the Union right] and established himself high up the mountain side, in full view of Chattanooga....

All night the point of Mission[ary] Ridge, on the extreme left, and the side of Lookout Mountain, on the extreme right [as viewed from below] blazed with the camp-fires of loyal troops. The day had been one of driving mists and rains, and much of Hooker's battle was fought above the clouds, which concealed him from [Meigs'] view, but from which his musketry was heard.[47] [Meigs credited God for hiding Hooker's troops from mortars on the top of Lookout Mountain.[48]]

The next, and final, day of the battle produced a feat for military annals—on top of the five hundred-foot Missionary Ridge "forty pieces of artillery, and no one knew how many muskets, stood ready to slaughter the assailants." Meigs continued:

Thomas sent out skirmishers, who drove in the rebel pickets, and even shook them in their intrenchments at the foot of Mission[ary] Ridge.

* * * * *

A general advance was ordered, and a strong line of skirmishers, followed by a deployed line of battle some two miles in length...moved rapidly and orderly forward.

The rebel pickets discharged their muskets and ran into their rifle-pits; our skirmishers followed on their heels; the line of battle was not far behind; and we saw the gray rebels swarm out of the long line of rifle-pits in numbers which surprised us, and spread over the base of the hill. A few turned and fired their pieces, but the greater number collected into the various roads which creep obliquely up its steep face, and went on to the top. Some regiments pressed on and began to swarm up the steep sides of the ridge. Here and there a color was advanced beyond the line. The attempt appeared most dangerous;...

With cheers answering to cheers the men swarmed upwards. They gathered to the lines of least difficult ascent and the line was broken. Color after color was planted on the summit, while musketry and cannon vomited their thunder upon them.[49]

Admiration as shown by Meigs, who stated "another victory [is] added to the chaplet of Unconditional Surrender Grant," was echoed throughout the North and propelled Grant into the lieutenant general rank and command over all the Union armies.[50] The casualties at Chattanooga were:

	North	South
Deaths	753	361
Wounded	4,722	2,160
Missing	349	4,146
	5,824	6,667 [51]

In evaluating the rout of the Rebels, not only the thinness of their lines must be considered, they also lacked food and supplies, as described by a Confederate private:

Our rations were cooked up by a special detail ten miles in the rear and were sent to us every three days; and then those three days' rations were generally eaten at one meal, and the soldiers had to starve the other two days and a half. The soldiers were...almost naked, and covered all over with vermin and camp-itch and filth and dirt. The men looked sick, hollow-eyed, and heart-broken.[52]

After Bragg was dislodged from Missionary Ridge, Sherman was sent to try to relieve the siege imposed by Longstreet on Burnside's Army of the Ohio at Knoxville, Tennessee. After learning of the outcome at Chattanooga, Longstreet gave up and retreated back to Virginia. Sherman's army had been under almost constant march or battle conditions since October 27, and at times men marched with bare feet.[53] But this was nothing compared to Longstreet's men. Longstreet had an open supply line but, nonetheless, was so short of basic supplies that Confederate Brigadier General E. Porter Alexander wrote the following after the war:

I recall some incidents illustrating how poorly our army was provided with even prime necessaries, although we were in our own country. We were so badly off for horse-shoes that on the advance to Knoxville we stripped the shoes from all the dead horses, and we killed for the purpose all the wounded and broken-down animals, both our own and those left behind by the enemy. During the siege the river brought down to us a number of dead horses and mules, thrown in within the town. We watched for them, took them out, and got the shoes and nails from their feet. Our men were nearly as badly off as the animals—perhaps worse, as they did not have hoofs. I have myself seen bloody stains on frozen ground, left by the barefooted where our infantry had passed. We of the artillery took the shoes off the drivers and gave them to the cannoneers who had to march.

Early in the advance Longstreet gave permission to the men to "swap" shoes with the prisoners whenever any were taken, but each man was strictly required to have something to "swap," and not leave the prisoner barefoot. It was quite an amusing sight (to us) to see a ragged rebel with his feet tied up in a sort of raw beef-hide moccasin, which the men learned to make, come up to a squad of prisoners, inspect their feet, and select the one he would "swap" with. Generally, however, the prisoners took it all very good-humoredly, guyed one another, and swapped jokes also with the swappers. It looked a little rough, but, as one of the victims said, "When a man is captured, his shoes are captured too."[54]

This description is in great contrast with the problems facing Meigs. He had to see that the ample supplies of the North were acquired at a reasonable cost, located strategically, and finally reached the Union armies.

Top quartermasters were in charge of key points on the Chattanooga supply line. Brigadier General Robert Allen, senior quartermaster in the valley of the Mississippi, transferred his headquarters from St. Louis to Louisville; Colonel James L. Donaldson was ordered from a depot in Baltimore to Nashville as the "senior and supervising quartermaster" of the Department of the Cumberland; and Major Langdon C. Easton was transferred from a depot at Fort Leavenworth to take over as chief quartermaster for the Army of the Cumberland. These were all graduates of West Point, two of whom (Allen and Donaldson) were classmates of Meigs in the class of 1836. Colonel Lewis B. Parsons, with headquarters in St. Louis, was put in charge of all transportation of supplies on the Western rivers.[55]

After the battle of Missionary Ridge, in anticipation of supplying a force to go against Johnston in northern Georgia, Meigs asked Daniel C. McCallum, the military superintendent of railroads in the East, to temporarily send whatever part of the construction corps from the eastern department that could be spared. On December 19 McCallum was ordered to proceed with the part of the construction corps to Chattanooga and to report to Meigs. This did not happen since Meigs was ordered back to Washington on December 26. For Christmas wife Louisa sent him a new uniform which he much appreciated since he "had been obliged to use the needle upon [his] trousers which had suffered in contests with hanging vines &...thick brambles."[56]

Chapter 24

A Quiet Interlude

On December 21, 1863, Grant moved his headquarters from Chattanooga to Nashville. The Army of the Cumberland, under Major General George Thomas, remained in the Chattanooga area confronting General Joseph Johnston's Army of Tennessee which had moved, down the Western & Atlantic Railroad, to Dalton, Georgia, about 38 miles south of Chattanooga.[1]

Work went on to improve the ability to get supplies from Nashville to Chattanooga. Meigs had some gunboats fitted at Bridgeport to facilitate trips from Bridgeport to Chattanooga and then on to Knoxville. The quiet nature of activities in January and February 1864 is reflected in Grant's request of Meigs for an "efficient and fearless" quartermaster to check up on quartermasters in the Department of the Cumberland. Fraud on the government was found and those relieved from duty brought to trial.[2]

Meigs was back in Washington rejecting unreasonable requisitions. He blocked a request by Thomas for 3,000 wagons, 4,000 horses, and 23,000 mules. Major General Quincy Gillmore, commanding Department of the South, was asked to reduce the use of marine transportation. "Cannot this immense expenditure be reduced with safety? The Government suffers under this drain."[3]

He also had to watch out for expenses at home. His wife and daughter Mary went to Philadelphia "for the purpose of seeking greater facilities for spending money on Mary's trousseau" than were available in Washington. Reporting to his father, Montgomery said they carried "off all the money [in the] house [which was] never abundantly furnished with that material."[4]

The marriage to Colonel Joseph Hancock Taylor, a nephew of Zachary Taylor and son of Brigadier General Joseph Pannel Taylor the Union commissary general, took place on March 30, 1864. Montgomery did not think it fitting, during a time of so much suffering, that the wedding should involve any expenditure or display that could be avoided, but, alas, the

221

"arrangements [were] ruled by the women" and beyond his control. A church wedding and reception with many people saw the couple united.[5]

When Colonel Daniel McCallum arrived at Chattanooga in January 1864, the rail connection to Nashville was not carrying enough forage for the animals there. McCallum found the Nashville to Chattanooga line to still be in bad condition—trains could "run only at the rate of 8 miles per hour" (a 19-hour one-way trip if it was uneventful) and accidents were frequent. He wanted two hundred locomotives and three thousand cars to supply an army moving south from Chattanooga with additions made as the line lengthened. "A construction corps of at least 1,000 men, under a competent head, with a full supply of tools and materials" was essential. The 70 locomotives and six hundred cars on hand in mid-January 1864 was woefully deficient.[6]

Locomotives and cars started rolling in. Before the offensive south started in May, 30 locomotives and 675 cars were added to the supply. Then, as the offensive was underway (May–September), another 89 locomotives and 1,056 cars were furnished. McCallum's needs were given priority by locomotive manufacturers to whom Stanton wrote in March 1864 explaining the military necessity. Sherman, who was to command the offensive southward against Johnston, anticipated the loss of six or more trains each month from "guerrillas and dashes at the road" which could not be prevented.[7]

Responding to a complaint by Thomas that his troops were required to work on the railroads, Meigs pointed out that

> [t]he Quartermaster's Department is expected to provide in a few weeks for military necessities a larger equipment than the railroad has ever possessed. We procure engines only by a species of impressment. The northern railroads generally have not enough for their own use, and the manufacturers have only supplied the United States by breaking contracts with railroad companies and giving us what they promised to others. This is done under military orders.[8]

As for troops working on the railroad, Meigs said that "[p]roperly organized and governed, the soldiers are not the less efficient guards for doing a few hours' work per day. Their health is better and they are better contented than when lying for weeks idle in camp, while civilians employed at high prices are toiling to accumulate supplies to enable the army to resume its activity."[9]

Anticipating future needs, Meigs wanted, as the army advanced, "that orders be given to set to work under guard all able-bodied men, black or white, civilian or military, who may come voluntarily or by capture within our lines. [Since the Union needed] every man, and it is cheaper to maintain a prisoner and guard him on the field than to send him a thousand miles to be guarded and fed and clothed in idleness, while a loyal workman must be taken from the workshop in which he is so much needed and sent, at high wages and great expense of transportation, to do the work made necessary by the destruction of our roads by the rebels.... The army should, from its own ranks and by capture, supply the labor needed." Meigs would pay all so working, including prisoners of war and impressed Negroes. An exception to forcing men to work would be deserters from the Rebel army.[10]

Meigs pushed for working prisoners of war when he was at Chattanooga in November 1863. A request to General in Chief Halleck for permission to use the prisoners for work was refused. Halleck did "not deem[] [it] expedient to employ prisoners of war on public works as laborers." Not liking this answer, when Meigs was back in Washington he wrote the editor of the *New York Times* and, asking that his name not be used, suggested that the subject was worthy of public print. Pointing out that the North had 40,000 to 50,000 prisoners of war who could be usefully employed, and that the prisoners would be more healthy and happy for the exercise—full fed in idleness they die. He surmised the only reason for this not having been ordered was "because the public mind ha[d] not yet been instructed and kn[ew] nothing of the laws or usages of war, but supposes that as a Christian nation [the North was] bound to support [the] Southern gentlemen in idleness, well fed, till we kill them with gout or inanition."[11]

In advocating the use of prisoners' labor, Meigs was extending his insistence that the prisoners in Union camps work to keep their camps in livable condition. The commissary general of prisoners organization had the questionable notion that prisoners should clean up the camps but not be required to put up fences designed to keep them penned in.[12]

A cavalry raid of four thousand, led by Brigadier General Judson Kilpatrick, was mounted from February 28 to March 2, 1864, with the object of freeing Union prisoners being held in Richmond. After getting within five miles of the city the effort was given up. A controversial question was raised with the death of Colonel Ulric Dahlgren, Rear Admiral John Dahlgren's son. The Confederacy said it found papers on Dahlgren's body indicating released prisoners were to be encouraged to burn the city and to kill Davis and his cabinet. When Lee asked Meade if such instructions were authorized by the United States, the authenticity of the documents was questioned, and any such instructions by the United States government disavowed.[13]

Depending on one's point of view, either a taunting or rewarding practice at the Union Point Lookout, Maryland, prisoner of war camp was use of a Negro regiment as guards. Particularly strange was the instance of a former slave guarding his former master. Meigs, who visited Point Lookout in March 1864, found the prisoners without regret at trying, and succeeding, to kill opposing soldiers. Their rationalization was that "they took chances of being shot themselves" and were not guilty of anything.[14]

After Point Lookout Meigs went to Fort Monroe and Norfolk where he observed that Major General Benjamin Butler, although not changing any hearts, had stopped the tongues of the Rebels. Butler was organizing black troops. At a review of a black cavalry unit of about seven hundred, Meigs said "None fell off their horses" when they charged "yelling & shouting," probably surpassing the ability of a like new white regiment. Within the next two months Butler expected to have 10,000 black troops.[15]

Except for a march and destroy mission into Mississippi launched by Sherman in February 1864, there was no major action taken by North or South in early 1864. But the South was struggling. The Confederate Congress found it necessary to ban the circulation of U.S. money within the Confederacy.[16]

A "chief part of [Sherman's] enterprise was to destroy the rebel cavalry commanded by General [Nathan Bedford] Forrest, [which was] a constant threat to [the Union] railway communications in Middle Tennessee." Another purpose was to discourage Confederate troops from interfering with the Union's use of the Mississippi River, hopefully, permitting the withdrawal of about 20,000 men from protecting the Mississippi for use in the upcoming campaign into Georgia.[17]

Sherman took a force of about 20,000 due east from Vicksburg along the Southern Mississippi Railroad to Meridian, some 125 miles from Vicksburg, practically all the way across Mississippi. The plan was for Brigadier General William Sooy Smith to come with cavalry of about seven thousand from the north, proceeding due south along the Mobile & Ohio Railroad, and to meet Sherman in Meridian. Smith was told to "disable [the railroad] as much as possible, [and to] consume or destroy the resources of the enemy along the road."[18]

Sherman met little resistance reaching Meridian on February 14 and spent five days destroying an arsenal and storehouses, and so much of the railroads going through Meridian as he could, before returning to Vicksburg. Smith never got there. He ran into Forrest and was forced to retreat incurring disfavor with Sherman which persisted even after the war—Sherman refused to "falsify history"—Smith's lack of success, according to Sherman, was a failure to follow Sherman's orders. Forrest was a threat to Union supply lines until the end of the war. As Sherman's troops marched back to Vicksburg, they were followed by about 10 miles of slaves.[19]

After Sherman's return from Meridian, he was thrust forward to a commanding position in the Union hierarchy. On March 18 he relieved Grant of command of the Military Division of the Mississippi. Grant, then in great favor with Lincoln, Stanton, and Congress, had delivered Vicksburg and saved Chattanooga over a six-month period.[20]

Congress enacted, and Lincoln approved on February 29, a law setting up the grade of lieutenant general, and, on March 2, the Senate confirmed Grant's nomination—his commission was signed March 6 and delivered by Lincoln on March 9. Meigs did not see in Grant "the high qualities knowledge & greatness which ought to combine to fit a man for the position" of general in chief, but he had seen no other man who had evidenced such qualities who had had success. After seeing Grant as a lieutenant general, Meigs found him to be the same "plain unaffected man" he had known at Chattanooga. Stanton met Grant for the first time at Louisville in October 1863, and after that often spoke of him to Meigs. He liked Grant because he "never complained, never disobeyed orders, never talked politics, never wanted what the Government could not furnish."[21]

Meade gained no favor with Lincoln after Gettysburg. Throughout the summer and fall of 1863 the Army of the Potomac was not used as an offensive weapon. Lee was willing to leave matters as they were because of the condition of his soldiers. He wrote the quartermaster general in Richmond in October 1863:

> The want of the supplies of shoes, clothing and blankets is very great. Nothing but my unwillingness to expose the men to the hardships that would have resulted from moving them into Loudoun [County in northern Virginia] in their present condition induced me to return to the Rappahannock. But I was averse to marching them over the rough roads of that region, at a season, too, when frosts are certain and snows probable, unless they were better provided [to] encounter them without suffering. I should, otherwise, have endeavoured to detain General Meade near the Potomac, if I could not throw him to the north side.[22]

Meade did not have the same excuse. His army was well supplied. According to Meigs, in February 1864, it was "in its normal state of good discipline & inactivity" and was receiving "37,000 bushels of grain & 700 tons of hay" daily—one horse or mule was fed for every man. In part he put the blame for inaction on the "public press that terrible group [which] tortures every man who by a little daring steps out of the cautious common path of mediocrity" and has the smallest stumble.[23]

On arriving back in Washington in January 1864, Meigs was prompted by the slow progress in the East to wonder if he might not have done more in a different field of service and, at times, to feel "as if the time must come when [he would] be called into the field to head some one of [the North's] great armies." This line of thought made him state he did not have enough rank for this to happen and to comment on how "the brillancy of military success" dazzled the people, Congress, and the administration whereas the efforts of his department, which made success possible, was not appreciated. He thought he had long since earned the rank of major

general and was discontented in seeing comrades with no better qualifications promoted over him. An example was William Franklin who he
had ranked at the time he displaced him as superintendent of the Capitol
extension in 1861. Franklin gave up his engineer position, went into field
commands, and was made a major general of volunteers in July 1862. In
March, Meigs asked his father to try to interest "some influential Pennsyl-
vanians" in urging Lincoln to give him a brevet promotion.[24]

Notwithstanding preparations for the anticipated struggle between
the giant armies of the war, the atmosphere in Washington in the quiet
months of 1864 was almost carnival-like. "The spirits of the people seem[ed]
to have cast off the weight which the war ha[d] laid upon society during
the past three years." Meigs explained this as a country which had "become accustomed to the war." The picture of Lincoln that appears on our
five dollar bills was taken before a large White House levee during this
period. At a soiree of the secretary of the navy were people from many
walks of life—"Senators & admirals generals & cabinet members mingl[ing]
with pretty girls & scrawny women diamonds & furs"; "Silks and cotton
mingl[ing] together in the throng." The party lasted until midnight when
the gas suddenly went out.[25]

The months of March and April found a restless Meigs. He was again
surrounded by paper work in new quarters at the Corcoran Art Building
(now the Renwick Museum) to which he moved in 1863. The marriage of
his daughter, who had returned from her honeymoon, had disrupted a
close relationship between mother and daughter with an upsetting, lonely
effect on the mother—Meigs thought she would adapt with time.[26]

The death of the head of the Corps of Engineers, Joseph Totten, who
was in that position during most of Meigs' career as an engineer, was a
sorrowful event. Stanton indicated his position would have been filled by
Meigs if he had still been an engineer. A position Meigs thought to have
"less labor & responsibility than [his] present one" but one more congenial to his tastes. Although a consummate organizer, Meigs' heart lay in
action, in building, and creating.[27]

Longing for the excitement and activity he found at Chattanooga, he
proposed to Grant and Stanton that he accompany the Army of the Potomac
as it went on the offensive. He predicted that when Grant moved out
"that it [would] thunder all round the heavens," and he wanted to be
present when the "death blow [was] given to the rebellion." The request
was denied. Stanton did not think he could be spared from Washington.[28]

Chapter 25
Pressure Everywhere

Although there may be controversy over whether Grant or Lincoln fathered the strategy of applying pressure along all fronts, and seeking to destroy armies rather than capture locations, Grant laid out implementing plans in April 1864. In Grant's words, he was going "to work all parts of the army together." The idea wasn't new—this was essentially what McClellan had in mind in November 1861, and what Lincoln ordered in January 1862. Lincoln, who worked at improving his commander in chief skills by studying books from the Library of Congress, may have read in Carl von Clausewitz's treatise On War: "Destruction of the enemy forces is the overriding principle of war." True, but the way to force an opposing army to fight was to threaten a location important enough that its fall would not be allowed without a fight.[1]

If the Federal armies were to advance into northern Georgia, a supply line, the first 151 miles of which (Nashville to Chattanooga) was through hostile territory, as would be later extensions, must be solid. The head of military railroads in the East, Colonel Daniel C. McCallum, made a report he found unpleasant but necessary in January 1864. The men who Meigs ordered to Nashville to work on the railroads between Nashville and Chattanooga were not being used; there were staggering deficiencies in the rails; and rolling stock needed to support an advance south of Chattanooga. On February 4, 1864, John B. Anderson was removed as general manager and McCallum ordered to take over. During 1864 McCallum employed, on average, 11,580 men in his operations in the West. Because these men, mostly civilians, were often in perilous circumstances there were times when "only by the force of military authority" were they kept on the job, but, generally, they voluntarily endured the inherent dangers knowing the success of the armies depended on the supply line.[2]

When Sherman took over at Chattanooga in March, he wanted a quartermaster on his staff with the same scope of authority that he, Sherman, had. Stanton told him that the quartermasters at Louisville

(Brigadier General Allen) and at Nashville (Colonel Donaldson) were not part of Sherman's staff but were "assigned to their duties by the Quartermaster-General, under the direction of the Secretary of War." On learning this, Sherman wrote, on April 6, to Meigs asking for a co-extensive quartermaster so he would not have to deal with "four independent departments, besides depot and district supervising quartermasters." Even though Meigs and Sherman came to an agreement for Allen to accompany Sherman into the field, Stanton disapproved.[3]

Sherman was not happy with Stanton's decision. He told Meigs:

> I will second any effort you will make looking to economy, and first to that end have your chiefs at the very points where they can see the causes and prevent waste. Old men as auditors can control the papers to the rear, but the causes are here. I would like Mr. Stanton to know this, my opinion.[4]

Sherman ended up with a quartermaster who did a first-class job—Langdon Easton who Meigs had brought in as chief quartermaster for the Army of the Cumberland in December 1863. After Stanton turned down the proposal for Allen to go with Sherman, Easton was made his chief quartermaster. Easton, a West Point graduate (1838), had quartermaster experience dating back to the Mexican War and had, for the first two and one-half years of the war, handled quartermaster chores for the far West from Fort Leavenworth, Kansas. By doing a good job, and being attached to a major army in major campaigns, he went from major to major general in the next 15 months.[5]

By April 12 there were plenty of supplies at Nashville—grain for 50,000 animals for the next eight months and rations for two hundred thousand men for four months; accordingly, Meigs told Sherman there should be no effort to increase supplies at Nashville since "[m]oney is needed for all purposes and should not be spent upon accumulating a surplus in Nashville." In this same letter Meigs, as a multi-dimensional person, asks for photographs of scenery around Nashville and Knoxville.[6]

Sherman was well aware of the importance of using all train space possible going south from Nashville—he wrote Allen on April 8 about "the Christian charities...perambulating [his] camps" and that, concerning the use of the trains, his "universal answer is that 200 pounds of powder or oats are more important to us than that weight of bottled piety." The immediate need was to "accumulate to the front at once as large a surplus as the capacity of the road [would] accomplish." Meigs wholly agreed. He said Sherman must "[r]esist the pressure of civilians and private donations and supplies" and use "the cars solely [for] transportation of military necessities." Troops should be marched. Sherman warned that Meigs "must make up [his] mind to heavy losses of stores [in 1864] as [the] best troops [were] at the front, and the enemy, being superior...in cavalry at all points, and having a cheap appreciation of horse-flesh, [would] make heavy swoops at [the] lines of communication."[7]

Meigs gave Sherman advice on tents. Through the use of shelter-tents, suitable for two men, half of which was carried by each soldier, the Army of the Potomac was able to have their tents up within one-half hour after stacking arms.[8]

Demands on the quartermasters were heavy during the quiescent months of January through April 1864. The major thrusts—Sherman to Atlanta and Grant to Richmond—had to have reserve supplies and adequate transportation to get those supplies to the armies as they maneuvered. In Kentucky, Tennessee, and St. Louis Meigs had experienced, energetic men to respond to Sherman's excellent quartermaster, Easton. In the East, Meigs could, and did, keep tight control over what went on. Grant also had an experienced and capable chief quartermaster in the Army of the Potomac, Brigadier General Rufus Ingalls, and in Washington Meigs relied on Colonel Daniel Rucker who commanded the quartermaster depot there from August 1861, through the war, and Colonel James Dana who was in charge of transportation in Washington for most of the war. The adjutant general's office also laid down the law as to "teamsters and other employees of the Quartermaster's Department" going to the front when required to do so—refusal to obey such an order could result in a trial before a military tribunal.[9]

May 4 kicked off Grant's plan. The Army of the Potomac, under Meade, with Grant's headquarters traveling with him, marched against Lee's Army of Northern Virginia while Major General Benjamin Butler was moving up the James River toward Richmond. About the same time, the Armies of the Ohio, Tennessee, and Cumberland, under the overall command of Sherman, proceeded against Johnston and the Army of Tennessee, and Major General Franz Sigel left Winchester, Virginia, going south up the Shenandoah Valley.[10]

Supplies were on Grant's mind. To ensure ready access to the abundance of the North, he went around Lee's right when he crossed the Rapidan River, across which the Army of the Potomac and the Army of Northern Virginia, had faced one another during the winter of 1863–1864. In this way, the Army of the Potomac was close to water supply routes under the control of the Union, rather than being dependent on lengthy rail and wagon train routes that could be intersected by Lee's cavalry.[11]

The Army of the Potomac, with 125,000 effective men, crossed the Rapidan with more than 4,000 wagons, 34,000 horses, and 22,000 mules. Only certain wagons, together with some pack animals, went with the troops—one-half the ammunition, intrenching tools, and ambulance wagons. The remainder were kept under the control of Ingalls. The troops carried on their persons 50 rounds of ammunition, "three days' full rations in their haversacks; three days' bread and small rations in their knapsacks, and three days' beef on the hoof." The supply trains had ten days' forage and ten of subsistence. The various commanders were advised no additional rations would be issued "under any pretext whatever" and to take great care to not let newspaper correspondents know the extent of the rations and forage being carried.[12]

Guarding the wagon train was a matter of concern. One step to do this was a Federal cavalry raid (May 9–25—10,000 strong, making a column 13 miles long when strung out) by Major General Philip Sheridan. The raid went all the way to Richmond, sustaining itself off Rebel land and supplies, disrupting Lee's supply line, and causing the Rebel cavalry to concentrate on Sheridan rather than Grant's wagon train. A telling loss to the Confederacy was the mortal wound suffered by Lee's head of cavalry, Jeb Stuart.[13]

Grant's continuous pressure meant continuous casualties. He occupied Lee with a series of bloody battles from the time he stepped out across the Rapidan River on May 4. At the battle of the Wilderness (May 5–7) Grant lost 17,666 to Lee's 7,500. Grant ordered his army forward by the left and, at Spotsylvania (May 8–20), lost another 17,500 with Lee's casualties of around 10,000.[14]

As Grant marched eastward a main supply and communication base was established at Belle Plain on the Potomac, slightly down river from Aquia landing, near Fredericksburg. As the army advanced, work went forward "making up for the consumption of food forage ammunition & men—replacing losses filling up the ranks & the wagons."[15] The wagon trains operated in a circuit. Supplies were taken from Belle Plain and the emptied wagons returned with the wounded.[16]

As a result of pressure from Clara Barton, who gave succor to the wounded during the war, and Senator Henry Wilson, Stanton ordered Meigs to take command in Fredericksburg to overcome a chaotic situation. On arrival he observed the sad sights of war: ambulances with freshly amputated stumps, churches and private homes filled with wounded, many lying on dirty floors without even a blanket below or above them. As of May 17 "27,000 wounded men ha[d] passed through Fredericksburg & 6,500 were there in the hospitals. Charitable women were at Belle Plain offering lemonade and otherwise giving comfort. Belle Plain also had men (20,000), forage for 50,000 animals, and food and ammunition for 100,000 men going forward."[17]

Meigs brought some order to the chaos and eliminated jolting wagon rides for the wounded to Belle Plain by having steamers come up the Rappahannock to Fredericksburg.[18]

By tactics and fighting Grant forced Lee back toward Richmond. These movements brought the armies to within 10 miles of Richmond by the time of the battle at Cold Harbor in June. Chaplain A. M. Stewart described what happened:

As to how we came here [Hanover Court House, near Cold Harbor] a volume would scarcely suffice to tell. What skirmishings and fightings—what long, long, weary marches by day and night—what countermarches, now far to the right, again away to the left—passing over hot, dusty roads, corduroy bridges, and pontoons; through mud, creeks, fields, woods, swamps, and sloughs; amid moonlight and thick darkness, showers, thunderstorms, and sunshine.

* * * * *

No matter; we are here on the south bank of the Pamunkey River, which we lately crossed on a pontoon bridge. Yes, here again on the *Peninsula*, although from another point than formerly approached. Again on *this Peninsula*, where, two years ago, we endured so much, suffered so terribly, and from whence we retreated so ingloriously. The future will tell whether this latter coming will prove more successful than the first.[19]

At Cold Harbor Grant made a bad decision. On June 3 he charged entrenched positions until some of the troops refused to go forward. In one hour Grant had seven thousand casualties compared to 1,500 for Lee. Failing in the direct assault Grant did not try further, and, after the armies more or less glared at one another for several days, Grant made the move which compelled Lee to march into the Richmond fortifications. The siege of Richmond, which lasted until the next spring, began.[20]

The move was one that could have been dangerous, but was carried off without serious challenge. With an objective of cutting Richmond off from supplies that were reaching it over the Richmond & Petersburg Railroad which was fed by the Norfolk & Petersburg, Weldon & Petersburg, and Petersburg & Lynchburg (also called the Southside) Railroads, Grant moved south and east around Richmond and Petersburg and established a new base of operations on the south shore of the James River at City Point. Grant had always seen this as a possible objective.[21]

The James River crossing is in the superlative category. The pontoon bridge, possibly, at 2,200 feet, the longest in military history, was used by "a train of wagons and artillery 35 miles long, a herd of 3,500 beef cattle, about half of the infantry of Meade's command and 4,000 cavalry." It took the army 48 hours to cross. The other half of the infantry crossed by steamboat ferries.[22]

After a fruitless assault on Petersburg on June 16 until mid-October, Grant made various efforts to break the lines of supply to Richmond and Petersburg and tried again on occasion to capture Petersburg or to break through to Richmond.[23]

By September 12 Grant had a railroad branch in place connecting City Point, a massive new supply depot at the confluence of the Appomattox and James Rivers, which he also used as his headquarters

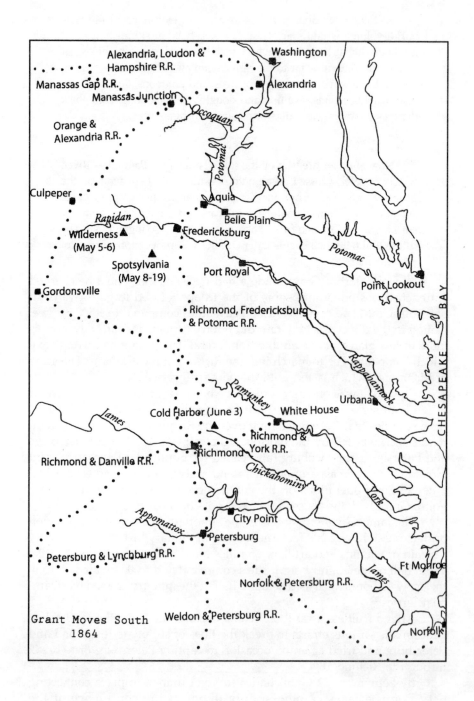

Grant Moves South
1864

for the remainder of the war, so that he could easily supply the forces in front of Petersburg. A drawback at City Point was the requirement that all supplies be brought to it by water—during the winter of 1864–1865 a problem was created when the northern ports of Philadelphia, Baltimore, Washington, and Alexandria were closed by ice.[24]

On an average day "40 steamboats, 75 sail vessels, and 100 barges...in the James River engaged in the transportation of supplies from northern ports." During this period the "[a]rmy's animals required 600 tons of grain and hay daily." Daily mail and passenger service was provided between City Point and Washington. City Point had 110 hospital buildings, and employed a "force of about 1,600 wheelwrights, carpenters, blacksmiths, saddlers, teamsters, laborers, and clerks" together with a construction corps of between two to three thousand.[25]

Grant complimented the Commissary and Quartermaster Departments for their "zeal and efficiency" in supplying the Army of the Potomac, with its ever-shifting base, for the 43 days of fighting from the Rapidan to the James River over "narrow roads, through a densely wooded country, with a lack of wharves at each new base from which to conveniently discharge vessels." He said that "the trains were made to occupy all the available roads between the army and [the] water base, and but little difficulty was experienced in protecting them." The water bases, referred to by Ingalls as "flying depots," changed as Grant went south—Aquia, Belle Plain, Fredericksburg, Port Royal (on the Rappahannock), White House (on the Pamunkey), and City Point (on the James).[26]

From mid-October until the spring offensive of 1865, Grant confined the troops in front of Richmond and Petersburg to "defense and extension of...lines and to offensive movements for crippling the enemy's lines of communication and to prevent [Lee from] detaching any considerable force to send" elsewhere. For the period June 15, 1864, through April 2, 1865, the casualties in and around Petersburg were 42,000 for the North and 28,000 for the South, and, for a similar period in and around Richmond, 15,000 for Grant and 5,000 for Lee.[27]

Butler's move up the James River with the Army of the James, which commenced about May 4, was of little help until it became part of the siege line around Petersburg. At Grant's request, Meigs and Brigadier General John Barnard, who was chief engineer of the Army of the Potomac under McClellan and was chief engineer for the Washington defenses, were sent to visit the Army of the James to "[s]ee what it had done what it was doing & [to] advise what should be done with it." They found that after some slight success Butler attacked the "advanced line of entrenchments south of Richmond" and was repulsed with severe loss. He then fell back into entrenched positions where he was safe, but also trapped by a relatively small Rebel force. A situation which earned Butler the sobriquet "Bottled Up" Butler. Meigs admired Butler's pluck and governing qualities but found him lacking in "knowledge of tactics necessary to enable him to handle troops on a battlefield."[28]

In Meigs' opinion "changes in command [would] materially improve the efficiency" of the Army of the James. But this was no time for change. With a November presidential election on the horizon, and Butler's influence within the Democratic Party, he stayed in command. However, 20,000 of Butler's army were transferred to the Army of the Potomac, and his remaining 10,000 stayed to hold on to his entrenched position.[29]

Grant wanted to constrain Lee's supplies as much as possible. To that end Sigel was to occupy as much of the Shenandoah Valley as he could since it was a storehouse Lee heavily relied on for sustenance of men and animals. Sigel quickly became a non-factor. Defeated by Confederate Major General John C. Breckinridge (former vice president to President Buchanan) at New Market, Virginia, around May 15 he was in full retreat to Strasburg, Virginia. The cadets of the Virginia Military Institute (ages 16 to 18 and 225 strong) went into military lore when they marched from VMI at Lexington, Virginia, some 70 miles south of New Market, to participate in the battle. In a heroic charge of a Union battery, the cadets had 8 killed and 46 wounded.[30]

During 1864, there were several ups and downs in the Shenandoah Valley. On May 21 Grant replaced Sigel with Major General David Hunter who, with augmented Union forces, took possession of New Market on June 1. Hunter marched southwest in the Valley and then went east through the Blue Ridge Mountains to threaten Lynchburg, Virginia, an important railroad junction. En route Hunter took some revenge against the VMI cadets by burning VMI as he passed through Lexington.[31]

Action in the Shenandoah Valley was of special interest to the Meigs' family. Lieutenant John Rodgers Meigs, the top graduate in his West Point class of 1863, was a staff officer there. The father worried. He told his father that, even "though of hopeful disposition & temperament," he felt it possible that they may have received the last letter they would ever receive from John. Since the war began, he prayed twice each day to the Almighty on John's behalf.[32]

The quartermaster general gave high marks to Hunter who did "an infinity of mischief to the rebellion by destroying depots stores mills railroads & that hot bed of insurrection the Virginia Military Institute."[33]

As the 1864 presidential election approached, casualty figures like those incurred by Grant during the summer and fall of 1864 were not helpful politically for a president caught between a Democratic peace party, headed by General McClellan, and a Republican Party with a wing looking forward to revenge on the South when it was defeated. In August Horace Greeley wrote that "Mr. Lincoln is already beaten." Not only Greeley thought this—Lincoln agreed.[34]

Meigs liked Lincoln who had "a fresh sense & honesty about him which it [was] always pleasant to come into contact with." Lincoln "honestly str[ove] to bring out a happy result the restoration of peace & union." As for his leading the nation into war, it was the washing out in blood of "the foul spot of slavery which used to be cast into [the United States'] teeth by England & France & all other Christian nations." Absent a "great statesman of high & commanding intellect character & reputation" it would be a "great misfortune to change [the] President in the midst of the war." For his part, Meigs stayed out of political entanglements as far as possible.[35]

Grant's losses were consistent with his notion that if the South could not be conquered otherwise, it would be "hammer[ed] continuously...until, by mere attrition...there should be nothing left to [it] but an equal submission with the loyal section of our common country to the constitution and laws of the land." Meigs observed that Grant "hesitated to do nothing needful even when certain that great slaughter was inevitable"; Grant had a single purpose, "vanquish the enemy" knowing that when "opposed by a splendid foe...it could not be done for nothing."[36]

Fortunately for Lincoln, shortly before the election the news from other battlefields, namely, Mobile Bay, Atlanta, and the Shenandoah Valley lifted the Northern psyche. It also brought Horace Greeley's *New York Tribune*, with a circulation of over 275,000, into Lincoln's camp.[37]

Mobile Bay, Alabama, and Wilmington, North Carolina, were the last ports where blockade runners could significantly evade the Northern blockade. Between August 6 and 23, 1864, Rear Admiral David Farragut led a combined naval and army assault on the outer fortifications of Mobile Bay. During the transit in the channel to the bay, Farragut, lashed high in the rigging of his command vessel, when warned of torpedoes, historical lore has it, shouted, "Damn the torpedoes, full speed ahead." The torpedoes were anchored mines lining the channel. When these outer defenses fell, the bay was closed to blockade runners.[38]

In the West, Sherman took the months of May, June, and half of July to force Johnston back to the outskirts of Atlanta. This was accomplished, except for the battle of Kenesaw Mountain, without direct confrontations between the full opposing armies. In general, Sherman would go around Johnston's flank and threaten the Western & Atlanta Railroad, which Johnston relied on as his line of communications and supply, and Johnston would fall back.[39]

Throughout Johnston's retreat of about 120 miles from Dalton, Georgia, to near Atlanta, Sherman had twice as big a force (roughly 100,000 to 50,000). Even though the only head-to-head struggle was the one at Kenesaw Mountain, there was continuous fighting and skirmishing which caused a drain on the manpower of each side. In May, Sherman lost 9,299 men compared to Johnston's loss of 8,638; June numbers, including

Sherman's rebuff at Kenesaw, were Union 7,530 to Confederate 3,948, a ratio which Sherman found acceptable in view of the relative strength of the armies.[40]

Johnston was successful in keeping his army intact; nonetheless, Sherman was, at the start of July 1864, threatening Atlanta, a key railroad hub and supply and manufacturing base of the Confederacy. Jefferson Davis may have made a pivotal mistake when he relieved Johnston with General John Bell Hood on July 18. Richmond was not gentle in the order relieving Johnston—in part, it states "you [Johnston] have failed to arrest the advance of the enemy to the vicinity of Atlanta, and express no confidence that you can defeat or repel him." Johnston did not take the order lying down—he responded with the observation that Sherman's army was much stronger, and that, comparatively, he held Sherman back longer than Lee had held back Grant; as for the Richmond inference that Hood was confident he could defeat Sherman, Johnston said, "Confident language by a military commander is not usually regarded as evidence of competence."[41]

Hood brought an entirely different attitude as to how Sherman should be treated. He attacked and was repulsed on July 20 (Peachtree Creek), July 22 (Decatur), and July 28 (Ezra Church)—results undesirable for the smaller army—in all, Hood lost more men in nine days (17,927) than Johnston had lost in two months. Also, he lost almost three times as many as did Sherman in those nine days (6,051).[42]

Hood gave up the offensive mode after these efforts and pulled in behind the fortifications of Atlanta. Sherman gradually swung around the city so as to cut the railroads coming into it from the south. On September 2, 1864, Hood gave up Atlanta. Just the tonic Lincoln needed before the election.[43]

Sherman was effusive as to how his supply line had been kept intact and used during the advance from Chattanooga to Atlanta:

> I must bear full and liberal testimony to the energetic and successful management of our railroads during the campaign. No matter when or where a break has been made, the repair train seemed on the spot, and the damage was repaired generally before I knew of the break. Bridges have been built with surprising rapidity, and the locomotive whistle was heard in our advanced camps almost before the echo of the skirmish fire had ceased. Some of these bridges...are fine substantial structures, and were built in an inconceivably short time, almost out of material improvised on the spot.

*   *   *   *   *

> Col. L. C. Easton, chief quartermaster, and Col. A. Beckwith, chief commissary, have also succeeded in a manner surprising to all of us in getting forward supplies. I doubt if ever an army was better supplied

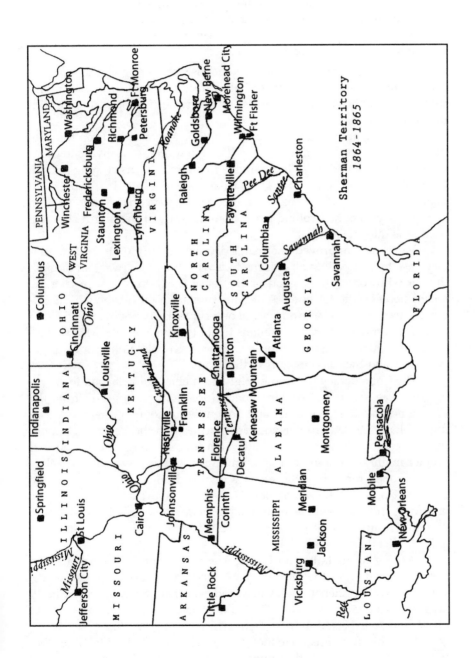

than this, and I commend them most highly for it, because I know that more solicitude was felt by the lieutenant-general commanding, and by the military world at large, on this than any other one problem involved in the success of the campaign....[44]

To Meigs' delight, brevet brigadier generalships were given to key personnel—to Colonel McCallum, military director of the U.S. Military Railroads, and the head quartermasters at Nashville (Donaldson) and with the army in the field (Easton).[45]

Sherman, at one stage, adopted a unique approach to keep the supply line full. When he was short of rolling stock on the Nashville to Chattanooga part, he told those in Nashville to not return cars coming in from Louisville and to use them to go to Chattanooga. When Louisville complained, they were told to make a similar forced loan on cars coming in to it. Soon, Sherman had rolling stock from all parts of the North showing up on the rails in Georgia.[46]

Meigs fully approved Sherman's decision to turn Atlanta into a military base by compelling all citizens to leave. "Sherman [was] an original thinker who act[ed] from good native sense & [did] not fear to take the means necessary to his end." A definite plus from this action was avoiding the need to feed a large number of non-combatants. Sherman and Hood agreed to a truce to permit Atlantans to get to a point on the Macon Railroad, and Quartermaster Easton provided such help as he could to get Atlantans and their possessions to that point.[47]

The Confederacy had some bright moments in the Shenandoah Valley after Lee dispatched Major General Jubal Early on June 12 from the Richmond area to stop Hunter and hopefully to mount a threat to Washington. Early chased Hunter not back northeast in the Valley, but rather into the mountains west of the Valley. On June 24 Meigs speculated that Hunter might be running out of ammunition and this was so. The Valley was left open for Early who rapidly marched north with about 10,000 infantry. On June 30 he was at New Market, Virginia, crossed the Potomac on July 5, and captured Hagerstown, Maryland, on the sixth. Washington reacted. Hunter was on his way and forces were coming to Washington and Maryland from several areas.[48]

Writing to his father on July 9, Meigs thought Early's advance "a curious repetition of the movements & strategy of former years"—a diversion down the Shenandoah Valley, and expected a hasty retreat by Early after a good deal of plunder. The quartermaster employees were organized, and he expected to have them armed during July 9.[49]

Early did not retreat. He took a path which could lead to either Baltimore or Washington. On the same day Meigs was speculating Early would retreat, a motley force, collected by Major General Lewis Wallace, tried to hold him in check at the Monocacy River near Frederick, Maryland. He was unable to do so, but his men fought well and caused a valuable day's delay for Early who was on his way to Washington.[50]

On the 10th of July Early was quite close to Washington which was in a state of great excitement. Help was on its way from Grant—about 10,000 troops under Major General Horatio Gouverneur Wright were embarking at City Point at 10:30 A.M. on the 10th.[51]

The morning of the 11th, Major General Alexander McCook, in command of the northern defenses of Washington, found that he only had a small number of men in place to meet any advance of Early. As the day wore on, several regiments of the Veteran Reserve Corps (invalids used for garrison duty in Washington) and detachments of dismounted cavalry reported for duty. By this time the enemy was in view but did nothing more than put out skirmishers. At 9 P.M. Meigs reported at Fort Stevens with about 1,500 quartermaster employees armed and equipped—they were at once ordered into rifle pits between Forts Stevens and Totten where they "lay upon their arms all night." An hour later 2,800 convalescents and men from hospitals arrived and were positioned in the rear.[52]

About midnight McCook received a telegram assigning commanders for intervals between the defensive forts on the northern perimeter facing Early. Meigs was given command of a line about two miles long extending from Stevens to Totten with five thousand men including some light artillery. The next day, the 12th, there was firing between the two forces but no real battle, and, when the sun rose on the 13th, Early was gone. The Union suffered about 250 killed and wounded.[53]

McCook characterized his force as a mixture of the "hale and hearty soldier, the invalid, the convalescent, the wounded, and the quartermaster's employees." Early left most likely because of the timely arrival of experienced forces which perchance landed from New Orleans and those under Wright sent by Grant from Petersburg. Wright immediately took up pursuit of Early but did not catch him before he was back across the Potomac.[54]

Meigs was proud of the part played by his department, and, while in the field, was delivered a brevet promotion to major general. On July 14 General Order No. 2 from the Headquarters Meigs' Division, signed by M. C. Meigs, Quartermaster General, Brevet Major General, relieved the employees from duty in the trenches and directed their return to Washington for resumption of their usual duties. Meigs decided that the Washington employees should continue as a military organization and attend, so far as practical, daily drills. He believed in recognizing service and told the Quartermaster's Brigade the Rebel army would "not soon again insult the majesty of a free people in their National Capital."[55]

Stanton established a cemetery near Fort Stevens. Meigs purchased an acre of ground in which Union soldiers who fell in front of Stevens were "buried with the feet of each toward a common centre, and the whole ground [was to be] enclosed by a substantial fence, and a monument [was] to be erected in the centre of the plot." This spot is at 6625 Georgia Avenue which is a continuation of Seventh Street, north of Washington. Sixty Rebels "were buried where they were found with no mark but the disturbed earth to show their resting place."[56]

Meigs' venom toward the South's aristocracy was strengthened by Early's raid. He commented to his father about complaints of Virginia Governor John Letcher over his house being burned. "Into how many families of the north & of the south too has [Letcher] not thrust fire & slaughter how many sons & brothers husbands & fathers have died through his consent.... He & such as he stink in the nostrils of all men who really comprehend the villainy of this treason."[57]

Early's demise as a Valley force originated with the appointment of Major General Philip H. Sheridan on August 7, 1864, to head the Army of the Shenandoah with the assignment of getting rid of the danger of invasion via the Valley. At 33 Sheridan, a West Point graduate (34th in a class of 49), had rapidly risen from being a quartermaster in southwestern Virginia to being a division commander at Chickamauga and Chattanooga. When Grant went east he made Sheridan head of the Army of the Potomac's cavalry corps. His cavalry raid that reached Richmond in May 1864, and which included the death in battle of Jeb Stuart, enhanced his reputation.[58]

It took a couple of months to eliminate Early from the Valley, and several hard-fought battles, but Sheridan was successful. During the first month there were cavalry and infantry skirmishes but, in the main, the opposing armies were relatively quiet. Sheridan was near Harpers Ferry while Early occupied the Winchester, Virginia, area some 25 miles to the southwest. During this time the South was benefitting from the crops of the Valley.[59]

The "working all parts of the army" strategy paid off when Lee withdrew some of Early's forces. Sheridan on learning of this went on the offensive at the third battle of Winchester (September 19) and caused Early to retreat to Fisher's Hill outside Strasburg, Virginia, 17 miles south. The Winchester battle was a companion piece to Sherman's taking Atlanta on September 2 and continued the momentum of public approval which kept Lincoln in office—a report of the battle, which described Early's army as "whirling through Winchester" with Union forces on their tail, caught the public fancy. Grant celebrated by ordering, as he had after Atlanta fell, a hundred-gun salute in front of Richmond.[60]

Early was dislodged from Fisher's Hill on September 22, and retreated south through New Market and then east out of the Valley. Sheridan undertook a laying waste campaign as he went back north in the Valley— the Valley would no longer be able to furnish the supplies Lee needed. Grant's orders were to "[t]ake all provisions, forage, and stock wanted for the use" of the Federal forces, and "such as [could not] be consumed destroy." Vouchers were to be given "for such as [was] taken from loyal citizens." Sheridan did such a good job that, at considerable expense to the treasury, quartermasters had to haul hay and oats some 40 miles to him.[61]

In Washington, following Early's retreat from its outskirts, Meigs was worried about money—he had been "carrying on the supply & equipment of the armies very much upon credit." His wife was off on an ocean visit to escape the oppressively hot weather, the work atmosphere was quiet; the confinement to the office was debilitating, but Meigs countered by early morning rides of 10 to 12 miles.[62]

Then, with everyone else, he was swept up in the excitement from the sequential Mobile Bay and Atlanta victories. He saw the end of the war with "Richmond [as] the final scene [with] fragments of the armies of rebellion...gathered round their capital...to be overwhelmed by Unconditional Surrender to Unconditional Grant." The euphoria continued with Sheridan's success in the Valley. To top it off his wife and daughters arrived back from the seashore.[63]

Suddenly the world took on a dreary cast. On the night of October 6 Stanton came to the Meigs' home and asked that Montgomery come outside. His initial thought was that Stanton had bad tidings—maybe it was that Grant had fallen, or a dreadful fate had befallen the president. Alas, it was news that 22-year-old Lieutenant John Rodgers Meigs was dead.[64]

Sheridan's personal memoirs written in 1888 described what happened:

> [A]bout dusk on the evening of October 3...my engineer officer, Lieutenant John R. Meigs, was murdered within my lines. He had gone out with two topographical assistants to plot the country, and late in the evening, while riding along the public road on his return to camp, he overtook three men dressed in our uniform. From their dress, and also because the party was immediately behind our lines and within a mile and a half of my headquarters, Meigs and his assistants naturally thought that they were joining friends, and wholly unsuspicious of anything to the contrary, rode on with the three men...but their perfidy was abruptly discovered by their suddenly turning upon Meigs with a call for his surrender. It has been claimed that, refusing to submit, he fired on the treacherous party, but the statement is not true, for one of the topographers escaped—the other was captured—and reported a few minutes later at my headquarters that Meigs was killed without resistance of any kind whatever, and without even the chance to give himself up.[65]

In the official account of his Valley campaign Sheridan said the "gallant Lieutenant Meigs, [his] chief engineer, [was a] young officer...endeared to [him] on account of his invaluable knowledge of the country, his rapid sketching, his great intelligence, and his manly and soldierly qualities."[66]

Because of the nature of the killing, Sheridan put out orders, to teach a lesson to those in the area supporting these men, for "all houses within an area of five miles to be burned." After Brigadier General George Armstrong Custer had burned a few houses in the village of Dayton, the next day he "was directed to cease his desolating work, but to fetch away all the able-bodied males as prisoners."[67]

Sheridan's version of what happened was not accepted in the South. The Southern version was that all six men were wearing waterproof ponchos, and when each group discovered the other was the enemy, they each shouted for the other to surrender, shots were fired, and Lieutenant Meigs was killed instantly. Another version, stated several years after the fact by the three Rebels, was that Lieutenant Meigs fired first severely wounding one of them, and then, return fire killed him. The Rebel who was wounded was thought by Montgomery Meigs to have been the one who killed his son, and he placed a $1,000 bounty on his head and caused him to go into hiding for several years.[68]

Words couldn't fill the loss but Stanton made an effort by calling John Meigs "[o]ne of the youngest and brightest of the military profession [who fell] an early victim to murderous rebel warfare." His funeral was attended by Lincoln, Seward, Stanton, and Halleck. John received posthumous brevets as captain and major for his meritorious service in the 1864 Valley battles of Opequon and Fisher's Hill, and his father found "much consolation in the memory of good deeds faithful service heroic endeavor [and] patriotic self-sacrifice."[69]

Chapter 26
It's Over

The calamitous war was coming to a close. The North had strong armies everywhere. The South was split at the Mississippi, and all ports, except for Wilmington, North Carolina, were under control of the navy's blockade. Nonetheless, when the Confederate Congress met on November 7, 1864, Davis bragged about the South's resistance to the much greater resources, material and human, of the North and opined that the South was holding its own in the unequal struggle because "a power higher than man ha[d] willed [their] deliverance." He shrugged off major Federal gains—in taking Atlanta, Sherman only gained control of the "narrow track of his march." Farragut at Mobile Bay only captured the "outer defenses of [the] Bay." And, even if Richmond had fallen, he said, "[T]he Confederacy would have remained as erect and defiant as ever."[1]

The bad news for the Confederacy became worse the next day when it was learned Lincoln was reelected. Lee voiced the hope after the Wilderness battle (May 1864) that if he could keep Grant out of Richmond for a few months that public opinion in the North would come around to letting the Confederacy alone. The election dashed this hope. Meigs thought a "strong decided majority [for Lincoln would] do more to dispirit the traitors than a great victory." And, when the results were known, the end of the war "must be near."[2]

McClellan's defeat (2.3 million votes for Lincoln and 1.8 for McClellan) was welcomed by Meigs.[3] When his son was killed his visceral dislike of McClellan poured out of his pen. He wrote:

Are [we] to cast [our] votes for the intriguer...the pliant tool of [New York politician and House member] Fernando Wood the corrupt & [a leader of the peace Democrats] Vallandigham the traitor or even for the general who after collecting into one vast golgotha two hundred thousand [men] held them in that pestiferous valley & petulantly & impudently whined & scolded & complained that the horror stricken people refused more victims to his shambles—beat a disgraceful retreat...&

shouted victory from a gunboat while his brave but deserted legions
were battling on Malvern Heights informing him by signal of the...fight
he should have led in person.

No No No![4]

After Atlanta (September 1864) Davis and Hood thought Sherman
was exactly where they wanted him. Over 120 miles from his primary
supply base at Chattanooga, connected by a single track railroad. Sherman
recognized his peril. Before Atlanta fell, he saw his army as being "two
hundred and fifty miles in advance of [his Nashville] base, dependent on
a single line of railroad for [its] daily food." After Atlanta fell, he knew he
could not stay there on the defensive.[5]

Davis made a speech "assuring [the Confederate] army that [it] would
make [Sherman's] retreat more disastrous than was that of Napoleon from
Moscow." On September 18 Hood started his army north, and for the next
25 days followed the Western & Atlantic Railroad back to Dalton, Georgia, tearing up the track as he went. Sherman followed him remarking
that Hood "can turn and twist like a fox...and wear out my army in pursuit." Hood did not understand Sherman. In a lengthy letter to Sherman
he set out "the terms and conditions on which he, Hood, would refrain
from burning the cotton in his line of march." Sherman's terse response
was "I hope you will burn all the cotton you can, for all you don't burn I
will."[6]

Sherman was ready for another game. To Grant on October 22:

> I am now perfecting arrangements to put into Tennessee a force able
> to hold the line of the Tennessee...and [myself] push into Georgia, and
> break up all its railroads and depots, capture its horses and negroes,
> make desolation everywhere, destroy the factories at Macon,
> Milledgeville, and Augusta, and bring up with 60,000 men on the sea-
> shore about Savannah or Charleston. I think this far better than de-
> fending a long line of railroad. I will leave General George H. Thomas
> to command all my division behind me, and take with me only the
> best fighting material. Of course I will subsist on the bountiful corn-
> fields and potato patches, as I am now doing luxuriously.[7]

Sherman was confident saying, "Where a million people live, I have no
fear of getting a share."[8]

In preparation for Sherman's arrival, Meigs ordered supplies shipped
to fill the warehouses at Hilton Head Island, a few miles up the coast from
Savannah, with additional supplies to be held afloat. But, to be ready if
Sherman came out elsewhere, supplies were also sent to Pensacola,
Florida, since his actual course would "depend upon the accidents of
[his] campaign."[9]

As Sherman prepared to leave Atlanta the city was being cleaned
out—Quartermaster Easton found this a formidable job; "more plunder

[had been accumulated] in the last two months than [he had] supposed could have been got...in six." In sending back to Chattanooga all that was not needed, a big task for the quartermasters was to be sure the railroad cars returning to Chattanooga only carried public property. Unceasing attempts were made "to get private freight, tobacco, furniture," etc., hauled.[10]

Near the end of October, Hood was at Florence, Alabama, where he was delayed for three weeks waiting for supplies and to be joined by Major General Nathan Bedford Forrest and his six thousand cavalrymen. The delay was costly. It allowed Sherman to send additional forces north to bolster a defense against what turned out to be a movement against Nashville.[11]

On November 19 Hood renewed his march north, and on the way to the destruction of his army in the next month. He did well until he reached Franklin, Tennessee, (November 30) where, irrationally, his army charged entrenched Union forces 13 times before the Yankees fell back to Nashville—this was at a cost of six Confederate generals killed or mortally wounded and total casualties of 6,252. The armies were of similar size (somewhere between 20,000 to 27,000) but the Yankees only had 2,326 casualties.[12]

Hood, aggressive as ever, chased the Union forces and surrounded them, with the Cumberland River to their back, at Nashville—the trouble was that there were more Yankees than Rebels (some 50,000–55,000 to under 30,000), including seven thousand quartermaster employees. Meigs, in rationalizing to his father why Thomas gave up much of Tennessee to Hood, noted that Hood's men were fatigued, had "eaten [their] supplies consumed ammunition & [suffered the loss of] 6,000 men in battle." His only fear was that Thomas was so well protected in the trenches in front of Nashville that he wouldn't go on the offensive before Hood slipped away. Grant had the same fear and repeatedly urged Thomas to go after Hood; in fact, he was on his way to Nashville from City Point when he learned Thomas had come out from behind his fortifications and routed Hood's army (December 15–16, 1864). The Army of Tennessee never posed a major threat again; it was shattered. Thomas was rewarded by a major generalship in the U.S. Army but had a sore feeling toward Grant who had come close to relieving him before he went on the offensive.[13]

Sherman started his March to the Sea on November 15 with a force of 63,680 men, and transportation consisting of 14,468 horses, 19,410 mules, 2,520 wagons, and 440 ambulances. The army took four days' grain, "[t]wenty days' rations of hard bread, five days' rations of soap, rice, and candles, eighty days' rations of salt" and 5,476 head of beef cattle. "The army marched by corps and on roads as near parallel to each other as could be found. Each corps had its pontoon train and each division its pioneer force, and with these organizations streams were crossed and roads repaired." Within the wagon trains of each corps, about midpoint, were empty wagons to be used for gathering forage and other supplies. Those empty wagons would be turned loose on the country and, when full, would fall in at the rear of the wagon train. Before abandoning Atlanta, anything of possible use to the Confederate war effort there was destroyed.[14]

Little resistance to Sherman's army was encountered, and on December 23 he entered Savannah and telegraphed Lincoln: "I beg to present to you, as a Christmas gift, the city of Savannah, with one hundred and fifty heavy guns and plenty of ammunition, and also about twenty-five thousand bales of cotton." During the nearly 40 days of his march he was out of touch with Washington. The only information it received of his army was from Southern papers. The North was spellbound by the suspense.[15]

The Quartermaster Department was ready for Sherman.[16] In addition to forage, rations, and ammunition waiting for him were:

Clothing.—30,000 sack coats; 30,000 trowsers; 60,000 shirts; 60,000 pairs drawers; 60,000 pairs socks; 100,000 pairs shoes and boots; 20,000 forage caps; 10,000 greatcoats; 20,000 blankets...; 10,000 waterproof blankets.

Equipage.—10,000 shelter-tents; 100 hospital tents; 10,000 knapsacks; 20,000 haversacks; 10,000 canteens; 2,000 camp kettles; 5,000 mess pans; 5,000 felling axes, two handles each; 1,000 hatchets, handled; 2,000 spades; 2,000 picks.

* * * * *

Transportation.—Wheel harness for 400 mules; lead harness for 800 mules; 10,000 pounds bar-iron, assorted; 5,000 pounds steel; 1,000 pounds harness leather; 40 sets shoeing tools and 40 extra hammers; thread, wax, needles, awls, &c., for repairing harness; 500 pounds wrought nails; 20 buttresses; 200 horse rasps; 100 large files, assorted; 50 shoeing knives, extra; 4,000 pounds manilla rope, assorted; 15,000 bushels smith's coal...; 200 extra wagon wheels; 50 extra ambulance wheels; 100,000 pounds horse and mule shoes; 10,000 pounds horse and mule shoe-nails.

* * * * *

50 extra king bolts; 500 linch pins; 200 wagon tongues; 400 extra whippletrees; 50 double trees, ironed ready for use; 100 coupling poles; 200 front hounds for wagons; 100 hind hounds for wagons; 200 mule hames, ironed ready for use; 200 mule collars; 500 wagon bows; 100 wagon whips; 1,000 open links, for repairing trace chains; 500 open rings; 100 water buckets.[17]

Included in the supplies were 150 barrels of salt for use of the animals which Meigs thought "after a long interior march, will feel the want of it." Salt was a scarce commodity in the South during the war. Without salt, meat and hides could not be preserved. Before the war about one bushel (50 pounds) of salt per individual per annum was required, much of which was imported. During the war the allotment was cut to between 20 to 30 pounds, and distribution from the salt sources was uneven since the railroads of the South were often preempted for military needs. The price per pound went from about one-fourth of a cent per pound to $5 or less depending on one's location within the Confederacy. The demand for salt led to illegal trading between North and South—cotton for salt.[18]

Meigs not only delivered congratulations to Sherman and exulted over Sherman proving "that an army can move more than twenty-five miles from a navigable river or railroad without perishing," he laid out the logistic facts that must be dealt with:

> I desire to call your attention to the difficulty, as well as the expense, of furnishing a large army with forage on the Atlantic coast. With all the exertions of the forage officer of this department, with a practically *unlimited command of money*, he has not been able to accumulate at Washington and at City Point enough long forage for the armies in Virginia to meet a few days' interruption by storm or ice. We can supply grain enough, but there is always a short supply of hay. He has agents in all the hay districts, and buys all that he can in the great markets. Still the armies complain of short allowance of hay. If you have more animals than you need for intended operations they should be sent off to some point where the country can subsist them, or else you will, I fear, lose many by the diseases resulting from constant feeding on grains without enough long forage. If you reduce the number of animals to the lowest point consistent with safety and efficiency the hay we can procure will subsist them in better condition. *The expense and difficulty of maintaining a large army stationary is enormous.* The wonderful resources of the Northern States have enabled us thus far to keep the Army of the Potomac fully supplied, except with hay, and of the want of that it complains bitterly. Should you rest upon the coast, as the Army of the Potomac has done, this hay question will be a great difficulty. I presume, however, that your army will be actively employed, and live, as it has heretofore, to some extent, upon the enemy. I hope so, and I believe that if there be a general officer in the service who can effect this, it is yourself. [Emphasis supplied.][19]

The "unlimited command of money" statement glossed over the fact that the Quartermaster Department was $180 million in debt in February 1865, and that Grant was calling for his army to be paid. Saying the money matters were the worst during the war, Halleck wrote Grant that his army had been treated better than those in the West and South, parts of which had not been paid for seven or eight months.[20]

At the end of January, with Sherman still in Savannah, Meigs warned him of the importance of not having steamers unnecessarily delayed inasmuch as payment had to be made for each day of delay, and also money could be saved if every requisition for coastal shipping was not made on an "urgent" basis. About the same time he wrote to Brigadier General Robert Allen, chief quartermaster, Louisville, that "[w]ith serious prospect of financial difficulty ahead it behooves us...to make every effort to limit the extravagance of the requisitions and consumption of commanding officers, who have heretofore spent the money and the supplies of this department as though it possessed the purse of Fortunatus and the granaries of Egypt."[21]

Music to Meigs' ears was Sherman's statement of December 25 that it would "not be long before [he would] sally forth again." Sherman wanted "enough provisions for 65,000 men and 40,000 horses and mules for sixty days" so as to be ready to move into South Carolina. In writing Grant about the troops to be left to hold Savannah when he moved north, he thought they should be white because "the people [were] dreadfully alarmed lest [Sherman should] garrison the place with negroes." "Now, no matter what the negro soldiers are," said Sherman, "you know that people have prejudices which must be regarded. Prejudice, like religion, cannot be discussed."[22]

The South did not have the men to confront the Federal armies. Davis complained to the Congress in November 1864 "that without the aid derived from recruiting their armies from foreign countries the [Northern] invaders would ere this have been driven from [Southern] soil." Davis, though exaggerating, had a point—one-fifth of the two million men who served in the Union army were foreign born, the bulk of whom were from Germany and Ireland, but many were surely naturalized citizens. Still, out of the over six hundred thousand alien passengers arriving in the United States during the years 1861–1864, many joined the army. One estimate was 180,000. But this foreign element was not the result of recruiting overseas—Secretary of State William Seward told the senate it was a "notorious fact...that a vigorous and continual tide of emigration [was] flowing from Europe" as a result of "the reciprocal conditions of industrial and social life in Europe and America." The South did not have the same benefit from Europe since emigration to the South virtually ceased during the war.[23]

A Confederate Act of February 17, 1864, which authorized "employment of slaves for service with the Army as teamsters or cooks, or in the way of work upon the fortifications, or in the Government workshops, or in hospitals and other similar duties" either by reimbursing their masters or impressment, produced less result than anticipated. In October 1864 the *Richmond Enquirer* advocated "conscription & arming of negroes granting them freedom."[24]

Davis had an epiphany about slaves and proposed a radical modification in the theory of the law. In the past slave labor was claimed in the same way as the government took any property. But slaves had another relation to the state—"that of a person." He proposed that slaves be taken over by the government both in their property and person senses and the masters be compensated. If this were done, a question would arise as to "what tenure" should be applied in the government's ownership. "Should [the slave] be retained in servitude, or should his emancipation be held out to him as a reward for faithful service, or should it be granted at once on the promise of such service; and if emancipated, what action should be taken to secure for the freedman the permission of the State from which he was drawn to reside within its limits after the close of the public service?" Davis favored a "policy of engaging to liberate the negro on his discharge after service faithfully rendered...to that of granting immediate manumission, or that of retaining him in servitude."[25]

Davis' action was one Meigs alerted his father to in December 1861: "Do not be surprised some morning at learning that Jeff Davis has proclaimed freedom to the blacks. Desperate men will do anything to uphold a failing cause." He didn't realize in 1861 how much fighting had to take place to make Davis desperate. Congress passed a bill authorizing use of slaves as soldiers which by March 13, 1865, was on its way to Davis. But it was too late.[26]

The Confederate bulwark, Fort Fisher, which guarded the entrance to the harbor at Wilmington, North Carolina, the last port for blockade runners was attacked. A combined military effort in December 1864, with the land forces under command of Major General Benjamin Butler and the naval forces under command of Rear Admiral David Porter, failed. Two weeks later, on January 15, 1865, under a different land commander Fisher was taken.[27]

Meigs was disgusted over Butler not trying a land assault against Fisher in the initial effort and, since Butler was "too powerful a man to be court-martialed," was afraid the Committee on the Conduct of the War would throw the blame on some *regular* officers. Meigs was wrong. West Point graduate Grant relieved Butler and effectively put an end to Butler's military career. Butler, not a stodgy man, may have appreciated the irony of his testifying before Congress about Fisher being impregnable at about the time word of its capitulation was received.[28]

After reaching Savannah, Sherman told Grant there was almost a popular demand for his army to go northward from Savannah into South Carolina. Many Georgians thought the South Carolinians should feel the utmost severities of war. Meigs was all for Sherman "eat[ing] out the bowels of the land of South Carolina" with its "aristocracy & devotion to slavery." Inasmuch as he went with Stanton to visit Savannah in early January, he probably told Sherman as much. He also hoped to influence Sherman to arm Negroes as they were liberated. A subject which he thought Sherman was "not up with the time on." An assessment which was probably correct. In speaking to Atlantans, Sherman said, "We don't want your Negroes"—a strange statement for a Northern leader more than a year and a half after the Emancipation Proclamation.[29]

Meigs found Savannah to be in poor condition—physically it was dingy and begrimed by bituminous coal smoke, and the people and animals were in need of food. He remained in Savannah after Stanton returned to Washington to arrange for disposal of $18,000,000 worth of captured cotton which Sherman considered a prize of war.[30]

With Sherman in Savannah and the Army of Tennessee destroyed, the South sent peace commissioners to Grant. They met with Lincoln on February 3 near Fort Monroe, Virginia. Lincoln reportedly told them

> that there would be no use in entering into any negotiations unless they would recognize, first: that the Union as a whole must be forever preserved, and second: that slavery must be abolished. If they were willing to concede these two points, then he was ready to enter into negotiations and was almost willing to hand them a blank sheet of paper with his signature attached for them to fill in the terms upon which they were willing to live with us in the Union and be one people.[31]

The negotiations came to nothing for reasons expressed by Meigs: "While Davis is in power no negotiation can be possible.... I expect nothing from him but the last ditch & the demand for recognition & separation." He knew his man. Davis and Lee must be faulted for not seeing the end was near and giving in to what was to be. General Joseph Johnston, who fought on to the end, knew that with Lincoln's reelection the North was united and the South was doomed.[32]

After a month of rest and refitting, Sherman set off. He followed a plan communicated to Grant on December 24:

> [T]he enemy will be in doubt as to my objective point after crossing the Savannah River, whether it be Augusta or Charleston, and will naturally divide his forces. I will then move either on Branchville or Columbia...; then, ignoring Charleston and Augusta both, occupy Columbia and Camden;...I would then favor a movement direct on Raleigh. The game is then up with Lee, unless he comes out of Richmond, avoids you, and fights me, in which event I should reckon on your being on his heels.[33]

Little resistance was encountered, other than from incessant rains, muddy roads needing to be corduroyed, swollen rivers, and swampy terrain. By February 16 the army reached the state capital at Columbia, and much of the city was burned, not by command, but by carelessness or vandalism of soldiers.[34]

On February 22, Washington's Birthday, Meigs rode out to hear and see a national salute (35 guns) from the 30 forts in the Washington area, at the same time rejoicing over the surrender of Charleston on February 18, which was made necessary by Sherman's bypassing it, and thought that the part of Charleston not useful to the army could "perish without a sigh from any loyal bosom." All forts, arsenals, and army headquarters in the United States fired the national salute "in honor of the restoration of the flag of the Union upon Fort Sumter."[35]

Before Lincoln's second inaugural, Meigs expressed concern over the president's safety:

> Tomorrow or every day he lives at the mercy of any returned fanatic. Any deserter or pretended deserter.
>
> To take precautions would be to change the whole custom of society here. Not only for the Pres[ident] but every high officer & official. Every body is always accessible.
>
> Nobody is guarded or armed except in the lines of fortifications & excepting the prisons & prisoners.
>
> The American people do not lean toward assassination.[36]

Meigs made a point of warning the president about the danger to him, but Lincoln did not like having guards around him and escaped from them whenever he could.[37]

From Columbia, Sherman proceeded to Fayetteville, North Carolina, arriving on March 10. During his trip the Confederates abandoned the city of Wilmington, and a steamship flying the Stars and Stripes, which came up the Cape Fear River from Wilmington, greeted Sherman's army at Fayetteville. The partial investment of Lee's army at Richmond would soon be reinforced with another major army unless some action was taken.[38]

The action was at Bentonville, North Carolina (near Goldsboro), on March 19–21, where General Joseph Johnston, who had been put back in command of such forces as the Confederacy had along the Atlantic coastal area on February 23, tried to overcome a part of Sherman's army but was unable to do so. Sherman had a force of about 60,000 men and Johnston only had 17,000.[39]

Leaving Bentonville, Sherman went to Goldsboro where he was joined by two corps which had come from the coast (Wilmington and New Berne). He now had three armies under his command (a newly designated Army of Georgia, the Army of the Ohio, and the Army of the Tennessee).[40]

Keeping supply routes open to Sherman's armies was the job of the quartermasters. A railroad line ran from Morehead City, North Carolina, to Goldsboro. Work proceeded to repair the railroad line, and cars and engines were shipped to North Carolina. When Sherman got to Goldsboro he immediately had on hand trains loaded with five days' rations, and shoes, and clothing to replace those worn out in the five hundred-mile march from Savannah. On the 22d of March Meigs left Washington for North Carolina to examine the supply operations. At Morehead City he found 117 vessels with supplies, and talked some with Sherman.[41]

On the 29th Meigs was in Goldsboro at Sherman's headquarters and wrote his father that when Sherman asked the owner of the house where Sherman was located about pitching headquarter tents on the man's lawn the owner objected that this would "spoil the grass which had cost him a good deal of money & care." Sherman immediately ordered the man and his family removed from the house and used it rather than the lawn for headquarters.[42]

Sherman went to City Point to confer with Grant and the president and on his return, about March 31, told the commanders that the next goal was to place the armies across the Roanoke River to gain contact with the Army of the Potomac.[43]

Grant was ready to put his spring offensive in motion. Major General Edward Canby was to move against Mobile, Alabama, Major General George Thomas to send out two large cavalry expeditions from Tennessee—one into Alabama and the other moving from East Tennessee toward Lynchburg, Virginia. Sherman was to move north from Goldsboro, North Carolina, Major General John Pope to move west of the Mississippi, and Major General Winfield Scott Hancock to guard against any offensive action by the Rebels in the Shenandoah Valley.[44]

Time was running out for the Confederacy. When Lee was asked for forces to oppose Sherman in South Carolina he wrote to Governor Andrew G. Magrath on January 27 that it would take Lee's whole force at Richmond and Petersburg to oppose Sherman and to move his men would result in Grant moving his. The implied question was whether the governor would rather have two large Union armies in South Carolina or do the best he could against the one on its way. Notwithstanding the situation, Lee took exception to Magrath's belief that to have Charleston fall would result in the loss of their cause. "Should [the] whole coast fall in the possession of [the North], with [the South's] people true, firm, and united, the war could be continued [and the South's] purpose accomplished." He saw no reason "for depression or despondency."[45]

Grant feared that Lee would abandon Richmond and Petersburg and go south to join up with Johnston in North Carolina. He planned movements to prevent this, if he acted before Lee did. The fear was well founded. In March, Davis and Lee decided Lee should move from Richmond and Petersburg as soon as possible. Grant moved first.[46]

The plan was for a movement on Grant's left to force Lee out of his entrenched positions protecting Richmond and Petersburg. Sheridan's cavalry, which had earlier come from Winchester capturing most of Early's command and destroying bridges, railroads, and parts of the James River Canal en route to White House (east of Richmond), was to block Lee from using the railroads going southwest and west from Richmond and Petersburg. Lincoln visited with Grant for several days before and after the start of the offensive, but he did not ask about Grant's plans, saying "[I]t [was] better he should not know them, and then he [could] be certain to keep the secret."[47]

Lee's armies were evaporating. On March 27 he reported 1,061 desertions from the infantry over the previous nine days and expected a considerable increase in the number when reports were received from the artillery and cavalry. He knew not how to stop it. Not only was the army shrinking (more than one hundred thousand deserters were scattered over the Confederacy, a situation understandable from the "most protracted and violent campaign that [was] known in history, contending against overwhelming numbers, badly equipped, fed, paid, and cared for in camp and hospital, with families suffering at home"), the War Department was in debt between $400 and $500 million, and the paper currency was at 60 to 1 when compared to coins of which only a small stock was in the treasury.[48]

Grant's movements started on March 29, and on April 2 Lee told Davis that Richmond was to be abandoned. This happened on the third. On learning that Richmond had surrendered bedlam broke loose in Washington, drums beating, flags waving, men shouting, and every other man drunk. Lee hoped to retreat toward Danville, Virginia, but the dogs of war were on his heels from every direction, and his force was constantly being reduced by desertions and losses in engagements. On April 7 Grant wrote to Lee asking for his surrender, and, with some further exchanges, this took place at Appomattox Court House on April 9. Lee's army had shrunk from about 60,000 to about 28,000.[49]

By April 11 Meigs, who wanted to be present when the Rebels fell, made his way from North Carolina to City Point where everyone was in a state of exultation. Sherman, who considered his army "in better condition [and] better equipped...than ever before," had set out after Johnston the day before. On April 12 Meigs traveled with Grant back to Washington.[50]

Meigs wasn't completely swept up in the excitement. Even though he thought Grant acted magnanimously in the terms imposed on Lee (essentially, lay down your arms, take your horses, agree to fight no more, and go home), he wanted "Congress [to] pass some law banishing [the Rebel] leaders if by military [action] or by Presidential pardon or clemency they escape immediate punishment." He looked upon all of them "as murderers of [his] son & of the sons of hundreds of thousands." Notwithstanding that they would be punished by God, he thought "[J]ustice seems not satisfied [if] they escape judicial trial & execution in this world by the government which they have betrayed attacked & whose people loyal & disloyal they have slaughtered."[51]

Meigs was in his office on Good Friday, April 14, attended church, and noted in his diary for that day that the "[C]ountry [was] drunk with joy." Then, around 10 that evening, he learned that Seward had been attacked at his home. Meigs walked the three blocks from his home to

Seward's and found him to be badly injured by knife wounds as was his son. Soon, Stanton and Gideon Welles arrived, and, after Meigs cleared the Seward house of sightseers, they proceeded by carriage to Ford's Theater where Lincoln had been shot by John Wilkes Booth.[52]

By the time they arrived, Lincoln had been carried to the Peterson home across from Ford's, and Meigs spent the night watching the dying president who breathed his last at 22 minutes past seven in the morning. The cabinet was present and Vice President Andrew Johnson looked upon the dying Lincoln, and retired. Meigs acted as a gatekeeper to the Peterson house. Lincoln was insensible from the time he was shot in the head.[53]

The dead president was taken to the White House, and on Tuesday, April 18, the public was allowed to view the body in the East Room, on Wednesday the funeral was held in the East Room, and then a procession took the body to the Rotunda of the Capitol where it lay in state until Friday morning when a special train started Lincoln's final journey to Springfield, Illinois. Meigs headed the quartermaster group in the procession from the White House to the Capitol, was in charge of the public's viewing of the body at the Capitol, and was part of the group, including the cabinet and Grant, which went with the body to the railroad station. In Lincoln's death Meigs suffered a loss of one who had always been kind and a friend to him.[54]

Following Lincoln's assassination Stanton took charge of trying to find those responsible. He jumped to the conclusion that Jefferson Davis was behind the assassination, set a reward of $100,000 to those capturing Davis, and bitterly denounced the Confederate government. He was in no mood to receive the news dispatched by Sherman. On April 17 Johnston asked Sherman for a cessation of hostilities to allow for negotiating terms of surrender. The generals met and Johnston wanted the surrender to encompass "the armies under Dick Taylor and Kirby Smith in the Gulf States, and those under Maury, Forrest, and others." Johnston assured Sherman he could get authority to sign for such a broad surrender.[55]

The next day Sherman and Johnston signed an agreement for a general surrender of Confederate armies which set off a firestorm of criticism of Sherman in the North. Sherman was a much better general than politician. The agreement proposed to deal with many sensitive political issues, for example, a general amnesty was granted to the extent the executive branch could give it. The agreement recognized that the signatories did not have the authority to enter into all the terms of the agreement, and it was pledged they would take steps to obtain the necessary authority.[56]

When Grant received a copy of the agreement he immediately knew it could not be approved and sent it on to the secretary of war. By April 24 Grant, together with Meigs who was asked by Stanton to accompany Grant, was at Sherman's headquarters with notice that the negotiations were not approved, and that Johnston should be offered surrender terms like those given Lee. This was done on the 26th when Sherman and Johnston signed a surrender of only those troops under Johnston's command.[57]

The South was disintegrating. Meigs found Raleigh, North Carolina, to be a beautiful town, even though many of Lee's paroled soldiers begged for food from "farmers who...dodged the conscription or from the wives & women of those who...died in the rebel ranks. The people feared more their own troops than they did the Yankees."[58]

By the fourth of May, the day Lincoln was laid to rest in Springfield after many funeral services as the train made its way westward, all forces east of the Mississippi had surrendered. Most of those west of the Mississippi were surrendered on May 26. Jefferson Davis was captured on May 11. Grant ended his report of operations from March 1864 to May 1865 with compliments not only to the Union men of East and West, but also to their opponents "whose manhood, however mistaken the cause, drew forth such herculean deeds of valor."[59]

Meigs reconstruction attitude was against "compromise or soft measures with traitors & murderers of...loyal people &...institutions." The murder of Lincoln, if possible, hardened his attitude. His anger was directed to the leaders of the South, not just those in government positions, but those planters who were influential in the secession. As for the "rank & file" they were not innocent but had less guilt. Disgust was directed to West Point graduates who had taken the oath to defend the Constitution of the United States against all enemies, were given a public education, and when an enemy arose "hastened to join" him.[60]

Lincoln's death on April 15 makes one think his destiny in life was to bring the Civil War to a successful conclusion. Although it took another month for all the surrenders to take place, the symbolism of a final chapter closing was Major General Robert Anderson hoisting the U.S. flag over Fort Sumter on April 14, four years after he marched out of Sumter under the eyes of his Confederate conquerors.[61]

Chapter 27

Disposing of Men and Materials, and Burying the Dead

To disband the Union armies as fast and cheaply as possible was the goal following the surrender of Lee and Johnston. It wasn't until May 26, when Confederate Lieutenant General Edmund Kirby Smith surrendered his command west of the Mississippi, that all "organized rebel force[s]" were accounted for, yet steps were well under way to muster out the volunteers before then.[1]

The armies of Grant and Sherman in Virginia and North Carolina marched to Washington and, in a grand parade, down Pennsylvania Avenue from the Capitol past the White House on May 23–24. Each day, for six hours, 66,000 troops, a total of 30 miles of soldiers, marched, leaving behind 60 miles of wagon trains.[2]

The Meigs' family had an excellent viewing position looking out the windows of the quartermaster general's office almost immediately opposite the White House. Meigs himself was in the reviewing stands. He asked as many of the family as could to come and see the review. A tent captured at Lookout Mountain, that of the quartermaster general of Georgia, was used to house guests. Meigs saw the accomplishments of the Union armies during the war as "a warning of the power and resources of a free people for any contest into which they heartily enter."[3]

"Two hundred and thirty-five thousand men were distributed from Washington...to their homes in the North—carried to every hamlet and village, camps of discharge being established in every state, at which the regiments rendezvoused until paid off, when the men dispersed." An estimated 60,000 men of the Army of the Tennessee moved to Louisville and were discharged from that point. "Sixty thousand prisoners of war...were sent to their homes in the Southern states." As much movement as possible was made by rail and river, which, dollar-wise, was cheaper than marching the men to points close to their homes. In the latter case the pay of the men would have continued, and the wagon trains necessary to support the men and animals would have been expensive. By August 7, 640,000 were gone, 800,000 through November 25, and by the start of 1866 almost a million. During this period over 100,000 employees of the Quartermaster Department were discharged.[4]

"Officers were sent to inspect the various depots and posts to report what stores should be sold and what preserved." Purchases were reduced and employees terminated. During the war the armies in the field averaged "one horse or mule to every two men" and "one wagon to twenty-four men." The surpluses were disposed of. Between May 8 and October 17, 1865, 53,794 horses and 52,516 mules were sold; and, by August 1866, the total of each sold exceeded one hundred thousand. In June 1866, in serviceable animals, the army was left with 8,891 cavalry horses, 566 artillery horses, and 15,362 mules. These sales were of "great advantage to the treasury and to the agricultural interests of the country." One beneficiary was brother Henry Meigs who bought a "General Meigs wagon" in Atlanta to use on his farm at Marietta, Georgia.[5]

Military railroads were, where possible, turned over to railroad companies of the "rebellious territories." "Questions of ownership, claims to material of the road tracks transferred either by rebel or by U. S. authority from one road to another, [were] left for decision of the courts." Nearly six hundred boats and barges were put up for sale.[6]

Of immediate concern with the end of hostilities was proper burial of the dead. During the war commanding officers had the responsibility of burying soldiers dying within their jurisdiction, but battle conditions did not lend themselves to careful interments. More often than not, soldiers were buried where they fell with little effort made to identify the person or place.[7]

Both the army and families were anxious to gather up the remains of those strewn over the whole country. The War Department did not pay to return bodies to their homes, but provided wagon transportation to trains or ports if practical. The Quartermaster Department was responsible to bury or rebury any remains not taken by family or friends.

Meigs gave the military job to Assistant Quartermaster Captain James M. Moore who was already involved in burials in the Washington area. One of his first acts was to prepare what was called a Roll of Honor—the names of soldiers who died in defense of the American Union interred in the national cemeteries at Washington, D.C., August 3, 1861 to June 30, 1865. The cover contained lines from an 1847 poem written by Theodore O'Hara in remembrance of Kentuckians dying in the Mexican War. Additional lines were used on future Rolls of Honor, and the following lines, which were on the first cover, are also on the McClellan Arch at the Arlington National Cemetery constructed in the 1870s as the entryway to the cemetery:

In fame's eternal camping ground
Their silent tents are spread
And glory guards with solemn round
The bivouac of the dead.

This poem had to be a Meigs' favorite. The reverse of the McClellan Arch also contains lines from it, as did bronze plaques in many of the national cemeteries.[8]

The McClellan Arch, consistent with the compulsion of Meigs to not only bring honor to his family name but also to display it prominently, had the name "Meigs" carved on the left column as the cemetery was entered. The road coming into the cemetery from the west is "Meigs Drive." Meigs published the first roll by a general order dated June 15, 1865. The preface notes that the Arlington National Cemetery was located on the "estate formerly the residence of the rebel general R. E. Lee," and that "many of those who...died in Washington as prisoners of war [received] the same care and attention as [did Union] soldiers." Although the Confederate deceased were buried with care, it took many years for the bitterness of the war to wear off so that their graves in national cemeteries could be decorated and included in memorial tributes. In 1906 Congress authorized construction of a Confederate memorial at Arlington.[9]

Because of the battles fought in the vicinity of the capital and the location of many hospitals in and near the city, burial space was needed early and late in the war. Initially, burials were made at relatively small burial grounds located at the Soldiers' Home (circa six acres) and in Alexandria (2-plus acres). A third cemetery, Harmony, was used to bury "all soldiers dying of infectious diseases, and contrabands." Grant's drive south in 1864 filled up the spaces at the Soldiers' Home and, in May 1864, the first burials were made at the Arlington National Cemetery, which, by the end of the war, had more than five thousand bodies with interments taking place daily. The first Roll of Honor spoke of Arlington as having "undulating [ground] which greatly enhance[d] the beauty of the cemetery" and the use of the mansion as "an office for the transaction of business, and for the reception of those who go to visit the graves of friends and relatives."[10]

Exactly how, what had been Lee's residence was selected as a cemetery and developed for that purpose, is not known. A composite explanation from several books about Arlington National Cemetery tells a story which can not be verified since the books do not give the basis for what is fact and, therefore, do not identify how much is speculation.

The composite story starts with Congress passing a law on June 7, 1862, and amending it by the act of February 6, 1863, which put a direct tax on property in the "Insurrection Districts within the United States." The Lee Arlington property fell within the scope of this law, and commissioners appointed to administer the law put a tax of $92.07 on it. Even though Mrs. Lee attempted to send payment through a relative, the tax commissioners refused to accept the money ruling the payment must be made in person by the owner. When the tax was not paid, the commissioners sold the property to the United States on January 11, 1864. This brought the paper title in line with the physical occupation of the property by Union troops since May 23, 1861.[11]

This last step is where Meigs became involved. Allegedly he "engineered a closed auction" of the property at which the government was the only bidder and acquired title to the property for the assessed value of $26,810. His actions are said to have been motivated by a hatred of Lee caused by "some real or imagined slight" or because of Lee turning against the United States.[12]

Supposedly, Meigs was afraid the Lees might at some point reoccupy the property and took steps to make that undesirable. Even before the property had been designated as a cemetery he had burials made on it—the first occurring on May 13, 1864. Then, on June 15, 1864, Meigs proposed to Stanton that Arlington House and two hundred acres around it be made a military cemetery, and, on the same day, Stanton approved. Burials near Arlington House began that day, or were directed to be made, and "[a]t Meigs' insistence, some graves were dug in Mrs. Lee's rose garden." "When Meigs came out to Arlington in August...he was furious. Instead of seeing the Lee house ringed with graves, he saw the mansion looking much as it always had.... [N]ear the old slave quarters was a neat looking cemetery filled with all of the bodies Meigs had wanted placed near the house. Enraged, he ordered twenty-six more bodies brought over from Washington right away, and in the hot August sun,...Meigs...stood by and personally supervised their burial in the rose garden just south of the house."[13]

Within the Meigs' family, the choice of Arlington came about as a result of a conversation between Lincoln and Meigs. Lincoln asked Meigs what to do with Arlington, and he replied: "The Romans sowed the fields of their enemies with salt; let us make it a field of honor."[14]

Regardless of what motivated Stanton and Meigs, the fact that up to two hundred acres were to be laid out around the Arlington Mansion shows that something more than a stopgap measure was being taken. The fact that title to the land was in the United States in 1864, albeit in 1882 the Supreme Court ruled that the tax sale was illegal and that title was still in the name of George Washington Custis Lee (who then sold it to the United States for $150,000), the possibility of the Lees ever resuming ownership was likely perceived by anyone knowing this as nil. But Meigs did not have this knowledge. In May 1865, he spoke of the land as "being appropriated" and, in November 1865, when President Johnson was refusing to confiscate Rebel property and was readily granting pardons to Rebel leaders, he expressed concern that the Lee family might question the title to the property which he thought had not been sold for taxes. He certainly didn't want Robert E. Lee to move back in, attributing the continuation of the war during the last year to Lee, but, if he did, he said the Lees would be sleeping "among ghosts."[15]

A believable explanation for Meigs' actions is: (1) burial sites were needed at a time when the war was reaching a crescendo, (2) because of his respect for those who gave their lives he wanted their burial locations to be in attractive settings, and (3) he did not want bodies to be moved once buried if that could be avoided. He "believ[ed] the dead, once decently buried should have rest." He also believed burials should not take place without the presence of a chaplain—he wrote to Stanton and asked that a chaplain be assigned full time at the Washington cemeteries where burials were taking place.[16]

If a feeling of vengeance influenced Meigs, he was not alone. A Washington paper, the *Morning Chronicle*, found the cemetery to be a "righteous use of the estate of the rebel General Lee," and accused him of the murder of "hundreds of Union heroes."[17]

On the other side, Mrs. Robert E. Lee was devastated by what happened. She wrote in 1866 that the graves of her mother and father, buried near Arlington House, were "surrounded closely by the graves of those who aided to bring all this ruin on the children and country. They are even planted up to the very door without any regard to common decency."[18]

A tribute to the unknown dead was made in September 1866 when a large pit (20 feet in diameter) was dug and lined for the common burial of the bones of 2,111 "gathered after the war from the fields of Bull Run and the route to the Rappahannock." The pit was topped with a large monument exhorting "grateful citizens" to "honor them as of their noble army of martyrs." This burial site is close by the Arlington Mansion.[19]

Arlington National Cemetery played a prominent role in the first Declaration Day, May 30, 1868, declared by Major General John Alexander Logan, of the veterans' group of the Grand Army of the Republic, to be a day to decorate the graves of those who died in defense of their country. As the custom gained popularity Congress made May 30 a national holiday in 1888 renaming it as Memorial Day. Completed in 1874, south of Arlington House, was a trellised structure used as an amphitheater.[20]

Following the publication of the first Roll of Honor, a vast burial and reburial program was carried out whereby most remains were placed in national cemeteries. By 1870 the program was concluded with "nearly 300,000 Civil War remains...reinterred in 73 national cemeteries,"—about 58 percent of the remains had been identified.[21]

During the next 10-year period (1870–1880), Congress expanded the right to be buried in national cemeteries, most significantly allowing veterans of the Civil War to be buried there. The prior law had limited burials to those dying during the war. In 1873 a law was passed providing for the "erection of a headstone at each grave." In 1881 Meigs wanted to make Arlington National Cemetery a special one—rather than limiting interments to soldiers, he would allow burial of "officers of the United

States, legislative, judicial, civil, and military, who may die at the seat of government or whose friends may desire their interment in a public national cemetery."[22]

The Meigs' suggestion was never adopted, but the existing rules did not keep him from having the remains of his grandfather (Josiah) and an uncle (Samuel Meigs) transferred from a Washington cemetery to Arlington. They died before 1823. This transfer took place after the death of Louisa Meigs in 1879. Also moved to the same location was their son John and their other three children who died before them. Graves nearby are those of his daughter Mary, her husband (a Civil War veteran), and their two sons, both of whom had military careers. Also close by are the graves of Colonel John Macomb and his wife Anna (Louisa's sister) who were always close to the Meigs' family, sharing a house with them during the war, and their son (Montgomery Meigs Macomb) and his wife. Montgomery and Louisa Meigs' grave site is Grave No. 1, in Section No. 1, at Arlington which adjoins Meigs Drive near the Arlington Mansion.

Chapter 28
Forty-Two Years and Out

Relatively, the Quartermaster Department became a minuscule operation after the war. The last year of the war saw it spending over $431 million. In the 12 months ending July 1, 1871, it spent $12 million, an approximate level at which expenditures remained until Meigs was involuntarily retired in 1882. Nonetheless, this was still a major part of the War Department appropriations.[1]

With peace the army became more obsessed with rank than it had been during the war when chances for promotion were always present. In dealing with the "old" army in 1861, Simon Cameron said he thought "promotion [was] the God of the officers." Understandably, "rank" which controlled "privilege, authority, and social standing" was important. To the consternation of officers of the line, the regular army had a disproportionate number of the higher ranks in staff organizations. The Quartermaster Department had 88 officers in 1869. Of these, 10 held brevets of major general and 22 of brigadier general. Although brevet ranks did not carry the pay of those ranks, immediately after the war officers wore the uniform of the brevet rank. Congress changed this in 1869 and 1870—uniforms of the regular rank were to be worn, and, according to Congress, officers would be officially addressed by their regular rank. However, military custom still caused the use of the brevet rank in social and, sometimes, official exchanges.[2]

Congress wrestled with the size and type of army needed in peacetime. Though some thought there should be no army, seeing it as a threat to a democracy, the majority were satisfied to keep its numbers low. The initial structuring in 1866 was for 54,000 headed by a four-star general (Grant), with one lieutenant general (Sherman), five major generals (six on duty in 1867: Halleck, Hancock, Meade, Sheridan, Daniel Sickles, Thomas), and 10 brigadier generals of the line. Eight of the 10 staff bureaus were to be headed by brigadier generals. However, it was not long before the overall numbers were cut to 37,000 in 1869; then to 27,000 in 1874 and, by 1888, the ranks of general and lieutenant general were phased out.[3]

The Quartermaster Department was allowed 90 officers in 1866 and by the mid-1870s was down to 57. A combination of the higher ranks not retiring and the reduction in allowed numbers stymied most promotions. In 1877, for the army as a whole, the expected time for a second lieutenant to become a major was about 25 years and for colonel about 35 years.[4]

In early 1867 Meigs became severely ill, and the quartermaster general duties were assumed by Daniel H. Rucker, who performed them until June 6, 1868, when Meigs returned to duty. To overcome what may have been exhaustion from overwork during the war, the Meigs' family—Montgomery (age 51), Louisa (51), Montie (20), and Loulie (13)—spent much of 1867–1868 in Europe. Secretary of State William Seward gave Montgomery a well-earned introduction to American diplomats abroad: "The prevailing opinion of this Country [is that] without the service of this eminent soldier the national cause must either have been lost or deeply imperilled in the last civil war." Except for Montie, who attended the Polytechnic School at Stuttgart, Germany, for most of the time, the family traveled to well-known sites.[5]

Before and during this period, bizarre and historic events occurred in Washington. Decisions as to how to treat the Southern states were being made, and a power struggle between Congress and President Andrew Johnson resulted in unseemly conduct by each. The insults exchanged were vicious—radical Republicans did not staunch rumors that the president was a drunk and maintained a "harem" of dissolute women at the White House, and Johnson said that radical Republicans were trying to destroy the fundamental principles of government and would like for him to be assassinated.[6]

Lincoln set forth his ideas for bringing seceding states back into the Union by a proclamation of December 3, 1863, which, in brief, accepted a loyal government if organized by a number taking an oath of allegiance equal to 10 percent of those voting in the 1860 election. In general, those participating in the rebellion would be pardoned and property restored. Southerners were required to accept the abolition of slavery, but were given discretion as to how they approached educating and providing for the freed "laboring, landless, and homeless class." Lincoln acknowledged that Congress had the final say. Congress, constitutionally, would decide when members sent by any Rebel state would be admitted.[7]

It took Congress six months to pass the Wade-Davis Bill which made it clear that Lincoln, in its view, was being too easy on the South. Wade-Davis, which Lincoln pocket-vetoed, insisted on no more slavery and would not let those who voluntarily bore arms against the United States participate in forming the new government. At this point, neither Congress nor Lincoln were insisting on voting rights for freedmen. Lincoln would have preferred for the "very intelligent" and Negro soldiers to have the vote but didn't insist upon it.[8]

On a personal level, Meigs had no doubts as to what should be done to the leaders of the South—string them up starting with Lee and Davis. They were all murderers. But he gave credit to the Southern soldiers who were of "a brave race."[9]

When it came to individuals he had an early test when Varina Davis, with whom the Meigs' family had social relations before the war, telegraphed asking for his help so she could come north to communicate with her husband imprisoned at Fort Monroe and to get their children out of an unhealthy climate. Meigs struggled with what to do, talked it over with Stanton, and finally decided to pass word back to Mrs. Davis through the commanding general at Savannah that her husband's health was better than when captured. He thought Varina shared her husband's guilt but had compassion for her situation. In general the plight of Southern women did not sway him—"[l]et the rebels take care of their own widows they have filled [the North's] hands with [its] own."[10]

When correspondence showed that his brother Henry was not repentant nor of any different view about slavery than he held before the war, he thought the family should let him stew in his own juices.[11]

The slavery question was still in the air on the national level and it was not until the 13th Amendment was ratified on December 6, 1865, that slavery was outlawed nationally. This, of course, added to the need to decide what to do with the new freedmen. Right after the war Meigs pushed hard for giving some acreage to each freed family. This would give the South a stable labor force and permit the freedmen to have property of their own to support their families—what additional time they had they could hire out to the larger landowners. The action to be taken though was for statesmen as the military power was dying out.[12]

The decision as to how to handle the freedmen was essentially in the hands of President Johnson. Johnson took a major step, during a time when Congress was not in session, by issuing an amnesty proclamation on May 29, 1865. In general it followed the Lincoln plan, giving amnesty to most Southerners who would take an oath of allegiance and restoring their property except as to slaves. However, excepted from the amnesty were many categories—Confederate officers above the rank of colonel; civil or diplomatic officers of the Confederacy; West Point or Naval Academy graduates who went over to the South; those having taxable property of a value over $20,000, and other groupings. The property Meigs would have given to freedmen would come from those with property in excess of $20,000 who would give up property for the freedmen as a condition of getting a pardon. He thought the distribution of property was more important to the integration of the freedmen into society than the right to vote; after all, women and children were not allowed to vote so letting the freedmen grow into that right was not without precedent.[13]

He managed to get his ideas before the president through Major General Oliver Howard who headed the Freedman's Bureau. As it worked out, Johnson did not accept the idea of taking property from the wealthy and gave pardons to Southerners on a wholesale basis. Johnson's attitude was that the Southern landowners had "lost everything but their lands & that the best way to restore peace & good will [was] to leave them intact except in some cases of particular guilt." This attitude, in Meigs' view, foretold trouble ahead. God would punish both sections of the country until the foul spot of limited freedom was erased. Johnson was throwing away his opportunity to have his name beside those of Washington and Lincoln as a great liberator. But the course was set, Johnson would issue many pardons before Congress could mandate a different course. To Meigs this demonstrated that "[w]hen the South assassinated Lincoln [it] did not make so great a mistake as at first supposed." In his view Johnson had too much "respect for the rights to which people who take his amnesty oath are restored." He asked: "Are we to pay Virginia for all the material which we clear from her soil to conquer her rebellion?"[14]

The country may have made the transition from slavery to freedmen in a more orderly and satisfactory manner if Meigs had been listened to.

At the end of May 1865, Meigs commented on expected treason trials. With many lawyers in positions of statesmanship, such trials would be conducted in accordance with law but, he feared, would result in too little "bloodthirstiness & slaughter." As for Davis, if he did not "deserve death then no murderer or traitor or assassin who has died since Caine was sent into exile has deserved death." It would be a blot on civilization to have to spend hundreds of thousands of dollars to prove Davis committed treason. However, he was thankful that he "had nothing to do with [the] matter & [was] perfectly willing to leave it to those whose duty [was] to deal with it." Although thinking Davis should die he did "not want to pronounce the sentence." These sentiments makes one think his bark may have been harsher than his bite.[15]

Toward the end of the year, with all the other Southern leaders being pardoned, he no longer thought Davis should be hanged and saw little point in spending a lot of money for a trial to prove something everyone knew, that is, that Davis was guilty of treason. He correctly speculated that in time "All parties [would] tire of Davis & that he [would] simply find his prison doors open." This is what happened. In May 1867 he was released on bond and was to live on until 1889, never asking for a pardon and spending three years writing a book, *The Rise and Fall of the Confederate Government*, which argues the South acted constitutionally in leaving the Union.[16]

Johnson, who dealt with a new 39th Congress elected in November 1864, but not meeting until December 1865, tried to follow Lincoln's plan. As of December 1865, all that was lacking was for Congress to seat the representatives and senators from the former Confederate states, but this did not happen. Instead Congress proceeded, over Johnson's vetoes, to keep the South under military control and legislated civil rights guarantees for freedmen. The philosophical approach to the Southern states was fought out in the 1866 congressional elections. The radical Republicans, those who favored the tougher approach, made gains so that they had a strong two-thirds majority in both Houses.[17]

Notwithstanding the results of the election, Johnson in his December 3, 1866, second annual message to Congress, was still pushing for the Lincoln-Johnson plan and said to do otherwise could end in "absolute despotism." Congress had both short- and long-term concerns. In the short term, it thought the provisional governments established under the Lincoln-Johnson plan were trying to virtually reinstate slavery through "black codes" passed by the legislatures which told freedmen what they could and could not do. In the long term, the radical Republicans foresaw readmitted states joining with Northern Democrats to control Congress. To offset this they wanted to give the freedmen the vote. These concerns gained credibility when the 14th Amendment to the Constitution designed to protect civil rights, which Congress referred to the states in June 1866, failed of ratification since all the former Confederate states rejected it.[18]

In its waning days, the 39th Congress took decisive action. An effort made in the House in January 1867 to impeach the president failed by two votes. Congress passed a Reconstruction Act which (1) divided the Rebel states into military districts and made them subject to military authority, (2) made the existing Southern governments provisional, (3) allowed male citizens 21 or more years old "of whatever race, color, or previous condition," to frame the state's constitution, and (4) would admit representatives and senators from new state governments, established according to law, to be seated in Congress once the state legislature approved the 14th Amendment. Putting its Reconstruction Act in place was only part of the radical Republican agenda. To gain some control over the army, Congress took two steps: it passed a Tenure of Office Act which prohibited the president from removing cabinet officers without Senate approval, and a Command of the Army Act which made the president and secretary of war go through the general of the army, at that time Grant, who held radical Republican ideas, to give orders to the army.[19]

The president's vetoes of the Reconstruction Act and the Tenure of Office Act were overridden on the same day they were issued, March 2, 1867. Purporting to act under the Tenure of Office Act, Johnson, during a congressional recess, on August 12, 1867, suspended Secretary of War Stanton who was not in agreement with Johnson's policies. After the Senate refused to sustain the suspension, Johnson chose to test the constitutionality of the Tenure of Office Act (which was declared unconstitutional in 1926) and on February 21, 1868, removed Stanton from office. Stanton barricaded himself in his office and remained as secretary until presidential impeachment proceedings started by the House of Representatives on February 24 failed in May 1868.[20]

Stanton resigned his office the day of the last vote in the Senate (May 26) and, in failing health, resumed the private practice of law. He was never able to recover his vigor, and before he could take office as a justice of the Supreme Court to which President Ulysses S. Grant nominated him about December 19, 1869, and Congress rapidly approved, death intervened. He passed away December 24.[21]

Meigs was in Texas on a western inspection trip, but undoubtedly was grieved by the death of his stalwart boss of the war years. They had had a good relationship. Many years later he said Stanton "was by nature excitable and nervous and [that they] could not depend upon his mood. But [that] he never faltered in his duty to his country and [the country owed] him a great debt.... He ought to have a statue." Earlier in 1869 an even more telling death changed Meigs' life—his father, to whom he had faithfully written letters for many years, died peacefully in his sleep on June 22. Montgomery recorded in his diary: "A good man has finished his course & is at rest."[22]

If Meigs had been present during the trying months Johnson had with Congress and Stanton in 1867 and 1868, instead of in Europe, it is doubtful if he would have been involved. His view was that after the war the army should not interfere with political matters—"reestablishing civil government should [be left] to the President & Congress." Nonetheless, he vigorously pushed for confiscation of land from Southern planters to be given in 40-acre parcels to freed households. This idea was subscribed to by Thaddeus Stevens, a leading radical Republican in the House, and, but for his death in 1868, might have been adopted.[23]

The white citizens of the South gradually gained control of the political establishments of their various states, but the radical Republicans and the 39th and 40th Congresses accomplished major objectives in the enactment of the 14th (ratified July 9, 1868) and 15th (ratified February 3, 1870) Amendments to the Constitution. The 14th in essence makes the Bill of Rights, the first 10 amendments, applicable to the states, and the 15th forbids denying the vote to any citizen "on account of race, color, or previous condition of servitude."

Meigs' postwar tenure as quartermaster general saw the army functioning in two primary areas. It did what was necessary for reconstruction in the South (taking up to one-third of the men), and protected the emigrants swarming into the West. "Travelers by the stage from Denver to Fort Leavenworth [Kansas], a distance of 683 miles, in the month of July, 1865, were never out of sight of wagon trains, belonging either to emigrants or to the merchants who transport[ed] supplies for the War Department, for the Indian Department, and for the mines and settlers of the central Territories." In the West the basic strategy was a "network of forts...comprehensive enough to cover all potential trouble spots," a strategy hobbled by a lack of troops to adequately man them.[24]

Major General Henry Halleck succinctly stated much of the Indian problem in 1867: "As their hunting grounds are gradually taken from them by the settlers, they are obliged either to rob or starve." The next year Major General William T. Sherman in a non-sequitur said, "[T]he existing war...was begun by the Indians without any provocation whatever on the part of the whites"; "the hungry Indian, who, deprived of his accustomed subsistence, will steal rather than starve, and will kill in order to steal." Sherman's conclusions: "With such opposing interests the races *cannot* live together, and it is the Indians who must yield." They were to be rounded up and put on reservations.[25]

The secretary of war in 1868 was Major General John Schofield who did not give the Indians any latitude:

> While good faith and sound policy alike require us to strictly observe existing treaties so long as the Indians maintain like good faith, when any tribe has violated its treaty it should no longer be regarded as a nation with which to treat, but as a *dependent uncivilized people*, to be cared for, fed when necessary, and governed.[26]

Nothing was said about the consequences if the United States violated a treaty. Schofield thought the Interior Department should be relieved of the management of Indian affairs if the army was going to have to act to protect railroads and frontier settlements.[27]

There is no indication in the official reports that Meigs found anything wrong with these statements. He referred to the Indians as "predatory and hostile savages" who murder our men and violate "our...women...with all the aggravations of savage barbarity." In 1874 he spoke of "the Apache savages, who have broken out of the reservations." Following Custer's last stand at Little Big Horn (June 1876) a national military cemetery was established on the battlefield on which a granite block had inscribed "the names of all who fell on that field contending against a savage enemy." The stone was a symbol "of the conflict between civilization and barbarism."[28]

It wasn't only the Indians the army was trying to control. The secretary of war's 1868 report refers to "lawless operations of a mysterious organization known as the 'Ku Klux Klan'" which was inspiring terror in Tennessee. The army in Mississippi, in 1869, was attempting to arrest "lawless characters guilty of murder" and outrages. These men were "[g]uarded and protected by their neighbors." In 1871 the Quartermaster Department incurred costs in "the return of a considerable force to the Southern states under the provisions of the enforcement bill."[29]

The Quartermaster Department supplied those protecting the settlers and miners "by heavy wagons, each drawn by ten oxen," carrying loads of 5,500 pounds, or lighter wagons, drawn by mules, for freight and passengers. Encroachment of settlements on the roads caused problems. Roads were initially "located upon the high and dry swells of the prairie, the most desirable land for agricultural purposes." There being no laws keeping farmers from fencing in his land "according to the unyielding lines of [their] rectangular boundaries" the roads were being forced along less desirable lines. Meigs recommended that "future land sales" reserve the "great and long-established trails" as public highways.[30]

The cost of supplying the army was expected to become cheaper with the advance of the Pacific railroads "two of which were rapidly moving Westward" in October of 1865. Wagon trains from Fort Leavenworth, Kansas, to Denver City, Colorado, in 1865 took 45 to 74 days. But, even with the railroads, posts north and south of the rail line had to be supplied by wagon routes "extending into the wilderness."[31]

The job of "overaw[ing] the predatory and hostile savages" was made more difficult by the Indians being supplied "improved arms and ammunition." Meigs suggested the army should be allowed "to take from every Indian, not a citizen, whenever it may be in the power of army commanders to do so, all fire-arms and ammunition therefor of whatever kind." He thought the arrow to be "a sufficiently effective weapon in the chase of the buffalo."[32]

In Meigs' view Congress did not adequately provide for the troops. Some improvement in their conditions was provided by replacing vermin-ridden wooden bunks with iron ones; "pillow-sacks" were issued together with a greater allowance of straw; chairs were supplied for the barracks; and military schools for instruction of soldiers and their children were established on the posts.[33] Although officers fared better than the enlisted, it was a harsh environment on the frontier—one description of enlisted life is:

> [L]iv[ing] in dark, dirty, overcrowded, vermin-infested barracks, sharing a straw-filled mattress with a "bunkie."...[B]ad food, badly prepared.... [L]abor[ing] long hours at menial tasks that neither required nor helped inculcate military skills.... [E]ndur[ing] strict discipline fortified by severe, often brutal penalties for transgressions. Occasionally...go[ing] out on scout or patrol or even campaign. Probably...never see[ing] combat.[34]

Reluctantly, Meigs gave up issuing old style uniforms—at the conclusion of the war he had more than one million uniforms in stock, a quantity sufficient for an army of 30,000 or more for many years. Even though changes in uniform were ordered in 1872, and some new uniforms were issued, in 1874 Congress mandated that some of the old-pattern clothing be used before new purchases were made. The troops complained and fought back. They would order a larger size trouser than they wore and have it cut down and restyled. The soldiers also cut the collars off their shirts, a change adopted by the quartermaster general who probably liked the economy of the collarless shirt.[35]

Keeping the old uniforms from being eaten by moths was a challenge. Chemicals were used with some success, and Meigs thought they could be controlled by putting bales of clothing in a vacuum, in which "[n]o living animal can survive long," and particularly so if carbonic acid is introduced. The moths held their own. Whatever was left in 1880 had been so ravaged that it was transferred to the National Home for Disabled Volunteers. Even some of the new-pattern uniforms were not acceptable—the "eyes of officers and soldiers...[would] not tolerate any difference [in color] distinguishable in ranks on parade." To an officer in Meigs' mold, notwithstanding the problems created for him, this was probably seen as a show of good esprit in the army.[36]

The Quartermaster Department was not reluctant to try out different ideas. In 1880 a use was made of the "[t]raveaux, i.e., ambulances consisting of two long poles with slings for sick and wounded men between them, the front ends of the poles being attached to a mule, the rear ends dragging on the ground" in imitation of the Indians. Metal hubs were adopted for wagons. Shoes and boots were made by attaching the uppers to the soles "by screwed brass wire, instead of wooden pegs or linen thread." Fire extinguishers and "small, portable force-pumps" were widely distributed.[37]

Steam-power and steam-heat were installed at the large depots at Philadelphia and Jeffersonville, Indiana. The services of the noted landscaper, Frederick Law Olmstead, were used to plan the grounds of these depots.[38]

An ongoing task requiring a lot of work at the quartermaster general's office was processing claims under the law of July 4, 1864, for "quartermaster's stores taken by the Army and delivered to and used by the Army during the...war in States not in rebellion." If the "Quartermaster-General [was] convinced of their justice, of the loyalty of the claimant, and that the stores [were] actually received or taken for the use of and used by the Army" he was to report such to the "Third Auditor [of the Treasury], with recommendation for settlement." Through June 30, 1878, 39,108 claims were filed for $29.6 million of which 18,162 (for $16.2 million) were rejected. At a time when "thirty-five or fifty cents" would buy a "passable breakfast or dinner" in Washington, and a congressman's salary was $5,000 per year, these were very large claims. Those recommended for settlement were 9,270 for a value of $4 million (about one-half the amount claimed). There were still 12,000 claims to be acted on.[39]

Congress decided to bar all claims not filed before January 1, 1880, and this set off a final surge of claims. Close to 20,000 claims had not been finally acted on when Meigs left office in 1882. In addition, he left about 12,000 miscellaneous claims for roughly $7 million most of which were for services rendered the army during the war.[40]

On May 1, 1869, the quartermaster general's office moved from the Corcoran Art Building, which it had occupied during the war, to one on 15th Street opposite the Treasury Building which was not fireproof. To safeguard the records related "to claims of vast amounts, and of great value to the people, who have just claims arising out of military service and military operations," Meigs suggested a fireproof building to be erected on the land west of the White House, occupied by the War and Navy Departments which would house all War Department bureaus. If constructed by use of "cast iron for the ornamental portions" such a building could be "erected in good style and at a moderate expense." In March 1871 Congress approved a new building on that land to house the Departments of State, War, and Navy, but it turned out to be a $10 million "gray granite mass," now called the Old Executive Office Building, not completed until 1888.[41]

A new building, under construction, didn't solve his immediate problem. His concern was somewhat diminished by the practice of forwarding all records in support of, or against, a claim to the third auditor of the treasury. But, when the third auditor said he could no longer store such records in a fireproof space as he had in the past, Meigs included in his 1878 annual report plans for a $200,000 fireproof brick building which could be used by both the Treasury and the War Department.[42]

Congress had earlier responded to Meigs' requests for fireproof buildings in Philadelphia and Jeffersonville, Indiana, for storage of clothing and the other vast quantities of material left over from the war. The plan for Jeffersonville was a rectangular building with an open courtyard center in which was erected a tower with space for a tank of water which could be discharged on any part of the building that should catch fire, and also for a watchman. The storerooms were relatively small with fire-resistant walls between them so any fire in one would not spread to those adjoining.[43]

His 1878 recommendation, which was repeated each year until he retired, was for a building similar to what had been built at Jeffersonville with the added observation that the open courtyard space could be roofed over if additional storage space was needed—he referred to this as a Hall of Records. He won the approval of President Rutherford Hayes, but Congress did not act.[44]

During his years as quartermaster general he had several official trips that must have delighted him. In 1869–1870 he traveled to Texas and the Southwest and had the company of his son Montie. Nightly, he would write his wife by the light of the campfire. California, Arizona, and western posts and railroad routes were explored in 1871 and 1872. And, in 1875–1876, by direction of President Grant he went to Europe to study the armies there. On this European trip he took his wife, daughter Loulie, and, as aide and secretary, his nephew Second Lieutenant Montgomery Meigs Macomb and his son Montie, respectively. These trips gave him plenty of chances to work on sketching and hunting, lifelong pursuits.[45]

General in Chief William T. Sherman was lavish in his praise in 1875 when Meigs was on his way to Europe: "I do honestly think and have often said that no Government ever had a more honorable and honest man in a most responsible position than General Meigs throughout his whole career in the army...to hold this high command."[46]

Meigs at age 65 did not leave office willingly. A confluence of events probably did him in. On September 19, 1881, President James Garfield, a Civil War comrade, was assassinated, and Chester Arthur became president. Earlier, the daughter of his subordinate, Colonel Daniel Rucker, married Lieutenant General Philip Sheridan.

The president ordered his retirement. By law he could retire any officer who had served more than 42 years or had reached 62 years of age. Rucker, who was near 70, was appointed to relieve him but only held the position for three days; then the job, and rank, passed to Rufus Ingalls (age 62) on March 16, 1882. A friend of Meigs speculated that Grant may have been the main force behind the president's action. Ingalls was the chief quartermaster in the field with the Army of the Potomac and the armies around Richmond in 1864 and had a warm relationship with Grant. If Meigs held any animosity against Grant, it was gone in 1885 when Grant was financially ruined and Meigs and others were pushing for Congress to put him on the retired list of the army with full pay. He said Grant's contributions to the country could not be justly estimated for at least a hundred years, but he knew the "change[s] [Grant] brought into the expenses in men, material and money of every campaign in which he took part" and it was strange that such "considerations [had] not long since been more fully and ably set before th[e] country and its legislature." After it was learned that Grant had cancer of the throat and was dying, Congress, on March 20, 1885, put him on the retired list at full pay. Grant died four months later.[47]

Meigs can be faulted for not voluntarily making room for these officers who served loyally for 30 years in important positions in the Quartermaster Department. They were both at, or near, the end of their military careers, and it was fitting for them to have the opportunity to be quartermaster general.

National Museum

The National Museum finished in 1881, designed by Montgomery Meigs, provided the least expensive government building to that time. Located next to the Smithsonian Castle, it was used to house and display Smithsonian acquisitions, then and now (today called the Arts and Industries Building). It was the site for President James Garfield's inaugural ball.

Washingtoniana Division, D.C. Public Library

Pension Building

The Pension Building, designed and supervised by Meigs, completed in 1887, has been used for a number of presidential balls. It is constructed of over 15 million bricks, the largest brick building in the world at that time. Some called it "Meigs' Old Red Barn," but it has stood the test of time. Recently, it was described as "one of this nation's most gloriously original public buildings," and by architect Philip Johnson, referring to its Great Hall, as "the most astonishing interior space in America."

Library of Congress

Frieze around Pension Building

A three-foot frieze runs completely around the building immediately above the first-floor windows. The figures are of Civil War forces: "a continuous parade of Union infantry, cavalry, artillery, navy, quartermaster, and medical units." The building was restored in the 1980s and is now home of the National Building Museum.

Author's Collection

Interior of Pension Building

Library of Congress

Interior of Meigs' home

The interior of the Pension Building is not nearly as ornate as the interior of the Meigs' home.

Library of Congress

Louisa Meigs

Library of Congress

Montgomery Meigs

National Archives

Brigadier General Meigs was photographed shortly after the war and Louisa, circa 1876, while they were in Europe. The picture *below* shows the son they lost to the war, John Rodgers Meigs, seated in the *middle* of the West Point Class of 1863.

John Rodgers Meigs and other cadets

Library of Congress

Meigs family grave site

Louisa and Montgomery Meigs are at rest together with son John Rodgers Meigs
at Grave Site No. 1 in Arlington National Cemetery.

Chapter 29
The Rest of His Life

To some extent during the war, and to a larger extent after the war, Montgomery Meigs participated in the civilian side of Washington. In the 1850s and 1860s there was a learned group, informally known as the Scientific Club, or The Saturday Club, which met on Saturday evenings "for the discussion of scientific subjects and for general scientific conversation"; the evenings closed with supper. Center to this group was Joseph Henry, the secretary of the Smithsonian Institute, a good friend of Meigs, and one who "used his scientific knowledge to concoct a punch with a base of pure alcohol" when the meetings were held at the Smithsonian.[1]

When Hugh McCulloch, later secretary of the treasury in the Lincoln, Johnson, and Arthur administrations, came to Washington in 1863, he was invited to join the group, notwithstanding his lack of knowledge of the sciences. He was told by Henry that finance was a subject in which the country was deeply interested, and the club wanted a member knowing something about it. This probably reflected Meigs' thinking since the wherewithal to pay for quartermaster purchases was a pragmatic problem he faced daily.[2]

At the time McCulloch started attending the get-togethers, the members, in addition to Meigs, were:

*Joseph Henry	whose most important work, in Meigs' mind, was in electromagnetism which laid the groundwork for the telegraph.[3]
*Alexander Dallas Bache	a physicist who was superintendent of the United States Coast Survey with a long-standing interest in terrestrial magnetism. He was the first president of the National Academy of Sciences.

---

* The club members who were also members of the National Academy of Sciences, as was Meigs, are shown by the asterisks.

Peter Parker	a medical missionary and diplomat in China
*Simon Newcomb	primarily a mathematical astronomer who received many rewards during his lifetime
*Julius E. Hilgard	a geodesist and a protégé of A. D. Bache who worked at the Coast Survey and was active in the area of weights and measures
George C. Schaeffer	a prodigy of learning who was a librarian in the Interior Department
*Andrew A. Humphreys	an engineer, scientist, and soldier who had distinguished Civil War service, both as a staff officer and as a line general, and chief of the Corps of Engineers after the war
Jonathan H. Lane	a man of large scientific acquirements whose hobby was to create by mechanical contrivances or chemical means intense cold
William B. Taylor	thought by some to be the most learned man in Washington who was an examiner at the Patent Office
Titian H. Peale	naturalist, artist, mechanician who, in his early years, accompanied expeditions to the upper Missouri, Columbia, and the South Sea, and, in his middle and later years, was a Patent Office examiner in Washington
Benjamin N. Craig	a clearheaded man employed in the Medical Museum
*James M. Gilliss	an observational astronomer who spent a number of years in Chile, and, during the Civil War, headed the Naval Observatory in Washington
J. N. McComb	a naval officer
Orlando M. Poe	an 1856 West Point graduate who performed important engineering duties during and after the war
*Frederick A. P. Barnard	an academic, president of the University of Mississippi when the war started, who came north, and was later president of Columbia College[4]

Club participation became so large in 1871, with as many as 50 attending, that a formal, restrictive organization was brought into being called the Philosophical Society of Washington. Together with Meigs and others committing themselves to the new organization were Aspah

Hall (an observer and mathematician at the Naval Observatory who discovered two satellites to Mars), General in Chief William T. Sherman, and Chief Justice Salmon P. Chase. An object of the Philosophical Society was to "help chart the course of national development." Only those with "a high apprehension of science" or "some familiarity with its principles" and the capability "of promoting the objects" of the organization were elected as members.[5]

Meetings, held twice a month in a room at Ford's Theater, were directed to "scrutinizing claims to advances in knowledge" by hearing and commenting on prepared papers. Joseph Henry held the highest office every year until his death in 1878, and Meigs and others "were so often returned to office that their names became synonymous with the Society itself." But his interest in clubs did not include social ones. In declining an 1881 invitation to join the Army & Navy Club in New York, he wrote: "I am not a club man. Have only belonged to one and was driven from that by finding the reading room intolerable from the smoking."[6]

Henry and the Smithsonian were the loadstones for science during Meigs' lifetime. The Smithsonian Institution carries that name as a result of an 1835 bequest ($515,169) by Englishman James Smithson conditioned on its use to make "an establishment for the increase and diffusion of knowledge among men." It was not until 1846 that Congress passed a law for the money to be used as specified by Smithson. Although supervised by the president, vice president, chief justice, secretaries of state, treasury, and war, and other public officials, primary oversight is by a Board of Regents of whom there were, in its first 50 years, 129 members, one of whom was Meigs.[7]

The executive officer of the board is the secretary who is appointed by the board, and, during Meigs' years, there were three talented, dedicated individuals—Joseph Henry (1846–1878), Spencer Baird (1878–1887), and Samuel P. Langley (1887–1906).[8]

The "Castle," as the original building for the Smithsonian is now known, was constructed in the years 1847–1852 and has had additions and changes over the years. Its ornate architecture, with its many towers, and distinctive brown freestone exterior, is in stark contrast to the brick building designated National Museum, 1879 (now known as the Arts and Industries Building), next to it designed by Meigs.[9]

In the late 1870s the Castle could no longer store the collections being accumulated, particularly those given to the Smithsonian after the 1876 Centennial Exhibition held in Philadelphia. Needed was as much exhibition space as could be provided for the $250,000 appropriated for what became the National Museum Building. The need for additional space was highlighted by Congress deciding that "all collections made by federal surveys [were to] be deposited in the National Museum." At the time there were four federally funded surveys studying "rock strata in the far west" and investigating "whether any use could be made of this last, unsettled part of the country." The surveys collected Indian artifacts and did fruitful work in the fields of "geology, botany, and paleontology." One survey was an army, one headed by Lieutenant George Montague Wheeler, which received support from the Quartermaster Department as did some of the others.[10]

Built in 1879–1881 the National Museum was described in 1897 as being "devoid of architectural pretensions," but the Meigs' design has held up over the years and presents to current eyes a pleasing, unique structure. In 1881 it was used for the inaugural ball for President James Garfield. That night, it resembled "a crystal palace" with "the whiteness of electric lights" setting off its rotunda and dome, and the rest of the building was aglow with "the yellowness of...thousands of gas burners." In 1884 it was described as a building

> of brick laid in black mortar, with ornamental lines near the cornice of buff and blue brick. The trimmings are of granite.... There is a central rotunda, octagonal in shape, with a dome, and four naves radiating from it, forming a Greek cross.... The roof, or roofs—for there are a series of them—are of iron. The main floors are covered with tile in fancy designs. The building is well lighted by numerous windows, in many of which are beautiful pictures photographed upon the glass, representing Indians, and scenes in the western Territories. In the rotunda is a deep basin with a fountain, constantly playing.
>
> The heating, water, and gas pipes are conducted through subterranean ducts, and there is a perfect network of telegraph and telephone wires.... [E]lectricity is made to do duty in many ways—lighting, moving clocks, burglar-alarms, call-bells, etc.

And, very important to Congress, it "cost less than 25 per cent as much for the accommodation afforded as any other permanent building ever erected."[11]

On December 26, 1885, Meigs was made a member of the Smithsonian Board of Regents and immediately placed on the Executive Committee. A landmark continuing to the present was established by the Smithsonian during his regency years. Animal specimens in the form of skins and skeletons were early objects of the museum. When Samuel Langley became secretary he wanted to expand the collection to live animals. To both facilitate studying animals and to call attention to the danger of killing off various indigenous species, such as the American buffalo, Langley wanted to confine them under somewhat natural conditions.[12]

Congress was convinced and, in 1889, appropriated money to acquire the needed land. The site selected, that of the current National Zoological Park, was only two miles from the White House in the valley of Rock Creek. Shortly before Meigs' death 185 animals, large and small, were placed on the zoo grounds. Up to that time they "had been kept huddled together...in a low shed and a few small paddocks upon the south side of the Smithsonian building."[13]

Meigs also was an active member of the National Academy of Sciences which was incorporated by an act of Congress signed on March 3, 1863. Formation of such an organization had been an idea in the air for a number of years that came to fruition during the Civil War when the need for the government to have some way of evaluating scientific developments became pressing. A key provision in the law was:

> The Academy shall, whenever called upon by any department of the Government, investigate, examine, experiment, and report upon any subject of science or art.

When invited to be a member in 1865 Meigs wrote to his father that it was probably a greater honor to be invited then than to have been one of the 50 persons named in the act incorporating the academy. Joseph Henry, president of the academy in 1867, agreed. Henry made the point that the academy was not responsible for the original 50 members but was for those since elected. In 1863 an original member thought the initial business of the academy should be to vote on which of the original members should be retained. To be elected was "a high honor" since the academy should be "exclusively composed of men distinguished for original research."[14]

Meigs chaired an academy committee in 1884 which recommended to Congress creation of a Department of Science to include the Coast and Geodetic Survey, the Geological Survey, a Meteorological Bureau (to take over the army Signal Service meteorological work), and an observatory "to investigate the laws of solar and terrestrial radiation and their application to meteorology." To take the weather service out of the army was a step favored by Commanding General Philip Sheridan and the secretary of war. Congress had established a commission to investigate conditions in the Signal Service and other agencies, with an eye to increasing the efficiency of all the organizations. As a first step the commission asked the National Academy of Sciences to give its views.[15]

Although Congress did not establish a new department, several of the recommendations of the committee came into being. The meteorological service was transferred in 1890 to the newly created Department of Agriculture. A Bureau of Standards was established, and an Astrophysical Observatory was organized under the Smithsonian Institution.[16]

Collection of weather data was a subject in which Meigs had a particular interest, an interest which could be traced to his grandfather, Josiah Meigs, who, as commissioner of the General Land Office, had the land offices spread throughout the United States collect meteorological data beginning in 1817. Josiah not only collected weather information he also asked for information concerning "the time of the migration of birds, the earliest appearance of flowers in the spring, the hibernation of animals, seismic disturbances, and anything relating to the antiquities of the country."[17]

The early 1800s was a time of debate over the effect of land clearance on climate. Thomas Jefferson thought "a change in climate was unquestionably taking place." When Joseph Henry became secretary of the Smithsonian in 1846, one of his first acts was to start "a system of extended meteorological observations for solving the problem of American storms," and, as telegraph lines came into being, Henry saw an opportunity, with the cooperation of telegraph companies, to warn people of storms that might be coming their way. A "system of daily telegraphic weather reports" was established.[18]

The demand put upon telegraph lines by the Civil War stopped this. Following the war, Henry urged the creation of a centralized system of collection of meteorological observations, and, in 1870, Congress set up a national weather service and gave the job to the army which assigned the task to the Signal Service. Over the period 1870–1880 the Signal Service made tentative steps toward providing flood warnings, showed an interest in giving hurricane warnings, encouraged state weather services, gained information from balloon flights, and rejected a plan to cause rain by shooting cannon into the sky.[19]

Although the Signal Service did a good job—by 1886, 132 regular stations reported and an accuracy in forecasts of a range of about 70–75 percent was reached—Meigs thought the job could more efficiently be done by others. He floated the idea to Professor Spencer F. Baird, then secretary of the Smithsonian, to have collections made by postmasters. A drawback with the Signal Corps was the army practice of rotating men between jobs. An alternative was to select six hundred to one thousand postmasters from the 50,000 in the country and train them to "read barometers, thermometers, wind vanes and rain gauges" which data would be telegraphed to Washington where, in the Post Office Department, an "office with a few experts, men devoted for life to the science of meteorology, could digest the reports and advance the science." The data could be collected at an expense of only a few dollars per year added to the postmaster's compensation.[20]

In the almost 30 years of active membership which Meigs had with the academy, the organization prepared 26 reports for the government. The studies were varied: "protection of bottoms of iron vessels from corrosion (1863)," "tests for purity of whiskey (1864)," "surveys of the Territories (1878)," "opium (1886–1887)," and "the north magnetic pole (1890)." Meigs was on a standing committee which handled many matters and another concerned with "proving and gauging distilled spirits and preventing fraud (1866)."[21]

From 1871 to 1875 he encouraged the academy to ask Congress to have experiments made on American coal deposits. Nothing seems to have come from this, but he received authority for the Quartermaster Department to run tests in the years 1879–1882. One of his last acts in office was to arrange for the publication and distribution of the results of these tests. In essence, the heat value of various coals was determined by boiling water, and, so as to tie the results in with earlier tests run by the navy in 1844, Meigs designed the boiler. The tests were conducted at the quartermaster general's office in Washington.[22]

Postwar Washington was a city with outstanding people, but it was a dismal place in which to live. During the war Washington had "endless train[s] of army wagons plough[ing] its streets with...their heavy wheels." "Across the Potomac, Arlington Heights were whitened by the tents of soldiers, from which the discharges of artillery or the sound of the fife and drum became so familiar that the dweller almost ceased to notice it." At night "swarms of rats, of a size proportional to their ample food supply" were afoot. With the excitement and activity of the war gone the city looked much as it had before, except somewhat worse for wear or tear, and an increase in population from about 75,000 to 125,000.[23]

Lands earmarked by L'Enfant for public use were either being used for other purposes or were "empty, weed-grown fields." Washington Canal (now Constitution Avenue) and Tiber Creek "were open sewers," Foggy Bottom (within which are now located the State Department and George Washington University) was a breeding ground of malaria, and the Potomac Flats "at low water a foul-smelling mudbank stretching from the White House to below the Long Bridge [now the 14th Street Bridge]." "[C]attle, geese and chickens roamed at will," stray dogs were plentiful, dead animals posed a hazard, and streets were "deep in dust or mud according to the weather." In 1870, Pennsylvania Avenue was "undrained, unpaved and unswept." Horace Greeley reportedly said: "The rents are high, the food is bad, the dust is disgusting, the mud is deep and the morals are deplorable."[24]

It is little wonder that around 1870 a clamor was made to move the capital to a more urban area and perhaps to the Midwest to be more centrally located. This threat, plus the general squalor, activated the local citizenry to take steps to improve the city. The years 1871–1874, although short in span, brought about much improvement together with some scandalous conduct.[25]

In 1871 Congress passed a law creating a territorial government for the District of Columbia with a powerful Board of Public Works. Working within and without the confines of this law, Alexander "Boss" Shepherd, a well-to-do Washingtonian and the de facto force behind the Board of Public Works and later as territorial governor, "transformed Washington into a metropolis with paved streets, good sidewalks, adequate water and sewage facilities, gas lights, and spacious parks; but at staggering cost." Cost overruns, corruption, and careless methods caused Congress to do away with the territorial government and put the District of Columbia under commission rule in 1874. Notwithstanding his high-handed actions, and the refusal of the Senate to make him one of the commissioners with the change of organization, Shepherd was appreciated for what he accomplished and was honored in later years. President Grant was a firm supporter of the work performed by the Board of Public Works.[26]

In the transformation Meigs played minor roles. The Board of Public Works, which had the job of modernizing the city, created an advisory panel to help in deciding how the work should proceed. After its initial report the panel (consisting of Meigs, Brigadier General Andrew Humphreys, chief of engineers, Major General Orville Babcock, commissioner of public buildings and grounds, Brigadier General Joseph K. Barnes, surgeon general, and Frederick Law Olmstead, chief engineer of the improvement of Central Park, New York) did not monitor the board's activities. The panel suggested which areas of the city should have priority—primarily, that the northwest quadrant, with the Capitol as focal point, should be first, together with selected roads leading out of the city (7th Street to be macadamized and 14th Street graded and leveled). It also recommended putting islands down the middle of streets and planting them with trees and shrubs—during the Boss Shepherd period 60,000 plus trees were planted.[27]

The board decided to use wood on some of the streets. But this was only after a committee made up of Meigs, Babcock, and Humphreys reported on its use. Wood was cut into blocks about 3x3x6 inches and had the advantage of low cost and the muffling of horses' hoofs and carriage wheels. The use of wood did not turn out well.[28]

The improvements paid off. In the early 1880s Washington was described as "one of the most singularly handsome cities on the globe" with "its parks and wide avenues" and public edifices. Henry James visited Washington for the first time in 1882 and said: "I shouldn't wonder if the place were the most agreeable of our cities....The pleasant thing here is the absence of business—the economy-empty streets, most of them rather pretty, with nothing going on in them."[29]

The last third of the 19th century was a hallmark-building period for the nation's capital. Two massive, granite structures and one monument which we admire today, with unique architectural features, were constructed. The State, War, and Navy Building, now the Old Executive Office Building next to the White House, was built between 1871 and 1888 at a cost of $10 million. In 1886 Congress authorized a building for the Library of Congress, the doors of which opened on November 1, 1897, at a cost of $6 million.[30]

Interest in the Washington Monument started in 1832, land was set aside for it in 1848, and the obelisk rose to 154 feet before construction was stopped in 1854 for lack of money. For the next 20 years, the monument remained as described by Mark Twain like a "factory chimney with the top broken off." In 1876 the "factory chimney" was examined and found to be "out of plumb" with a foundation showing an "increasing departure from horizonality." After Congress provided money for the project in 1878 the foundation was strengthened, and construction started again but only after a board, including Meigs, Brigadier General Horatio G. Wright (chief of engineers), and another Corps of Engineers officer, according to an unverified report, told President Rutherford Hayes that the "existing masonry was sufficient and the remaining four hundred feet of the monument [could be] built upon it." The capstone was set on December 6, 1884. At a dedication ceremony on February 21, 1885, President Chester A. Arthur declared the monument to be for "the immortal name and memory of George Washington." The cost was $1.2 million.[31]

The high cost of these public works contrasted markedly with the $300,000 spent on the Meigs designed National Museum built in 1879–1881, and set the stage for a crowning achievement.[32]

When Meigs was put adrift by the army in February 1882, he was not ready to be put on the shelf. He wrote to Secretary of War Robert Lincoln in an effort to get the job of extending the Washington Aqueduct and said he was "not too old to have lost all desire to be useful."[33] Over the years, increasing demands upon the aqueduct created a need for greater line pressure, and complaints about muddy water needed to be addressed. Congress passed a law in July 1882 authorizing steps long advocated by Meigs in testimony and speeches, including the construction of a tunnel to a new reservoir on high ground north of the Capitol. He did not get the job. However, he was still respected enough, three years after his death, for a letter he had written to be cited as a basis for finishing the tunnel which had been suspended after poor engineering and management had brought it to a standstill.[34]

Any disappointment over not getting the aqueduct job was more than assuaged when Congress, on August 7, 1882, appropriated money for a "brick and metal fire-proof building for the use of the Pension Office" to be built under the "supervision of General M. C. Meigs...retired." Congress wanted a $300,000 building and got a $900,000 one, but what a one. Not only did this assignment put Meigs "to work...in the line in which [his] tastes,...inclinations, and...experience...naturally led [him]," it also helped with income. He was certain that he could "live comfortably upon the pay which the Government [gave] worn out officers," but he was not so sure about his unmarried daughter Loulie who liked to have a good income. She would not like to lose a "carriage & horses."[35]

With the death of his wife in November 1879, Loulie took over running his house. When he got into financial straits in 1886, and needed to borrow money to make improvements on real estate he owned in Washington, he called the situation to Loulie's attention asking that she restrict her expenses. Their reserve funds were dissipated and economy was imperative. Certainly not in response to this, but Loulie changed their arrangement. By June 1886 she agreed to marry and accompany Archibald Forbes, a Scotsman and noted newspaper correspondent and author, back to England. Forbes was somewhat older (48) than Loulie (31), but Montgomery thought she needed "a strong man to guide her own strong will." Her marriage to a foreigner caused him to worry about the estate he anticipated leaving to Loulie. He arranged it so that his "children's heritage" would not go to a foreign family if Loulie should die without children, but took care that Loulie should have funds if she, "in a land which [would] always be a foreign country to [her was] left [by] one of the manifold accidents of life destitute & alone."[36]

Loulie's departure did not leave Meigs alone. His daughter Mary and her family (two girls and three boys) came from Omaha to live with him after the death of her husband, Colonel Joseph Hancock Taylor, in 1885. One of Mary's daughters, about 19 then, described her grandfather, who was lame, as always being immaculately dressed and constantly reading. He was a dignified, kindly, punctual man, about six feet tall who kept his weight at two hundred pounds. His house, which was built in 1868–1869, was a wondrous place filled with interesting and stimulating things. His library was full of books.[37]

In constructing the Pension Building he more or less had a free hand; he was both architect and engineer. Striking interior columns were planned, 72 feet high and 7 feet in diameter, which could hardly fail to be impressive. If the money held out he wanted to top it off with an iron dome covered with tiles, but it didn't, and he settled for a cheaper tent roof. The building was started in November 1882, and, when completed in 1887, evoked the comment that "the like of [it was] not to be seen anywhere else in the country." The same can be said today. Many presidential balls have been held in its great hall.[38]

Not everyone was an admirer of the Pension Building. At times it was referred to as "Meigs's Old Red Barn." General Sheridan, after inspecting in under Meigs' guidance, told him there was only one fault in it. "What is that?" asked Meigs. "It is fireproof"—was the unexpected answer.[39]

Meigs was particularly pleased with the working conditions created for federal employees. Each office had window light, and no doors were installed so that air could circulate freely from the outside into and out of the building. In the year of occupancy 8,622 days in lost time due to illness was avoided. For a man who liked to deal in superlatives, it was gratifying that he had built the largest brick building in the world containing over 15 million bricks.[40]

Meigs was not a man to let an opportunity for ornamentation pass. One of the most impressive features of the building is the three-foot high frieze that completely wraps the building about 19 feet above the ground. His original conception was of a "procession of soldiers" with invalids, wounded, old men and women at the end. On the inside of the building, 244 niches about two and a half feet high were located around the cornice of the center bay. Into these went life-sized busts primarily of American Indians based on molds lent by the Smithsonian; included were busts of Meigs, his wife, and father. Meigs learned at some point that some of the molds were of convicted murderers.[41]

Over time the building fell into disrepair and escaped being re-modeled and added on to or being torn down. Today, it has been com-pletely restored and refurbished and is the home of the National Building Museum.[42]

Although Meigs was still looking for projects in 1886 when he pre-pared design ideas for a city post office and municipal offices, the Pension Building was his last construction project. He was starting to show his age. In 1887 he was incapacitated for active exercise. He wrote Loulie in Scotland that he was finding that "12 or 14 hours work fatigues [him] as it did not when [he] was 60." But he was thankful that he was being allowed to erect "a very Great Building which [would] in centuries to come...[be] the means of preserving the name of [the] family from absolute oblivion."[43]

The military tradition of the Meigs' line was carried on by Mary's sons. One went to West Point and the other to the Naval Academy. One reached the rank of colonel and the other vice admiral. Meigs' namesake, the son of his Corps of Engineers brother-in-law, John Navarre Macomb (West Point class of 1832), and sister-in-law, Anna Rodgers Macomb, Mont-gomery Meigs Macomb did well at West Point graduating fourth in the class of 1874.[44]

The Meigs' son Montie did not enter the military but worked as a civil engineer for the Corps of Engineers spending most of his profes-sional life at Rock Island Arsenal, Illinois, working on control of the Mis-sissippi River. He joined the Rock Island District in 1874 at a time when his uncle, Colonel John N. Macomb, was in charge and was assigned to make a comprehensive survey of the upper Mississippi River. A few years later he was made responsible for the Des Moines Rapids Canal at Keokuk, Iowa, and remained there until he retired in 1926. He was affectionately referred to as "Major" Meigs after he convincingly stood up against charges of ineptness and wastefulness made against the corps in 1877.[45]

As the time for the census to be taken in June 1890 approached, Mont-gomery Meigs put his mind on the future. He observed that Malthus had said in 1798 that the population of a country, with ample space, would double every 25 years. Finding this to be close to what had happened in the United States over the previous two hundred years, and with an expected population in 1890 of 67,240,000, he projected that by the year 1990 there would be a population of 1,206,400,000, plus 85,957,000 Negroes. Notwithstanding that he was wrong by a billion, his other remarks are interesting.

With such a population "of intelligent, educated, industrious people, of one race and blood, under one free government, armed with all that science teaches and man has invented—[he asked] who will wish to interfere with their happiness? Who will attack them?" Although he was wrong about who would have such a population, his questions are pertinent at the end of the 20th century.

Another of his observations casts a shadow over the less populous regions of the earth. He said, "[T]he Anglo-Saxon race will occupy the continent from the Isthmus to the Arctic, and, when crowded therein, must spread over South America, or perish. [Just as] the prairie wolf disappears when man drives off or subjugates the animals on which he lives...so will the weaker races give way to the stronger. It has been thus in all history, and the law still holds."

He foresaw an easier life for people; electric engines to do the heavy work, allowing more time for enjoyment. He thought that "[i]n all probability, electricity [would] heat as well as light...houses, and...cook...food. It [would] drive other as well as our city passenger railroads. And it is not probable that man [had] yet discovered all the resources laid up by the creator to be discovered and utilized by his creatures when needed for their happiness and comfort."[46]

After a sudden illness death came at his home on January 2, 1892, at age 75. Funeral services were held at St. John's Church:

> It was just 10:30 when the cavalry detachment arrived.... A bugle blast sounded out and the columns wheeled from H Street into 16th and formed a single line of men and horses, facing the church, just as the hearse bearing the casket reached the door on the south. A few sharp orders were given...and in a few moments the 150 men, divided into three troops, marked by bright guidons, sat motionless on their horses, the line of yellow capes extending as far north as I street.[47]

After the church service the body was taken to Arlington and on a caisson draped in the national colors and tied with black knots. As the procession of 150 cavalrymen, batteries of artillery, and foot soldiers started for Arlington the band played a dirge.[48]

At Arlington the body was prepared for the sarcophagus overlying the grave of Louisa Meigs, and, if General Meigs' instructions were followed, his head was covered with plaster of Paris or hydraulic cement in fine powder duly tempered with water but not in such quantity as to incur any risk by swelling of fracturing the sarcophagus. The instructions were for the lid to be secured from infiltration of water and that he be left to await the resurrection.[49]

In his life he lived up to the expectations of his father: he brought credit to the Meigs' name, and left evidence of his works in Washington, D.C. The markings on his tombstone, "Soldier Engineer Architect Scientist Patriot," were earned. Rest in peace Montgomery Cunningham Meigs, you served your family and country well.

Notes

Information about abbreviations used in chapter notes:

B&L	Robert Underwood Johnson and Clarence Clough Buel, eds., *Battles and Leaders*, 4 vols. (1887-88; reprint, Secaucus, N.J.: Castle, 1982).
Calendar	E. B. Long with Barbara Long, *The Civil War Day By Day* (New York: A Da Capo Paperback, 1971).
Cullum	George W. Cullum, *Biographical Register of the Officers and Graduates of the U.S. Military Academy*, 3d ed., vol. 1 (Boston: Houghton, Mifflin and Company, 1891).
DAB	Allen Johnson and Dumas Malone, eds., *Dictionary of American Biography*, 10 vols. (New York: Charles Scribner's Sons, 1927-1936).
Dictionary	Mark Mayo Boatner III, *The Civil War Dictionary* (revised edition, New York: Vintage Books, 1991).
MCM Journal (Nicolay Papers)	Transcribed copy of M. C. Meigs' journal, written in shorthand, for the period March-September 1861, found in John G. Nicolay's papers (container 13) at the Library of Congress, Manuscript Reading Room.
Meigs Conduct of the War	Montgomery Meigs, "General M. C. Meigs on the Conduct of the Civil War," *The American Historical Review* 26, no. 2 (1920-21): 285-303.
Meigs Journal (Transcribed)	"Journals, Montgomery C. Meigs Papers," Manuscript Division, Library of Congress, transcribed by William Mohr for the United States Senate Bicentennial Commission,

	examined in the office of House Curator with the understanding that "the source is an unedited and unverified transcript of a work in progress."
Meigs Papers	Montgomery Meigs' papers held by the Library of Congress, Manuscript Reading Room. The notations following Meigs Papers are to the accession numbers, of which there are two (18,202 and 18,202.1), the reel numbers within the applicable accession, and the approximate exposure number on the microfilm copy of the papers. The exposure number is often followed by the date of the document being cited. Where a reel contains a series of letters, more or less, chronological, the date of the letter is helpful for locating the document cited.
OR	*The War of the Rebellion, A Compilation of the Official Records of the Union and Confederate Armies*, published by the Government Printing Office between 1880 and 1900. The compilation consists of four different series, designated *OR* I, *OR* II, etc., but, in the main, is in the first series. The first series has 52 volumes many of which are made up of from 2 to 5 parts, each part having separate pagination. Hence, *OR* I, vol. 1, pt. 2, 32 is a reference to *Official Records*, series I, volume 1, part 2 at page 32.
Pocket Diary	A typed copy of parts of a pocket diary kept by Meigs during the Civil War which is found at Meigs Papers (18,202) reel 12, 0037 et seq. (renumbering of exposures starts after 0428).
QMG	Annual reports of the Quartermaster General for the year shown.
SecWar	Annual reports of the Secretary of War for the year shown.

Preface

1. Henry B. Meigs, *Record of the Descendants of Vincent Meigs* (Baltimore, Md.: J. S. Bridges & Co., 1901), appendix, 268.

2. Jeanne Fogle, *Two Hundred Years* (Arlington, Va.: Vandamere Press, 1991), 68.

3. James G. Blaine, *Twenty Years in Congress*, vol. 2 (1886), 30, as quoted in the *Dictionary of American Biography*, Montgomery Cunningham Meigs.

Chapter 1

1. Sherrod E. East, "Banishment of Captain Meigs," *Records of the Columbia Historical Society* 40-41 (1939): 135.
2. Harry C. Ways, *The Washington Aqueduct, 1852-1992* (United States Corps of Engineers, 1996), 29, 31.
3. Meigs Journal (Transcribed), 1/4/59.
4. Ibid., 1/1/59.
5. *OR* I, vol. 52, pt. 1, 3-5; Meigs Journal (Transcribed), 2/21/61.
6. Meigs Journal (Transcribed), 2/21/61; Pocket Diary, 1/18/61; Meigs Papers (18,202.1), reel 5, 0167 (1/23/61).
7. East, 138; Meigs Papers (18,202.1), reel 5, 0177 (2/1/61).
8. Meigs Papers (18,202.1), reel 5, 0174 (2/1/61). Those exiting Buchanan's Cabinet were: Howell Cobb (Treasury) in December 1860, John B. Floyd (War) in December 1860, Jacob Thompson (Interior) in January 1861, and Philip Thomas (Treasury) in January 1861. See Elbert B. Smith, *The Presidency of James Buchanan* (Lawrence: The University Press of Kansas, 1975), 143, 179, 184.
9. Pocket Diary, 2/12/61, 2/20/61; East, 142; *OR* III, vol. 1, 331.

Chapter 2

1. Henry Meigs, 231.
2. Ibid., 231.
3. Ibid., at various pages, and *DAB* for each.
4. *DAB*, Josiah Meigs; Henry Meigs, 232.
5. Meigs Papers (18,202.1), reel 14, 0523-25, reel 15, 011.
6. *DAB* Charles D. Meigs; Henry Meigs, 234, 268 et seq.; J. Forsyth Meigs, *Memoir of Charles D. Meigs* (Philadelphia: Lindsay & Blakiston, 1876), 9, 28-30.
7. Meigs Papers (18,202), reel 16, 0606.
8. Ibid., reel 12, typed journal entry for 7/15/1874 (002).
9. Henry Meigs, 268 et seq.
10. *DAB*, Montgomery Meigs; Meigs Papers (18,202), reel 22, 0544.
11. Meigs Papers (18,202), reel 16, 0604.
12. Edward C. Boynton, *History of West Point* (2d ed., D. Van Nostrand, 1871), 322; Stephen E. Ambrose, *Duty, Honor, Country, A History of West Point* (Baltimore: Johns Hopkins Press, 1966), 9.
13. Ambrose, 9-10.
14. *Statutes at Large* 2 (1802): 132, sec. 26-28; Boynton, 320; Ambrose, 10, 12-13, 22, 25.
15. Ambrose, 36.
16. Ibid., 38-39, 43-44; Boynton, 322.
17. Boynton, 313; George S. Pappas, *To The Point, The United States Military Academy 1802-1902* (New York: Praeger Publishing, 1993), 218, 231-32; Ambrose, 70-71; James L. Morrison, *The Best School In The World* (Kent, Ohio: The Kent State University Press, 1986), 8-10. Act of April 29, 1812, ch. 72, sec. 3, provided that West Point graduates should serve five years unless sooner discharged.
18. Ambrose, 73-76; Pappas, 128, 200; Morrison, 24, 88.
19. Pappas, 109, 164-65, 249; Morrison, 24, 43, 87-88.
20. Pappas, 163-64.
21. Ambrose, 89, 97; Henry Petroski, *Engineers of Dreams* (New York: Alfred A. Knopf, Inc., 1995), 23-25.

22. Ambrose, 107, 111-12, 116-17, 120-124; Pappas, 231-32.

23. Ambrose, 108-10; Pappas, 200-209, 223-27.

24. *Official Register of Officers and Cadets, U.S. Military Academy, West Point, 1818-1837; Cullum* at Class of 1836.

25. Meigs Papers (18,202.1) reel 15, 0266 (12/12/81).

26. *Official Register of Officers and Cadets, U.S. Military Academy, West Point 1818-1837;* Jennie Forsyth Jeffries, comp., *A History of the Forsyth Family* (Indianapolis: W. B. Burford, 1920), 50-51; *DAB*, John Forsyth.

27. Meigs Papers (18,202.1), reel 11, 0525.

28. *Cullum* at Class of 1829 (22d in Class standing); John Frances McDermott, *Seth Eastman Pictorial Historian of the Indian* (Norman: University of Oklahoma Press, 1961), 3-5, 12, 23; Sarah E. Boehme, *Seth Eastman, A Portfolio of North American Indians* (Afton, Minn.: Afton Historical Society Press, 1995), 6.

29. Ambrose, 71, 150.

30. Pappas, 227, 240-41.

31. Ibid., 211, 241-42.

32. Ibid., 228.

33. Ibid., 228-29.

34. Ibid., 203, 216, 228.

Chapter 3

1. *Cullum* at Class of 1836; Meigs Papers (18,202), reel 22, 0544.

2. John K. Mahon, *History of the Second Seminole War 1835-1842* (Gainesville, Fla.: University of Florida Press, 1967), 116.

3. Ibid., 72; 21st Congress, 1st Session, ch. 148, *Statutes at Large* 4 (5/28/1830): 411; Samuel Eliot Morison, *The Oxford History of the American People* (New York: Oxford University Press, 1965), 446-52.

4. *Mahon,* 85-86, 88-105; *Cullum* at Class of 1836.

5. *Mahon*, 315-18, 321, 323-25.

6. Russell F. Weigley, *History of the United States Army* (New York: The Macmillan Company, 1967), 163.

7. Weigley, *History*, 163, 164, 166; *Historical Sketch of the Corps of Engineers* (letter from the chief of engineers to the secretary of war, GPO, 1876), 33, 35, 37, 39 (cited hereafter as *Historical Sketch*).

8. George S. Pappas, *To The Point, The United States Military Academy 1802-1902* (New York: Praeger Publishing, 1993), 221-22; *Historical Sketch*, 37.

9. *Dictionary*.

10. *DAB*.

11. *SecWar (1847)*, 75, and *(1849)*, 188.

12. *Cullum* at Class of 1836; Meigs Papers (18,202), reel 22, 0544; Douglas Southall Freeman, *R. E. Lee*, vol. 1 (New York: Charles Scribner's Sons, 1934-35), 137-40.

13. Freeman, 140; *Encyclopedia Brittanica* (1947 Edition) for St. Louis; Meigs Papers (18,202.1), reel 4, 014 (8/5/1837); *Secretary of War Annual Report 1838*, 237-38.

14. Meigs Papers (18,202.1), reel 4, 014-015 (8/5/1837); Freeman, 144.

15. Freeman, 143-47; Meigs Papers (18,202), reel 16, circa 0011 (statement dictated by Meigs' granddaughter Louisa Taylor Alger), 12.

16. Ibid., 148.

17. *Cullum* at Class of 1836; Meigs Papers (18,202.1), reel 22, 0544-45; Henry B. Meigs, *Record of the Descendants of Vincent Meigs* (Baltimore, Md.: J. S. Bridges & Co., 1901), 88; *DAB*, John Rodgers.

18. Meigs Papers (18,202.1), reel 7, 0007 (2/24/41).

19. *Cullum* at Class of 1836; Meigs Papers (18,202.1), reel 22, 0545.

20. Henry Meigs, 88.

21. National Archives, Office of the Chief of Engineers, RG 77, "Meigs letter to Chief of Engineers (10/9/1845), and Chief of Engineers letter (7/20/1845)," entries 6 and 17.

22. Morison, 546-47.

23. *Cullum* at Class of 1836; Meigs Papers (18,202.1), reel 14, 0526.

24. Article I, section 8.

25. John W. Reps, *Washington On View* (Chapel Hill, N.C.: The University of North Carolina Press, 1991), 1- 2, 10, 14-15.

26. Ibid., 2-3, 10.

27. Ibid., 2.

28. Ibid., 6, 39.

29. Ibid., 10, 31, 32, 40, 42.

30. Ibid., 57.

31. Ibid., 76.

32. Charles Dickens, *American Notes For General Circulation* (1842; reprint, Penquin Classics, 1985), 162-64.

33. William Tindall, *History of the City of Washington* (Knoxville, Tenn.: H. W. Crew & Co., 1914), 361; Bicentennial Edition, *Historical Statistics of the United States*, 93rd Congress, House Document No. 93-78; Donald D. Dodd, comp., *Historical Statistics of the States of the United States* (Westport, Conn.: Greenwood Press, 1993).

34. Tallmadge A. Lambert, "Observations on the Development of the Nation's Capital," *Records of the Columbia Historical Society* 2 (1897): 282-83; Joseph T. Kelly, "Memories of a Lifetime in Washington," *Records of the Columbia Historical Society* 31-32 (1928): 119; Hal H. Smith, "Historic Washington Homes," *Records of the Columbia Historical Society* 11 (1907): 244, 258, 263-66; Richard M. Lee, *Mr. Lincoln's City* (McLean, Va.: EPM Publications, 1981), 12-13.

35. Wilhelmus Bogart Bryan, *A History of the National Capital*, vol. 2 (New York: The Macmillan Company, 1914-16), 104-17, 355; Kelly, 118-19; Tindall, *History*, 360-61.

36. Kelly, 119.

37. Ibid., 123, 127; Tindall, *History*, 363, 366; Junior League of Washington, edited by Thomas F. Roncek, *The City of Washington* (New York: Alfred A. Knopf, 1979), 300.

38. Bryan, 309-12.

39. Kelly, 125; Tindall, *History*, 362.

Chapter 4

1. *Cullum* at Class of 1836.

2. John Y. Cole, "LC in the 19th Century—An Informal Account," *Library of Congress Professional Association* (1972): 2-3; William C. Allen, *The Dome of the United States Capitol: An Architectural History*, Senate Document 102-7, 102d Congress, 1st Session (1992), 6-7.

3. Harry C. Ways, *The Washington Aqueduct, 1852-1992* (United States Corps of Engineers, Baltimore District, 1996), 3-4; *Senate Executive Document No. 48*, 32d Congress, 2d Session, 11 (cited hereafter as *No. 48*); History of the Washington Aqueduct, 1852-1952, Washington District, Corps of Engineers, 1953, 2-3 (cited hereafter as Aqueduct, 1852-1952).

4. Aqueduct, 1852-1952, 3.

5. *No. 48*, 1-2.

6. Ibid., 8, 30.

7. Meigs Papers (18,202.1), reel 4, 072.

8. *Cullum* at Class of 1836; *No. 48,* 2; Ways, 10.

9. National Geographic, *"The Washington Aqueduct and Cabin John Bridge,"* National Geographic 8, no. 12 (1897): 338-39 (cited hereafter as National Geographic); *No. 48*, 2, 12.

10. *No. 48*, 11-12.

11. Ibid., 12.

12. Ibid., 13-14.

13. National Geographic, 339; *National Intelligencer*, 11/10/1853; *Congressional Globe*, 8/14/1856, 2106.

14. National Geographic, 338-39; Ways, iv, 7, 56; *No. 48*, 24.

15. *Statutes at Large* 10 (3/3/1853): 206; *National Intelligencer*, 11/10/1853.

16. *National Intelligencer*, 11/10/1853; Ways, 14; Harold K. Skramstad, "The Engineer as Architect in Washington: The Contribution of Montgomery Meigs," *Records of the Columbia Historical Society)* 47 (1969-70): 268.

17. Ways, 13.

18. Russell F. Weigley, *Quartermaster General of the Union Army* (New York: Columbia University Press, 1959), 63, 74; Meigs Journal (Transcribed) 5/4/54, 6/10/54.

19. Weigley, *Quartermaster General*, 51; Meigs Journal (Transcribed), 5/2/54, 4/25/56, 1/21/57, 5/3/57.

20. Aqueduct, 1852-1952, 8.

21. *No. 48*, 17; Aqueduct, 1852-1952, 35-36; American Society of Civil Engineers, *Civil Engineering Landmarks of the Nation's Capital* (Washington: American Society of Civil Engineers, National Capital Section, Committee on History and Heritage, 1982), 22.

22. *No. 48*, 29.

23. National Geographic, 339; *Senate Mis. Doc. No. 83*, 38th Congress, 1st Session (3/22/1864), 12-13; *Secretary of War Annual Report 1858*, 53.

24. Aqueduct, 1852-1952, 15-16.

25. Charles S. Whitney, *Bridges, Their Art, Science, & Evolution* (New York: Greenwich Press, 1983), 59, 61, 67; Fact sheet and letter from the West Virginia Department of Transportation dated January 6, 1997, to author.

26. National Geographic, 343; Aqueduct, 1852-1952, 15; Meigs Journal (Transcribed), 2/8/1856, 3/19/1856.

27. Aqueduct, 1852-1952, 15.

28. Ways, 52; *Senate Mis. Doc. No. 83*, 38th Congress, 1st Session (3/22/1864), 24-25; P. O. Macqueen, "Cabin John Bridge," *The Military Engineer* 24, no. 138 (1932): 567-68.

29. Ways, 57; Meigs Journal (Transcribed), 3/22, 29/1858, 4/3/1858.

30. *National Intelligencer*, 11/10/1853.

31. Henry B. Meigs, *Record of the Descendants of Vincent Meigs* (Baltimore, Md.: J. S. Bridges & Co., 1901), 88; Meigs Journal (Transcribed), 1/29/1854, 7/19/1854; Meigs Papers (18,202.1), reel 14, 0527.

32. National Geographic, 343-44; *Senate Mis. Doc. No. 83*, 38th Congress, 1st Session (3/22/1864), 4; Aqueduct, 1852-1952, 63; Mrs. Neal Fitzsimons, "The Building of the Cabin John Bridge," *Montgomery (Maryland) County Historical Society* 16, no. 1 (Feb. 1973): 7.

33. Aqueduct, 1852-1952, 21, 23-24.

34. Aqueduct, 1852-1952, 14; Ways, 29, 31.

35. Weigley, 88.

36. *Senate Mis. Doc. No. 83*, 38th Congress, 1st Session (3/22/1864), 26; Meigs Papers (18,202.1), reel 5, 2/25/64, 3/20/64.

Chapter 5

1. John W. Reps, *Washington on View* (Chapel Hill, N.C.: The University of North Carolina Press, 1991), 21; Fred J. Maroon, *The United States Capitol* (New York: Stewart, Tabori &

Chang, 1993), 46; *Plan of the City Intended for the Permanent Seat of the Government of the United States*, U.S. Coast and Geodetic Survey, 1887, based on L'Enfant's 1791 plan.

2. *The United States Capitol: A Brief Architectural History*, House Document 101-144, 101st Congress, 1st Session (1990), 2 (cited hereafter as *Capitol*).

3. *Capitol*, 3-5.

4. Ibid., 7-8; William C. Allen, *The Dome of the United States Capitol: An Architectural History*, Senate Document 102-7, 102d Congress, 1st Session (1992), 4 (cited hereafter as *Dome*).

5. *Capitol*, 5, 8-12.

6. *Capitol*, 10-12; Maroon, 37; *Dome*, 5.

7. *Statutes at Large* 9 (9/30/1850): 538; Glenn Brown, *History of the United States Capitol* (1900, 1902; reprint, New York: De Capo Press, 1970), 115-16, 119; *Capitol*, 13-14.

8. *Capitol*, 14; Brown, 119.

9. Brown, 119, and Plate 164; *Senate Rep. Com. No. 273*, 31st Congress, 2d Session, Feb. 8, 1851; *Capitol*, 14.

10. Brown, 122.

11. *Senate Rep. No. 1*, 33rd Congress, Special Session, 19-20.

12. *Documentary History, United States Capitol Building and Grounds*, House Report 646, 58th Congress, 2d Session (1904), 582 (cited hereafter as *Documentary*); *SecWar (1853)*, 32, 76; Brown, 125-26.

13. *Congressional Globe*, 8/14/1856, 2102 (cited hereafter as *Globe*).

14. *SecWar (1853)*, 69; Maroon, 38.

15. *SecWar (1853)*, 32-33; *Globe*, 6/21/1860, 3210; Meigs Papers (18,202.1), reel 20, 095.

16. *SecWar (1853)*, 33, 85-86; *DAB*, Bache and Henry.

17. Meigs Papers (18,202.1), reel 11, 0684-89.

18. *SecWar (1858)*, 751; Brown, 126-27; *Globe*, 8/14/1856, 2104; *SecWar (1853)*, 83; *Documentary*, 614-15.

19. *SecWar (1853)*, 72.

20. *SecWar (1853)*, 80; Meigs Papers (18,202), reel 23, 0100.

21. *Globe*, 8/14/1856, 2104.

22. Ibid., 6/21/1860, 3212; Benjamin Perley Poore, *Perley's Reminiscences*, vol. 1 (1886; reprint, New York: AMS Press, 1971), 486.

23. Brown, 153; Maroon, 115.

24. *SecWar (1853)*, 71.

25. *Dome*, 18, 36.

26. *Documentary*, 465; *Dome*, 36; Maroon, 42, 80.

27. *Documentary*, 610-11; *Globe*, 2/21/1855, 847-48.

28. Letters of Thomas Walter found in a file maintained by Sarah H. Turner, archivist, Office of the Architect of the Capitol (referred to hereafter as TUW together with the date of the letter): TUW (to Chas. Fowler) 3/15/55, (to Richard Stanton) 12/8/57.

29. Meigs Journal (Transcribed) 1/31/54, 11/4/54.

30. Ibid., 11/4/54.

31. Ibid., 11/4/54.

32. TUW (to John Rice) 10/12/57.

33. Meigs Papers (18,202), reel 13, 0391.

34. *Dome*, 36; *National Intelligencer (Washington)*, Dec. 7, 1857.

35. *SecWar (1858)*, 751-752.

36. Ibid., 750-751; *Globe*, 6/1/1858, 2589; *Capitol*, 13; *Dome*, 36.

37. *SecWar (1858)*, 752; *Documentary*, 443.

38. *Documentary*, 609; *Dome*, 6-7, 13.

39. Meigs Journal (Transcribed) 5/31/54, 12/11, 20, 26, 29/54.

40. Ibid., 12/24, 31/54, 1/2, 10, 20, 23, 25, 27, 31/55, 2/21/55; *Globe*, 2/22/1855, 893-94.

41. Meigs Journal (Transcribed) 2/24/55; *Dome*, 17-18.

42. Meigs Journal (Transcribed) 3/2/55; *Statutes at Large* 10 (3/3/1855): 663.

43. Meigs Journal (Transcribed) 2/2/55.

44. *Dome*, 18.

45. Ibid., 19-22.

46. I. T. Frary, *They Built The Capitol* (Richmond: Garrett and Massie, 1940), 192; Brown, 141-42, 203-4.

47. *Dome*, 24; *SecWar (1855)*, 119.

48. Meigs Journal (Transcribed) 12/31/54; *Dome*, 24, 26-28.

49. *Dome*, 26-27, 31, 34.

50. Ibid., 37.

51. TUW (to wife) 5/20/57, (to Chas. Heebner) 11/19/57, (to wife) 11/20/57; Meigs Journal (Transcribed), 5/5/57, 5/23/57, 6/8/57, 7/23/57, 8/20/57, 10/18/57, 10/21/57, 11/21/57, 5/24/58, 6/28/58, 1/15/59.

52. TUW (to John Rice) 9/7/57, (to Meigs) 9/7/57; Meigs Journal (Transcribed), 12/26/57.

53. TUW (to Meigs) 9/7/57.

54. *Senate Mis. Doc. No. 29*, 36th Congress, 1st Session, 5-8, 64-83, 102, 131-36.

55. TUW (to John Rice) 10/2, 22/57, 11/2, 4, 6/57, 12/4, 8/57.

56. Copy in TUW at 12/4/57.

57. TUW (to Richard Stanton) 12/8/57, (to John Rice) 12/9/57, (to Gridley I. F. Bryant) 12/14/57, (to John Rice) 12/22/57.

58. Meigs Journal (Transcribed) 12/26/57, 12/30/57.

59. TUW (to John Rice) 1/8/58, (to J. B. Floyd) 1/21/58.

60. *Pennsylvania Magazine of History and Biography*, ch. 25 (1901), 75-78; Meigs Journal (Transcribed), 3/10/58.

61. Meigs Journal (Transcribed) 2/18/58; Dunbar Rowland, col. and ed., *Jefferson Davis, His Letters, Papers and Speeches*, vol. 5 (Jackson, Miss.: Mississippi Department of Archives and History, 1923), 166 n. 3, 167-68.

62. *Dome*, 38; Meigs Journal (Transcribed) 3/19/58, 6/28/58.

63. *SecWar (1859)*, 561, *(1858)*, 758.

64. Meigs Journal (Transcribed) 1/22/58, 6/26/58.

65. Ibid., 1/30/58.

66. TUW (to John Rice) 9/4/58.

67. Meigs Journal (Transcribed) 5/20/57, 6/5/57, 7/1/57, 7/26/57, 9/4/57, 10/13/57, 10/21/57, 11/21/57, 12/31/57, 1/13/58, 1/25/58, 3/7/58, 3/9/58.

68. Ibid., 1/20/58.

69. TUW (to wife) 8/10/58; Meigs Journal (Transcribed), 8/25, 26/58.

70. Meigs Journal (Transcribed) 9/15, 16, 24/58.

71. Ibid., 10/5/58; Brown, 134; *Dome*, 38.

72. Meigs Journal (Transcribed) 10/7, 13, 27/58; *Dome*, 38-39.

73. Meigs Journal (Transcribed) 10/27/58.

74. Ibid., 11/19, 24/58, 3/16/59.

75. Ibid., 6/8, 22/59.

76. Ibid., 6/25/59.

77. Ibid., 9/5/59.

78. Ibid., 6/25/59.

79. Meigs Papers (18,202.1), reel 12, 018 (9/5/59); Russell F. Weigley, *Quartermaster General of the Union Army* (New York: Columbia University Press, 1959), 91-94.

80. Brown, 134, 135; *House Report No. 78*, 36th Congress, 2d Session, 6.

81. *SecWar (1859)*, 567; *Dome*, 41.

82. Meigs Journal (Transcribed) 11/6/59, 11/10/59, 12/9/59.

83. Meigs Papers (18,202), reel 14, 0628, 0665, reel 17, 0384, reel 26, 0218; (18,202.1), reel 21, 0102.

84. *Globe*, 6/11/1860, 2820-21.

Chapter 6

1. House of Representatives, 34th Congress, 1st Session, *Mis. Doc. 65*, 2-3; Meigs Journal (Transcribed) 2/15/56, 12/19/57.

2. Glenn Brown, *History of the United States Capitol* (1900, 1902; reprint, New York: De Capo Press,1970), 134; *OR* I, vol. 52, pt. 1, 139.

3. William C. Allen, *The Dome of the United States Capitol: An Architectural History*, Senate Document 102-7, 102d Congress, 1st Session (1992), 36 (cited hereafter as *Dome*); *Documentary History, United States Capitol Building and Grounds*, House Report 646, 58th Congress, 2d Session (1904), 612; *Congressional Globe*, 3/25/1862, 1348 (cited hereafter as *Globe*).

4. Adolf K. Placzek, ed. in chief, *Macmillan Encyclopedia of Architects* (New York: Free Press, 1982), 367, 369; *Dome*, 40-41; Brown, 203.

5. *Dome*, 75; Meigs Papers (18,202), reel 23, 0102 et seq.

6. *Dome*, 15-16, 19-20, 49.

7. United States Capitol Historical Society, *We, the People* (Washington: The National Geographic Society, 1985), 114 (cited hereafter as *We*).

8. *House Document 101-144*, 101st Congress, 1st Session, 14, 17, 33.

9. *Dome*, 70; I. T. Frary, *They Built The Capitol* (Richmond: Garrett and Massie, 1940), 196-98; Brown, 139-41, 203.

10. Brown, 139-40.

11. Ibid., 140.

12. *Globe*, 6/1/1858, 2588; *Globe*, 3/2/1859, 1588.

Chapter 7

1. Charles E. Fairman, *Art and Artists of the Capitol* (Washington: GPO, 1927), 144; William Allen, *The Dome of the United States Capitol: An Architectural History*, Senate Document 102-7, 102d Cong., 1st Sess. (1992), 8 (cited hereafter as *Dome*); *DAB*, Edward Everett.

2. Fairman, 142-44; *DAB*, Thomas Crawford, Hiram Powers.

3. Fred J. Maroon, *The United States Capitol* (New York: Stewart, Tabori & Chang, 1993), 69; Glenn Brown, *History of the United States Capitol* (1900, 1902; reprint, New York: De Capo Press, 1970),183; *Documentary History, United States Capitol Building and Grounds*, House Report 646, 58th Congress, 2d Session, 1904, 653 (cited hereafter as *Documentary*); Fairman, 172-74.

4. Brown, 177; I. T. Frary, *They Built the Capitol* (Richmond: Garrett and Massie, Richmond, 1940), 220; Fairman, 183, 201.

5. William C. Davis, *Jefferson Davis, The Man and His Honor* (New York: Harper Collins, 1991), 236-37; Thomas U. Walter, *The Architectural Review and American Builders Journal* (Claxton,

Renisen & Haffelfinger, 1869), 344; Fairman, 170-71; Meigs Journal (Transcribed) 1/26/57, 2/12/57; S. Pub. 104-40, *The Statue of Freedom* (Architect of the Capitol).

6. Fairman, 143.

7. Mary Sayre Haverstock, "George Washington Sat Here . . . and Here," *American Heritage* 24, no. 1 (Dec. 1972): 26.

8. Fairman, 147-48, 158 note.

9. Ibid., 149.

10. *Statutes at Large 13* (7/2/1864): 344, 347.

11. Fairman, 150.

12. Ibid., 156-57.

13. Maroon, 145; Brown, 191.

14. Fairman, 160-61.

15. Ibid., 161; *Dome*, 66; Maroon, 42, 146.

16. Maroon, 83.

17. *SecWar (1855)*, 16; Fairman, 159, 161; Maroon, 42, 146.

18. Brown, 191; Maroon, 146, 155.

19. *Congressional Globe*, 5/19/1858, 2243-44, 6/15/1860, 3045 (cited hereafter as *Globe*).

20. Brown, 191; *Dome*, 67; Maroon, 78.

21. *Globe*, 5/19/1858, 2243; Maroon, 158; *Documentary*, 745; *SecWar (1856)*, 220.

22. Brown, 191; *Dome*, 66, 71; Maroon, 103; United States Capitol Historical Society, *We, the People* (Washington: The National Geographic Society, 1985), 77, 94 (cited hereafter as *We*).

23. Russell F. Weigley, "Captain Meigs and the Artists of the Capitol: Federal Patronage of Art in the 1850's," *Records of the Columbia Historical Society* 47 (1969-70): 296 n. 16.

24. Fairman, 151; Maroon, 14-15, 39, 42, 66-67, 102-3; *We*, 95.

25. *Globe*, 5/26/1856, 623.

26. Fairman, 165; *Documentary*, 650-56.

27. *Documentary*, 653.

28. *Statutes at Large* 11 (8/18/1856): 81, 86; *Documentary*, 659.

29. *Statutes at Large* 11 (6/12/1858): 319, 323.

30. *Documentary*, 733.

31. Ibid., 749; Fairman, 189; *Statutes at Large* 12 (6/25/1860): 104, 105, 110; Meigs Papers (18,202) reel 14, 0509; Harold K. Skramstad, "The Engineer as Architect in Washington: The Contribution of Montgomery Meigs," *Records of the Columbia Historical Society* 14 (1911): 274.

32. *Documentary*, 746.

33. Ibid., 730.

34. *Globe*, 5/28/58, 2462.

35. *Statutes at Large* 12 (6/25/1860): 105; *Globe*, 6/15/1860, 3044-45.

36. *Globe*, 6/16/1860, 3045.

37. Ibid.

38. Ibid., 5/28/1858, 2462.

39. Ibid., 5/28/1858, 2463.

40. Ibid., 5/28/1858, 2463.

41. Weigley, "Artists of the Capitol", 301 n. 23.

42. Maroon, 70.

Chapter 8

1. Sherrod E. East, "The Banishment of Captain Meigs," *Records of the Columbia Historical Society* 40-41 (1939): 132.

2. *Statutes at Large* 11 (3/3/1857): 221, 225; Meigs Journal (Transcribed) 3/5/57, 5/4/57, 5/23/57, 7/22/57.

3. East, 114, 119; *SecWar (1856)*, 346-56; *Statutes at Large* 11 (3/3/1857): 221, 225; Meigs Journal (Transcribed) 5/23/57.

4. Meigs Journal (Transcribed) 3/12/57, 4/25/57.

5. Ibid., 4/16/57, 5/5/57, 5/6/57, 7/1/57; *DAB*, John B. Floyd.

6. Meigs Journal (Transcribed) 5/14/57; East, 100-101.

7. East, 100-101.

8. Ibid., 102.

9. Ibid., 104.

10. Ibid., 104; Meigs Journal (Transcribed) 7/22, 26, 27/57.

11. *SecWar (1857)*, 225-30, *(1858)*, 48-54.

12. East, 106.

13. Ibid., 107.

14. Ibid., 108-10.

15. Ibid., 112-13, 116.

16. Meigs Journal (Transcribed) 5/20/57, 6/18/57, 9/4/57, 10/13/57, 10/21/57, 11/6/57, 11/16/57.

17. Ibid., 8/6/57, 11/15/57, 11/21/57.

18. Ibid., 5/23/57, 6/8/57, 7/23/57, 8/20/57, 10/18/57, 11/21/57, 5/24/58, 6/28/58, 1/15/59.

19. Ibid., 5/23/57, 10/8/57, 11/21/57, 12/31/57, 2/19/58, 3/24/58, 9/24/58, 10/27/58, 3/18/59, 6/25/59, 8/19/59, 9/5/59, 12/9/59, 2/28/61.

20. *SecWar (1859)*, 677, 679-80, 682-83, *(1858)*, 51-52; *Secretary of the Interior, Annual Report, 1860*, 564.

21. Russell F. Weigley, *Quartermaster General of the Union Army* (New York: Columbia University Press, 1959), 100-103.

22. *Statutes at Large* 12 (6/25/1860): 104, 106.

23. *Congressional Globe*, 6/21/1860, 3208-11.

24. Ibid., 3211, 3213.

25. History of the Washington Aqueduct, 1852-1952, Washington District, Corps of Engineers, 1953, 32; East, 121-23.

26. East, 122-23.

27. Ibid., 124, 127.

28. *Statutes at Large* 2 (4/10/1806): 359, 367.

29. East, 129.

30. Ibid., 130.

31. Ibid., 131.

32. Meigs Papers (18,202.1), reel 5, 0102 (8/11/60).

33. Weigley, *Quartermaster General*, 105-07, 109.

34. Meigs Papers (18,202.1), reel 5, 0163; East, 132.

35. East, 132-33.

Chapter 9

1. *OR* I, vol. 52, pt. 1, 3.

2. Henry B. Meigs, *Record of the Descendants of Vincent Meigs* (Baltimore, Md.: J. S. Bridges & Co., 1901), 57; Meigs Papers (18,202), reel 16, 0188 (8/20/65), (18,202.1), reel 1, 0456 (11/1/60); Pocket Diary, 10/25/60.

3. Meigs Papers (18,202.1), reel 6, circa 0869.

4. Ibid., reel 1, 0448 (11/22/60).

5. MCM Journal (Nicolay Papers), 28 (4/25/61); Meigs Papers (18,202.1), reel 1, 0455, 0457 (11/1/60).

6. Meigs Papers (18,202.1), reel 1, 0458 (12/24/60).

7. Ibid., reel 5, circa 0164 (1/19/61).

8. *OR* I, vol. 52, pt. 1, 3-5.

9. *Calendar*, 11/6/60; Samuel Eliot Morison, *The Oxford History of the American People* (New York: Oxford University Press, 1965), 605; Congressional Quarterly, *Presidential Elections 1789-1992* (Washington: Congressional Quarterly Inc., 1995).

10. Richard N. Current, ed. in chief, *Encyclopedia of the Confederacy* (New York: Simon & Schuster, 1993), 1379.

11. Sherrod E. East, "The Banishment of Captain Meigs," *Records of the Columbia Historical Society* 40-41 (1939): 138; Pocket Diary, 1/18/61; *OR* I, vol. 52, pt. 1, 3; Meigs Papers (18,202.1), reel 5, circa 0175 (2/4/1861).

12. Meigs Papers (18,202.1), reel 2, 0560-61.

13. Ibid., reel 5, circa 0173 (2/1/61).

14. Ibid., reel 5, circa 0127 (9/20/60), (18,202.1), reel 12, circa 0100 (12/12/60).

15. Ibid., reel 5, circa 0173 (2/1/61); East, 142; Pocket Diary, 2/12, 20/61.

16. East, 141.

17. Meigs Papers (18,202.1), reel 5, circa 0175 (2/4/61).

18. *DAB* for Floyd, Joseph Johnston and Beauregard.

19. W. A. Swanberg, *First Blood* (New York: Charles Scribner's Sons, 1957), 60.

20. *OR* III, vol. 1, 302.

21. William Davis, *First Blood, Fort Sumter to Bull Run* (The Civil War, Time-Life Series, 1983), 27; Richard P. Weinert, "The Confederate Regular Army," *Military Affairs* 26, no. 3 (1962): 100; F. B. Heitman, *Historical Register of the United States Army* (Washington: National Tribune, 1890), 842 et seq.

22. *OR* III, vol. 1, 8-9.

23. *OR* III, vol. 1, 52.

24. *House Report No. 85*, 36th Congress, 2d Session, 10-12; John Bassett Moore, col. and ed., *The Works of James Buchanan*, vol. 12 (Philadelphia: J. P. Lippincott Company, 1908-11), 203; James Ford Rhodes, *History of the United States from The Compromise of 1850*, vol. 3 (New York: Harper & Brothers Publishers, 1900), 239-40; *OR* III, vol. 1, 15, 35-36.

25. Edward A. Pollard, *The First Year of the War* (London: Henry Stevens, 1863), 67; Winfield Scott, *Memoirs of Lieut-General Scott, LL.D.* (1864; reprint, Freeport, N.Y.: Books for Libraries Press, 1970), 615-16.

26. Swanberg, 112-13; Samuel Wylie Crawford, *The Genesis of the Civil War* (New York: Charles L. Webster and Company, 1887), 150-51; Edward A. Pollard, *Lee and His Lieutenants* (New York: E. B. Treat & Co., 1867), 799-800.

27. *House of Representatives Report No. 78*, 36th Congress, 2d Session, February 12, 1861, 12-13, 18; Rhodes, 237-38.

28. Harry C. Ways, *The Washington Aqueduct, 1852-1992* (United States Corps of Engineers, 1996), 52, 154; History of the Washington Aqueduct, 1852-1952, Washington District, Corps of Engineers, 1953, 18; Meigs Journal (Transcribed) 2/20/61.

29. Meigs Papers (18,202.1), reel 5, circa 0181 (2/27/61).

30. Ibid.

31. Ibid.

32. May Meigs Olds, "Memories of the Old Meigs Home and Historical Events in the Neighborhood, 1863-1913," *Records of the Columbia Historical Society* 46/47 (1947): 85, 87; Meigs Papers (18,202.1), reel 12, circa 0574 (2/27/61).

33. Meigs Papers (18,202.1), reel 12, circa 0574 (2/27/61); Meigs Journal (Transcribed) 3/1/61.

34. William C. Allen, *The Dome of the United States Capitol: An Architectural History*, Senate Document 102-144, 102d Congress, 1st Session (1992), 54 (cited hereafter as *Dome*); Meigs Papers (18,202.1) reel 5, circa 0197 (3/6/61).

35. Meigs Papers (18,202.1), reel 5, circa 0197 (3/6/61).

36. Ibid., circa 0206 (3/17/61); Meigs Journal (Transcribed) 3/8/59, 3/21/61.

37. *Dome*, 54.

38. Charles E. Fairman, *Art and Artists of the Capitol* (Washington: GPO, 1927), 201-4; *Congressional Globe*, 3/25/1862, 1349; *Dome*, 51, 67.

39. *Statutes at Large* 12 (4/16/1862): 617; *Documentary History, United States Capitol Building and Grounds*, House Report 646, 58th Congress, 2d Session, 1904, 808-11; Glenn Brown, *History of the United States Capitol* (1900, 1902; reprint, New York: De Capo Press, 1970), 210; Ways, 65.

40. *Dome*, 60; Brown, 137-38.

Chapter 10

1. Samuel Wylie Crawford, *The Genesis of the Civil War* (New York: Charles L. Webster and Company, 1887), 21; Jefferson Davis, *Rise and Fall of the Confederate Government*, vol. 1, (1881; reprint, New York: Thomas Yoseloff, 1958), 208.

2. Henry Steele Commager, *Documents of American History*, 4th ed. (New York: Appleton-Century-Crofts, Inc., 1948), 367-69 (Extract from the Fourth Annual Message to Congress, December 3, 1860).

3. *OR* I, vol. 1, 79, 108-11, 125-29.

4. Ibid., 110, 115-18.

5. Ibid., 124.

6. *OR* I, vol. 1, 114, 132, 134; Charles Winslow Elliott, *Winfield Scott, The Soldier and the Man* (New York: The Macmillan Company, 1937), 685.

7. *Message of the President of the United States (July 4, 1861)*, Senate Ex. Doc. No. 1, 37th Congress, 1st Session, 3 (cited hereafter as Lincoln 7/4/1861); also printed at *OR* III, vol. 1, 311.

8. Lincoln 7/4/1861, 4-5.

9. Ibid., 5; Winfield Scott, *Memoirs of Lieut-General Scott, LL.D.* (1864; reprint, Freeport, N.Y.: Books for Libraries Press, 1970), 622, 624-25; *OR* I, vol. 1, 395.

10. Richard N. Current, ed. in chief, *Encyclopedia of the Confederacy* (New York: Simon & Schuster, 1993), 1380; Philip Van Doren Stern, *Prologue to Sumter* (Bloomington: Indiana University Press, 1961), 19; John G. Nicolay and John Hay, eds., *Complete Works of Abraham Lincoln*, vol. 6 (New York: Francis D. Tandy Company, New and Enlarged Edition, 1905), 194-95 (3/15/61).

11. *Meigs on the Conduct of the War*, 299.

12. Nicolay and Hay, vol. 6, (3/15/61) 192-220, (3/29/61) 227-231; Jefferson Davis, 266-74, 675-76; *Meigs on Conduct of War*, 299; *DAB*, Winfield Scott, Joseph G. Totten; Meigs Papers (18,202.1), reel 15, 0166 (10/31/81).

13. *Meigs on Conduct of War*, 299; Meigs Papers (18,202.1), reel 15, 0167-0170 (10/31/81).

14. *Meigs on Conduct of War*, 299-300.

15. Ibid., 300; *OR* I, vol. 1, 201.

16. Ibid., 300; Meigs Papers (18,202.1), reel 3, circa 0069 (4/8/1861); James Cooley, "The Relief of Fort Pickens," *American Heritage* (Dec. 1972): 76.

17. *Meigs on Conduct of War*, 300; Cooley, 76; Stern, 440.

18. *OR* I, vol. 1, 365; *Meigs on Conduct of War*, 301; Meigs Papers (18,202.1), reel 15, 0172, 0175 (10/31/81).

19. Meigs Papers (18,202.1), reel 3, circa 0069 (4/8/61), reel 15, 0170 (10/31/81); Stern, 446.

20. Nicolay and Hay, vol. 6, 232-33 (4/1/61).

21. *Meigs on Conduct of War*, 301; Nicolay and Hay, vol. 6, 238-39 (4/2/61); *OR* I, vol. 1, 393; Cooley, 77, 85.

22. Cooley, 86; Fletcher Pratt, *Civil War on Western Waters* (New York: Henry Holt and Company, 1956), 22; *B&L*, vol. 1, 346.

23. *OR* I, vol. 1, 240.

24. *Meigs on Conduct of War*, 302.

25. Cooley, 87; Crawford, 414-15.

26. Stern, 452; Cooley, 87; Meigs Papers (18,202.1), reel 15, 0174 (10/31/81).

27. *Meigs on Conduct of War*, 302; *OR* I, vol. 1, 393, 397.

28. *OR* I, vol. 1, 394; National Geographic Society, *Battlefields of the Civil War* (National Geographic Society, 1974), map; *OR* I, vol. 1, 395; Stern, 453; *OR* I, vol. 1, 394-96.

29. *OR* I, vol. 1, 396; MCM Journal (Nicolay Papers), 13 (4/14/61).

30. *OR* I, vol. 1, 397; Stern, 453.

31. *OR* I, vol. 1, 397-99, 461.

32. MCM Journal (Nicolay Papers), 19 (4/14/61).

33. Meigs Papers (18,202.1), reel 15, 0167 (10/31/61).

34. Lincoln 7/4/61, 5-6.

35. Jefferson Davis, 273-74; *OR* I, vol. 1, 297; W. A. Swanberg, *First Blood* (New York: Charles Scribner's Sons, 1957), 292.

36. *OR* I, vol. 1, 14.

37. Jefferson Davis, 288-89; *OR* I, vol. 1, 14-15, 18, 24.

38. Lincoln 7/4/1861, 6.

39. Jefferson Davis, 292, 294.

40. Stern, 19; Current, 1379.

41. *OR* I, vol. 1, 399, 465, 468.

Chapter 11

1. *OR* III, vol. 1, 303; John G. Nicolay and John Hay, eds., *Complete Works of Abraham Lincoln*, vol. 6 (New York: Francis D. Tandy Company, New and Enlarged Edition, 1905), 246.

2. Jefferson Davis, *The Rise and Fall of the Confederate Government*, vol. 1 (1881; reprint, New York: Thomas Yoseloff, 1958), vol. 1, 232-33; *OR* III, vol. 1, 316-17.

3. Jefferson Davis, 328, 339-40; *Dictionary*, Joseph Johnston; *Calendar*, 4/17/61.

4. Meigs Papers (18,202.1), reel 5, 0415 (5/6/62).

5. *Calendar*, 4/19/61; A. Howard Meneely, *The War Department, 1861* (New York: Columbia University Press, 1928), 116.

6. Meneely, 117; William C. Davis, *First Blood, Fort Sumter to Bull Run* (Alexandria, Va.: Time-Life Books, 1983), 10; Philip Van Doren Stern, *Prologue to Sumter* (Bloomington: Indiana University Press, 1961), 445; Richard Wheeler, *Sword Over Richmond* (New York: Harper & Row, 1986), 5.

7. *OR* III, vol. 1, 22-26; Jefferson Davis, vol. 1, 326; *OR* III, vol. 5, 605.

8. Meneely, 117-18.

9. MCM Journal (Nicolay Papers), 32 (5/1/61); Meneely, 127-28.

10. Jefferson Davis, vol. 1, 304-7, 326-28.

11. MCM Journal (Nicolay Papers), 21, 23 (4/21/61), 28 (4/25/61).

12. Ibid., 31-32 (5/1/61), 33 (5/3/61).

13. Ibid., 33 (5/3/61), 33-34, 37-38 (5/6-9/61).

14. Ibid., 36 (5/9/61), 37-38 (5/10/61).

15. Ibid., 38-39 (5/10/61), 40 (5/14/61).

16. Ibid., 37 (5/10/61); Meigs Papers (18,202.1), reel 12, 0198 et seq. (5/14/61); OR III, vol. 3, 599 et seq.

17. Meigs Papers (18,202.1), reel 12, 0198 et seq. (5/14/61).

18. Ibid.

19. MCM Journal (Nicolay Papers), 41-43 (5/15/61).

20. Ibid., 43 (5/15/61), 46 (5/18/61).

21. OR I, vol. 1, 423; Cullum at Class of 1836; MCM Journal (Nicolay Papers), 44 (5/17/61), 46-47 (5/18/61), 54-55 (5/27/61); Nicolay and Hay, vol. 6, 290 (6/13/61); Meigs Journal (Transcribed) 5/22/58.

22. MCM Journal (Nicolay Papers), 36 (5/9/61), 39 (5/10/61); Glenn Brown, *History of the United States Capitol* (1900, 1902; reprint, New York: De Capo Press, 1970), 203; Howard K. Beale, ed., *Diary of Gideon Welles* (New York: W. W. Norton & Company, 1960), vol. 1, 25; Meigs Papers (18,202), reel 16, 056 (11/58); Meigs Journal (Transcribed) 12/7/54, 3/8/59.

23. Meigs Papers (18,202.1) reel 12, 0188 (5/3/1861), reel 15, 0179 (10/31/81); MCM Journal (Nicolay Papers), 56 (6/1/61).

24. MCM Journal (Nicolay Papers), 57 (6/1/61).

25. Ibid., 39 (5/10/61), 55 (5/27/61), 69 (6/11/61), 71 (6/13/61); Cullum at Class of 1836.

26. DAB, Francis Preston Blair; Meigs Papers (18,202.1), reel 0256 (6/21/61).

27. Meigs Papers (18,202), reel 20, 091 (6/12/61), (18,202.1) reel 3, 0064-65 (7/6/1861).

28. Meigs Papers (18,202), reel 20, 090 (6/12/61).

29. MCM Journal (Nicolay Papers), 50 (5/23/61); OR III, vol. 1, 145-46, 303-4; Margaret Leech, *Reveille in Washington* (New York: Time Reading Program, Special Edition, 1962), 101; Calendar, 5/23, 24/61.

30. Jefferson Davis, vol. 1, 338; B&L, vol. 1, 126 et seq.

31. B&L, vol. 1, 135.

32. OR III, vol. 1, 301, 306; Meigs Papers (18,202) reel 20, 089 (6/12/61).

33. MCM Journal (Nicolay Papers) 71 (6/14/61), 72 (6/18/61), 72 (6/20/61); Virginia Jeans Laas, ed., *Wartime Washington, The Civil War Letters of Elizabeth Blair Lee* (Champaign, Ill.: University of Illinois Press, 1991), 48; Meigs Papers (18,202.1), reel 5, 0236 (6/25/61), 0239 (7/4/61).

34. MCM Journal (Nicolay Papers), 73 (6/22/61), 73 (6/24/61).

35. Meigs Papers (18,202.1), reel 5, 0234 (6/22/61), 0306 12/13/61.

Chapter 12

1. OR III, vol. 1, 303, 316; Statutes at Large 12 (7/22/1861): 268.

2. MCM Journal (Nicolay Papers), 74 (6/25/61).

3. Ibid., 75 (6/25/61).

4. Ibid., 76 (6/25/61); Meigs Papers (18,202.1), reel 5, 0253 (7/30/61).

5. MCM Journal (Nicolay Papers), 77-78 (6/29/61).

6. Ibid., 78 (6/29/61); Meigs Papers (18,202.1), reel 5, 0243 (7/18/61).

7. MCM Journal (Nicolay Papers), 80 (7/6/61), 81 (7/16/61); Meigs Papers (18,202.1), reel 5, 0243 (7/18/61); *Dictionary*, Robert Patterson, Beauregard, McDowell; Russell F. Weigley, *Quartermaster General of the Union Army* (New York: Columbia University Press, 1959), 173.

8. MCM Journal (Nicolay Papers), 82 (7/16/61).

9. Charles Winslow Elliott, *Winfield Scott, The Soldier and the Man* (New York: The Macmillan Company, 1937), 722; A. Howard Meneely, *The War Department, 1861* (New York: Columbia University Press, 1928), 176, 185.

10. *DAB*, Greeley; Meneely, 184-88.

11. *First Manassas (First Bull Run)*, National Park Service Brochure (GPO: 1994).

12. MCM Journal (Nicolay Papers), 80-83 (7/15-17/61); Meigs Papers (18,202.1), reel 5, 0243 (7/18/61).

13. Meigs Papers (18,202.1), reel 3, 0054 et seq.

14. *Dictionary*, Robert Patterson, Banks, McDowell; *Calendar*, 7/21/61; *DAB*, Banks; Meigs Papers (18,202.1), reel 12, 0189 (5/21/61); Shelby Foote, *The Civil War, Fort Sumter to Perryville* (New York: Vintage Books, 1986), 435.

15. *Calendar*, 7/21/61, 7/29/61.

16. Meigs Papers (18,202.1), reel 5, 0253, 0255 (7/30, 8/1/61); Pocket Diary, 7/21/61; MCM Journal (Nicolay Papers), 86 (7/21/61).

17. Meigs Papers (18,202.1), reel 5, 0255 (8/1/61), 0462 (7/18/62); *OR* I, vol. 2, 356.

18. *OR* I, vol. 2, 376-77, 380.

19. Meigs Papers (18,202.1), reel 12, 0390 (12/15/61).

20. Ibid., reel 5, 0253(7/30/61); *DAB*, McDowell; *Calendar*, 7/22/61.

Chapter 13

1. *OR* I, vol. 8, 389.

2. *Calendar*, 701; *B&L*, vol. 1, 264.

3. *Calendar*, 703.

4. *B&L*, vol. 1, 263-65; *Calendar*, 5/10/61.

5. *B&L*, vol. 1, 266-67, 289; *House Ex Doc. No. 19*, 37th Congress, 1st Session, 3, 6-9, 19-20; *Calendar*, 8/10/61.

6. Andrew Rolle, *John Charles Fremont* (Norman: University of Oklahoma Press, 1991), 200.

7. *B&L*, vol. 1, 278-79; *OR* I, vol. 3, 390.

8. *DAB*, Fremont.

9. Ibid.

10. *B&L*, vol. 1, 278.

11. *B&L*, vol. 1, 279, 286; *Senate Report 108*, 37th Congress, 3d Session, Joint Committee on the Conduct of the War, Part III, 151; *OR* I, vol. 3, 543; Russell F. Weigley, *Quartermaster General of the Union Army* (New York: Columbia University Press, 1959), 191.

12. *OR* I, vol. 3, 463-65.

13. *House Report No. 2*, 37th Congress, 2d Session (Government Contracts, circa July, 1862), LII, LVII (cited hereafter as *House Report No. 2*); Erna Risch, *Quartermaster Support of the Army, A History of the Corps 1775-1939* (Washington: Quartermaster Historians Office, Office of the Quartermaster General, 1962), 408; *OR* I, vol. 7, 546.

14. Roy P. Basler, ed., *The Collected Works of Abraham Lincoln*, vol. 4 (Brunswick, N.J.: Rutgers University Press, 1953-55), 513, note 1; Virginia Jeans Laas, ed., *Wartime Washington, The Civil War Letters of Elizabeth Blair Lee* (Champaign, Ill.: University of Illinois Press, 1991), 79.

15. Basler, vol. 4 , 513, note 1.

16. MCM Journal (Nicolay Papers), 94-95 (9/18/61).

17. Ibid., 95 (9/18/61).

18. *Dictionary*, McKinstry; MCM Journal (Nicolay Papers), 94 (9/18/61); Weigley, *Quartermaster General*, 193.

19. Basler, vol. 4, 515-16.

20. *OR* I, vol. 3, 549.

21. *OR* I, vol. 3, 549; Risch, 344; Weigley, *Quartermaster General*, 188.

22. *OR* I, vol. 3, 532-33.

23. Ibid., 547.

24. *OR* I, vol. 3, 549, 553; *Dictionary*, Curtis; *Calendar*, 11/2/61.

25. *House Report No. 49*, 37th Congress, 3d Session (3/3/63), 24; *Dictionary*, Robert Allen.

26. *OR* I, vol. 3, 463-65.

27. Ibid., vol 8, 385.

28. *Statutes at Large* 12 (1/22/1862): 332; OR I, vol. 8, 385-87.

29. *House Report No. 2*, LIX; OR I, vol. 8, 396.

30. *House Report No. 2*, LVI.

31. *OR* I, vol. 8, 387-88.

32. *Calendar*, 11/19/61; *B&L*, vol. 1, 337; Shelby Foote, *The Civil War, Fort Sumter to Perryville* (New York: Vintage Books, 1986), 292.

33. John G. Nicolay and John Hay, eds., vol. 7, *Complete Works of Abraham Lincoln* (New York: Francis D. Tandy Company, New and Enlarged Edition, 1905), 129-30; Charles Dana, *Recollections of the Civil War* (1898; New and Enlarged Edition Reprint, New York: Collier Books, 1963), 29.

Chapter 14

1. Meigs Papers (18,202.1), reel 12, 0332 (8/27/61).

2. *QMG (1865)*, *OR* III, vol. 5, 213.

3. Ibid.

4. John G. Nicolay and John Hay, eds., *Complete Works of Abraham Lincoln*, vol. 7 (New York: Francis D. Tandy Company, New and Enlarged Edition, 1905), 189-90 (5/26/62).

5. Ibid., 192 (5/26/62).

6. *OR* III, vol. 1, 175; Erna Risch, *Quartermaster Support of the Army, A History of the Corps 1775-1939* (Washington: Quartermaster Historians Office, Office of the Quartermaster General, 1962), 368; *House Report No. 2*, 37th Congress, 2d Session, 306, 311, 470 (cited hereafter as *House Report No. 2*).

7. *OR* I, vol. 2, 603; OR III, vol. 1, 228 (5/23/61); *House Report No. 2*, XV, 548, 551.

8. *House Report No. 2*, 306, 312, 323.

9. *Calendar*, 4/20/61, 5/13/61; Risch, 368; Virgil Carrington Jones, *The Civil War At Sea*, vol. 1 (New York: Holt, Rinehart, Winston, 1960), 166.

10. *B&L*, vol. 1, 632-34, 673-91.

11. Ibid., 660-69.

12. *House Report No. 2*, XL, 485.

13. Ibid., III; *Congressional Globe*, 4/25/62, 1835, 4/30/62, 1888.

14. *QMG (1865)*, OR III, vol. 5, 235.

15. *House Report No. 2*, XV-XVI; Samuel Richey Kamm, *The Civil War Career of Thomas A. Scott* (Philadelphia: University of Pennsylvania, 1940), 2; Meigs Papers (18,202.1), reel 14, 0769-70 (circa 8/1871).

16. *House Report No. 2*, XVII-XVIII, 489-90; OR III, vol. 1, 325-26.

17. *House Report No. 2,* XV, XVIII-XIX.

18. *OR* III, vol. 1, 325-26, 749, 751-52, 762-63; *House Report No. 2,* XXIX, 559-60, 563; *House Ex Doc. No. 18,* 37th Congress, 2d Session; Kamm, 74-75.

19. *DAB,* Cameron; Pocket Diary, 1/14/62; Russell F. Weigley, *Quartermaster General of the Union Army* (New York: Columbia University Press, 1959), 211-12.

Chapter 15

1. *SecWar (1861), OR* III, vol. 1, 699; Charles R. Shrader, *U.S. Military Logistics, 1607-1991* (Westport, Conn.: Greenwood Press, 1992), 296, 300; *Meigs Conduct of the War,* 292.

2. *Congressional Globe,* 8/1/61, 370 (cited hereafter as *Globe*); *House Report No. 2,* 37th Congress, 2d Session, (7/8/61), 137 (cited hereafter as *House Report No. 2*).

3. *Globe* 8/1/61, 370.

4. *Globe,* 8/2/61, 403; *OR* III, vol. 1, 378-79.

5. *Globe,* 8/2/61, 403, 406; *Statutes at Large* 12 (3/2/1861): 220, (6/2/1862): 411, (7/17/1862): 600.

6. *Globe,* 8/2/61, 403-5.

7. *OR* III, vol. 1, 425; Erna Risch, *Quartermaster Support of the Army, A History of the Corps 1775-1939* (Washington: Quartermaster Historian's Office, Office of the Quartermaster General, 1962), 348, 351-52; *OR* III, vol. 1, 393, 594, 682-83.

8. *OR* III, vol. 2, 732-33; Risch, 354-55; *QMG (1862), OR* III, vol. 2, 803.

9. *QMG (1862), OR* III, vol. 2, 803; Risch, 354-55.

10. *QMG (1862), OR* III, vol. 2, 803; Risch, 348.

11. Risch, 357-58; Meigs Papers (18,202), reel 26, 0218 (10/1/61).

12. *OR* III, vol. 2, 483, 732.

13. Ibid., vol. 1, 615; Philip Haythornthwaite, *Uniforms of the American Civil War* (UK: Blandford Press, 1975), plate 6, 138.

14. *House Report No. 2,* XLII.

15. Ibid., XLV, 486-488; Risch, 361.

16. *Quartermaster General Annual Report, 1862, OR* III, vol. 2, 786-88.

17. *Calendar,* 1/15/62; *OR* III, vol. 1, 866; Meigs Papers (18,202.1), reel 5, 0359 (2/3/62).

18. *OR* III, vol. 1, 866-67.

19. Ibid., 649.

20. Ibid., 868.

21. *OR* III, vol. 1, 712; *Meigs Conduct of the War,* 292.

22. *Secretary of the Treasury Annual Report, 1862,* 8-9; Chester L. Krause, Robert F. Lemke and Robert E. Wilhite, ed., *Standard Catalog of United States Paper Money,* 13th ed. (Iola, Wisc.: Krause Publication, 1994), 4; John Steele Gordon, *Hamilton's Blessing* (New York: Walker and Company, 1997), 71-72.

23. *Secretary of the Treasury Annual Report, 1864,* 23; Gordon, 68, 70, 75-79, Appendix, 202.

24. Ibid., *1862,* 2.

25. *OR* I, vol. 12, pt. 1, 643, pt. 3, 60-61, 589.

26. Risch, 376.

27. Ibid., n. 161; *House Ex. Doc. No. 60,* 37th Congress, 2d Session, 5, 38 (cited hereafter as *No. 60*).

28. Don E. Fehrenbacher and Virginia Fehrenbacher, eds. and comps., *Recollected Words of Abraham Lincoln* (Stanford, Calif.: Stanford University Press, 1996), 113.

29. Risch, 379, 382, 420; *OR* I, vol. 11, pt. 1, 159.

30. Shelby Foote, *The Civil War, Fort Sumter to Perryville* (New York: Vintage Books, 1986), 761.

31. *OR* III, vol. 1, 682.

32. Charles A. Dana, *Recollections of the Civil War* (Collier Books, New York, N.Y., 1963), 34.

33. Dana, 82; *OR* III, vol. 1, 682, vol. 2, 805-6; Meigs Papers (18,202.1), reel 14, 0823 (6/24/81).

34. Russell F. Weigley, *Quartermaster General of the Union Army* (New York: Columbia University Press, 1959), 231-35; Risch, 393-94.

35. *Statutes at Large* 13 (7/4/1864): 394; Weigley, *Quartermaster General*, 224, 234-35; Risch, 337.

Chapter 16

1. *B&L*, vol. 1, 288.

2. Ibid., 399.

3. Ibid., 368, 399-401.

4. John D. Milligan, *Gunboats Down the Mississippi* (Annapolis, Md.: United States Naval Institute, 1965), 3-4.

5. Ibid., 4-5, 7; *Official Records of the Union and Confederate Navies*, serial 1, vol. 22, 277 (cited hereafter as *ORN*).

6. Milligan, 5-7, 11-13.

7. Ibid., 15-17, 19-21; *ORN* serial 1, vol. 22, 297, 314; Meigs Papers (18,202.1), reel 2, 0653.

8. Milligan, 17; *ORN* serial 1, vol. 22, 314.

9. *Statutes at Large* 12 (7/17/1861): 261, 263; Milligan, 21; *House Ex Doc No. 5*, 37th Congress, 2d Session; *OR* I, vol. 52, pt. 1, 199; *Statutes at Large* 12 (12/24/1861): 331.

10. *Senate Report No. 108*, 37th Congress, 3d Session, Joint Committee on the Conduct of the War, Part III, 153.

11. Milligan, 22-25; *ORN* serial 1, vol. 22, 523.

12. Milligan, 37-49; William M. Fowler, Jr., *Under Two Flags* (New York: W. W. Norton & Company, 1990), 144-45.

13. *DAB*, John B. Floyd.

14. Meigs Papers (18,202.1), reel 5, 0393 (3/2/62), 0401 (3/29/62), 0415 (5/6/62).

15. *Calendar*, 8/28/61 (Hatteras), 9/17/61 (Ship Island), 11/7/61 (Port Royal), 4/3/62 (Pass Christian), 4/3/62 (Apalachicola), 4/29/62 (New Orleans).

16. *Calendar*, 3/10/62, 4/6-7/62, 6/3/62, 6/6/62.

17. *Statutes at Large* 12 (7/16/1862): 587; Milligan, 93-94; Erna Risch, *Quartermaster Support of the Army, A History of the Corps 1775-1939* (Washington: Quartermaster Historian's Office, Office of the Quartermaster General, 1962), 413; *Dictionary*, David Dixon Porter; *OR* III, vol. 2, 644.

18. Milligan, 97.

19. Ibid., 65-70; *B&L*, vol. 1, 454.

20. Milligan, 71-77; *B&L*, vol. 1, 453-54, 456-59.

Chapter 17

1. *DAB*, McClellan; Richard Wheeler, *Sword Over Richmond* (New York: Harper & Row, 1986), 32.

2. Meigs Papers (18,202.1), reel 2, 0582 (10/8/61), reel 5, 0253 (7/30/61), 0255 (8/1/61), 0264 (8/25/61), 0301 (12/1/61), 0359 (2/3/62); MCM Journal (Nicolay Papers), 92 (7/27/61).

3. Meigs Papers (18,202.1), reel 5, 0260 (8/22/61), 0264 (8/25/61), 0265 (8/27/61), 0301 (12/1/61).

4. Meigs Papers (18,202.1), reel 5, 0271 (9/4/61), 0323 (12/18/61); *OR* III, vol. 1, 613-14.

5. *OR* I, vol. 5, 9; *Senate Report 108*, 37th Congress, 3d Session, Joint Committee on the Conduct of the War, Part I, 160 (cited hereafter as *Senate Report 108*); Meigs Papers (18,202.1), reel 5, 0301 (12/1/61); *B&L*, vol. 2, 436.

6. *Senate Report 108*, Part I, 153-54.

7. *Meigs Papers* (18,202.1), reel 5, 0291 (10/8/61), 0301 (12/1/61), 0323 (12/18/61); reel 7, 0799.

8. *Senate Report 108*, Part I, 154.

9. Ibid.

10. *Meigs Conduct of the War*, 292.

11. Ibid.

12. Ibid., 292, 302.

13. Ibid., 292-93.

14. *DAB*, Stanton; Meigs Papers (18,202.1), reel 5, 0359 (2/3/62), 0365 (2/9/62), 0367 (2/11/62); Wheeler, *Sword*, 95-96.

15. William O. Stoddard, *Abraham Lincoln: The True Story of a Great Life* (New York: Fords, Howard, & Hulbert, 1884), 316-18.

16. Virginia Jeans Laas, ed., *Wartime Washington, The Civil War Letters of Elizabeth Blair Lee* (Champaign, Ill.: University of Illinois Press, 1991), 152.

17. Stoddard, 282, 286.

18. *OR* I, vol. 5, 41; Frank Abial Flower, *Edwin McMasters Stanton* (Akron, Ohio: The Saalfield Publishing Company, 1905), 158-59.

19. Roy P. Basler, ed., *The Collected Works of Abraham Lincoln*, vol. 5 (Brunswick, N.J.: Rutgers University Press, 1953-55), 122-23; *OR* I, vol. 5, 42-45.

20. John Nivens, *Salmon P. Chase* (New York: Oxford University Press, 1995), 277; Meigs Papers (18,202.1), reel 5, 0408 (4/29/62).

21. *OR* I, vol. 5, 46, 47.

22. Ibid., 50.

23. Meigs Papers (18.202.1), reel 5, 0390 (3/9/62).

24. *OR* I, vol. 9, 20-21.

25. Ibid., 22-23.

26. *OR* I, vol. 5, 50-51, vol. 9, 21-23; Meigs Papers (18.202.1), reel 5, 0390 (3/9/62); Wheeler, *Sword*, 77.

27. *OR* I, vol. 9, 28; Stoddard, 297; William Tindall, *The True Story of the Virginia and the Monitor* (Richmond, Va.: Old Dominion Press, 1923), 18-19.

28. *OR* I, vol. 5, 18; *B&L*, vol. 2, 166.

29. *OR* I, vol. 5, 50; *Meigs Conduct of the War*, 291.

30. *B&L*, vol. 2, 166; *OR* I, vol. 5, 51, 55; Wheeler, *Sword*, 92.

31. *OR* I, vol. 5, 45.

32. *OR* I, vol. 5, 64, vol. 9, 27; Tindall, *Monitor*, 80.

33. *OR* I, vol. 10, pt. 2, 28-29.

34. *Calendar*, 3/17/62; *B&L*, vol. 2, 166; *Meigs Conduct of the War*, 296.

35. *Dictionary*, "Shenandoah Valley, Jackson"; *Calendar*, 3/23/62.

36. *B&L*, vol. 2, 168, 170.

37. Meigs Papers (18,202.1), reel 5, 0408 (4/29/62); Herman Hattaway and Archer Jones, "The War Board, the Basis of the United States First General Staff," *Military Affairs* 46, no. 1 (1982): 1-5; Flower, 159; Meigs Papers (18,202.1), reel 12, 0421 (3/12/62).

38. Meigs Papers (18,202.1), reel 5, 0424 (5/15/62), 0447 (6/17/62), 0454 (7/8/62).

39. *B&L*, vol. 2, 171; Meigs Papers (18,202.1), reel 5, 0408 (4/29/62), 0409 (5/4/62); *Senate Report 108*, Part I, 296-97.

40. Meigs Papers (18,202.1), reel 6, 085 (4/15/62).

41. *Meigs Conduct of the War*, 292.

42. *OR* I, vol. 11, pt. 1, 129-30.

43. *B&L*, vol. 2, 172.

44. *OR* I, vol. 11, pt. 1, 159.

45. Wheeler, *Sword*, 191; Stephen W. Sears, *To the Gates of Richmond* (New York: Ticknor & Fields, 1992), 104 ; *B&L*, vol. 2, 167, 173.

46. Wheeler, *Sword*, 193, 264-65, 317; Shelby Foote, *The Civil War, Fort Sumter to Perryville* (New York: Vintage Books, 1986), 418.

47. Wheeler, *Sword*, 188, 192.

48. Meigs Papers (18,202.1), reel 5, 0403 (4/6/62).

49. *B&L*, vol. 2, 173.

50. Ibid., 173-74.

51. Foote, *Fort Sumter to Perryville*, 413-15; Wheeler, *Sword*, 176-77; *Calendar*, 5/11/62.

52. *OR* I, vol. 11, pt. 1, 27-28; Meigs Papers (18,202.1), reel 12, 0421 (3/12/62); *Dictionary*, Totten, Joseph Taylor, Ripley.

53. Meigs Papers (18,202.1), reel 5, 0430 (5/26/62); Wheeler, *Sword*, 218; Foote, *Fort Sumter to Perryville*, 437; *Calendar*, 5/25/62.

54. Meigs Papers (18,202.1), reel 7, 085 (4/15/62).

55. Foote, *Fort Sumter to Perryville*, 435; *Dictionary*, "Shenandoah, Jackson"; Meigs Papers (18,202.1), reel 5, 0430 (5/26/62), 0432 (5/28/62); Wheeler, *Sword*, 211.

56. Meigs Papers (18,202.1), reel 5, 0432 (5/28/62); Russell F. Weigley, *Quartermaster General of the Union Army* (New York: Columbia University Press, 1959), 260.

57. *Calendar*, 5/29/62; Foote, *Fort Sumter to Perryville*, 452; Meigs Papers (18,202.1), reel 5, 0424 (5/15/62).

58. *DAB*, Thomas Jonathan Jackson; Foote, *Fort Sumter to Perryville*, 452-53, 464.

59. *B&L*, vol. 2, 175-78.

60. *B&L*, vol. 2, 178; Meigs Papers (18,202.1), reel 5, 0447 (6/17/62); Sears, 46; Wheeler, *Sword*, 288.

61. *B&L*, vol. 2, 170; Samuel Richey Kamm, *The Civil War Career of Thomas A. Scott* (Philadelphia: University of Pennsylvania, 1940), 127; *OR* III, vol. 2, 109; Foote, *Fort Sumter to Perryville*, 437.

62. *B&L*, vol. 2, 178, 437; Meigs Papers (18,202.1), reel 5, 0447 (6/17/62); Wheeler, *Sword*, 277.

63. Wheeler, *Sword*, 285.

64. *B&L*, vol. 2, 180, 315, 317; Sears, *Gates of Richmond*, 285-86; *OR* I, vol. 11, pt. 1, 83; pt. 2, 315; pt. 3, 238.

65. *B&L*, vol. 2, 183; *OR* I, vol. 11, pt. 1, 60, 70; Sears, *Gates of Richmond*, 319-20; Sears, 263-64; James A. Huston, *The Sinews of War: Army Logistics 1775-1953* (Washington: Office of the Chief of Military History, United States Army, 1966), 221-22.

66. *B&L*, vol. 2, 185-86; Foote, *Fort Sumter to Perryville*, 517.

67. Wheeler, *Sword*, 339.

68. Ibid., 344.

69. Ibid., 346.

70. *OR* I, vol. 11, pt. 1, 73-74.

71. *Meigs Conduct of the War*, 296; Basler, vol. 4, 12/31/61; *B&L*, vol. 2, 315, 317.

72. Meigs Papers (18,202.1), reel 5, 0454 (7/8/62).

Chapter 18

1. *B&L*, vol. 2, 183; *Senate Report 108*, 37th Congress, 3d Session, Joint Committee on the Conduct of the War, Part I, 28 (cited hereafter as *Senate Report 108*).

2. Meigs Papers (18,202.1), reel 5, 0471 (7/29/62).

3. Ibid.

4. *OR* I, vol. 11, pt. 1, 81; *Calendar*, 8/3/62; *B&L*, vol. 2, 454.

5. *OR* I, vol. 11, pt. 1, 82-83; pt. 2, 315; pt. 3, 337-38; Meigs Papers (18,202.1) reel 5, 0471 (7/29/62), 0513 (10/22/62).

6. *Meigs Conduct of the War*, 297.

7. *OR* I, vol. 11, pt. 1, 80-81.

8. Ibid., 82, 85; *Calendar*, 8/4/62.

9. *OR* I, vol. 11, pt. 1, 86-87.

10. Ibid., 87-88.

11. Ibid., 89, 91.

12. *Calendar*, 7/13/62, 8/9/62, 8/13-14/62.

13. *Calendar*, 8/18/62, 8/20-21/62; *B&L*, vol. 2, 451, 460, 548-52; *OR* I, vol. 11, pt. 1, 105.

14. *OR* I, vol. 11, pt. 1, 93, 98; William O. Stoddard, *Abraham Lincoln: The True Story of a Great Life* (New York: Fords, Howard, & Hulbert, 1884), 304.

15. *Calendar*, 8/25/62, 8/27-31/62, 9/2/62.

16. *Calendar*, 8/30/62.

17. *OR* I, vol. 19, pt. 2, 590-91.

18. *Calendar*, 9/3/62; Shelby Foote, *The Civil War, Fort Sumter to Perryville* (New York: Vintage Books, 1986), 668-69.

19. *OR* I, vol. 11, pt. 1, 98; *Calendar*, 8/29/62, 9/3/62.

20. *B&L*, vol. 2, 549-52; *OR* I, vol. 11, pt. 1, 105.

21. Don E. Fehrenbacher and Virginia Fehrenbacher, eds. and comps., *Recollected Words of Abraham Lincoln* (Stanford, Calif.: Stanford University Press, 1996), 193, 208-9, 472-73; Frank Abial Flower, *Edwin McMasters Stanton* (Akron, Ohio: The Saalfield Publishing Company, 1905), 178-79.

22. Fehrenbacher and Fehrenbacher, 223.

23. Meigs Papers (18,202.1), reel 5, 0498 (9/23/62).

24. Fehrenbacher and Fehrenbacher, 472-73; Meigs Papers (18,202.1), reel 5, 0492 (9/16/62).

25. *OR* I, vol. 19, pt. 2, 225-26.

26. *Calendar*, 9/17/62; Meigs Papers (18,202.1), reel 5, 0521 (10/2/62).

27. *Senate Report 108*, Part I, 41.

28. Meigs Papers (18,202.1), reel 5, 0498 (9/23/62); OR I, vol. 19, pt. 2, 339-40, 342-43.

29. *Senate Report 108*, Part I, 41-42.

30. Ibid., 41-43.

31. Ibid., 43-44.

32. Ibid., 44-45.

33. Ibid., 45.

34. Ibid., 45; *OR* I, vol. 19, pt. 2, 417.

35. *OR* I, vol. 19, pt. 2, 422.

36. Ibid., 423-24.

37. Ibid., 423-24.

38. *Senate Report 108*, Part I, 45-46.

39. Ibid., 46.

40. Ibid., 46.

41. Ibid., 47.

42. Ibid., 47.

43. Ibid., 47-48.

44. Ibid., 48.

45. Ibid., 48.

46. Meigs Papers (18,202.1), reel 5, 0559 (10/26/62).

47. *OR* I, vol. 19, pt. 2, 521.

48. Ibid., 491-93.

49. Ibid., 502-4.

50. Ibid., 490-91, 502.

51. *Senate Rep. Com. No. 71*, 37th Congress, 3d Session, 2; Meigs Papers (18,202.1), reel 5, 0693 (11/18/62); *B&L*, vol. 3, 70.

52. Meigs Papers (18,202.1), reel 5, 0691, 0693 (11/18/62).

53. Flower, 195, 197.

54. Pocket Diary, 11/12/62.

55. Meigs Papers (18,202.1), reel 5, 0513 (10/22/62).

56. Ibid., 0535 (11/16/62).

57. *Statutes at Large* 12 (8/6/1861): 319; (7/17/62) 589-92; *Calendar*, 5/24/61, 5/30/61, 7/30/61, 8/8/61; James M. McPherson, *Marching Toward Freedom* (New York: Facts on File, 1994), 16-17.

58. *Calendar*, 7/22/62; John G. Nicolay and John Hay, eds., *Complete Works of Abraham Lincoln*, vol. 8, (New York: Francis D. Tandy Company, New and Enlarged Edition, 1905), 36 (9/22/62); Meigs Papers (18,202.1), reel 5, 0537 (11/23/62).

59. *SecWar (1862)*, *OR* III, vol. 2, 910-12; Meigs Papers (18,202.1), reel 12, 0311-13.

60. Nicolay and Hay, vol. 8, 161 (1/1/63).

61. Meigs Papers (18,202.1), reel 5, 0537 (11/23/62).

62. James D. Richardson, *A Compilation of the Messages and Papers of the Confederacy*, vol. 1 (Nashville, Tenn.: United States Publishing Company, 1905), 271, 276, 290-91.

63. Henry Steele Commager, *Documents of American History*, 4th ed. (New York: Appleton-Century-Crofts, Inc., 1948), 421.

64. Foote, *Fort Sumter to Perryville*, 809; *Calendar*, 11/4/62; Frank Donovan, *Mr. Lincoln's Proclamation* (New York: Dodd, Mead & Company, 1964), 113-14.

Chapter 19

1. Samuel Richey Kamm, *The Civil War Career of Thomas A. Scott* (Philadelphia: The University of Pennsylvania, 1940), 108.

2. Ibid.

3. Ibid., 112-13.

4. A. Wilson Greene and Gary W. Gallagher, *National Geographic Guide to the National Battlefield Parks* (Washington: 1992), 100; Ulysses S. Grant, *Memoirs and Selected Letters* (New York: The Library of America, 1990), 222-23.

5. *Calendar*, 4/7/62.

6. *B&L*, vol. 2, 718-22.

7. *Dictionary*, Corinth; *B&L*, vol. 2, 722.

8. *DAB*, Halleck, John Pope; *Calendar*, 7/17/62.

9. *B&L*, vol. 2, 722, 725, vol. 3, 1.

10. *B&L*, vol. 2, 722, 725, 737, vol. 3, 35.

11. *DAB*, Don Carlos Buell; *B&L*, vol. 2, 725, vol. 3, 35; *Calendar*, 7/23/62.

12. *B&L*, vol. 3, 2, 4, 45-46.

13. *B&L*, vol. 3, 8, 13, 46, 50-51; Shelby Foote, *The Civil War, Fort Sumter to Perryville* (New York: Vintage Books, 1986), 711.

14. *Calendar*, 10/8/62.
15. *Calendar*, 10/3-4/62; Meigs Papers (18,202.1), reel 5, 0691 (11/18/62).
16. *DAB*, Buell, Rosecrans; *Calendar*, 10/24/62, 10/30/62; *B&L*, vol. 3, 49; Meigs Papers (18,202.1), reel 5, 0524 (11/5/62).
17. *Calendar*, 12/31/62; Greene and Gallagher, 108-10; Meigs Papers (18,202.1), reel 5, 0571 (1/25/63), 0582 (2/15/63).
18. *DAB*, Rosecrans; *Dictionary*, "Thanks of Congress."
19. *OR* I, vol. 20, pt. 2, 326, 328.
20. Ibid., 326-27.
21. Ibid., 327-28, 331.
22. Ibid., 332-33.
23. Ibid., 332, 338-39.
24. *DAB*, Rosecrans; *OR* I, vol. 23, pt. 2, 146, 271-72, 284, 288-89, 300-4.
25. *OR* I, vol. 23, pt. 2, 320-21; *Calendar*, 6/23/63.
26. *OR* III, vol. 3, 580-81.
27. Ibid., 580, 884-86; Russell F. Weigley, *Quartermaster General of the Union Army* (New York: Columbia University Press, 1959), 267-68.
28. *OR* III, vol. 3, 580-81.

Chapter 20

1. *Calendar*, 12/11-13/62.
2. Meigs Papers (18,202.1), reel 5, 0535 (11/16/62).
3. *Calendar*, 12/13/62.
4. *DAB*, William Buel Franklin; *Senate Rep. Com. No. 71*, 37th Congress, 3d Session, Joint Committee on the Conduct of the War, 18 (cited hereafter as *Senate Report 71*).
5. Meigs Papers (18,202.1) reel 5, 0524 (11/5/62).
6. *Senate Report 71*, 3-4, 11.
7. Meigs Papers (18,202.1), reel 5, 0691 (11/18/62).
8. *Senate Report 71*, 4, 11.
9. Ibid., 4, 12-14; *Calendar*, 12/11-13/62.
10. *OR* I, vol. 21, 103-4.
11. Meigs Papers (18,202.1) reel 5, 0543 (11/30/62).
12. Ibid., 0546 (12/7/62).
13. Ibid., 0546 (12/7/62).
14. Ibid., 0546 (12/7/62); *OR* I, vol. 21, 817.
15. *OR* I, vol. 21, 817-18; vol. 25, pt. 2, 544; vol. 27, pt. 3, 230.
16. *OR* I, vol. 21, 818; vol. 27, pt. 3, 843; vol. 29, pt. 2, 11, 40.
17. *Senate Report No. 108*, 37th Congress, 3d Session, Joint Committee on the Conduct of the War, Part I, 676.
18. *OR* I, vol. 21, 916.
19. Ibid.
20. *Secretary of the Treasury Annual Report, 1862*, 7, 12.
21. *OR* I, vol. 21, 965-67.
22. *Calendar*, 1/19-21/63; Richard Wheeler, *Voices of the Civil War* (New York: A Meridian Book, 1990), 247.
23. *Calendar*, 1/22-24/63.
24. *OR* I, vol. 21, 967.

25. Wheeler, *Voices*, 221-22.
26. Meigs Papers (18,202.1), reel 5, 0537 (11/25/62), 0546 (12/7/62).

Chapter 21

1. Shelby Foote, *The Civil War, Fredericksburg to Meridian* (New York: Vintage Books, 1986), 104-5.
2. James D. Richardson, *A Compilation of the Messages and Papers of the Confederacy*, vol. 1 (Nashville, Tenn.: United States Publishing Company, 1905), 276-77.
3. Foote, *Fredericksburg to Meridian*, 116; Meigs Papers (18,202.1), reel 5, 0568 (1/18/63).
4. Meigs Papers (18,202.1), reel 5, 0565 (1/9/63).
5. Ibid., 0576 (2/1/63), 0581 (2/12/63); *Statutes at Large* 12 (2/7/1863): 641.
6. Meigs Papers (18,202.1), reel 5, 0561 (12/29/62).
7. John G. Nicolay and John Hay, eds., *Complete Works of Abraham Lincoln*, vol. 8 (New York: New and Enlarged Edition, Francis D. Tandy Company, 1905), 52-53 (9/62).
8. Nicolay and Hay, vol. 11, 45-46 (3/4/65).
9. Meigs Papers (18,202.1), reel 5, 0335 (12/25/61).
10. Meigs Papers (18,202), reel 16 (3/2/63), 072 (6/27/63).
11. Captain Robert E. Lee, *Recollections and Letters of General Robert E. Lee* (New York: Garden City Publishing Co., Inc., 1904), 105-6.
12. *Congressional Globe*, part 1, 1/15/1863, 327 (cited hereafter as *Globe*).
13. Ibid., 1/15/1863, 328.
14. Ibid., 1/16/1863, 359; Meigs Papers (18,202.1), reel 12, 0593 (1/16/63).
15. *Globe*, 1/16/1863, 358-60; Meigs Papers (18,202.1), reel 5, 0568 (1/18/63), reel 12, 0594 (1/16/63), 0597 (1/17/63), 0606 (1/23/63).
16. *Globe*, 1/15/1863, 327; see *Dictionary* for men listed.
17. John Y. Simon, ed., *The Papers of Ulysses S. Grant*, vol. 7 (Carbondale, Ill.: Southern Illinois University Press, 1979), 301.
18. Henry B. Meigs, *Record of the Descendants of Vincent Meigs* (Baltimore, Md.: J. S. Bridges & Co., 1901), 270-71; Meigs Papers (18,202.1), reel 5, 0593 (3/10/63).
19. Meigs Papers (18,202.1), reel 5, 0622 (5/7/63), 0630 (5/23/63); Russell F. Weigley, *Quartermaster General of the Union Army* (New York: Columbia University Press, 1959), 49.
20. Meigs Papers (18,202), reel 16 (3/2/63), 078 (7/12/63), (18,202.1), reel 5, 0359 (2/3/62), 0524 (11/5/62), 0605 (4/5/63), 0614 (4/21/63), 0634 (5/30/63).
21. Meigs Papers (18,202.1), reel 1, 0693 (1/8/62), reel 5, 0341 (1/4/62), 0576 (2/1/63).
22. *DAB*, John Rodgers; Meigs Papers (18,202.1), reel 5, 0608 (4/16/63), 0614 (4/21/63); *Calendar*, 4/7/63.
23. Meigs Papers (18,202), reel 16, 085 (8/23/63).
24. Meigs Papers (18,202.1), reel 5, 0576 (2/1/63), 0605 (4/5/63); *B&L*, vol. 3, 154-55; Richard Wheeler, *Voices of the Civil War* (New York: A Meridian Book, 1990), 249-52.
25. Meigs Papers (18,202.1), reel 5, 0614 (4/21/63); *B&L*, vol. 3, 156-57; *Dictionary*, "Chancellorsville Campaign"; Archer Jones, *Civil War Command & Strategy* (New York: The Free Press, 1992), 156-57, 227, 274.
26. *B&L*, vol. 3, 159-62; *Calendar*, 4/27-5/1/63; *Dictionary*, "Chancellorsville Campaign".
27. *B&L*, vol. 3,161-63; *Calendar*; 5/2/63; A. Wilson Greene and Gary W. Gallagher, *National Geographic Guide to the Civil War National Battlefield Parks* (Washington: 1992), 140.
28. *Calendar*, 5/3-5/63, 5/10/63.
29. Meigs Papers (18,202.1), reel 5, 0624 (5/10/63), 0634 (5/30/63).
30. Ibid., 0634 (5/10/63).
31. *OR* III, vol. 2, 654-55; Weigley, *Quartermaster General*, 269.

32. *OR* I, vol. 25, pt. 2, 486, 489-90, 544.

33. Ibid., 203-4, 486-87, 544-47.

34. Meigs Papers (18,202.1), reel 5, 0617 (4/28/63).

Chapter 22

1. Meigs Papers (18,202.1), reel 5, 0640 (6/7/63).

2. Herman Haupt, *Reminiscences of General Herman Haupt* (1901; reprint, North Stratford, N.H.: Arno Press Inc., 1981), 204-5.

3. Haupt, 205-7.

4. Shelby Foote, *The Civil War, Fredericksburg to Meridian* (New York: Vintage Press, 1986), 430-33; Hudson Strode, *Jefferson Davis, Confederate President* (New York: Harcourt, Bruce and Company, 1959), 402-6.

5. Meigs Papers (18,202), reel 16, 072 (6/27/63); Haupt, 207; *Calendar,* 6/16-24/63.

6. Russell F. Weigley, *Quartermaster General of the Union Army* (New York: Columbia University Press, 1959), 273-74.

7. Meigs Papers (18,202), reel 16, 072 (6/27/63); *Calendar,* 6/9/63.

8. *Calendar,* 6/9/63.

9. Weigley, *Quartermaster General,* 274-75.

10. Richard Wheeler, *Voices of the Civil War* (New York: A Meridian Book, 1990), 282-83.

11. *Dictionary,* "Gettysburg Campaign"; *Calendar,* 7/1-3/63; Foote, *Fredericksburg to Meridian,* 577, 595.

12. Captain Robert E. Lee, *Recollections and Letters of General Robert E. Lee* (New York: Garden City Publishing Co., Inc., 1904), 102.

13. Haupt, 223.

14. Meigs Papers (18,202), reel 16, 075 (7/5/63); *OR* I, vol. 27, pt. 3, 543, 567.

15. *OR* I, vol. 27, pt. 3, 568-69.

16. Meigs Papers (18,202.1), reel 5, 0537 (11/23/62), 0654 (7/13/63), (18,202), reel 16, 083 (7/21/63).

17. *OR* I, vol. 27, pt. 1, 92-93, 109; Haupt, 243.

18. Meigs Papers (18,202), reel 16, 075 (7/5/63), (18,202.1), reel 5, 0668 (8/16/63); *OR* I, vol. 51, pt. 2, 741-42.

19. *OR* I, vol. 27, pt. 3, 591.

20. Meigs Papers (18,202.1), reel 5, 0605 (4/5/63); *Calendar,* 4/10/63.

21. *Calendar,* 10/3-4/62.

22. Ibid., 12/20/62; *OR* I, vol. 21, 967.

23. *Dictionary,* "Vicksburg Campaign"; *Calendar,* 3/29/63, 4/15/63, 4/16/63.

24. *Calendar,* 4/17/63, 4/29/63, 4/30/63, 5/2/63.

25. Ibid., 5/14/63, 5/16/63, 5/19/63, 5/22/63, 7/4/63; Foote, *Fredericksburg to Meridian,* 613.

26. James A. Huston, *The Sinews of War: Army Logistics 1775-1953* (Washington: Office of the Chief of Military History, United States Army, 1966), 231.

27. Foote, *Fredericksburg to Meridian,* 613-15; Grant, 381, 384, 388-89.

28. Meigs Papers (18,202.1), reel 5, 0660 (8/5/63), (18,202), reel 16, 085 (8/23/63).

29. Meigs Papers (18,202.1), reel 5, 0662 (8/9/63); Varina Davis, *Jefferson Davis, A Memoir by His Wife,* vol. 2 (New York: Belford Company, 1890), 454-61.

30. Meigs Papers (18,202.1), reel 5, 0662 (8/9/63), 0668 (8/16/63).

31. Weigley, *Quartermaster General,* 284.

32. Meigs Papers (18,202), reel 16, 085 (8/23/63), 087 (8/25/63).

33. Ibid., 087 (8/25/63).

34. Meigs Papers (18,202.1), reel 5, 0662 (8/9/63).

35. *Calendar*, 6/23-24/63, 8/16/63, 9/2/63, 9/9/63.

36. Ibid., 9/9/63, 9/17/63, 9/20/63

37. Ibid., 9/20-21/63.

Chapter 23

1. Shelby Foote, *The Civil War, Fort Sumter to Perryville* (New York: Vintage Books, 1986), 252; Shelby Foote, *The Civil War, Red River to Appomattox* (New York: Vintage Books, 1986), 845; David Herbert Donald, *Lincoln* (New York: Simon & Schuster, 1995), 475; *OR* I, vol. 30, pt. 4, 10.

2. John Niven, *Salmon P. Chase* (New York: Oxford University Press, 1995), 333; William Tecumseh Sherman, *Memoirs of General W. T. Sherman* (New York: The Library of America, 1990), 375-76; Ulysses S. Grant, *Memoirs and Selected Letters* (New York: The Library of America, 1990), 390; *OR* I, vol. 31, pt. 2, 568-71.

3. *Calendar*, 9/23/63.

4. *OR* I, vol. 29, pt. 2, 154-55, vol. 30, pt. 3, 479.

5. *OR* I, vol. 30, pt. 3, 810, 942.

6. Meigs Papers (18,202.1), reel 5, 0678 (9/27/63); *OR* I, vol. 29, pt. 1, 157, vol. 30, pt. 4, 246-47.

7. Samuel Richey Kamm, *The Civil War Career of Thomas A. Scott* (Philadelphia: University of Pennsylvania, 1940), 130; *OR* I, vol. 29, pt. 1, 150, 157.

8. Kamm, 181-82; *OR* III, vol. 3, 910.

9. Meigs Papers (18,202.1), reel 5, 0678 (9/27/63); *QMG (1864)*, *OR* III, vol. 4, 879.

10. Kamm, 165, 174-75; *Calendar*, 10/2/63.

11. Meigs Papers (18,202), reel 16, 093 (10/4/63); *OR* I, vol. 29, pt. 1, 186; *B&L*, vol. 3, 676; James Huston, *The Sinews of War: Army Logistics 1775-1953* (Washington: Office of the Chief of Military History, United States Army, 1966), 209-10.

12. *OR* I, vol. 30, pt. 4, 78, 208; Kamm, 171.

13. *OR* I, vol. 52, pt. 1, 617; *B&L*, vol. 3, 676; *Quartermaster General Annual Report, 1864*, *OR* III, vol. 4, 879.

14. *QMG (1864)*, *OR* III, vol. 4, 879; Charles A. Dana, *Recollections of the Civil War* (Collier Books, New York, N.Y., 1963), 126.

15. *QMG (1864)*, *OR* III, vol. 4, 879.

16. Kamm, 167; Dana, 124; *QMG (1864)*, *OR* III, vol. 4, 879-80; *OR* I, vol. 52, pt. 1, 617-18.

17. *OR* I, vol. 30, pt. 4, 31, 57.

18. Ibid., 101-2.

19. Ibid., 206, 208; *B&L*, vol. 3, 683.

20. Dana, 125.

21. *OR* I, vol. 30, pt. 4, 307, 413.

22. Ibid., 413, 426.

23. *Calendar*, 10/17/63; *B&L*, vol. 3, 681-82; Meigs Papers (18,202), reel 16, 095 (10/22/63).

24. Meigs Papers (18,202), reel 16, 095 (10/22/63).

25. Sherman, 383; *OR* I, vol. 31, pt. 2, 571, vol. 32, pt. 2, 5-6.

26. *OR* I, vol. 31, pt. 1, 678, 729.

27. *B&L*, vol. 3, 678; *OR* I, vol. 31, pt. 1, 666; *Calendar*, 10/23/63; Meigs Papers (18,202), reel 16, 097 (10/25/63).

28. *B&L*, vol. 3, 714.

29. *Calendar*, 10/26, 27/63; *B&L*, vol. 3, 678, 687-89.

30. *Calendar*, 10/28/63; Meigs Papers (18,202), reel 16, 099 (10/30/63).

31. Meigs Papers (18,202), reel 16, 099 (10/30/63).
32. *OR* I, vol. 31, pt. 3, 15, 124; Meigs Papers (18,202), reel 16, 099 (10/30/63), 0102 (11/4/63).
33. *OR* I, vol. 31, pt. 2, 55-56; Meigs Papers (18,202), reel 16, 0104 (11/11/63); Sherman, 388.
34. *B&L*, vol. 3, 683; also see *OR* I, vol. 31, pt. 1, 729.
35. *OR* I, vol. 31, pt. 3, 162, 216.
36. Meigs Papers (18,202), reel 16, 093 (10/4/63), 099 (10/30/63), 0102 (11/4/63), 0104 (11/11/63).
37. Ibid., 0104 (11/11/63), 0106 (11/17/63).
38. Ibid., 0104 (11/11/63).
39. Ibid., 0106 (11/17/63).
40. Ibid., 0104 (11/11/63), 0115 (12/5/63).
41. Kamm, 168-69; *OR* I, vol. 29, pt. 1, 175, vol. 31, pt. 2, 63, vol. 31, pt. 3, 190, 195, 219, vol. 52, pt. 1, 618; *OR* III, vol. 4, 942.
42. *OR* I, vol. 31, pt. 3, 195, 230, 264.
43. *Calendar*, 11/15/63; *OR* I, vol. 31, pt. 2, 77, pt. 3, 96; A. Wilson Greene and Gary W. Gallagher, *National Geographic Guide to the Civil War Battlefield Parks* (Washington: 1992), 113-14; *B&L*, vol. 3, 746.
44. *B&L*, vol. 3, 695-96; *Calendar*, 11/30/63, 12/16/63.
45. *B&L*, vol. 3, 707; Meigs Papers (18,202), reel 26, 0398.
46. *OR* I, vol. 31, pt. 2, 77 et seq.; Meigs Papers (18,202), reel 16, 0111 (12/5/63), 0114 (12/8/63).
47. *OR* I, vol. 31, pt. 2, 77-78.
48. Meigs Papers (18,202), reel 16, 0111 (12/5/63).
49. *OR* I, vol. 31, pt. 2, 78-79.
50. Ibid., 79; *Calendar*, 2/29/64.
51. *Calendar*, 11/25/63.
52. Richard Wheeler, *Voices of the Civil War* (New York: A Meridian Book, 1990), 364.
53. Sherman, 405-6, 410; Meigs Papers (18,202), reel 16, 0111 (12/5/63), 0114 (12/8/63).
54. *B&L*, vol. 3, 750.
55. *OR* I, vol. 31, pt. 3, 106-7, 109; *QMG (1864)*, *OR* III, vol. 4, 880-81; *Dictionary*, Robert Allen, James Donaldson, Langdon Easton.
56. *OR* I, vol. 31, pt. 3, 422, 444, 496; Meigs Papers (18,202.1), reel 5, 0157 (12/25/63).

Chapter 24

1. William Tecumseh Sherman, *Memoirs of General W. T. Sherman* (The Library of America, 1990), 414; *B&L*, vol. 4, 99.
2. Meigs Papers (18,202.1), reel 5, 0703 (12/11/63); *OR* I, vol. 32, pt. 2, 104-5, 118, 334-35.
3. *OR* III, vol. 4, 16; *OR* I, vol. 32, pt. 2, 351-52, 354; *OR* I, vol. 35, pt. 1, 472.
4. Meigs Papers (18,202.1), reel 5, 0728 (1/25/64).
5. Meigs Papers (18,202.1), reel 5, 0766 (3/22/64), 0767 (3/22/64), 0771 (3/30/64), 0835 (6/27/64).
6. *OR* I, vol. 32, pt. 2, 144-45.
7. *SecWar (1865)*, Appendix I, Part I, Report of Brevet Brig. Gen. D. C. McCallum, 18 (cited hereafter as McCallum); *OR* I, vol. 38, pt. 5, 4.
8. *OR* I, vol. 32, pt. 2, 437-38.
9. Ibid., 438.
10. Ibid., 438.
11. *OR* II, vol. 6, 589, 632, 893-94.

12. *OR* II, vol. 4, 129, 324.

13. *B&L*, vol. 4, 95-96.

14. Meigs Papers (18,202.1), reel 5, 0754 (3/6/64).

15. Ibid., 0756 (3/9/64).

16. *Calendar*, 2/6/64.

17. Sherman, 414, 417-18, 422.

18. *B&L*, vol. 4, 247 footnote; Sherman, 452.

19. Sherman, 420, 422-23; National Geographic Society, *Battlefields of the Civil War* (National Geographic Society, 1974), map notation at Meridian, Mississippi; Meigs Papers (18,202.1), reel 5, 0758 (3/13/64).

20. Sherman, 463.

21. *OR* I, vol. 32, pt. 3, 26; *Calendar*, 3/9/64; Meigs Papers (18,202.1), reel 5, 0746 (3/1/64), 0758 (3/13/64); Frank Abial Flower, *Edwin McMasters Stanton* (Akron, Ohio: The Saalfield Publishing Company, 1905), 383.

22. Captain Robert E. Lee, *Recollections and Letters of General Robert E. Lee* (New York: Garden City Publishing Co., Inc., 1904), 103-4.

23. Meigs Papers (18,202.1), reel 5, 0738 (2/7/64).

24. Ibid., 0728 (1/25/64), 0738 (2/7/64), 0764 (3/20/64), 0769 (3/26/64); *Dictionary*, William Franklin.

25. Meigs Papers (18,202.1), reel 5, 0738 (2/7/64), 0787 (4/21/64); *Calendar*, 2/9/64; Russell F. Weigley, *Quartermaster General of the Union Army* (New York: Columbia University Press,1959), 230.

26. Meigs Papers (18,202.1), reel 5, 0769 (3/26/64), 0793 (4/20/64), 0792 (4/27/64).

27. Ibid., 0787 (4/21/64); *Dictionary*, Joseph Totten.

28. Meigs Papers (18,202.1), reel 5, 0769 (3/26/64), 0780 (4/5/64), 0794 (4/20/64), 0787 (4/21/64).

Chapter 25

1. *B&L*, vol. 4, 99, 101-4, 112, 248; William Tecumseh Sherman, *Memoirs of General W. T. Sherman* (The Library of America, 1990), 489-90; Roy P. Basler, ed., *The Collected Works of Abraham Lincoln*, vol. 5 (Brunswick, N.J.: Rutgers University Press, 1953-55), 98 (1/13/62); David Herbert Donald, *Lincoln* (New York: Simon & Schuster, 1995), 334; *OR* I, vol. 38, pt. 1, 1-2, 4; *OR* I, vol. 5, 41; Geoffrey Parker, ed., *Cambridge Illustrated History of Warfare* (New York: Cambridge University Press, 1995), 5.

2. *OR* III, vol. 4, 943-44; *SecWar (1865)*, Appendix I, Part I, Report of Brig. Gen D. C. McCallum, 12-13, 26, 34-35.

3. *OR* I, vol. 32, pt. 3, 148, 270, 280-81, 301-2, 435, 532.

4. *OR* I, vol. 38, pt. 4, 19-20.

5. Ibid., 33; *Cullum* at Class of 1838.

6. *OR* I, vol. 32, pt. 3, 330, 434, vol. 38, pt. 4, 4.

7. *OR* I, vol. 32, pt. 3, 301-2, 434, 503-4.

8. *OR* I, vol. 29, pt. 2, 421, vol. 32, pt. 3, 435.

9. *Dictionary*, James Dana, Langdon Easton, Rufus Ingalls, Daniel Rucker; *OR* III, vol. 4, 241.

10. *B&L*, vol. 4, 114, 117; *Calendar*, 5/4/64, 5/7/64.

11. *B&L*, vol. 4, 102, 106-7.

12. *OR* I, vol. 33, 853-54, 919-22, vol. 36, pt. 1, 277; vol. 38, pt. 1, 7.

13. *B&L*, vol. 4, 189-92; *OR* I, vol. 38, pt. 1, 8-9.

14. *Calendar*, 5/6/64, 5/19/64; A. Wilson Greene and Gary W. Gallagher, *National Geographic Guide to the Civil War National Battlefield Parks* (Washington: 1992), 143.

15. Meigs Papers (18,202.1), reel 5, 0799 (5/10/64), 0804 (5/17/64).

16. *OR* I, vol. 36, pt. 1, 278.

17. Meigs Papers (18,202.1), reel 5, 0806 (5/21/64).

18. Russell F. Weigley, *Quartermaster General of the Union Army* (New York: Columbia University Press, 1959), 294-95.

19. Richard Wheeler, *Voices of the Civil War* (New York: A Meridian Book, 1990), 395.

20. *Calendar*, 6/3/64; *B&L*, vol. 4, 218.

21. Benjamin Butler, *Private and Official Correspondence of Gen. Benjamin F. Butler* (Privately Issued, 1917), vol. 4, 7-9, 82-83, 94-95 (cited hereafter as *Butler Papers*).

22. James Huston, *The Sinews of War: Army Logistics 1775-1953* (Washington: Office of the Chief of Military History, United States Army, 1966), 235.

23. *OR* I, vol. 38, pt. 1, 15-16, 20-21.

24. *OR* I, vol. 38, pt. 1, 21, vol. 46, pt. 2, 298.

25. Erna Risch, *Quartermaster Support of the Army, A History of the Corps 1775-1939* (Washington: Quartermaster Historian's Office, Office of the Quartermaster General, 1962), 435-38.

26. *OR* I, vol. 36, pt. 1, 278, pt. 3, 77-79, 208, vol. 38, pt. 1, 12, vol. 40, pt. 3, 35.

27. *OR* I, vol. 38, 22; Greene and Gallagher, 148-49.

28. OR I, vol. 38, pt. 1, 9; Harold B. Raymond, "Ben Butler: A Reappraisal," *Colby Library Quarterly*, series 6, no. 11 (1964): 450; *Butler Papers*, vol. 4, 254, 263; Meigs Papers (18,202.1), reel 5, 0812 (5/26/64); *OR* I, vol. 36, pt. 3, 43, 68-69, 77, 177-78.

29. Meigs Papers (18,202.1), reel 5, 0812 (5/26/64); Ulysses S. Grant, *Memoirs and Selected Letters* (New York: The Library of America, 1990), 570; *Butler Papers*, vol. 4, 263.

30. *B&L*, vol. 4, 103-4, 114, 482-84.

31. *B&L*, vol. 4, 485-86.

32. Meigs Papers (18,202.1), reel 5, 0835 (6/27/64), reel 6, 077 (10/7/64).

33. Ibid., 0828 (6/24/64).

34. *DAB*, Salmon Chase; Samuel Eliot Morison, *The Oxford History of the American People* (New York: Oxford University Press, 1965), 693.

35. Meigs Papers (18,202.1), reel 6, 002 (7/2/64), 045 (8/31/64), 051 (9/16/64).

36. *OR* I, vol. 38, pt. 1, 2; Frank Abial Flower, *Edwin McMasters Stanton* (Akron, Ohio: The Saalfield Company, 1905), 195.

37. *DAB*, Greeley.

38. Morison, 695; *DAB*, David Farragut; *B&L*, vol. 4, 391, 406-7.

39. *B&L*, vol. 4, 252-53; Sherman, 496, 503-04, 511-15; *OR* I, vol. 38, pt. 1, 59-61; Hugh McCulloch, *Means and Measures of Half a Century* (1888; reprint, New York: De Capo Press, 1970), 285.

40. *B&L*, vol. 4, 252-53; Sherman, 515, 517-18, 520, 533-34; McCulloch, 285.

41. *B&L*, vol. 4, 253, 274-75.

42. *Calendar*, 7/20/64, 7/22/64, 7/28/64.

43. *B&L*, vol. 4, 254.

44. *OR* I, vol. 38, pt. 1, 83-84.

45. Meigs Papers (18,202.1), reel 6, 062 (9/27/64).

46. Huston, 235.

47. *OR* I, vol. 39, pt. 2, 356; Grant, 511; Meigs Papers (18,202.1), reel 6, 0107 (11/7/64).

48. *B&L*, vol. 4, 492-93; Meigs Papers (18,202.1), reel 5, 0828 (6/24/64); *DAB*, David Hunter; *Calendar*, 7/6/64, 7/7/64.

49. Meigs Papers (18,202.1), reel 6, 009 (7/9/64).

50. *Calendar*, 7/9/64.

51. *OR* I, vol. 37, pt. 2, 193, vol. 40, pt. 3, 127.

52. *OR* I, vol. 37, pt. 1, 231, 255, 258.

53. *OR* I, vol. 37, pt. 1, 231-33, 255-56, 259, vol. 37, pt. 2, 236.

54. *OR* I, vol. 37, pt. 1, 234, 259; *Calendar*, 7/11/64, 7/13/64, 7/14/64.

55. *OR* I, vol. 37, pt 1, 259, pt. 2, 308, 385-87.

56. Meigs Papers (18,202.1), reel 6, 024 (7/29/64), (18,202), reel 26, 090; *OR* I, vol. 37, pt. 1, 256.

57. Meigs Papers (18,202.1), reel 6, 024 (7/29/64).

58. *B&L*, vol. 4, 501; *DAB*, Philip Sheridan; *Dictionary*, Philip Sheridan.

59. *B&L*, vol. 4, 501-5; Meigs Papers (18,202.1), reel 6, 024 (7/29/64).

60. *B&L*, vol. 4, 505-6; Shelby Foote, *The Civil War, Red River to Appomattox* (New York: Vintage Press, 1986), 554-55.

61. *B&L*, vol. 4, 511-13; *OR* I, vol. 38, pt. 1, 18-19; Meigs Papers (18,202.1), reel 6, 0122 (11/18/64).

62. Meigs Papers (18,202.1), reel 6, 009 (7/9/64), 031 (7/24/64), 024 (7/29/64), 027 (8/6/64), 029 (8/12/64), 042 (8/25/64).

63. Ibid., 047 (9/4/64), 052 (9/20/64), 060 (9/22/64).

64. Ibid., 077 (10/7/64).

65. P. H. Sheridan, *Personal Memoirs of P. H. Sheridan*, vol. 1 (New York: Charles L. Webster & Company, 1888), 308.

66. *OR* I, vol. 43, pt. 1, 56-57.

67. Sheridan, 308; Roy Morris, Jr., *Sheridan* (New York: Crown Publishers, Inc., 1992), 208.

68. Morris, 207-8.

69. *OR* I, vol. 43, pt. 2, 318; Meigs Papers (18,202.1), reel 2, 0199; Weigley, *Quartermaster General*, 309.

Chapter 26

1. James D. Richardson, *A Compilation of the Messages and Papers of the Confederacy*, vol. 1 (Nashville, Tenn.: United States Publishing Company, 1905), 482-84.

2. Richard Wheeler, *Voices of the Civil War* (New York: A Meridian Book, 1990), 389; Meigs Papers (18,202.1), reel 6, 0107 (11/7/64), 0111 (11/9/64).

3. *Calendar*, 11/8/64.

4. Meigs Papers (18,202.1), reel 6, 077 (10/7/64).

5. William Tecumseh Sherman, *Memoirs of General W. T. Sherman* (New York: The Library of America, 1990), 560; *OR* I, vol. 38, pt. 1, 28.

6. *B&L*, vol. 4, 254, 425-26, 441; Simon Newcomb, *The Reminiscences of An Astronomer* (Boston: Houghton, Mifflin and Company, 1903), 244.

7. *OR* I, vol. 39, pt. 3, 394-95.

8. Ibid., 728.

9. Ibid., 395, 614, 727.

10. Ibid., 626; *OR* I, vol. 52, pt. 1, 701-2.

11. *B&L*, vol. 4, 441.

12. *B&L*, vol. 4, 441; *Calendar*, 11/30/64.

13. *OR* I, vol. 44, 755, vol. 45, pt. 2, 251, 561; *Calendar*, 12/16/64; Ulysses S. Grant, *Memoirs and Selected Letters* (New York: The Library of America, 1990), 656-61; Meigs Papers (18,202.1), reel 6, 0150 (12/14/64).

14. *OR* I, vol. 52, pt. 1, 702-3; *B&L*, vol. 4, 663.

15. *B&L*, vol. 4, 666; *Calendar*, 12/22/64; *OR* III, vol. 5, 214.

16. Meigs Papers (18,202.1), reel 6, 0132 (11/28/64); *OR* I, vol. 44, 568.

17. *OR* I, vol. 44, 637-38.

18. *OR* I, vol. 44, 568-69; Ella Lonn, *Salt As A Factor In The Confederacy* (New York: Walter Neale, Publisher, 1933), 13-18, 43-44, 145-47, 160-70, 205, 207.

19. *OR* I, vol. 44, 715-16.

20. *OR* I, vol. 46, pt. 2, 547-48, 561-62.

21. *OR* I, vol. 47, pt. 2, 180; *OR* III, vol. 4, 1054.

22. *OR* I, vol. 44, 807, 841.

23. Richardson, 487; *Calendar,* 703, 707; Ella Lonn, *Foreigners in the Union Army and Navy* (Westport, Conn.: Greenwood Press, Publishers, 1969), 406-17, 574-77, 582; *OR* III, vol. 4, 455-57.

24. Richardson, 493; Meigs Papers (18,202.1), reel 6, 092 (10/22/64).

25. Richardson, 493-94.

26. Meigs Papers (18,202.1), reel 5, 0306 (12/13/61); Richardson, 547.

27. *B&L,* vol. 4, 655, 658-61.

28. Meigs Papers (18,202.1) reel 6, 0163 (12/31/64); *OR* I, vol. 38, pt. 1, 35, vol. 46, pt. 2, 29; Harold B. Raymond, "Ben Butler: A Reappraisal," *Colby Library Quarterly,* series 6, no. 11 (1964): 453-54.

29. *B&L,* vol. 4, 683; *OR* I vol 44, 799; Meigs Papers (18,202.1), reel 6, 0146 (12/24/64), 0172 (1/6/65); *OR* I, vol. 47, pt. 2, 18; Wheeler, *Voices,* 422.

30. Meigs Papers (18,202.1), reel 6, 0179 (1/13/65), 0182 (1/16/65); *OR* I, vol. 46, pt. 2, 157, vol. 47, pt. 2, 35-37.

31. Grant, 686.

32. Meigs Papers (18,202.1) reel 6, 0187 (2/6/65), 0231 (4/24/65).

33. *OR* I, vol. 44, 797.

34. *B&L,* vol. 4, 686-87.

35. Meigs Papers (18,202.1), reel 6, 0198 (2/22/65); *OR* I, vol. 47, pt. 2, 512.

36. Meigs Papers (18,202.1), reel 6, 0201 (3/3/65).

37. Ibid., reel 20, 0147.

38. *B&L,* vol. 4, 687-88.

39. Ibid., 692-95, 698, 700-1, 705.

40. Ibid., 754.

41. Meigs Papers (18,202), reel 16, 0129 (3/21/65), 0132 (3/29/65), (18,202.1), reel 6, 0217 (4/11/65); *OR* I, vol. 47, pt. 3, 19, 32.

42. Meigs Papers (18,202), reel 16, 0132 (3/29/65).

43. *B&L,* vol. 4, 754.

44. *OR* I, vol. 38, pt. 1, 41.

45. *B&L,* vol. 4, 683.

46. *OR* I, vol. 38, pt. 1, 41; Grant, 691.

47. *OR* I, vol. 38, pt. 1, 39-41; Grant, 689-90; *B&L,* vol. 4, 709; *Calendar,* 3/23/65-4/8/65.

48. *OR* I, vol. 46, pt. 2, 1258, pt. 3, 1353-54, vol. 51, 1065-66.

49. *OR* I, vol. 38, pt. 1, 44; Grant, 696; *B&L,* vol. 4, 709, 725, 742; *Calendar,* 3/29/65; Newcomb, 344.

50. Meigs Papers (18,202.1), reel 6, 0217 (4/11/65).

51. Ibid., 0217 (4/11/65).

52. Meigs Papers (18,202), reel 3 (4/14/65); Russell F. Weigley, *Quartermaster General of the Union Army* (New York: Columbia University Press, 1959), 322-23; Dorothy Meserve Kunhardt and Philip B. Kunhardt Jr., *Twenty Days* (Memphis, Tenn.: Castle Books, 1965), 61.

53. Meigs Papers (18,202), reel 3 (4/14-15/65); Weigley, *Quartermaster General*, 322-23; Kunhardt and Kunhardt, 61.

54. Meigs Papers (18,202), reel 3 (4/20/65), (18,202.1), reel 16, 0654; Weigley, *Quartermaster General*, 323; Kunhardt and Kunhardt,119, 132.

55. *B&L*, vol. 4, 755-56; Kunhardt and Kunhardt,100.

56. *B&L*, vol. 4, 756.

57. Ibid., 757.

58. Meigs Papers (18,202.1), reel 6, 0231 (4/24/65).

59. *OR* I, vol. 38, pt. 1, 50-51; Kunhardt and Kunhardt, 140-73, 218-302.

60. Meigs Papers (18,202.1), reel 6, 0101 (11/4/64), 0228 (4/21/65).

61. Wheeler, *Voices*, 466; *Calendar*, 4/14/65.

Chapter 27

1. *SecWar (1865)*, *OR* III, vol. 5, 507, 515-16.

2. *Calendar*, 5/23-24/65; Meigs Papers (18,202), reel 16, 0144 (5/25/65), 0146 (5/26/65).

3. *QMG (1865)*, *OR* III, vol. 5, 249; Meigs Papers (18,202), reel 16, 0142 (5/20/65), 0144 (5/25/65), reel 17, 0021.

4. *QMG (1865)*, 217, 232-33; *SecWar (1865)*, 518; *SecWar (1866)*, *OR* III, vol. 5, 1031.

5. *QMG (1865)*, 217, 221; *QMG (1866)*, Papers Accompanying the *Report of the Secretary of War*, 105-6; *SecWar (1865)*, 527-28; Meigs Papers (18,202.1), reel 1, 0471 (2/13/61).

6. *QMG (1865)*, 230, 234.

7. Monro MacCloskey, *Hallowed Ground Our National Cemeteries* (New York: Richard Rosen Press, Inc., 1968), 21-23, 29.

8. *QMG (1865)*, 241-42; Mark Hughes, *Bivouac of the Dead* (Bowie, Md.: Heritage Books, Inc., 1995), 10, 15; Philip Bigler, *In Honored Glory, Arlington National Cemetery: The Final Post* (Arlington, Va.: Vandamere Press, 1987), xiii-xv.

9. Bigler, 34; Quartermaster Department, *Roll of Honor* (GPO, 1865) (cited hereafter as *Roll of Honor*).

10. *QMG (1864)*, *OR* III, vol. 4, 903-4; Dean W. Holt, *American Military Cemeteries* (Jefferson, N.C.: McFarland & Company, 1995), 17, 418; *Roll of Honor* (1865).

11. Brent Ashabranner, *A Grateful Nation* (New York: G. P. Putnam's Sons, 1990), 30; MacCloskey, 137; *Statutes at Large* 12 (1862): 422, 640; Bigler, 23-24.

12. Peter Andrews, *In Honored Glory* (New York: G. P. Putnam's Sons, 1966), 19-20.

13. Ashabranner, 32, 35; Andrews, 21-22; MacCloskey, 137-38; Hughes, 7; James Edward Peters, *Arlington National Cemetery* (Kensington, Md.: Woodbine House, 1986), 23-27, 155; Bigler, 27; John Vincent Hinkel, *Arlington Monument To Heroes* (Englewood, N.J.: Prentice Hall, New Edition, 1970), 20-24 (includes photo copy of Meigs' letter and Stanton approval).

14. Meigs Papers (18,202), reel 16, 0021, reel 17, 0024.

15. Meigs Papers (18,202), reel 16, 0138 (5/3/65), 0265 (11/13/65).

16. 106 U.S. 196 (1882); Hughes, 19; Bigler, 28-29; Enoch Aquila Chase, "The Arlington Case," *Records Of Columbia Historical Society* 31-32, 1928.

17. Bigler, 30-31.

18. Ibid., 29.

19. Ashabranner, 35.

20. Bigler, 35-37.

21. MacCloskey, 31-36.

22. *QMG (1881)*, 235.

Chapter 28

1. *QMG* for 1865, 1866, 1868, 1871, and 1880; *SecWar* (1867), 20.

2. Robert M. Utley, *Frontier Regulars 1866-1891* (Lincoln: University of Nebraska Press, 1973), 20-21, 83 n. 100; MCM Journal (Nicolay Papers), 670 (6/10/61).

3. Utley, 11-15, 59-61; *Statutes at Large* 14 (7/28/1866): 332; 15 (3/3/69) 315; 18 (6/16/74) 72; F. B. Heitman, *Historical Record of the United States Army (1789-1889)* (Washington: National Tribune, 1890), 880; *SecWar (1867)*, 23, 26, 29, 30.

4. Utley, 14-15, 19.

5. *QMG (1868)*, 156; Meigs Papers (18,202), reel 17, 0134 (5/28/67).

6. J. G. Randall, *The Civil War And Reconstruction* (Boston: D. C. Heath and Company, 1937), 741-42; Benjamin Perley Poore, *Perley's Reminiscences*, vol. 2 (1886; reprint, New York: AMS Press, 1971), 229.

7. Henry Steele Commager, *Documents of American History*, 4th ed. (New York:Appleton-Century-Crofts, Inc., 1948), 429 (Proclamation of Amnesty and Reconstruction, December 8, 1863).

8. Commager, 436 (Wade-Davis Bill, July 8, 1864); Randall, 705.

9. Meigs Papers (18,202), reel 16, 0207 (9/5/65).

10. Meigs Papers (18,202), reel 16, 0156 (6/28/65), 0162 (7/5/65), (18,202.1), reel 6, 0257 (6/22/65); Meigs Journal (Transcribed) 1/10/56, 12/7/57, 4/3/58.

11. Meigs Papers (18,202), reel 16, 0158 (7/1/65), 0162 (7/5/65), 0189 (8/21/65), (18,202.1), reel 6, (7/17/65).

12. Meigs Papers (18,202), reel 16, 0175 (7/20/65), 0219 (9/16/65).

13. Ibid., 0194 (8/27/65), 0219 (9/16/65), 0231 (10/5/65).

14. Ibid., 0209 (9/8/65), 0231 (10/5/65), 0238 (10/10/65), 0240 (10/13/65), 0240 (10/13/65), 0269 (11/24/65).

15. Meigs Papers (18,202), reel 16, 0197 (8/26/65), (18,202.1), reel 6, 0249 (5/31/65).

16. Meigs Papers (18,202.1), reel 6, 0269 (11/24/65); *DAB*, Jefferson Davis.

17. Commager, 12 (Veto of Freedmen's Bureau Bill, February 19, 1866), 15 (Veto of the Civil Rights Act, March 27, 1866), 14 (The Civil Rights Act, April 9, 1866); Randall, 748; James H. Whyte, *The Uncivil War* (New York: Twayre Publishers, 1958), 54.

18. Commager, 20 (Second Annual Message to Congress, December 3, 1866); Randall, 722, 724-30; Whyte, 45-46.

19. Randall, 761-63; Commager, 30 (The First Reconstruction Act, March 2, 1867), 35-36 (Tenure of Office Act, March 2, 1867), 37 (Command of the Army Act, March 2, 1867); Whyte, 57.

20. Randall, 764, 766, 777; 272 U.S. 52 (1926).

21. Benjamin P. Thomas and Harold M. Hyman, *Stanton* (New York: Alfred A. Knopf, 1962), 608, 614-39.

22. Meigs Papers (18,202.1), reel 16, 0467 (11/30/83); Russell F. Weigley, *Quartermaster General of the Union Army* (New York: Columbia University Press, 1959), 352-53.

23. Samuel Eliot Morison, *The Oxford History of The American People* (New York: Oxford University Press, 1965), 714-15, 719, 722; Meigs Papers (18,202), reel 16, 0407 (4/24/65).

24. Utley, 12, 46-47; *QMG (1865)*, 244.

25. *SecWar (1867)*, 30, *(1868)*, 11.

26. *SecWar (1868)*, 17.

27. *SecWar (1868)*, 17.

28. *QMG (1868)*, 159, 169, *(1874)*, 125, *(1879)*, 9-10.

29. *SecWar (1868)*, 13, *(1869)*, 17; *QMG (1871)*, 129.

30. *QMG (1865)*, 244.

31. *QMG (1865)*, 244, *(1869)*, 213.

32. *QMG (1868)*, 167-68.

33. *QMG (1871)*, 127, *(1872)*, 142, *(1876)*, 126, *(1878)*, 262, *(1880)*, 316.

34. Utley, 80-81.

35. *QMG (1865)*, 223, *(1870)*, 148, *(1872)*, 142, *(1876)*, 127, *(1877)*, 192, *(1878)*, 262.

36. *QMG (1871)*, 125, *(1872)*, 139, 141, *(1874)*, 122-23, *(1875)*, 190, *(1879)*, 10, *(1880)*, 331.

37. *QMG (1870)*, 147, *(1872)*, 141, *(1873)*, 110, 119, 121, *(1874)*, 123, *(1876)*, 131, *(1877)*, 180, *(1880)*, 322.

38. *QMG (1876)*,128.

39. *QMG (1878)*, 255, *(1879)*; Constance McLaughlin, *Washington, Capital City, 1879-1950* (Princeton, N.J.: Princeton University Press, 1963), 78-79.

40. *QMG (1880)*, 326, *(1881)*, 226-27, *(1882)*, 266; Act of March 3, 1879.

41. *QMG (1869)*, 208-9; *The Old Executive Office Building, A Victorian Masterpiece* (The Executive Office of the President, 1984).

42. *QMG (1878)*, 255-56.

43. *QMG (1865)*, 224, *(1866)*,103-4, 108, *(1867)*, 531, *(1868)*, 163, *(1873)*, 114, *(1877)*,189.

44. *QMG (1879)*, 225, *(1880)*, 326-27, *(1881)*, 227-28; Victor Gondos, Jr., *J. Franklin Jameson and the Birth of the National Archives 1906-1926* (Philadelphia: University of Pennsylvania Press, 1981), 7.

45. Henry B. Meigs, *Record of the Descendants of Vincent Meigs* (Baltimore, Md.: J. S. Bridges & Co., 1901), 266; Meigs Papers (18,202), reel 17, 0184 (5/11/75), 0210, (18,202.1) reel 1, 12/5/69 et seq., 0315 (1/6/70).

46. Meigs Papers (18,202), reel 17, 0218 (5/29/75).

47. *QMG (1882)*, 250; Charles R. Shrader, *U. S. Military Logistics, 1607-1991* (Westport, Conn.: Greenwood Press, 1992), Appendix A; *Meigs Papers* (18,202), reel 17, 0289 (2/8/82); Roy Morris, Jr., *Sheridan* (New York: Crown Publishers, 1992), 377-78; Meigs Papers (18,202.1), reel 18, 0637, 0676 (1/12/85); Ulysses S. Grant, *Memoirs and Selected Letters* (New York: The Library of America, 1990), 1158-59.

Chapter 29

1. J. Kilpatrick Flack, *Desideratum in Washington, The Intellectual Community in the Capital City 1870-1900* (Cambridge, Mass.: Schenkman Pub. Co., 1975), 59; *Meigs Papers* (18,202), reel 16, 001 et seq. at 14.

2. Hugh McCulloch, *Men and Measures of Half a Century* (1888; reprint, New York: De Capo Press, 1970), 261-62.

3. Meigs Papers (18,202), reel 22, 0598 (3/7/83).

4. McCulloch, 262, 265-69; *DAB* for Henry, Bache, Parker, Newcomb, Hilgard, Humphreys, Peale, Gilliss, Poe, and Barnard; Frederick W. True, *A History of the First Half-Century of the National Academy of Sciences, 1863-1913*, vol. 1 (1913; reprint, New York: Arno Press, 1980), vol. 1, 337-44.

5. Flack, 60-61, 64; *DAB*, Aspah Hall.

6. Flack, 61-62, 65; Meigs Papers (18,202.1) reel 14, 0734 (5/18/81).

7. Flack, 19-20, 58-59; William Jones Rhees, *The Smithsonian Institution, Documents Relative To Its Origin And History, 1835-1899*, vol. 1 (1901; reprint, North Stratford, N.H.: Arno Press, 1980), preface; George Brown Goode, *The Smithsonian Institution, 1846-1896* (1897; reprint, North Stratford, N.H.: Arno Press, 1980), 59, 62-65, 76.

8. Goode, 59-62, 834, 838, 840.

9. Cynthia R. Field, Richard E. Stamm, Heather P. Ewing, *The Castle* (Washington: Smithsonian Institution Press, 1993); Goode, 76, 254-57.

10. Goode, 261-62, 329-30, 839; Flack, 86-87, 89; *QMG (1871)*, 131, *(1872)*, 148, *(1874)*, 124, *(1876)*, 121, *(1878)*, 256.

11. Goode, 261-62, 329-30; Constance Mc Laughlin Green, *Washington Capital City 1879-1950* (Princeton, N.J.: Princeton University Press, 1963), 82; Jane W. Gemmill, *Notes on Washington* (Philadelphia: E. Claxton & Company, 1884), 183-84.

12. Goode, 76, 103, 445-47.

13. Ibid., 449-51, 453.

14. Meigs Papers (18,202.1), reel 6, 0172 (1/6/65); True, 6-8, 13-15; Flack, 66.

15. True, 295-98; *Senate Miscellaneous Document No. 82*, 49th Congress, 1st Session (1886); David R. Whitnah, *History of the United States Weather Bureau* (Champaign, Ill.: University of Illinois Press, 1961), 52, 54-55.

16. True, 298-99.

17. Goode, 648, 663-64; Milton Conover, *The General Land Office* (Baltimore: John Hopkins Press, 1923), 17-18; Meigs Papers (18,202), reel 16, 001 et seq. at pages 7-8.

18. Goode, 650, 656-57; Whitnah, 5.

19. Goode, 672-73, 678; Whitnah, 19-21, 23, 29-33, 39-40.

20. Whitnah, 21, 23, 29-30; Meigs Papers (18,202), reel 23, 026 et seq.

21. True, 207, 239-47, 348-49.

22. True, footnote on 41-42; *QMG (1882)*, 366-67, 370.

23. Simon Newcomb, *The Reminiscences of An Astronomer* (Boston: Houghton, Mifflin and Company, 1903), 334-35.

24. Albert E. Cowdrey, *A City for the Nation* (Washington: Historical Division, Office of Administrative Services, Office of the Chief of Engineers, 1978), 24, 31; Richard M. Lee, *Mr. Lincoln's City* (McLean, Va.: EPM Publications, Inc. 1981), 15; William M. Maury, *Alexander "Boss" Shepherd and the Board of Public Works* (Washington: George Washington University 1975), 1-2, 14, 32, 34; William Tindall, "A Sketch of Alexander Robey Shepherd," *Records of the Columbia Historical Society* 14 (1910): 55-56.

25. Maury, 2, 4.

26. *DAB*, Alexander Robey Shepherd; Maury, 4, 13, 18, 22, 32, 34-44, 48-49; Tindall, *Shepherd*, 55, 60-61.

27. Maury, 6, 27-30; Franklin T. Howe, "The Board of Public Works," *Records of the Columbia Historical Society* 3 (1899): 261-63.

28. Maury, 35; Howe, 274.

29. Maury, 51; Cowdrey, 24-26; Flack, 17.

30. John Y. Cole, "LC in the 19th Century—An Informal Account," *Library of Congress Professional Association* (1972): 7-10; *The Old Executive Office Building, A Victorian Masterpiece* (The Executive Office of the President, 1984); H. P. Caemerer, *Washington, The National Capital*, Senate Document No. 332, 71st Congress, 3d Session, 311.

31. Louis Torres, *"To the Immortal name and memory of George Washington"* (Washington: Historical Division, Office of Administrative Services, Office of the Chief of Engineers, 1985), 6-8, 15-16, 23, 32, 39, 42, 54, 56-59, 82, 86-87, 97; Cowdrey, 27-28.

32. Goode, 329; Rhees, 778, 834.

33. Meigs Papers (18,202.1), reel 14, 0635 (2/19/81), (18,202), reel 21, 0237 (6/19/82).

34. Harry C. Ways, *The Washington Aqueduct, 1852-1992* (United States Corps of Engineers, Baltimore District, 1996), 70-73, 76, 81-83, 86.

35. Meigs Papers (18,202.1), reel 15, 0389 (2/6/82), reel 17, 0123 (3/25/84), (18,202), reel 23, 0507 (3/8/87); Linda Brody Lyons, *A Handbook to the Pension Building* (Washington: National Building Museum, 1989) 7, 10.

36. Meigs Papers (18,202), reel 23, 057 (1/30/86), 0217 (6/9/86), 0311-0315 (10/6/86), (18,202.1), reel 14, 0590 (1/18/81); Henry B. Meigs, *Record of the Descendants of Vincent Meigs* (Baltimore, Md.: J. S. Bridges & Co., 1901), 88; Stanley J. Kunitz, ed., *British Authors of the Nineteenth Century* (New York: The H. W. Wilson Company, 1936).

37. Meigs Papers (18,202), reel 16, 001 et seq. at pages 1-3, 12-13, 31-32.

38. Ibid., reel 22, 0326 (12/10/82); Lyons, 13, 55.

39. Lyons, 58; Joseph T. Kelly, "Memories of a Lifetime in Washington," *Records of the Columbia Historical Society* 31/32 (1930): 126-27.

40. Lyons, 14-16, 22-23, 59-62.

41. Ibid., 25-26, 36-37; Meigs Papers (18,202), reel 21, 0357 (9/13/82).

42. Lyons, 59-62.

43. Meigs Papers (18,202), reel 23, 0225 (6/10/86), 0307 (10/6/86), 0455 (1/23/87).

44. *Cullum* at Classes of 1832, 1874, 1889; Henry Meigs at Appendix page 308; Meigs Papers (18,202), reel 16, 001 et seq. at page 3.

45. Roald Tweet, *A History of the Rock Island District U. S. Army Corps of Engineers 1866-1983* (Rock Island, Ill.: U. S. Army Engineers District, Rock Island, 1984), 7-10, 103-04, 113.

46. Meigs Papers (18,202.1) reel 20, 053.

47. Ibid., reel 21, 0111; Meigs Papers (18,202), reel 16, 001 et seq. at page 31.

48. Meigs Papers (18,202.1), reel 21, 0111, (18,202), reel 16, 0613.

49. Meigs Papers (18,202), reel 16, 0613.

Bibliography

Manuscript Sources

Meigs, Montgomery. Papers. Library of Congress, Manuscript Reading Room.

Meigs, Montgomery. Shorthand journal (March–September 1861), transcribed. John G. Nicolay's papers (container 13), Library of Congress, Manuscript Reading Room.

Meigs, Montgomery. Journals (12/1854–12/1859; 2/1861–5/1861), Library of Congress, Manuscript Reading Room, transcribed. Transcribed by William Mohr for the United States Senate Bicentennial Commission, examined in the office of House Curator with the understanding that "the source is an unedited and unverified transcript of a work in progress."

Walter, Thomas U. Letters. File maintained by Sarah H. Turner, archivist, Office of the Architect of the Capitol.

Government Documents

Annual Reports of the Quartermaster General, and the Secretaries of the Interior, Treasury, and War.

Architect of the Capitol. The Statue of Freedom. S. Pub. 104–40.

Chief of Engineers. Letter to the Secretary of War, "Historical Sketch of the Corps of Engineers." GPO, 1876.

Corps of Engineers. History of the Washington Aqueduct, 1852–1952. Washington District, Corps of Engineers, 1953.

Executive Office of the President. The Old Executive Office Building, A Victorian Masterpiece. 1984.

National Park Service. First Manassas (First Bull Run), brochure. GPO, 1994.

Official Register of Officers and Cadets, U.S. Military Academy, West Point, 1818–1837.

National Archives. Office of the Chief of Engineers, RG 77, "Letters to and from Chief of Engineers (1845)." Entries 6 and 17.

Plan of the City Intended for the Permanent Seat of the Government of the United States. U.S. Coast and Geodetic Survey, 1887, based on L'Enfant's 1791 plan.

Quartermaster Department. Roll of Honor. GPO, 1865.

The War of the Rebellion, A Compilation of the Official Records of the Union and Confederate Armies. 4 series, 70 vols. GPO, 1882–1900.

The War of the Rebellion, A Compilation of the Official Records of the Union and Confederate Navies. 26 vols. GPO, 1894–1922.

Congressional Documents

Senate, *Architect's plans for enlargement of Capitol*, 31st Cong., 2d sess., Senate Rep. Com. No. 273.

Senate, *Presidential message communicating report with surveys, plans, and estimates for supplying cities of Washington and Georgetown with water*, 32d Cong. 2d sess., Senate Ex. Doc. No. 48.

Senate, *Report of Select Commitee to investigate abuses, bribery, or fraud*, 33rd Cong., special sess., senate Rep. No. 1.

House, *Sundry reports on construction of new dome on Capitol*, 34th Cong., 1st sess., House Mis. Doc. 65.

Senate, *Letter on dome and porticoes of Capitol*, 36th Cong., 1st sess., Senate Mis. Doc. No. 29.

House, *Abstracted Indian trust bonds, and supplement*, 36th Cong., 2d sess., House Report No. 78.

House, *Forts, arsenals, arms, etc.*, 36th Cong., 2d sess., House Report No. 85.

Senate, *Message of the President of the United States (July 4, 1861)*, 37th Cong., 1st sess., Senate Ex. Doc. No. 1.

House, *Copies of reports made by General William S. Harney during command of United States forces in Missouri*, 37th Cong., 1st sess., House Ex. Doc. No. 19.

House, *Investigation of government contracts*, 37th Cong., 2d sess., House Report No. 2.

House, *Armed flotilla on western rivers*, 37th Cong., 2d sess., House Ex. Doc. No. 5.

House, *Answer to resolution of House on transportation of troops and munitions of war by railroad, etc.*, 37th Cong., 2d sess., House Ex. Doc. No. 18.

House, *Copies of papers in Quartermaster General's bureau on purchase of horses*, 37th Cong., 2d sess., House Ex. Doc. No. 60.

House, *Investigation of government contracts*, 37th Cong., 3rd sess., House Report No. 49.

Senate, *Conduct of the War, report on battle of Fredericksburg*, 37th Cong., 3rd sess., Senate Report Com. No. 71.

Senate, *Conduct of the War, vol. 1, Army of the Potomac, vol. 2, Battle of Bull Run; Battle of Ball's Bluff, and vol. 3, Western department, or Missouri; Miscellaneous subjects*, 37th Cong., 3rd sess., Senate Report No. 108.

Senate, *Supplemental report of chief engineer of Washington aqueduct*, 38th Cong., 1st sess., Senate Mis. Doc. No. 83.

Senate, *Testimony taken before joint commission authorized to investigate scientific bureaus of Government*, 49th Cong., 1st sess., Senate Mis. Doc. No. 82.

House, *Documentary History, United States Capitol Building and Grounds*, 58th Cong., 2d sess., House Report 646.

House, *Historical Statistics of the United States, Bicentennial Edition*, 93rd Cong., House Document, No. 93–78.

House, *The United States Capitol: A Brief Architectural History*, 101st Cong., 1st sess. House Document 101–144.

Books and Articles

Allen, William C. *The Dome of the United States Capitol: An Architectural History*. Senate Document 102–7, 102d Cong., 1st sess (1992).

Ambrose, Stephen E. *Duty, Honor, Country, A History of West Point*. Baltimore: John Hopkins Press, 1966.

American Society of Civil Engineers. *Civil Engineering Landmarks of the Nation's Capital*. American Society of Civil Engineers, National Capital Section, Committee on History and Heritage, 1982.

"Interesting Historical Letter, An." *Pennsylvania Magazine of History and Biography* 25 (1901): 77–79.

Andrews, Peter. *In Honored Glory*. New York: G. P. Putnam's Sons, 1966.

Ashabranner, Brent. *A Grateful Nation*. New York: G. P. Putnam's Sons, 1990.

Basler, Roy P., ed. *The Collected Works of Abraham Lincoln*. 9 vols. Brunswick, N.J.: Rutgers University Press, 1953.

Beale, Howard K., ed. *Diary of Gideon Welles*. New York: W. W. Norton & Company, 1960.

Bigler, Philip. *In Honored Glory, Arlington National Cemetery: The Final Post*. Arlington, Va.: Vandamere Press, 1987.

Boatner III, Mark Mayo. *The Civil War Dictionary.* New York: Vintage Books, Revised Edition, 1991.

Boehme, Sarah E. *Seth Eastman, A Portfolio of North American Indians.* Afton, Minn.: Afton Historical Society Press, 1995.

Boynton, Edward C. *History of West Point.* New York: Second Edition, D. Van Nostrand, 1871.

Brown, Glenn. *History of the United States Capitol.* 1900, 1902. Reprint, New York: De Capo Press, 1970.

Bryan, Wilhelmus Bogart. *A History of the National Capital.* 2 vols. New York: The Macmillan Company, 1916.

Butler, Benjamin. *Private and Official Correspondence of Gen. Benjamin F. Butler.* 5 vols. Privately issued, 1917.

Caemerer, H. P. *Washington, The National Capital.* Senate Document No. 332, 71st Cong., 3rd sess.

Chase, Enoch Aquila. "The Arlington Case." *Records of Columbia Historical Society* 31–32 (1930): 175–207.

Congressional Globe.

Cole, John Y. "LC In The 19th Century—An Informal Account." *Library of Congress Professional Association,* 1972.

Commager, Henry Steele. *Documents of American History.* 4th ed. New York: Appleton-Century-Crofts, Inc., 1948.

Conover, Milton. *The General Land Office.* Baltimore: John Hopkins Press, 1923

Cooley, James. "The Relief of Fort Pickens." *American Heritage,* Dec. 1972.

Cowdrey, Albert E. *A City for the Nation.* Washington: Historical Division, Office of Administrative Services, Office of the Chief of Engineers, 1978.

Crawford, Samuel Wylie. *The Genesis of the Civil War.* New York: Charles L. Webster and Company, 1887.

Cullum, George W. *Biographical Register of the Officers and Graduates of the U.S. Military Academy.* Boston: Houghton, Mifflin and Company, Third Edition, 1891.

Current, Richard N., ed. in chief. *Encyclopedia of the Confederacy.* New York: Simon & Schuster, 1993.

Dana, Charles. *Recollections of the Civil War.* 1898. Reprint, New York: Collier Books, 1963.

Davis, Jefferson. *Rise and Fall of the Confederate Government.* 2 vols. 1881. Reprint, Thomas Yoseloff, 1958.

Davis, Varina. *Jefferson Davis, A Memoir by His Wife.* New York: Belford Company, 1890.

Davis, William C. *Jefferson Davis, The Man and His Honor.* New York: Harper Collins, 1991.

———. *First Blood, Fort Sumter to Bull Run.* Alexandria, Va.: The Civil War, Time-Life Series, 1983.

Dickens, Charles. *American Notes for General Circulation.* 1842. Reprint, New York: Penguin Classics, 1985.

Dodd, Donald D., comp. *Historical Statistics of the States of the United States.* Westport, Conn.: Greenwood Press, 1993.

Donald, David Herbert. *Lincoln.* New York: Simon & Schuster, 1995.

Donovan, Frank. *Mr. Lincoln's Proclamation.* New York: Dodd, Mead & Company, 1964.

East, Sherrod E. "Banishment of Captain Meigs." *Records of the Columbia Historical Society* 40–41 (1940): 97–148.

Elliott, Charles Winslow. *Winfield Scott, The Soldier and the Man.* New York: The Macmillan Company, 1937.

Encyclopedia Brittanica. 1947 Edition.

Fairman, Charles E. *Art and Artists of the Capitol.* Washington: GPO, 1927.

Fehrenbacher, Don E., and Virginia Fehrenbacher, eds. and comps. *Recollected Words of Abraham Lincoln.* Stanford, Calif.: Stanford University Press, 1996.

Field, Cynthia R., Richard E. Stamm, and Heather P. Ewing. *The Castle.* Washington: Smithsonian Institution Press, 1993.

Fitzsimons, Mrs. Neal. "The Building of the Cabin John Bridge." *Maryland: Montgomery County Historical Society*, Feb. 1973.

Flack, J. Kilpatrick. *Desideratum in Washington, the Intellectual Community in the Capital City 1870–1900.* Cambridge, Mass.: Schenkman Pub. Co., 1975.

Flower, Frank Abial. *Edwin McMasters Stanton.* Akron, Ohio: The Saalfield Publishing Company, 1905.

Fogle, Jeanne. *Two Hundred Years.* Arlington, Va.: Vandamere Press, 1991.

Foote, Shelby. *The Civil War, Fort Sumter to Perryville.* New York: Vintage Books, 1986.

———. *The Civil War, Fredericksburg To Meridian.* New York: Vintage Books, 1986.

———. *The Civil War, Red River to Appomattox.* New York: Vintage Books, 1986.

Fowler, William M., Jr. *Under Two Flags.* New York: W. W. Norton & Company, 1990.

Frary, I. T. *They Built The Capitol.* Richmond: Garrett and Massie, 1940.

Freeman, Douglas Southall. *R. E. Lee.* 4 vols. New York: Charles Scribner's Sons, 1934–35.

Gemmill, Jane W. *Notes on Washington.* Philadelphia: E. Claxton & Company, 1884.

Gondos, Victor, Jr. *J. Franklin Jameson and the Birth of the National Archives 1906–1926.* Philadelphia: University of Pennsylvania Press, 1981.

Goode, George Brown. *The Smithsonian Institution, 1846–1896.* 1897. Reprint, New York: Arno Press, 1980.

Gordon, John Steele. *Hamilton's Blessing.* New York: Walker and Company, 1997.

Grant, Ulysses S. *Memoirs and Selected Letters.* New York: The Library of America, 1990.

Green, Constance McLaughlin. *Washington Capital City 1879–1950.* Princeton, N.J.: Princeton University Press, 1963.

Greene, A. Wilson, and Gary W. Gallagher. *National Geographic Guide to the National Battlefield Parks.* Washington: 1992.

Hattaway, Herman, and Archer Jones. "The War Board, the Basis of the United States First General Staff." *Military Affairs* 46, no. 1 (1982): 1–5.

Haupt, Herman. *Reminiscences of General Herman Haupt.* 1901. Reprint, North Stratford, N.H.: Arno Press Inc., 1981.

Haverstock, Mary Sayre. "George Washington Sat Here . . . and Here." *American Heritage* (Dec. 1972).

Haythornthwaite, Philip. *Uniforms of the American Civil War.* United Kingdom: Blandford Press, 1975.

Heitman, F. B. *Historical Register of the United States Army.* Washington: National Tribune, 1890.

———. *Historical Record of the United States Army (1789–1889).* Washington: National Tribune, 1890.

Hinkel, John Vincent. *Arlington Monument To Heroes.* New edition, Englewood, N.J.: Prentice Hall, 1970.

Holt, Dean W. *American Military Cemeteries.* Jefferson, N.C.: McFarland & Company, 1992.

Howe, Franklin T. "The Board of Public Works." *Records of the Columbia Historical Society* 3 (1899): 257–78.

Hughes, Mark. *Bivouac of the Dead.* Bowie, Md.: Heritage Books, Inc., 1995.

Huston, James A. *The Sinews of War: Army Logistics 1775–1953.* Washington: Office of the Chief of Military History, United States Army, 1966.

Jeffries, Jennie Forsyth, comp. *A History of the Forsyth Family.* Indianapolis: W. B. Burford, 1920.

Johnson, Allen, and Dumas Malone, ed. *Dictionary of American Biography*. 10 vols. New York: Charles Scribner's Sons, 1927–1936.

Johnson, Robert Underwood, and Clarence Clough Buel, eds. *Battles and Leaders of the Civil War*. 4 vols. 1887–88. Reprint, Secaucus, N.J.: Castle, 1982.

Jones, Virgil Carrington. *The Civil War At Sea*. 3 vols. New York: Holt, Rinehart, Winston, 1960.

Jones, Archer. *Civil War Command & Strategy*. New York: The Free Press, 1992.

Junior League of Washington, and Thomas F. Roncek, ed. *The City of Washington*. New York: Alfred A. Knopf, 1979.

Kamm, Samuel Richey. *The Civil War Career of Thomas A. Scott*. Philadelphia: University of Pennsylvania, 1940.

Kelly, Joseph T. "Memories of a Lifetime in Washington." *Records of the Columbia Historical Society* 31–32 (1930), 117–49.

Krause, Chester L., Robert F. Lemke, and Robert E. Wilhite, ed. *Standard Catalog of United States Paper Money*. 13th ed. Iola, Wisc.: Krause Publication, 1994.

Kunhardt, Dorothy Meserve, and Philip B. Kunhardt, Jr. *Twenty Days*. Memphis, Tenn.: Castle Books, 1965.

Kunitz, Stanley J., ed. *British Authors of the Nineteenth Century*. New York: The H. W. Wilson Company, 1936.

Laas, Virginia Jeans, ed. *Wartime Washington, The Civil War Letters of Elizabeth Blair Lee*. Champaign, Ill: University of Illinois Press, 1991.

Lambert, Tallmadge A. "Observations on the Development of the Nation's Capital." *Records of the Columbia Historical Society* 2 (1897): 272–92.

Lee, Captain Robert E. *Recollections and Letters of General Robert E. Lee*. New York: Garden City Publishing Co., Inc., 1904.

Lee, Richard M.. *Mr. Lincoln's City*. McLean, Va.: EPM Publications, Inc. 1981.

Leech, Margaret. *Reveille in Washington*. Special ed. New York: Time Reading Program, 1962.

Long, E. B., with Barbara Long. *The Civil War Day By Day*. New York: A Da Capo Paperback, 1971.

Lonn, Ella. *Salt As A Factor In The Confederacy*. New York: Walter Neale, Publisher, 1933.

———. *Foreigners in the Union Army and Navy*. Westport, Conn.: Greenwood Press, Publishers, 1969.

Lyons, Linda Brody. *A Handbook to the Pension Building*. Washington: National Building Museum, 1989.

MacCloskey, Monro. *Hallowed Ground Our National Cemeteries*. New York: Richard Rosen Press, Inc., 1968.

Macqueen, P. O. "Cabin John Bridge." *The Military Engineer* 24, no. 138 (1932): 566–68.

Mahon, John K. *History of the Second Seminole War 1835–1842*. Gainesville, Fla.: University of Florida Press, 1967.

Maroon, Fred J. *The United States Capitol*. New York: Stewart, Tabori & Chang, 1993.

Maury, William M. *Alexander "Boss" Shepherd and the Board of Public Works*. Washington: George Washington University, 1975.

McCulloch, Hugh. *Men and Measures of Half a Century*. 1888. Reprint, New York: De Capo Press, 1970.

McDermott, John Frances. *Seth Eastman Pictorial Historian of the Indian*. Norman: University of Oklahoma Press, 1961.

McLaughlin, Constance. *Washington, Capital City, 1879–1950*. Princeton, N.J.: Princeton University Press, 1963.

McPherson, James M. *Marching Toward Freedom*. New York: Facts on File, 1994.

Meigs, Henry B. *Record of the Descendants of Vincent Meigs*. Baltimore, Md.: J. S. Bridges & Co., 1901.

Meigs, J. Forsyth. *Memoir of Charles D. Meigs*. Philadelphia: Lindsay & Blakiston, 1876.

Meigs, Montgomery. "General M. C. Meigs on the Conduct of the Civil War." *The American Historical Review* 26, no. 2 (1920–21): 285–303.

Meneely, A. Howard. *The War Department, 1861*. New York: Columbia University Press, 1928.

Milligan, John D. *Gunboats Down the Mississippi*. Annapolis, Md.: United States Naval Institute, 1965.

Moore, John Bassett, col. and ed. *The Works of James Buchanan*. 12 vols. Philadelphia: J. P. Lippincott Company, 1908–11.

Morison, Samuel Eliot. *The Oxford History of the American People*. New York: Oxford University Press, 1965.

Morris, Roy, Jr. *Sheridan*. New York: Crown Publishers, 1992.

Morrison, James L. *The Best School In The World*. Kent, Ohio: The Kent State University Press, 1986.

National Geographic Society. *Battlefields of the Civil War*. National Geographic Society, 1974.

National Geographic Society. "The Washington Aqueduct and Cabin John Bridge." *National Geographic* 8, no. 12 (1897).

National Intelligencer.

Newcomb, Simon. *The Reminiscences of An Astronomer.* Boston: Houghton, Mifflin and Company, 1903.

Nicolay, John G., and John Hay, eds. *Complete Works of Abraham Lincoln.* 12 vols. New York: New and Enlarged Edition, Francis D. Tandy Company, 1905.

Niven, John. *Salmon P. Chase.* New York: Oxford University Press, 1995.

Olds, May Meigs. "Memories of the Old Meigs Home and Historical Events in the Neighborhood, 1863–1913." *Records of the Columbia Historical Society* 46/47 (1947): 81–95.

Pappas, George S. *To The Point, The United States Military Academy 1802–1902.* New York: Praeger Publishing, 1993.

Parker, Geoffrey, ed. *Cambridge Illustrated History of Warfare.* New York: Cambridge University Press, 1995.

Peters, James Edward. *Arlington National Cemetery.* Kensington, Md.: Woodbine House, 1986.

Petroski, Henry. *Engineers of Dreams.* New York: Alfred A. Knopf, Inc., 1995.

Placzek, Adolf K., ed. in chief. *Macmillan Encyclopedia of Architects.* New York: Free Press, 1982.

Pollard, Edward A. *The First Year of the War.* London: Henry Stevens, 1863.

———. *Lee and His Lieutenants.* New York: E. B. Treat & Co., 1867.

Poore, Benjamin Perley. *Perley's Reminiscences.* 2 vols., 1886. Reprint, New York: AMS Press, 1971.

Pratt, Fletcher. *Civil War on Western Waters.* New York: Henry Holt and Company, 1956.

Presidential Elections 1789–1992. Washington: Congressional Quarterly, 1995.

Randall, J. G. *The Civil War and Reconstruction.* Boston: D. C. Heath and Company, 1937.

Raymond, Harold B. "Ben Butler: A Reappraisal." *Colby Library Quarterly,* ser. 6, no. 11 (1964).

Reps, John W. *Washington on View.* Chapel Hill, N.C.: The University of North Carolina Press, 1991.

Rhees, William Jones. *The Smithsonian Institution, Documents Relative To Its Origin and History, 1835–1899.* 1901. Reprint, North Stratford, N.H.: Arno Press, 1980.

Rhodes, James Ford. *History of the United States from the Compromise of 1850.* 4 vols. New York: Harper & Brothers Publishers, 1900.

Richardson, James D. *A Compilation of the Messages and Papers of the Confederacy.* 2 vols. Nashville, Tenn.: United States Publishing Company, 1905.

Risch, Erna. *Quartermaster Support of the Army, A History of the Corps 1775–1939.* Washington: Quartermaster Historian's Office, Office of the Quartermaster General, 1962.

Rolle, Andrew. *John Charles Fremont.* Norman: University of Oklahoma Press, 1991.

Rowland, Dunbar, col. and ed. *Jefferson Davis, His Letters, Papers and Speeches.* Jackson, Miss.: Mississippi Department of Archives and History, 1923.

Scott, Winfield. *Memoirs of Lieut-General Scott, LL.D.* 1864. Reprint, Freeport, N.Y.: Books for Libraries Press, 1970.

Sears, Stephen W. *To the Gates of Richmond.* New York: Ticknor & Fields, 1992.

Sheridan, P. H. *Personal Memoirs of P. H. Sheridan.* 2 vols. New York: Charles L. Webster & Company, 1888.

Sherman, William Tecumseh. *Memoirs of General W. T. Sherman.* New York: The Library of America, 1990.

Shrader, Charles R. *U.S. Military Logistics, 1607–1991.* Westport, Conn.: Greenwood Press, 1992.

Simon, John Y., ed. *The Papers of Ulysses S. Grant.* 7 vols. Carbondale, Ill.: Southern Illinois University Press, 1979.

Skramstad, Harold K. "The Engineer as Architect in Washington: The Contribution of Montgomery Meigs." *Records of the Columbia Historical Society* 47 (1969–70): 266–84.

Smith, Elbert B. *The Presidency of James Buchanan.* Lawrence, Kans.: The University Press of Kansas, 1975.

Smith, Hal H. "Historic Washington Homes." *Records of the Columbia Historical Society* 11 (1907): 243–67.

Stern, Philip Van Doren. *Prologue to Sumter.* Bloomington: Indiana University Press, 1961.

Stoddard, William O. *Abraham Lincoln: The True Story of a Great Life.* New York: Fords, Howard, & Hulbert, 1884.

Strode, Hudson. *Jefferson Davis, Confederate President.* New York: Harcourt, Bruce and Company, 1959.

Swanberg, W. A. *First Blood.* New York: Charles Scribner's Sons, 1957.

Thomas, Benjamin P., and Harold M. Hyman. *Stanton.* New York: Alfred A. Knopf, 1962.

Tindall, William. *History of the City of Washington.* Knoxville, Tenn.: H. W. Crew & Co., 1914.

————. "A Sketch of Alexander Robey Shepherd." *Records of the Columbia Historical Society* 14 (1911): 49–66.

————. *The True Story of the Virginia and the Monitor.* Richmond, Va.: Old Dominion Press, 1923.

Torres, Louis. *"To the Immortal Name and Memory of George Washington."* Washington: Historical Division, Office of Administrative Services, Office of the Chief of Engineers, 1985.

True, Frederick W. *A History of the First Half-Century of the National Academy of Sciences, 1863–1913.* 2 vols. 1913. Reprint, New York: Arno Press, 1980.

Tweet, Roald. *A History of the Rock Island District U.S. Army Corps of Engineers 1866–1983.* Rock Island, Ill.: U.S. Army Engineers District, Rock Island, 1984.

United States Capitol Historical Society. *We, the People.* Washington: The National Geographic Society, 1985.

Utley, Robert M. *Frontier Regulars 1866–1891.* Lincoln, Nebr.: University of Nebraska Press, 1973.

Walter, Thomas U. *The Architectural Review and American Builders Journal.* Philadelphia: Claxton, Remisen & Haffelfinger, 1869.

Ways, Harry C. *The Washington Aqueduct, 1852–1992.* United States Corps of Engineers, 1996.

Weigley, Russell F. *History of the United States Army.* New York: The Macmillan Company, 1967.

————. *Quartermaster General of the Union Army.* New York: Columbia University Press, 1959.

————. "Captain Meigs and the Artists of the Capitol: Federal Patronage of Art in the 1850s." *Records of the Columbia Historical Society* 47 (1969–70): 285–305.

Weinert, Richard P. "The Confederate Regular Army." *Military Affairs* 26, no. 3 (1962): 97–107.

Wheeler, Richard. *Sword Over Richmond.* New York: Harper & Row, 1986.

————. *Voices of the Civil War.* New York: A Meridian Book, 1990.

Whitnah, David R. *History of the United States Weather Bureau.* Champaign, Ill.: University of Illinois Press, 1961.

Whitney, Charles S. *Bridges, Their Art, Science, & Evolution.* New York: Greenwich Press, 1983.

Whyte, James H. *The Uncivil War.* New York: Twayre Publishers, 1958.

Index

Page number references in *italics* refer to photographs and maps.

A

acoustics, for House chamber, 28–29, 32, 41, 43
Adams, John Quincy, 26
Alabama, secedes, 72
Alexander, E. Porter, 219
Alexandria, 16–17; at time Washington, D.C., was being established, 15–16; port for transport of Union soldiers, 135, 166
Allen, Robert, Fremont's quartermaster, 106–9, *162*; quartermaster for Mississippi Valley, 220, 228, 248
Amendments to Constitution. *See* Constitution
American Institute of Architects, 42–43
American Philosophical Society, 21
"Anaconda plan," advocated by Scott, 99
Anderson, John B., 216–17, 227
Anderson, Robert, 76, 80–81, 87, 255
Andrews, C. F., 42
Apotheosis of George Washington, 49
Appomattox Court House, Va., surrender at, 253
Aqueduct. *See* Washington Aqueduct
Aqueduct Bridge (now Key Bridge), 17
Aquia landing, a "flying depot," 187–89, 201, 230, 233. *See also* Rivers and Creeks: Aquia
Architect of the Capitol, 43
Arkansas, secedes, 88
Arlington Heights, 92, 95, 101, 284
Arlington Mansion or House, home of Robert E. Lee. *See* Lee property
Arlington National Cemetery, 5, 258–61; Confederate memorial authorized, *258*
Armed Liberty. *See* Freedom
Army of Georgia, 251
Army of Northern Virginia, 139, 186–87, 229

Army of Virginia, 164, 166, 179, 181
Army of Tennessee, 205, 207, 221, 229, 245, 250
Army of the Cumberland, 181, 207, 210–14, 216–17, 220–21, 228–29
Army of the James, 233–34
Army of the Mississippi, 179
Army of the Ohio, 179–80, 207, 210, 219, 229, 251
Army of the Potomac, 102, 108, 131–36, 141, 164–68, 170–72, 174–75, 179, 181, 187–89, 191–92, 197, 199–201, 209, 225–26, 229, 233–34, 247, 252, 272
Army of the Shenandoah, 240
Army of the Tennessee, 179, 229, 251, 256
arsenals and armories: Harper's Ferry, W.Va., 61; Meridian, Miss., 224; Pittsburgh, Pa., 75; Rock Island, Ill., 288; St. Louis, Mo., 103–4; Springfield, Mass., 76; Virginia State, 75; Watervliet, 76; Washington, D.C., 16, 58
Art Commission, 49, 51–52
Arthur, Chester A., 272, 286
Arts and Industries Building. *See* National Museum
Astrophysical Observatory, 282
Atlanta, Ga., 240, 243–44, 246; as rail point 180; as military objective, 229; as base, 238. *See also* Battles: Atlanta
Atlanta (ship), CSS, 197
Atlantic (ship), USS, 85–86

B

Babcock, Orville, 285
Bache, Alexander Dallas, 28, 278
Baird, Spencer F., 280, 283
Ball, Edward, 49–50

339